The Elements of Life

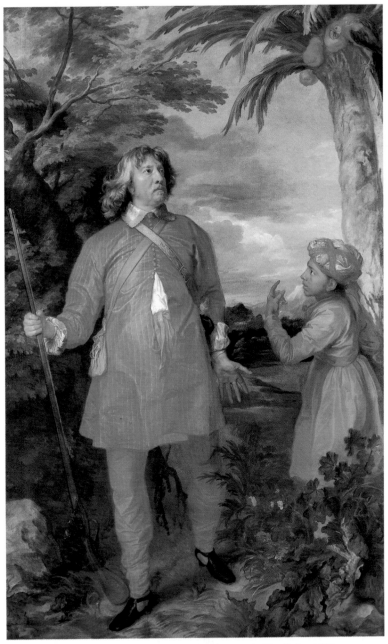

Sir Anthony Van Dyck, *William Feilding, Earl of Denbigh*, *c.*1633,
National Gallery, London

The Elements of Life

*Biography and Portrait-Painting in
Stuart and Georgian England*

RICHARD WENDORF

CLARENDON PRESS · OXFORD

1990

Oxford University Press, Walton Street, Oxford OX2 6DP

Oxford New York Toronto
Delhi Bombay Calcutta Madras Karachi
Petaling Jaya Singapore Hong Kong Tokyo
Nairobi Dar es Salaam Cape Town
Melbourne Auckland

and associated companies in
Berlin Ibadan

Oxford is a trade mark of Oxford University Press

Published in the United States
by Oxford University Press, New York

British Library Cataloguing in Publication Data
Wendorf, Richard
The elements of life: biography and portrait-painting
in Stuart and Georgian England.
1. European portrait paintings, to 1900
2. Biographical prose, to 1900. Critical studies
I. Title
757'094
ISBN 0–19–811720–5

Library of Congress Cataloging in Publication Data
Wendorf, Richard
The elements of life: biography and portrait-painting in Stuart
and Georgian England/Richard Wendorf.
p.   cm.
Includes index.
1. Great Britain—History—Stuarts. 1603–1714—Biography—History
and criticism.   2. Great Britain—History—1714–1837—Biography-
-History and criticism.   3. Art and literature—Great Britain-
-History.   4. Biography (as a literary form)   5. Portrait painting.
British.   I. Title.
DA377.W46   1990
941.06—dc20   89–15997
ISBN 0–19–811720–5

Typeset by Latimer Trend & Company Ltd, Plymouth
Printed and bound in
Great Britain by Biddles Ltd,
Guildford and Kings Lynn

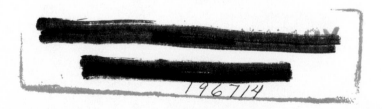

For Diana,
in her own guise

Acknowledgements

LIKE many books, this book began as something quite different from what it has become. I originally intended to examine the relationships between Boswell's *Life of Samuel Johnson* and the various forms of portraiture that his voluminous text digested: letters, journals, 'ana', the character-sketch, the dramatic representation of conversation, perhaps (I thought) even portrait-painting itself. As so often happens, what at first appeared to be an intriguing subject for a chapter in one book eventually emerged as the central focus of a separate and very different kind of work, one that has taken much longer to complete while profoundly changing my own career as a scholar. I therefore take great pleasure in acknowledging the many debts I have incurred while attempting to formulate new questions about English painting that would, in turn, generate fresh ways of approaching those literary texts with which I thought I was already familiar.

The seed-ground for this study of verbal and visual portraiture has been the Henry E. Huntington Library and Art Gallery, where (while I was supposed to be completing my study of William Collins) I became convinced of the importance of exploring the relations between these two arts in the seventeenth and eighteenth centuries. I am indebted to Martin Ridge for inviting me to work at the Huntington, and to Robert Wark for continuing to share his knowledge of British painting with me. The opening chapters of this book were completed while I was the recipient of a senior research fellowship from the American Council of Learned Societies. Grants from the Yale Center for British Art and the American Philosophical Society enabled me to work in New Haven and London; I owe special thanks to Duncan Robinson and Barbara Mulligan at Yale, where I was able to present some of the ideas in this book in more tentative form.

I am also grateful to the following institutions for allowing me to work in their collections: the Art Institute of Chicago (Richard Brettell and Sam Carini), the Ashmolean Museum, the Beinecke Library, the Bodleian Library, the British Library and British Museum, the Courtauld Institute, the National Gallery, the National Portrait Gallery and its library and archives (Robin Gibson and Susan Foister), the New York Public Library, the Newberry Library, the Paul Mellon Centre for Studies in British Art (Christopher White and Michael Kitson), Princeton University

Library, the Tate Gallery, the Victoria and Albert Museum, and Yale University Library.

Northwestern University has generously underwritten the production of the illustrations in this book and has provided me, over the years, with numerous grants-in-aid. The chairpersons of both the English and Art History departments at Northwestern—Gerald Graff and Martin Mueller, Larry Silver and Sandra Hindman—have been unstinting in their support and friendship. I owe a similar debt to my former dean, Rudolph H. Weingartner, who accelerated work on this project by granting me a leave of absence, and then later slowed it down by asking me to join his administration. I am pleased to say that both tasks have been completed at the same time, largely because of the generous support I have enjoyed from those who served with me in the dean's office, and from no one more than Lois Cichowicz, who (with Kirstie Felland and Marjorie Weiner) was responsible for preparing the manuscript for the press. I also owe a special debt to Russell Maylone and Rolf Erickson for many acts of kindness while I worked in the Northwestern University Library, and to Robert Mayer and Laura Rosenthal for serving as my research assistants.

Earlier versions of some of the material in this book have already appeared in print: much of the first chapter in *Articulate Images: The Sister Arts from Hogarth to Tennyson*, ed. Wendorf (Minneapolis: Univ. of Minnesota Press, 1983), 98–124; the discussion of Walton, in the second chapter, in *Modern Philology*, 82 (1985), 269–91; the section on Jonathan Richardson (in the fifth chapter) in *New Literary History*, 15 (1983–4), 539–57; and the sixth chapter, on Hogarth, in the *Art Journal*, 46 (1987), 200–8. Permission to reprint this material has been granted by the University of Minnesota Press, the University of Chicago Press, the Johns Hopkins University Press, and the College Art Association of America. Kim Scott Walwyn of the Oxford University Press deserves many thanks for the considerable care and patience she has devoted to this book over a period of several years.

Many important articles, catalogues, and monographs devoted to biography and portrait-painting have appeared in the past decade, and I have recorded my indebtedness to—or arguments with—their authors and editors in the notes to this book. But critical activity within one's own field should not be relegated to footnotes alone. The present study would be significantly different if I had not been able to share in the work of W. J. T. Mitchell and Wendy Steiner on the relations between verbal and visual art, or in Ronald Paulson's studies of English literature and painting. The same is true of numerous other scholars: Svetlana Alpers

(Dutch portraiture), Judith Anderson (early English biography), Richard Brilliant (portraiture), Christopher Brown (Van Dyck), William Epstein (biographical theory), John Kerslake (English portrait-painting), Roger Lonsdale (Richardson), Peter Millard (North), Nicholas Penny and David Mannings (Reynolds), and J. Douglas Stewart (Kneller). Four scholars, in particular, have dramatically changed our understanding of British portraiture; my debts to Oliver Millar, David Piper, Roy Strong, and the late Ellis Waterhouse are present throughout this book.

I have also relied on the advice of the many colleagues who have read parts of the manuscript of this study, particularly Leonard Barkan, Peter Berek, Elizabeth Dipple, William Epstein, Stephen Fix, James King, Roger Lonsdale, Bruce Redford, John Riely, Charles Ryskamp, and James Winn. Robin Robbins provided numerous corrections and suggestions, and my two most indefatigable readers—Jean Hagstrum and Lawrence Lipking—have once again made this a better book than it otherwise would have been. So, too, have the twelve members of the National Endowment for the Humanities Summer Seminar I directed on portraiture in 1987; rarely does someone have the opportunity to share his work with so many lively scholars at such an appropriate time. I take great pleasure in thanking both the Endowment (especially Kenneth Kolson) and my colleagues in the seminar (they know who they are) for their contributions to this book.

Contents

List of Plates

All images are paintings in oil unless otherwise indicated.

Abbreviations

Anecdotes of Painting	Walpole, Horace, *Anecdotes of Painting in England*, 2nd edn. (3 vols.; London, 1765).
Baker	Baker, C. H. Collins, *Lely and the Stuart Portrait Painters: A Study of English Portraiture Before and After Van Dyck* (2 vols.; London: Medici Society, 1912).
Baldini and Mandel	Baldini, Gabriele and Gabriele Mandel, *L'opera completa di Hogarth pittore* (Milan: Rizzoli, 1967).
Beckett, *Hogarth*	Beckett, R. B., *Hogarth* (London: Routledge, 1949).
Beckett, *Lely*	—— *Lely* (London: Routledge, 1951).
Boswell, *Life*	*Boswell's Life of Johnson*, ed. George Birkbeck Hill and rev. L. F. Powell (6 vols.; Oxford: Clarendon Press, 1934–50; 2nd edn. of vols. v–vi, 1964).
Brief Lives	Aubrey, John, *'Brief Lives', chiefly of Contemporaries, set down by John Aubrey, between the Years 1669 and 1696*, ed. Andrew Clark (2 vols.; Oxford, 1898).
Buckeridge	Buckeridge, Bainbrigge, *An Essay towards an English School of Painting*, 3rd edn. (1754; rpt. London: Cornmarket Press, 1969).
Burke	Burke, Joseph, *English Art 1714–1800* (Oxford: Clarendon Press, 1976).
Compleat Angler	Walton, Izaak, *The Compleat Angler 1653–1676*, ed. Jonquil Bevan (Oxford: Clarendon Press, 1983).
Compleat Walton	*The Compleat Walton*, ed. Geoffrey Keynes (London: Nonesuch Press, 1929).
Cust	Cust, Lionel, *Anthony Van Dyck: An Historical Study of His Life and Works* (London: Bell, 1900).
Darbishire	*The Early Lives of Milton*, ed. Helen Darbishire (London: Constable, 1932).
Dick	*Aubrey's Brief Lives*, ed. Oliver Lawson Dick, 3rd edn. (London: Secker and Warburg, 1958).
English Miniature	Murdock, John *et al.*, *The English Miniature* (New Haven: Yale Univ. Press, 1981).
Evelyn, *Dairy*	Evelyn, John, *The Diary of John Evelyn*, ed. E. S. de Beer (6 vols.; Oxford: Clarendon Press, 1955).

Evelyn, *Godolphin*   —— *The Life of Mrs. Godolphin*, ed. Harriet
                          Sampson (London: Oxford Univ. Press, 1939).

Glück   Glück, Gustav, *Van Dyck* (Klassiker der Kunst,
                          Stuttgart and Berlin: Deutsche Verlags-Anstalt,
                          1931).

Goldsmith, *Works*   *Collected Works of Oliver Goldsmith*, ed. Arthur
                          Friedman (5 vols.; Oxford: Clarendon Press,1966).

Gowing   Gowing, Lawrence, *Hogarth* (London: Tate
                          Gallery, 1971).

Hagstrum   Hagstrum, Jean H., *The Sister Arts: The Tradition
                          of Literary Pictorialism from Dryden to Gray*
                          (Chicago: Univ. of Chicago Press, 1958).

Hiscock, *Family Circle* Hiscock, W. G., *John Evelyn and His Family Circle*
                          (London: Routledge, 1955).

Hiscock, *John Evelyn*   —— *John Evelyn and Mrs. Godolphin* (London:
                          Macmillan, 1951).

Hogarth, *Analysis*   Hogarth, William, *The Analysis of Beauty*, ed.
                          Joseph Burke (Oxford: Clarendon Press, 1955).

Hunter   Hunter, Michael, *John Aubrey and the Realm of
                          Learning* (London: Duckworth, 1975).

Johnson, *Lives*   Johnson, Samuel, *Lives of the English Poets*, ed.
                          George Birkbeck Hill (3 vols.; Oxford:
                          Clarendon Press, 1905).

Johnson, *Savage*   Johnson, Samuel, *Life of Savage*, ed. Clarence
                          Tracy (Oxford: Clarendon Press, 1971).

Kerslake   Kerslake, John, *Early Georgian Portraits* (National
                          Portrait Gallery, 2 vols.; London: HMSO, 1977).

Killanin   Killanin, Lord, *Sir Godfrey Kneller and His Times,
                          1646–1723* (London: Batsford, 1948).

Larsen   Larsen, Erik, *L'opera completa di Van Dyck* (2
                          vols.; Milan: Rizzoli, 1980).

Millar, *Age of Charles I* Millar, Oliver, *The Age of Charles I: Painting in
                          England 1620–1649* (London: Tate Gallery, 1972).

Millar, *Lely*   —— *Sir Peter Lely 1618–80* (London: National
                          Portrait Gallery, 1978).

Millar, *Tudor, Stuart*   —— *The Tudor, Stuart, and Early Georgian Pictures
                          in the Collection of Her Majesty the Queen* (2 vols.;
                          London: Phaidon Press, 1963).

Millar, *Van Dyck*   —— *Van Dyck in England* (London: National
                          Portrait Gallery, 1982).

Millard   North, Roger, *General Preface and Life of Dr. John
                          North*, ed. Peter Millard (Toronto: Univ. of
                          Toronto Press, 1984).

North, *Lives*   —— *The Lives of the Right Hon. Francis North,*
                                Baron Guilford; the Hon. Sir Dudley North; and the
                                Hon. and Rev. Dr. John North . . . together with the
                                Autobiography of the Author, ed. Augustus Jessopp
                                (3 vols.; London: 1890).

Paulson, *Emblem*   Paulson, Ronald, *Emblem and Expression: Meaning*
                                in English Art of the Eighteenth Century (London:
                                Thames and Hudson; Cambridge, Mass.: Harvard
                                Univ. Press, 1975).

Paulson, *Hogarth*   —— *Hogarth: His Life, Art, and Times* (2 vols.;
                                New Haven and London: Yale Univ. Press for
                                the Paul Mellon Centre for Studies in British Art,
                                1971).

Penny   *Reynolds*, ed. Nicholas Penny (London: Royal
                                Academy of Arts, and Weidenfeld and Nicolson,
                                1986).

Piozzi, *Anecdotes*   Piozzi, Hesther Lynch, *Anecdotes of the Late*
                                Samuel Johnson, LL.D., in *Memoirs and Anecdotes of*
                                Dr. Johnson, ed. Arthur Sherbo (London: Oxford
                                Univ. Press, 1974), 57–161.

Piper, *Catalogue*   Piper, David, *Catalogue of Seventeeth-Century*
                                Portraits in the National Portrait Gallery 1625–1714
                                (Cambridge: Cambridge Univ. Press, 1963).

Piper, *English Face*   —— *The English Face* (1957; rpt. London:
                                National Portrait Gallery, 1978).

Piper, *Image of the Poet*   —— *The Image of the Poet: British Poets and their*
                                Portraits (Oxford: Clarendon Press, 1983).

Pope-Hennessy   Pope-Hennessy, John, *The Portrait in the*
                                Renaissance (Princeton: Princeton Univ. Press,
                                1966).

Reynolds, *Discourses*   Reynolds, Sir Joshua, *Discourses on Art*, ed.
                                Robert R. Wark, 2nd edn. (New Haven and
                                London: Yale Univ. Press for the Paul Mellon
                                Centre for British Art, 1975).

Reynolds, *Portraits*   —— *Portraits*, ed. Frederick W. Hilles (London:
                                Heinemann; New York: McGraw-Hill, 1952).

Richardson, *Essay*   Richardson, Jonathan, *An Essay on the Theory of*
                                Painting, 2nd edn. (1725; rpt. Menston,
                                Yorkshire: Scolar Press, 1971).

Stauffer   Stauffer, Donald A., *English Biography Before 1700*
                                (Cambridge, Mass.: Harvard Univ. Press, 1930).

Stewart, *Kneller* 1971   Stewart, J. Douglas, *Sir Godfrey Kneller* (London:
                                Bell, National Portrait Gallery, 1971).

Stewart, *Kneller* 1983 —— *Sir Godfrey Kneller and the English Baroque Portrait* (Oxford: Clarendon Press, 1983).

Stewart, 'Pin-ups or Virtues?' Stewart, J. Douglas, 'Pin-ups or Virtues? The Concept of the "Beauties" in Late Stuart Portraiture', in *English Portraits of the Seventeenth and Eighteenth Centuries* (Los Angeles: William Andrews Clark Memorial Library, 1974).

Strong, *Cult of Elizabeth* Strong, Roy, *The Cult of Elizabeth: Elizabethan Portraiture and Pageantry* (London: Thames and Hudson, 1977).

Strong, *English Icon* —— *The English Icon: Elizabethan and Jacobean Portraiture* (London: Routledge; New York: Pantheon, 1969).

Strong, *Portraits* —— *Portraits of Queen Elizabeth I* (Oxford: Clarendon Press, 1963).

Strong, *Tudor and Jacobean* —— *Tudor and Jacobean Portraits* (National Portrait Gallery, 2 vols.; London: HMSO, 1969).

Thraliana *Thraliana: The Diary of Mrs. Hester Lynch Thrale (Later Mrs. Piozzi) 1776–1809*, ed. Katharine C. Balderston, 2nd edn. (2 vols.; Oxford: Clarendon Press, 1951).

Walton, *Lives* Walton, Izaak, *The Lives of John Donne, Sir Henry Wotton, Richard Hooker, George Herbert, and Robert Anderson*, ed. George Saintsbury (London: Oxford Univ. Press, 1927).

Waterhouse Waterhouse, Ellis, *Painting in Britain 1530 to 1790*, 4th edn. (Harmondsworth: Penguin, 1978).

Whinney and Millar Whinney, Margaret, and Millar, Oliver, *English Art 1625–1714* (Oxford: Clarendon Press, 1957).

Wimsatt Wimsatt, William Kurtz, *The Portraits of Alexander Pope* (New Haven: Yale Univ. Press, 1965).

Yung Yung, Kai Kin, *Samuel Johnson 1709–82* (London: Herbert, 1984).

Better for Us, perhaps, it might appear,
Were there all harmony, all virtue here;
That never air or ocean felt the wind;
That never passion discompos'd the mind:
But ALL subsists by elemental strife;
And Passions are the elements of Life.

Pope, *An Essay on Man*

History, like nature, is cognizable only insofar as it
is perceived selectively, insofar as it is divided up
into domains of happening, their elements discriminated,
and these elements unified in structures of relationships,
which structures, in turn, are conceived to manifest
specifiable rules, principles, or laws which give to them
their determinate forms.

Hayden White, 'The Problem of Style
in Realistic Representation'

Human beings are too important to be treated as mere
symptoms of the past.

Lytton Strachey, *Eminent Victorians*

1

Representing Historical Character

IN the autumn of 1691 a thief entered the Ashmolean Museum in Oxford and successfully made away with several objects, including two paintings that belonged to the peripatetic John Aubrey. Aubrey had begun to deposit his most valuable belongings in the museum three years earlier, worried that his manuscripts would be plagiarized or that their more scandalous contents might leave him open to costly law suits. He believed that the Ashmolean, founded over a decade earlier, would prove to be a safe depository, that here, at least, his work would not be 'cast away as Rubbish' or torn to pieces and used to stop guns by the young relatives of his collaborators.[1] But Aubrey was to be somewhat disappointed even in this belief, for on 22 October he wrote to his friend, the naturalist John Ray, that among the missing items were 'my picture in miniature by Mr S. Cowper, (which at an auction yields 20 guineas,) and Archbishop Bancroft's, by Hillyard, the famous illuminer in Queen Elizabeth's time'.[2] Aubrey had met Samuel Cooper in the 1650s or early 1660s; by 1661 he had sat to him for his portrait. They became good friends, and it was in Cooper's studio that Aubrey was able to reintroduce another friend, Thomas Hobbes, to the newly restored Charles II.[3] Cooper's portrait of Hobbes, Aubrey wrote, was 'as like as art could afford, and one of the best pieces that ever he did: which his majesty, at his returne, bought of him, and conserves as one of his great rarities in his closet at Whitehall'.[4] In his *Brief Lives* Aubrey four times referred to Cooper as 'the prince of limners of this last age'; it is doubtful, on the other hand, whether Cooper ever had an opportunity to savour Aubrey's work as a verbal miniaturist, for his sketches of friends and near-contemporaries were often as unfinished and disorganized as they were brief.[5] But the impulses both artists shared emerge clearly throughout their work: a natural tendency to work 'in little' and at close range; a relish for the accuracy and immediacy of the

[1] Hunter, pp. 86–7.
[2] Anthony Powell, *John Aubrey and His Friends* (1948; rev. edn., New York: Barnes and Noble, 1964), 217–18.
[3] *Brief Lives*, i. 339–40.
[4] Ibid. i. 338.
[5] See e.g. his fragmentary notes on Cooper, 'his majestie's alluminer and my honord friend' (ibid. i. 182–3).

ad vivum portrait; and a keen eye for those minute particulars that set an individual apart from his or her contemporaries.

John Aubrey's interest in painting was not confined to his friendship with Samuel Cooper, but the nature of their relationship serves to accentuate the unusual similarity of their work, their common dedication to the principle of *multum in parvo*. We can isolate an even closer relationship between biographer and portrait-painter—one bordering on collaboration—almost exactly a century later, as James Boswell laboured to complete his monumental life of Samuel Johnson. Sir Joshua Reynolds, who had painted at least five portraits of Johnson and who would eventually read proof-sheets of the *Life*, had been prompted by Boswell to prepare his own character-sketch of their friend. In complying with Boswell's request, Reynolds began by speculating about the restrictions of his own art:

The habits of my profession unluckily extend to the consideration of so much only of character as lies on the surface, as is expressed in the lineaments of the countenance. An attempt to go deeper and investigate the peculiar colouring of his mind, as distinguished from all other minds, nothing but your earnest desire can excuse the presumption even of attempting.[6]

But attempt it he did, not only in the traditional form of the character-sketch but also in two imaginary dialogues that, as I shall argue later, are intimately tied both to his conception of human nature and to his ability to explore—on canvas—the complexities of the characters he portrayed.

Boswell, for his part, would call his painstakingly detailed narrative a 'Flemish picture' in which he marked 'the most minute particulars' of his friend,[7] and in a revealing entry in his journal he (like Reynolds) would draw upon a different form of portraiture in order to emphasize the limitations in his own art:

The great lines of characters may be put down. But I doubt much if it be possible to preserve in words the peculiar features of mind which distinguish individuals as certainly as the features of different countenances. The art of portrait painting fixes the last, and musical sounds with all their nice gradations can also be fixed. Perhaps language may be improved to such a degree as to picture the varieties of mind as minutely.[8]

Perhaps; but in the *Life* itself Boswell would have to counter the inherent

---

[6] Reynolds, *Portraits*, p. 66.

[7] Boswell, *Life*, iii. 191. Further references to this edition are provided in the text.

[8] *Boswell: The Ominous Years, 1774–1776*, ed. Charles Ryskamp and Frederick A. Pottle (London: Heinemann; New York: McGraw-Hill, 1963), 168.

deficiencies of language by casting the sound of Johnson's conversation as the index of his mind and by establishing a series of visual metaphors by which Johnson's character could consistently be revealed. He was assisted, moreover, by Reynolds, who shared his character-sketch with Boswell and also presented him with his earliest portrait of Johnson, which Boswell would include as the frontispiece to the *Life*. Boswell appropriately draws our attention to this picture during his description of his first meeting with Johnson in the back-parlour of Tom Davies's bookshop:

> I found that I had a very perfect idea of Johnson's figure, from the portrait of him painted by Sir Joshua Reynolds soon after he had published his Dictionary, in the attitude of sitting in his easy chair in deep meditation, which was the first picture his friend did for him, which Sir Joshua very kindly presented to me, and from which an engraving has been made for this work. (i. 392)

The production of this engraving and the introduction of the original portrait at this point in the narrative are both highly problematical, as we shall see, but it is clear that Boswell wanted to stress his close friendship with Reynolds, a relationship in which both artists were responsible for revisions in the other man's work. Boswell dedicated the first edition of the *Life* to Reynolds, and mourned his death in the second; and though he collected material for a projected life of Reynolds, he later abandoned it, for his friend 'had not those prominent features which can be seized, like Johnson's'.[9] Reynolds, however, had painted Boswell's portrait in 1785; when Boswell died it passed to his relatives, who eventually consigned it to the attic, its face against the wall.

The relationships I have been describing—between brother artists and sister arts—are the primary subject of this book. By providing a comparative study of biography and portrait-painting in England during the seventeenth and eighteenth centuries, I attempt to establish the grounds of comparison between two arts that have often been linked in a casual way (as when, for instance, we refer to a short biography as a portrait or sketch), but whose historical interrelations remain almost completely unexplored.[10] By focusing on the great age of English

---

[9] Quoted by Frank Brady, *James Boswell: The Later Years 1769–1795* (New York: McGraw-Hill, 1984), 466.

[10] Wendy Steiner and David M. Lubin are the only scholars to look critically at the relationship between these two forms of portraiture; see Steiner's *Exact Resemblance to Exact Resemblance: The Literary Portraiture of Gertrude Stein* (New Haven: Yale Univ. Press, 1978), ch. 1, and Lubin's *Act of Portrayal: Eakins, Sargent, James* (New Haven: Yale Univ. Press, 1985). More recently, Nadia

portraiture—from the arrival of Van Dyck to the publication of Boswell's *Life*—I hope to show that, despite their obvious differences, visual and verbal portraits often shared similar assumptions about the representation of historical character. By approaching one form of portraiture in terms of the other, moreover, I hope to shed fresh light on many of the most important texts and images produced in Stuart and Georgian England.

Because comparisons between visual and verbal artistic forms have so often proved to be treacherous, I want to be as precise as possible about the inter-artistic relations I intend to explore: (1) Theoretical parallels between portrait-painting and biography, particularly when the comparisons or analogies are drawn by a biographer or portrait-painter. (2) Statements by painters and biographers about how characters should be determined or represented. (3) The description by a painter or writer of a particular work—or of a particular problem in characterization or representation—in terms of a related form of portraiture. (4) Relationships between biographers and painters, including their collaboration (and extending, as in the case of Van Dyck, to collaboration between the painter and his patron). (5) Combined forms of portraiture: series of portraits, multiple texts, and (especially) the combination of word and image. (6) Iconicism, which I define as the incorporation of images or other pictorial motifs in biographical works, or of verbal or literary motifs in visual portraits. (7) Spatial form in narrative; the manipulation of time in pictorial images. (8) The comparative portrayal of the same subject (or type of subject) in both artistic forms. (9) Visual and verbal portraits created by the same artist. (10) The parallel development of pictorial and biographical form, and the significance of formal change as an indication of changing conceptions of the self.

Tscherny, 'Reynolds's Streatham portraits and the art of intimate biography', *Burlington Magazine*, 128 (1986), 4–10, attempts to draw a parallel between several of Reynolds's portraits of friends and the development of an honest, 'intimate' form of biography that 'peaked during the 1780s...' (p. 7). The equation of honesty with intimacy is misleading, however, and numerous forerunners in both biography and portrait-painting can be mapped, as I shall show, in the 17th and early 18th cents. For other discussions, see André Maurois, *Aspects of Biography*, trans. Sydney Castle Roberts (New York: Appleton, 1929), 50, 110, 176–7; Leon Edel, *Writing Lives: Principia Biographica* (New York: Norton, 1984), 159–60 and *passim*; Ira Bruce Nadel, *Biography: Fiction, Fact and Form* (New York: St Martin's, 1984), 62; Charles A. Le Guin, 'The Language of Portraiture', *biography*, 6 (1983), 333–41; *Biography as an Art: Selected Criticism 1560–1960*, ed. James L. Clifford (London: Oxford Univ. Press, 1962), 136, 162, 164; and the index to David Novarr, *The Lines of Life: Theories of Biography, 1880–1970* (West Lafayette, Ind.: Purdue Univ. Press, 1986). For parallels between autobiography and self-portraits, see William L. Howarth, 'Some Principles of Autobiography', *New Literary History*, 5 (1974), 363–81, and María A. Salgado, 'Mirrors, Portraits, and the Self', *Romance Quarterly*, 33 (1986), 439–52. The thematic and representational functions of the portrait in other forms of narrative—particularly the novel—have been examined by Theodore Ziolkowski, *Disenchanted Images: A Literary Iconology* (Princeton: Princeton Univ. Press, 1977), ch. 3, and Françoise Meltzer, *Salome and the Dance of Writing: Portraits of Mimesis in Literature* (Chicago: Univ. of Chicago Press, 1987).

There is inevitably a good degree of overlap among the relations I attempt to isolate, just as there are several important figures whose work or career can be characterized as exhibiting many (occasionally all) of these inter-artistic features. The painter Jonathan Richardson, for example, repeatedly drew explicit comparisons between his own art and that of biography, both in his theoretical works and in his life of Milton. He described his biographical text in terms of his work as a painter, provided his own frontispiece, enjoyed a close relationship with Pope, and drew multiple portraits of himself and of his son as well as combined (and composite) portraits of several English poets. As a double agent—a practitioner of both forms of portraiture—Richardson raises interesting questions about the comparative accuracy or idealization to be found in 'life-writing' and 'face-painting' in the first half of the eighteenth century. His formal choices, moreover, provide as clear an understanding as we are likely to find of how he conceived not just of individual character (in the highly polemical biography of Milton) but of the poetical character itself.

It should be clear that as these issues become broader and more ambitious, the relations between visual and verbal portraiture correspondingly become more analogical or metaphorical, and Wendy Steiner has wisely warned us to steer between what she calls the Scylla of the old-fashioned four-term relation linking painting and literature and the Charybdis of its three-term counterpart.[11] But any attempt to draw searching comparisons between the arts will have to brave these waters at some point; success will ultimately lie in how carefully the terms are defined and in how stable the point of comparison can be made. It might be argued, for example, that any comparison between Aubrey and Cooper is necessarily a four-term proposition: Aubrey's brief lives are to the tradition of biographical writing as Cooper's miniatures are to the tradition of portrait-painting (or, more precisely, to the history of limning). The very notion of a common third term (their interest in portraits in miniature) dissolves, in other words, once we acknowledge the differences between the artistic traditions in which they worked. At the same time, any comparison between these two figures becomes closer and more stable when we examine their personal relationship, their knowledge of each other's work, their characteristic focus on the human face, their frequent portrayal of the same subject, and, as I shall finally argue, the extent to which their decision to work 'in little' enabled them to

---

[11] See *The Colors of Rhetoric: Problems in the Relation between Modern Literature and Painting* (Chicago: Univ. of Chicago Press, 1982), 5.

achieve naturalistic effects that anticipate a much more modern form of portraiture.

The most convincing (and most lasting) scholarship on relations between the arts continues to focus on a carefully defined common subject (Steiner's stable third term) or on the relative concord or conflict between word and image in the same artistic work.[12] Inter-artistic comparisons become impressionistic (at best) or entirely useless (at worst) when the essential differences between different genres are unwittingly collapsed. As Patricia Meyer Spacks has argued, 'If we conclude . . . that autobiography and the novel in eighteenth-century England shared common modes, we are not declaring an identity of genres: only an important bond of shared assumptions, shared techniques, and shared demands on the reader.'[13] What is true of two analogous literary forms is even truer when the works to be compared are drawn from artistic media that employ essentially different means of imitation. A parallel built upon the doctrine of *ut pictura poesis* does not imply that the biographer must imitate the painter, nor the painter the writer. The parallel simply suggests that the functions of the two arts, the impulses that lie behind them, some of their methods (and many of their effects) are often strikingly similar, and that what the painter accomplishes with the brush and what the biographer achieves with the pen deserve the same kind of comparative analysis that has been devoted to poetry and painting. As Jean Hagstrum emphasizes in his study of the sister-arts tradition, Horace did not specifically warrant the interpretive 'Let a poem be like a painting'; he meant by his phrase only 'As a painting, so also a poem' or 'As sometimes in painting, so occasionally in poetry'.[14] In Aristotle's discussion of painting and poetry the two arts are cousins rather than sisters. 'Each of the mimetic arts achieves its proper pleasure in its proper medium', Hagstrum argues; 'Each must take into perpetual account its own peculiar limitations', and this modified family relationship also characterizes the two arts that I compare.[15] Although I explore the common grounds of comparison between biography and portrait-paint-

---

[12] In addition to the work of Hagstrum, Steiner, and Ronald Paulson, I am thinking specifically of W. J. T. Mitchell, *Iconology: Image, Text, Ideology* (Chicago: Univ. of Chicago Press, 1986); Leonard Barkan, *The Gods Made Flesh: Metamorphosis and the Pursuit of Paganism* (New Haven: Yale Univ. Press, 1986); and two books by Ernest B. Gilman: *The Curious Perspective: Literary and Pictorial Wit in the Seventeenth Century* (New Haven: Yale Univ. Press, 1978) and *Iconoclasm and Poetry in the English Reformation: Down Went Dagon* (Chicago: Univ. of Chicago Press, 1986).

[13] *Imagining a Self: Autobiography and Novel in Eighteenth-Century England* (Cambridge, Mass.: Harvard Univ. Press, 1976), 301; her parallel is built upon Paul Alpers's definition of a 'mode' (see pp. 300–1).

[14] Hagstrum, p. 9.

[15] Ibid. 6.

ing during a period in which both arts flourished, it should be borne in mind that the differences between these two arts may tell us as much about them as do their similarities. This book is primarily a history of related forms; but in its devotion to the analysis of individual texts and images, it can also be read as a study of the evolution of English biography, on the one hand, and of English portrait-painting, on the other.

i. Parallels between the Arts

When Hazlitt remarked that 'Portrait-painting is the biography of the pencil' (the brush), he was in fact drawing an analogy that had become a commonplace in the aesthetic theory of the preceding two centuries.[16] Even Samuel Johnson, that most unpainterly of biographers, relied upon the parallel in *Rambler* no. 60 when he stated that 'We know how few can portray a living acquaintance, except by his most prominent and observable particularities, and the grosser features of his mind; and it may be easily imagined how much of this little knowledge may be lost in imparting it, and how soon a succession of copies will lose all resemblance of the original.'[17] Jonathan Richardson was even more emphatic:

A Portrait is a sort of General History of the Life of the Person it represents, not only to Him who is acquainted with it, but to Many Others, who upon Occasion of seeing it are frequently told, of what is most Material concerning Them, or their General Character at least; The Face; and Figure is also Describ'd and as much of the character as appears by These, which oftentimes is here seen in a very great Degree.[18]

At other times he argued that 'to sit for one's Picture, is to have an Abstract of one's Life written, and published, and ourselves thus consign'd over to Honour, or Infamy'.[19] Indeed,

Painting gives us not only the Persons, but the Characters of Great Men. The Air of the Head, and the Mien in general, gives strong Indications of the Mind, and illustrates what the Historian says more expressly, and particularly. Let a Man read a Character in my Lord *Clarendon*, (and certainly never was there a better Painter in that kind) he will find it improv'd by seeing a Picture of the same Person by *Van Dyck*.[20]

[16] Hazlitt, *The Champion*, 25 Dec. 1814; I quote from Reynolds, *Discourses*, p. 330.
[17] *The Rambler*, ed. W. J. Bate and Albrecht B. Strauss, vols. iii–v of *The Yale Edition of the Works of Samuel Johnson* (New Haven: Yale Univ. Press, 1969), iii. 323.
[18] *The Whole Art of Criticism*, in *Two Treatises* (1719), 45; see below, pp. 136–9.
[19] Richardson, *Essay*, pp. 13–14.
[20] Ibid. 10.

Not everyone agreed, of course. Although William Mason was an amateur painter, he never invoked the parallel in his life of Thomas Gray, nor did he attempt to achieve what we might define as pictorial effects. With the assistance of John Evelyn, the Earl of Clarendon accumulated one of the finest collections of portraits in England; but in his character-sketches in *The History of the Rebellion* he took little interest in the outward appearances of men, or, when he did, he usually created a visual impression only to draw a forceful contrast between a man's internal and external characteristics.[21] And even when a biographer did draw an explicit comparison, he could, like Conyers Middleton, wield the metaphor to warn against the dangers inherent in each form of portraiture: biographical panegyrists 'work up their characters as painters do their portraits; taking the praise of their art to consist, not in copying, but in adorning nature; not in drawing a just resemblance, but giving a fine picture; or exalting the man into a hero . . .'.[22] Qualifications such as these are exceptions, however, to a conviction that we shall see articulated throughout the following chapters of this book. The parallel between biography and portrait-painting appealed to practical experience as well as to common sense, and it was grounded (as I have shown elsewhere) in influential arguments posed by Aristotle, Plutarch, and Dryden.[23] The root of the comparison lies in the focus of both biography and portrait-painting on historical figures: no matter how artfully or imaginatively it is constructed, portraiture must also be faithful to historical fact, to contemporary standards of accuracy (if not to our own).

As a consequence of this double relation, portraiture embodies what Frank Brady has characterized as an open rather than closed structure:

Imaginative works are closed forms, while memorial works are open ones. *Don Quixote* is a self-limiting novel; nothing more can be learned about its hero because he was not a real person. But the *Life of Johnson* is permeable, so to speak; the adequacy of its Johnson can be checked by information from other sources . . . At most, novels can be compared; biographies can be corrected.[24]

---

[21] I take a closer look at Clarendon (and the character-writers generally) in 'Ut Pictura Biographia: Biography and Portrait Painting as Sister Arts', in *Articulate Images: The Sister Arts from Hogarth to Tennyson*, ed. Wendorf (Minneapolis: Univ. of Minnesota Press, 1983), 103–5.

[22] Quoted in *Biography as an Art*, ed. Clifford, p. 38.

[23] See 'Ut Pictura Biographia', in *Articulate Images*, ed. Wendorf, pp. 99–102.

[24] *James Boswell: The Later Years 1769–1795*, p. 424. There is an interesting parallel to Brady's argument in Spacks, *Imagining a Self*, p. 10, where she states that we can be more confident about imaginary characters than about ourselves. Recent scholarship on fact and fiction (or imaginative shaping) in biographical works begins with Ralph W. Rader, 'Literary Form in Factual Narrative: The Example of Boswell's *Johnson*', in *Essays in Eighteenth-Century Biography*, ed. Philip B. Daghlian (Bloomington: Indiana Univ. Press, 1968), 3–42, rpt. in *Boswell's 'Life of Johnson': New Questions, New Answers*, ed. John A. Vance (Athens: Univ. of Georgia Press, 1985), 25–52. See also Ina Schabert,

Everything that Hayden White and others have taught us about the problematical nature of historiography and historical fact should make us deeply suspicious of the sharp polarization in Brady's distinctions between 'memorial' and 'imaginative' form, but the fundamental relation he draws between portraiture and documentation cannot be entirely ignored. Biographies and portraits not only record facts and include documents, they function *as* documents themselves. Perhaps the most famous example is Van Eyck's portrait of the Arnolfini, where the painting not only commemorates a wedding, but also serves (according to contemporary custom) as the marriage certificate itself.[25] We can see this same double function at work in Van Dyck's portrait of *Charles I in Three Positions* (Plate 1),[26] an unusual painting that is, as I shall argue later, as ambitious and suggestive as any of the other portraits that Van Dyck painted of the king. But this painting was originally conceived (by its subject, if not by its painter) as a pictorial document, a combination of different poses that would enable Bernini to sculpt a marble bust of Charles. Van Dyck could have completed this commission by painting three separate portraits of the king—in full-profile, three-quarter profile, and full-frontal poses—but he chose, instead, to create a more complex portrait in which the king is forced to confront himself. If we turn to biographical writing, we can isolate similar functions in Aubrey's fragmentary narratives (which would be retailed by other hands) and in Mason's life of Gray, where the desire to have the poet 'become his own biographer' is so strong that the resulting biography (if one can call it that) is, among other things, a critical edition of Gray's correspondence.[27]

Biographies and painted portraits, however, are not merely historical, factual, documentary works of art; they often serve as *personal* documents, attempts to capture—on paper or on canvas—what is lost or certain to

'Fictional Biography, Factual Biography, and their Contaminations', *biography*, 5 (1982), 1–16; William R. Siebenschuh, *Fictional Techniques and Factual Works* (Athens: Univ. of Georgia Press, 1983); and Frank Brady, 'Fictional Techniques in Factual Works', *The Eighteenth Century: Theory and Interpretation*, 26 (1985), 158–70. For the historical relations, see J. Paul Hunter, 'Biography and the Novel', *Modern Language Studies*, 9 (1979), 68–84. The works by Hayden White to which I allude include *Metahistory: The Historical Imagination in Nineteenth-century Europe* (Baltimore: The Johns Hopkins Univ. Press, 1973), *Tropics of Discourse: Essays in Cultural Criticism* (Baltimore: The Johns Hopkins Univ. Press, 1978), and 'The Problem of Style in Realistic Representation: Marx and Flaubert', in *The Concept of Style*, ed. Berel Lang (Philadelphia: Univ. of Pennsylvania Press, 1979), 213–29 (from which I draw one of the epigraphs for this book).

[25] See Erwin Panofsky, 'Jan van Eyck's "Arnolfini" Portrait', *Burlington Magazine*, 64 (1934), 117–27.

[26] Glück, no. 389; Millar, *Tudor, Stuart*, no. 146; Millar, *Van Dyck*, no. 22; also see Michael Vickers, 'Rupert of the Rhine: A new portrait by Dieussart and Bernini's Charles I', *Apollo*, 107 (1978), 161–9.

[27] *The Poems of Mr. Gray. To Which are Prefixed Memoirs of His Life and Writings by W. Mason, M.A.*, 2nd edn. (1775), 5.

fade. After the death of Colonel John Hutchinson, for instance, his widow
completed a biography of her husband that was intended to provide
consolation for herself and instruction for her children. Lucy Hutchinson
includes a full description of her husband for 'such of you as have not
seene him to remember his person', but she finally concedes that 'In all his
naturall and ordinary inclinations and composure there was somthing
extraordinary and tending to vertue, beyond what I can describe or can be
gather'd from a bare dead description . . .'. There was, she writes, 'a life of
spiritt and power in him that is not to be found in any copie drawne from
him'.[28] Even in a much more conventional narrative, Abraham Hill's
commemorative life of Isaac Barrow, we hear that 'All I have said, or can
say, is far short of the Idea which Dr *Barrow's* Friends have formed of him,
and that Character under which he ought to appear to them who knew
him not. Besides all the defects on my part, he had in himself this
disadvantage of wanting foils to augment his lustre, and low places to give
evidence to his heights . . .'. 'I have laid together a few sticks for the
Funeral-fire,' Hill concludes, 'dry Bones which can make but a Sceleton,
till some other hand lay on the Flesh and Sinews, and cause them to live
and move.'[29] Behind the standard topos here of unworthiness or inadequacy—which we shall also see in the work of Walton, Evelyn, and Mrs
Piozzi—we can sense the frustration that Hutchinson and Hill share as
they measure their own imitative structures against the palpable memory
of a virtuous life, of 'a life of spiritt and power'. Verbal and visual
portraits are always re-creations, re-presentations. And yet re-placement is
never quite dis-placement; the art of presence is inextricably tied to the
reality of absence.

   The commemorative or memorial instinct is therefore extremely
powerful in portraiture, and it poses its own dilemmas. There is a
strong tendency, on the one hand, for portraits and biographies to flatter
or idealize their subjects. Johnson told Boswell that ' "We may know
historical facts to be true, as we may know facts in common life to be true.
Motives are generally unknown. We cannot trust to the characters we find
in history, unless when they are drawn by those who knew the persons; as
those, for instance, by Sallust and by Lord Clarendon." '[30] But personal
knowledge may impose personal bias. Middleton remarked that when we
sit down to write a biography 'with the disposition of a friend, it is natural

---

[28] *Memoirs of the Life of Colonel Hutchinson*, ed. James Sutherland (London: Oxford Univ. Press, 1973), 3, 5.
[29] *Some Account of the Life of Dr Isaac Barrow*, in *English Biography in the Seventeenth Century: Selected Short Lives*, ed. Vivian De Sola Pinto (London: Harrap, 1951), 162.
[30] Boswell, *Life*, ii. 79.

for us to cast a shade over his failings, to give the strongest colouring to his virtues; and, out of a good character, to endeavour to draw a perfect one',[31] and even Johnson admitted that 'he that writes the life of another is either his friend or his enemy, and wishes either to exalt his praise or aggravate his infamy . . .'.[32] If anything, this danger is even greater for the portrait-painter, who must reconcile his or her livelihood with the competing claims of the painting's sitter, patron, function, and artistic integrity. Fidelity to nature compels the painter to balance virtues and imperfections, beauties and blemishes; but painters, like biographers, also inherited an aesthetic tradition, most recently championed by Dryden, that encouraged them to ennoble nature without entirely deserting it (the portraitist may 'shadow the more imperfect side').[33] Jonathan Richardson was thus both echoing Dryden and anticipating Reynolds when he wrote that 'The Business of Painting is not only to represent Nature, but to make the Best Choice of it; Nay to Raise, and Improve it from what is Commonly, or even Rarely Seen, to what never Was, or Will be in Fact, tho' we may easily conceive it Might be.'[34] A portrait should not be too flattering, for 'the Character must be seen throughout, or it ceases to be a Compliment';[35] but Richardson, like Reynolds after him, argues that something must be left to the imagination. The particular paradox for Richardson, as we shall see, lies in the tension between the unimaginative nature of the portraits he painted in order to earn a living (which rarely rise above the literal) and the idealizing impulse that we find in his biography and portraits of Milton.

On the other hand, there is a competing impulse in commemorative portraiture (and especially in biography) to commemorate the dead by being as exacting, as thorough, as exhaustive as possible. In planning his 'Great Biographical Monument' of Johnson, Boswell cast himself in the role of an embalmer: 'I tell every body it will be an Egyptian Pyramid in which there will be a compleat mummy of Johnson that Literary Monarch.'[36] In the *Life* itself he lamented that, had Johnson's 'other friends been as diligent and ardent as I was, he might have been almost

---

[31] Quoted in *Biography as an Art*, ed. Clifford, p. 38.

[32] *The Idler and the Adventurer*, ed. W. J. Bate, John M. Bullitt, and L. F. Powell, vol. ii of *The Yale Edition of the Works of Samuel Johnson* (New Haven: Yale Univ. Press, 1963), 263 (*Idler*, no. 84).

[33] See Wendorf, '*Ut Pictura Biographia*', in *Articulate Images*, pp. 99–103, and 'Dryden, Charles II, and the Interpretation of Historical Character', *Philological Quarterly*, 57 (1977), 82–103.

[34] *The Science of a Connoisseur*, in *Two Treatises* (1719), 13.

[35] Richardson, *Essay*, p. 79.

[36] *The Correspondence and Other Papers of James Boswell Relating to the Making of the 'Life of Johnson'*, ed. Marshall Waingrow (New York: McGraw-Hill, n.d. [1969]), 96. On Boswell as preserver, see Paul Alkon, 'Boswellian Time', *Studies in Burke and His Time*, 14 (1973), 239–56.

entirely preserved' (i. 30). More complete preservation could be accomplished by combining portraits and other visual motifs with written
narratives, and the models for this kind of composite art are the second
edition of Vasari's *Vite* (1568) and Perrault's *Les Hommes illustres*,
published in 1696 and translated into English in 1704 (but lacking the
engraved portraits).[37] And yet the actual incorporation of visual images in
narrative texts rarely transcended the frontispiece.[38] The task for Boswell—and for Roger North before him—involved the manipulation of a
vast store of primary and secondary documents (registers and wills,
conversation, anecdotes, letters, published and unpublished writings), and
the challenge facing each writer was also the same as they attempted to
exercise control over the gleanings of an entire life (what Aubrey would
call the scattered fragments of a shipwreck). Consider the irony of
Boswell's fate: for all of his diligence and devotion, to be attacked today
for imposing his own conception of Johnson on the *Life* (a conception
that does not do justice to the psychological complexity of Johnson's
character, or so the argument runs) and yet, during his own lifetime, to be
vilified for invading Johnson's privacy and thereby procuring the very
materials that make more subtle interpretations of Johnson possible.[39]

[37] See T. S. R. Boase, *Giorgio Vasari: The Man and the Book* (Princeton: Princeton Univ. Press, 1979),
66–72, and Einur Rud, *Vasari's Life and Lives: The First Art Historian* (London: Thames and Hudson,
1963), 15–21. For a recent work modelled on Perrault, see Rémy G. Saisselin, *Style, Truth and the
Portrait* (Cleveland: Cleveland Museum of Art, n.d. [1963]).

[38] The joint appearance of portraits and biography was a feature of a few English books in the 18th
cent., such as Thomas Birch's *Heads of Illustrious Persons of Great Britain* (1743), but the more popular
form combining the two arts is one that continues to flourish today, in which the portrait of a writer
serves as the frontispiece to his or her own work or to a book written about him or her. This is a
practice that became respectable even for living writers by the middle of the 17th cent.: Milton,
displeased with William Marshall's engraved portrait of him for the *Poems* of 1645, appended four
lines in Greek that pointed out the artist's incompetence; see David Piper, 'The Development of the
British Literary Portrait up to Samuel Johnson', *Proceedings of the British Academy*, 54 (1968; pub.
1970), 51–72. Later engravings were more accurate (and more flattering), and by the turn of the
century the pictorial frontispiece had become an established feature of literary works. As Addison
pointed out in the first number of the *Spectator*, 'I have observed, that a Reader seldom peruses a Book
with Pleasure, 'till he knows whether the Writer of it be a black or a fair Man, of a mild or cholerick
Disposition, Married or a Batchelor, with other Particulars of the like nature, that conduce very much
to the right Understanding of an Author'; see *The Spectator*, ed. Donald F. Bond (Oxford: Clarendon
Press, 1965), i. 1. The relationship between frontispieces and the printed works in which they appear
deserves more attention than I can devote to it here, as does the decorative arrangement of portraits
and books in 18th-cent. libraries. For an interesting approach to the latter, see David Piper, 'The
Chesterfield House Library Portraits', in *Evidence in Literary Scholarship: Essays in Memory of James
Marshall Osborn*, ed. René Wellek and Alvaro Ribeiro (Oxford: Clarendon Press, 1979), 179–95, who
quotes Carlyle: 'the Portrait was a small lighted *candle* by which the Biographies could for the first time
be *read*, and some human interpretation be made of them' (p. 179).

[39] For recent attacks on Boswell, see especially Donald J. Greene, ' " 'Tis a Pretty Book, Mr.
Boswell, But—" ', *Georgia Review*, 32 (1978), 17–43, rpt. in *Boswell's 'Life of Johnson': New Questions,
New Answers*, ed. Vance, pp. 110–46; and Richard B. Schwartz, *Boswell's Johnson: A Preface to the 'Life'*
(Madison: Univ. of Wisconsin Press, 1978). For contemporary assaults on Boswell—and for the
general issue of biographical discretion—see James L. Clifford, 'How Much Should a Biographer
Tell?', in *From Puzzles to Portraits: Problems of a Literary Biographer* (Chapel Hill: Univ. of North
Carolina Press, 1970), 113–33.

There is an interesting logic, after all, in Foucault's association of 'panopticism', the punitive imposition of total surveillance, with the attempt 'to reconstitute all the sordid detail of a life in the form of knowledge, to fill in the gaps of that knowledge and to act upon it by a practice of compulsion'.[40] The metaphor of the pyramid (in which biographical treasures are stored) must be balanced against the metaphor of the prison; like the panopticon, biographies and painted portraits also hold their subjects up to the light.

ii. Distinctions

The parallels portrait-painters and biographers draw between their works inevitably throw their differences as well as their similarities into high relief. We can sense these distinctions in Boswell's fascination with the ability of paintings to 'fix' their subjects and, by the same token, in Reynolds's conviction (perhaps, more precisely, his worry) that painting can reveal 'so much only of character as lies on the surface, as is expressed in the lineaments of the countenance'. Other important distinctions are implicit in the broad comparisons we have already examined. Most portraits, for example, are painted of men and women who are still living, who are often, in fact, portrayed at a triumphant stage in their careers. Portraits are usually commissioned by sitters—or by those who wish to honour them—but they need not be taken from the life, nor even presented to the persons they represent. Johnson probably did not sit for Reynolds's second portrait of him, completed in 1769, which represented a more idealized version than the earlier 'Dictionary Johnson' portrait of 1756–7. The full-length sketches we have of Pope were clandestinely drawn and secretly circulated.[41] But it is nevertheless true that a portrait is more 'occasional' than a biography: it can mark both a special event and a specific age in the sitter's life. Biographies, on the other hand, almost always celebrate—or at least chronicle—the dead. We sense a fullness and a perspective in biography that are lacking in portraiture: the *oeuvre* or career is complete; the lives often close with miscellaneous tributes, even inscriptions from the tomb.

One of the occasions a portrait captures is the sitting itself; biographical subjects, on the other hand, rarely stand still. The degree of self-consciousness is thus greater in the creation of visual portraiture: the sitters usually know that their portrait is being painted, and that they are

---

[40] Michel Foucault, *Discipline and Punish: The Birth of the Prison*, trans. Alan Sheridan (New York: Vintage, 1979), 252. For a more extended treatment of this parallel, see William H. Epstein, *Recognizing Biography* (Philadelphia: Univ. of Pennsylvania Press, 1987), 132–3.
[41] See Wimsatt, pp. 298–9.

officially posing for it.[42] But this heightened self-consciousness is not restricted to portrait-painting, even if it is more common there; it can also be found in biography, and in the relationship between the biographer and his subject. The most famous example is of course Boswell, who by 1768 had received Johnson's permission to publish his letters posthumously, and who by 1772 was entertaining 'a constant plan to write the *Life* of Mr. Johnson'.[43] Johnson was therefore in effect 'sitting' for his portrait—at first unconsciously, later fully aware of Boswell's designs—until his death in 1784. We must therefore consider Boswell's manipulation of major events and scenes in these years in a double context: when Boswell drew Johnson out on fanciful subjects—as in their tour of the Hebrides—or when he forced Johnson into uncomfortable situations—the dinner at Dilly's, or the prolonged conversation with Edwards—he was both learning about Johnson's character and at the same time manufacturing episodes that would be dramatically re-created in the *Life*.

At the same time, portrait-painting is more fully mimetic than biography; its representation of its subject is both more palpable and more immediate. A portrait is a more readily identifiable image of its subject; it strikes the viewer with what Richardson called 'velocity', and produces its effects, Reynolds added, at 'a single blow'.[44] Dryden also recognized this distinction in his 'Parallel Betwixt Painting and Poetry': 'I must say this to the advantage of painting, even above tragedy, that what this last represents in the space of many hours, the former shows us in one moment. The action, the passion, and the manners of so many persons as are contained in a picture are to be discerned at once, in the twinkling of an eye . . .'.[45]

But mimetic immediacy may also have its disadvantages. Boswell was impressed by the way in which the features drawn in a portrait were firmly 'fixed', but he might also have pointed out that this very act of fixing character must exclude the dramatic, conversational, and temporal elements that would most enliven his own work. By achieving its mimetic effects more quickly and directly, the portrait imposes strict limitations on its ability to represent a character's development, inconsistencies, or complexity. Like the character-sketch, the portrait attempts to encapsulate the essence of its subject; but unlike the 'character', it normally freezes its

---

[42] I quote an interesting passage on the self-conscious sitter from Henry James's *The Europeans* in 'Ut Pictura Biographia', in *Articulate Images*, pp. 111–12.

[43] *Correspondence and Other Papers of James Boswell*, ed. Waingrow, p. li.

[44] Richardson, *The Science of a Connoisseur*, in *Two Treatises* (1719), 17; Reynolds, *Discourses*, p. 65.

[45] 'Of Dramatic Poesy' and Other Critical Essays, ed. George Watson (London: Dent; New York: Dutton, 1962), ii. 189.

subject at a particular time. As Richardson noted, 'In Picture we never die, never decay, or grow older.'[46]

This distinction has recently been stressed by critics who object to any casual comparison of these two arts. Jean Starobinski argues that 'Biography is not portrait; or if it is a kind of portrait, it adds time and movement. The narrative must cover a temporal sequence sufficiently extensive to allow the emergence of the contour of life.'[47] This same point is made by Georges May in his discussion of autobiography and self-portraiture: 'Entries in a diary, or ... texts of the kind of Montaigne's disconnected, probing looks at himself, are more akin to self-portraits than to autobiography. The reason for this statement is that, in order fully to deserve its name, autobiography must, like biography, encompass an entire life, or at least a good part of a life. Short of this, a crucial element is missing, namely the experience of the passing of time.'[48]

Comments such as these reflect the fundamental difference that exists not only between biography and portrait-painting, but between any literary (temporal) and visual (spatial) art. This dichotomy has been drawn most stringently by Lessing in *Laocoön* (1766), and it has been the ambitious project of recent criticism, spearheaded by Joseph Frank and W. J. T. Mitchell, to temper his conclusions by emphasizing the role of spatial form in literary works.[49] Considerably less attention has been paid, however, to the function of temporal design within the plastic arts.[50] 'A painter must compensate the natural deficiencies of his art', Reynolds told his students. 'He has but one sentence to utter, but one moment to exhibit. He cannot, like the poet, or historian, expatiate, and impress the mind with great veneration for the character of the hero or saint he represents.'[51]

The portrait-painter must therefore take full advantage of the 'pregnant moment'—the sublime, single blow. The artist may wish to capture a distinct and significant moment in a subject's life, similar to the 'break-through' stage that is associated with crucial episodes in biography and autobiography,[52] or choose to suspend time by creating an idealized

---

[46] Richardson, *Essay*, p. 7.

[47] 'The Style of Autobiography', in *Autobiography: Essays Theoretical and Critical*, ed. James Olney (Princeton: Princeton Univ. Press, 1980), 73.

[48] 'Autobiography and the Eighteenth Century', in *The Author and His Work: Essays on a Problem in Criticism*, ed. Louis L. Martz and Aubrey Williams (New Haven: Yale Univ. Press, 1978), 323–4.

[49] See, in particular, Mitchell, 'Spatial Form in Literature: Toward a General Theory', *Critical Inquiry*, 6 (1980), 539–67, and *Iconology: Image, Text, Ideology* (Chicago: Univ. of Chicago Press, 1986).

[50] The only significant exception is Wendy Steiner, *Pictures of Romance: Form against Context in Painting and Literature* (Chicago: Univ. of Chicago Press, 1988), ch. 1, but see also Etienne Souriau, 'Time in the Plastic Arts', *Journal of Aesthetics and Art Criticism*, 7 (1949), 294–307.

[51] Reynolds, *Discourses*, p. 60.

[52] See e.g. Karl J. Weintraub, 'Autobiography and Historical Consciousness', *Critical Inquiry*, 1 (1975), 821–48, and Georges May, 'Autobiography and the Eighteenth Century', pp. 324–6.

portrait in which the subject is released from temporal contingencies. These alternatives can be illustrated in two important paintings by Reynolds that I shall return to, in greater detail, in the closing chapters of this book. In Reynolds's first portrait of Johnson (Plate 2), we find the painter depicting his subject at a moment that clearly marked a watershed in Johnson's career.[53] The portrait was finished in 1756 or 1757, shortly after Johnson had published his monumental *Dictionary of the English Language*, which was to serve as the foundation of his literary reputation. Reynolds consequently portrays Johnson as a writer: he sits at a small table with pen and paper in hand; his head, slightly tilted, reflects the tradition of portraying literary men, especially poets, in a moment of creative reverie. But if Reynolds succinctly captures a specific moment in Johnson's career, there is also a certain temporal ambiguity in the portrait: what, exactly, is Johnson composing here? One commentator has suggested that the picture is a 'portrait of the Lexicographer as poet, on the brink of the perfect definition',[54] but how can this be true if the *Dictionary* itself has already been published? (The *Dictionary*, an inkstand, and a larger table were in fact added to the painting sometime before Boswell had it engraved for the *Life of Johnson*.) Surely more than one moment of time is implied in this portrait, even if Johnson is not portrayed at work on the *Dictionary* itself. Reynolds depicts his friend as he appeared in the middle of the decade, but he simultaneously emphasizes the process of writing that links this specific moment with the broader contour of Johnson's life. In Lessing's terms, it is both a portrait of a significant moment with coexistent images, and a portrait of the consecutive activity that makes this particular achievement possible.[55]

Reynolds manipulates temporal (and spatial) design quite differently in his portrait of *Mrs Siddons as the Tragic Muse* (Plate 3).[56] This painting suggests a particular time only in the sense that it represents Sarah Siddons as the reigning queen of the English stage. She is not, however, portrayed in a specific role, nor is she even portrayed as herself in 1784.

[53] Boswell, *Life*, iv. 448; Yung, no. 39.

[54] David Piper, 'The Development of the British Literary Portrait', p. 71 (see also Piper, *Image of the Poet*, p. 93).

[55] Gotthold Ephraim Lessing, *Laocoön*, ed. Edward Allen McCormick (Indianapolis: Bobbs-Merrill, 1962), 95.

[56] C. H. Collins Baker, *Catalogue of British Paintings in the Henry E. Huntington Library and Art Gallery* (San Marino, Calif.: Huntington Library, 1936), 75–7; Waterhouse, *Reynolds* (London: Phaidon Press, 1973), no. 100; Penny, no. 151. Of the many important discussions of this painting in the context of Reynolds's theory and practice of portraiture, see Robert E. Moore, 'Reynolds and the Art of Characterization', in *Studies in Criticism and Aesthetics, 1660–1800*, ed. Howard Anderson and John S. Shea (Minneapolis: Univ. of Minnesota Press, 1967), 332–57, and Robert R. Wark, *Ten British Pictures, 1740–1840* (San Marino, Calif.: Huntington Library, 1971), 43–57.

Instead she is shown personifying the tragic muse, both the Melpomene of earlier portraiture and the tragic spirit in general. Reynolds attempts to elevate her above the ordinary circumstances of life: 'the whole beauty and grandeur of the art consists, in my opinion, in being able to get above all singular forms, local customs, particularities, and details of every kind.'[57] He therefore portrays her in a traditionally regal pose, situated upon a conventionally lofty throne, surrounded by the iconographical figures of tragedy (Pity and Fear), and impersonating a generalized, archetypal figure. The cloudy foreground of the painting, and the equally indeterminate background (are the figures attendants or statues?), reveal an intentional suppression of any distinct spatial design that would divert attention from the central figure. In similar fashion, time appears to have been abolished here, or at least infinitely extended. Reynolds suggests the transcendence of his figure by portraying her 'out of herself', having relinquished her own individuality as she takes on a more ambitious role. Reynolds in fact uses the equivalence (or equivocation) of 'as' here as one possible solution to the dilemma of representing historical character (his subject is Sarah Siddons, and yet it is not).[58] But for all of his emphasis on ideal characterization in this famous portrait, Reynolds still manages to depict an individual character, appropriately captured in the dramatic activity that gave Siddons her distinctive vitality.

In neither of these portraits, however, can Reynolds completely suggest the actual development of character, or even the gradual unfolding of unchanging characteristics. If we wish to sense the 'experience of the passing of time' we must turn to a series of portraits of the same person, painted at different stages in his or her career, such as Reynolds's three portraits of Keppel or his five paintings of Johnson. And yet it would be imprudent for us to conclude that Stuart and Georgian biography, with all of its narrative resources, actually provides precisely this sense of individual or psychological development, at least as we understand it today. As we shall see, Roger North is one of the very few writers to take an interest in the incremental stages by which humans grow into a sense of their vocation or identity, and yet even he remarked in the life of his

---

[57] Reynolds, *Discourses*, p. 44.

[58] Joel Weinsheimer, 'Mrs. Siddons, The Tragic Muse, and the Problem of *As*', *Journal of Aesthetics and Art Criticism*, 36 (1978), 317–28, argues that 'as' marks a 'double absence of relation', because a portrait itself is only a likeness. Reynolds certainly creates an intentional distance between his representation and the actual Mrs Siddons, but the terms in which Weinsheimer defines this distinction are not entirely clear: 'as means similarity or likeness' and a 'portrait is a likeness', but these are really two different kinds of similarity. Reynolds is more interested in the tension produced by his audience's realization that there is something *different* about Mrs Siddons in this painting, and something *familiar* about 'The Tragic Muse'.

brother John that 'all men living' have a 'natural temper and propensities
... which came into the world with them, and are in their power to alter
no more than complexion or stature'.[59] We shall discover a similar tension
in Walton between the conflicting elements of life and the portrait of an
accomplished self in which they are embedded, and what is especially true
of Walton's life of Donne is not entirely untrue of Boswell's life of
Johnson, nor of Johnson's life of Savage.

iii. Iconic Portraiture

The most distinctive similarity between biography and portrait-painting—the relationship that most fully justifies our thinking of them as
sister arts—lies in their central focus on human identity and achievement
and, increasingly during this period, on the importance and distinctiveness of the individual. But when we attempt to trace the history of the self,
as Lionel Trilling has warned, 'we of course know that we are dealing
with shadows in a dark land. Our predications must be diffident, our
conclusions can be only speculative.'[60] Perhaps this would be less so if
painters and biographers had been more explicit about the ways in which
they conceived of human character, especially during a period in which
scepticism about the integrity and permanence of the self was the focus of
heated philosophical and theological discourse.[61] But the only direct
formulation I have discovered is an unusual passage that Richardson
included in *The Science of a Connoisseur* (1719):

We possess but one Single Point, the whole Circumference of Eternity belongs to

[59] Millard, p. 102.

[60] *Sincerity and Authenticity* (London: Oxford Univ. Press, 1972), 54. I have found the following
essays and books on the conception of character or the self in this period to be especially helpful:
Miriam J. Benkowitz, 'Some Observations on Woman's Conception of Self in the 18th Century', in
Women in the 18th Century and Other Essays, ed. Paul Fritz and Richard Morton (Toronto: Hakkert,
1976), 37–54; John O. Lyons, *The Invention of the Self: The Hinge of Consciousness in the Eighteenth Century*
(Carbondale: Southern Illinois Univ. Press, 1978); John Archer, 'Character in English Architectural
Design', *Eighteenth-Century Studies*, 12 (1978–9), 339–71; Patrick Coleman, 'The Idea of Character in
the *Encyclopédie*', *Eighteenth-Century Studies*, 13 (1979–80), 21–48, and 'Character in an Eighteenth-
Century Context', *The Eighteenth Century: Theory and Interpretation*, 24 (1983), 51–63; Alexander Gelley,
'Character and Person: On the Presentation of Self in Some Eighteenth-Century Novels', *The
Eighteenth Century: Theory and Interpretation*, 21 (1980), 109–27; Stephen D. Cox, '*The Stranger Within
Thee': Concepts of the Self in Late-Eighteenth-Century Literature* (Pittsburgh: Univ. of Pittsburgh Press,
1980); and Martin Price, *Forms of Life: Character and Moral Imagination in the Novel* (New Haven: Yale
Univ. Press, 1983).

[61] In 'Locke and the Scriblerians: The Discussion of Identity in Early Eighteenth-Century
England', *Eighteenth-Century Studies*, 16 (1982–3), 1–25, Christopher Fox reveals that the origin of
much of Hume's theory of the unstable or impermanent self was rooted in Locke and, indeed, in
ferocious theological arguments early in the century.

Others. We talk of Years, we are Creatures but of a Day, a Moment! the Man I was Yesterday is now no more; If I live till to Morrow, That Man is not yet born: What the *Self* shall be is utterly unknown; what Ideas, what Opinions, what Joys, what Griefs, nay what Body, all is yet hid in the Womb of Time; but This we are sure of, I shall not be the Same, the present Fabrick will be demolish'd for ever. What is past we know, but 'tis vanish'd as a Morning Dream; we are moving on; and every Step we take is a Step in the Dark. (p. 178)

Reiterating Locke and anticipating Hume, Richardson provides an interesting analogue in this passage to his unusual practice of drawing a pencil sketch either of himself or of his son each morning;[62] but the observations themselves—extraordinary as they are—bear little relation to Richardson's work as a biographer or as a painter in oil. Reynolds, as we shall see, was particularly interested in the inherent contradictions in human character, but he offered no systematic theory of these inherent conflicts; they must be reconstructed from a variety of sources and applied to his work as a painter with great care. Even Hume himself remains a shadowy figure in this landscape, for 'no trace' of his sceptical formulations of human identity can be found in his individual portraits of characters in the monumental *History of England*.[63]

We shall therefore have to look elsewhere if we are to discover evidence of changing conceptions of the self. We need to examine who is portrayed, in which guise, and for what purpose; and we need to focus as well on the relations between artists and their subjects or patrons. But we can also gauge these conceptual changes by interpreting representational form as an implicit theory of characterization. Pose, setting, format, narrative length and continuity, authorial voice, the presence or absence of a concluding character-sketch—the formal structures of biography and portrait-painting indicate not only what *should* but also what *can* be said about the subjects they portray. The formal choices writers and painters make may well reveal their attitudes toward social, political, or professional decorum, but they are also tied to epistemological issues, to the question of how human character is to be understood and, ultimately, to the problem posed by contemporary philosophy, which is whether it can be understood at all. The comparative development of visual and verbal portraiture tends to accentuate these formal characteristics, especially when the structures of one medium are literally or metaphorically incorporated into the other: this is what I call iconicism.

---

[62] On Richardson's habits as a draughtsman, see Kerslake, i. 230 (whose source is Walpole).

[63] See James Noxon, 'Human Nature: General Theory and Individual Lives', in *Biography in the 18th Century*, ed. J. D. Browning (New York: Garland, 1980), 8–27 (I quote from p. 10).

In choosing the word 'iconic' to characterize these works, I am, at least in part, augmenting conventional uses of this word in the analysis of literary texts. Hagstrum, for instance, employs the term to describe poetry or prose 'of which a work of graphic art is the subject', a definition that is often more loosely associated with *ekphrasis*.[64] Biographical texts can be iconic or *ekphrastic* in this sense when they describe a portrait or re-enact its iconographic drama or significance, but I have not found it useful to restrict iconicism to these fairly infrequent occurrences. A much broader definition has been provided by the semiotician C. S. Peirce, who distinguishes between conventional (arbitrary) and relational (natural) signs by calling the first 'symbols' and the second 'icons' (an intermediate sign, which points to its referent, is called an 'index').[65] Because Peirce's schema focuses on the relative power of mimetic or imitative forms, his definitions have been particularly useful to theorists interested in refining distinctions between literature and painting and to critics wishing to suggest the ways in which literary texts strive to achieve *enargeia* or vividness.[66] Wendy Steiner, for example, argues that a portrait, unlike a biography, physically resembles its subject: 'Writing can never be iconic of a visual object in the same way painting can.'[67] These distinctions are crucial to understanding spatial and temporal form—and they will prove to be useful in establishing the shorthand effect that visual portraits have when they are referred to in biographical narratives—but, with their primary focus on iconicity in literature, they are of limited use in the study of visual images.

Iconicism, as I define it, provides a common ground of comparison between complex verbal and visual structures. Iconic biography may well partake of the particular forms of iconicity that Hagstrum and Peirce have isolated, but it can be characterized, in a more general sense, as an incorporation or adaptation of visual images and aesthetic effects, often with explicit reference to (or dependence upon) painted portraits. Iconic portraits, by the same token, disclose a reliance upon traditional iconographical motifs (which are rooted in literature) and, in many of the examples I shall examine, the literal inscription of the written word.[68] Because of its frequent combination of word and image, iconic portraiture bears an obvious and often close resemblance to emblematic literature and paint-

---

[64] Hagstrum, p. 18.

[65] For a clear discussion of Peirce's distinctions, see Steiner, *The Colors of Rhetoric*, pp. 19–20.

[66] See e.g. Max Nänny, 'Iconicity in literature', *Word and Image*, 2 (1986), 199–208, who offers a somewhat different approach to Peirce's definitions.

[67] Steiner, *Exact Resemblance to Exact Resemblance*, p. 13.

[68] For more detailed discussions of iconic biographies and portraits, see below, chs. 2–3.

ing. Shaftesbury, after all, chose the words 'emblematical' and 'enigmatical' to denote 'mixed' or combined forms of 'designatory' systems in his *Second Characteristics*, and there will be times, in fact, when I shall invoke the terms 'iconic' and 'emblematic' almost interchangeably.[69] But I have refrained from characterizing these texts and images primarily as 'emblematic' portraits for two reasons: first, because emblems are sharply defined artefacts that still enjoyed great currency in England during the seventeenth century; second, because our common use of the word 'emblematic' continues to suggest a moralistic or didactic function that is frequently but not always characteristic of Stuart and especially Georgian portraiture. 'Iconicism', moreover, reveals in its very name both its relation to the iconographic interpretation of Western painting and its roots in religious and political icons.[70] It is true, as Steiner argues, that writing cannot 'be iconic of a visual object in the same way painting can', but when we turn to biographical form in the hands of Walton and Evelyn we shall see that they wished to establish the same devotional relationship between reader and text that painters had traditionally created between the beholders of images and the icons they worshipped.

Although it is never precisely parallel, the comparative history of biography and portrait-painting might be thought of as the intertwining and gradual unravelling of visual and verbal forms or, more precisely, of the waxing and waning reliance of one art on the other in order to determine or reinforce meaning. Throughout the late seventeenth and early eighteenth centuries we shall discover an increasing reluctance to combine word and image in English portraiture, or at least to have 'necessary recourse to what is absolutely of the emblem-kind', as the iconoclastic Shaftesbury tartly put it.[71] But we must turn first to Walton, Van Dyck, and their contemporaries, for their highly iconic structures provided a conceptual framework for depicting historical character that was never entirely repudiated by their most prominent successors.

---

[69] Anthony, Earl of Shaftesbury, *Second Characters or the Language of Forms*, ed. Benjamin Rand (Cambridge: Cambridge Univ. Press, 1914), 91.

[70] For the political icon, I am indebted to Strong, *English Icon*; for the religious, Sixten Ringbom, *Icon to Narrative: The Rise of the Dramatic Close-Up in Fifteenth-Century Devotional Painting* (Acta academiae Aboensis, ser. *a*, xxxi. 2; Åbo: Åbo Akademi, 1965).

[71] *Second Characteristics*, p. 58. Cf. Sir Horace Walpole's praise of Hogarth in *Anecdotes of Painting in England*, ed. Ralph N. Wornum (1849), iii. 725: 'Another instance of this author's genius is his not condescending to explain his moral lessons by the trite poverty of allegory. If he had an emblematic thought, he expressed it with wit, rather than by a symbol'.

2

Iconic Biography:
Izaak Walton and John Evelyn

SURVEYING the three major branches of historical writing (annals, lives, narratives) in *The Advancement of Learning*, Sir Francis Bacon pointed to his contemporaries' relative disregard for biographical works: 'For *Lives*, I do find it strange that these times have so little esteemed the virtues of the times, as that the writing of lives should be no more frequent. For although there be not many sovereign princes, or absolute commanders . . . yet are there many worthy personages that deserve better than dispersed report or barren elogies.'[1] Writing almost ninety years later, in 1694, Edward Phillips was eager to revise Bacon's estimate of the popularity of biographical writing, which had greatly burgeoned with the passage of time: 'Of all the several parts of History, that which sets forth the Lives, and Commemorates the most remarkable Actions, Sayings, or Writings of Famous and Illustrious Persons . . . as it is not the least useful in it self, so it is in highest Vogue and Esteem among the Studious and Reading part of Mankind.'[2] And of the eight biographers Phillips chose to single out for praise, fully half—Fulke Greville, Thomas Stanley, Izaak Walton, and 'the Great *Gassendus* of *France*'—were men whose works had been written following Bacon's assessment in 1605.[3] Phillips could indeed look back with pride at modern biography, one of whose most significant achievements in the preceding century had been its gradual evolution into an eclectic literary form that could no longer be easily classified under the broad headings of historical writing. Had Phillips also been aware of the unusually large number of memoirs and lives that still remained in manuscript, he could have borne even stronger witness to an age of biography in which great richness was often the product of extraordinary variety.

[1] Bacon, *The Advancement of Learning*, ed. G. W. Kitchin, introd. Arthur Johnston (London: Dent, 1973), 77. Bacon actually surveys a wide area of historical writing in the original edition of 1605; in the expanded and Latinized version of 1623—*De Augmentis Scientiarum*—he focuses more precisely on chronicles, annals, and lives.

[2] Edward Phillips, *The Life of Mr. John Milton*, in Darbishire, p. 49.

[3] Phillips also singles out Plutarch, Diogenes Laertius, Cornelius Nepos, and Machiavelli. Stanley 'made a most Elaborate improvement to the foresaid *Laertius*'; Gassendi wrote biographies of Epicurus and Pieresc.

Among the most interesting features of seventeenth-century biography is its increasing emphasis on relatively 'private' individuals, on those other 'worthy personages' mentioned by Bacon who were neither sovereign princes nor absolute commanders. But when Bacon himself turned biographer, in 1622, he wrote *The History of the Reign of King Henry the Seventh*; Edward Phillips, on the other hand, wrote the life of his uncle, John Milton. It was in fact a period in which the definition of 'great and worthy men' was steadily broadened, and in which traditional collections of lives, such as Fuller's *History of the Worthies of England* or the biographical interludes in Clarendon's histories, were published side by side with William Winstanley's *Lives of the Most Famous English Poets* and Phillips's *Theatrum Poetarum*.

This gradual biographical movement towards the 'private' individual is clearly marked in the career of Gilbert Burnet. His earliest biography, *Memoirs of the Lives and Actions of James and William Dukes of Hamilton and Castle-Herald* (1677), is quite close in form and spirit to what Bacon called historical 'narrative', and it shares with Greville's life of Sidney an often exasperating tendency to present its subjects primarily as illustrious characters in the public life of the nation.[4] But in his later work, and especially in his lives of the Earl of Rochester and Sir Matthew Hale, Burnet attempted to portray characters whose private qualities (and holy deaths) made them figures of interest and emulation. His life of Rochester is intimate by necessity: '*I . . . saw him only in one light*', on his deathbed, debating the most fundamental tenets of his religion.[5] In the preface to his life of Hale, Burnet sounded a theme he had already introduced in his memoirs of the Dukes of Hamilton and Castle-Herald: biographies of 'heroes and princes, which are commonly filled with accounts of the great things done by them', are normally—and in spite of the firm example of Plutarch—plagued by bias and flattery.[6] In his life of Hale, however, Burnet followed this line of reasoning to its logical conclusion by conceding that biographies of public men are of little use to the common reader:

but the lives of private men, though they seldom entertain the reader with such a variety of passages as the other do; yet certainly they offer him things that are

---

[4] Burnet acknowledges his focus in his preface, where he discourses on the sad state of contemporary biographies of 'great persons', which are 'full of gross partiality and flattery, and often swelled with trifling and impertinent things' ((Oxford, 1852), vii–viii).

[5] Burnet, *Some Passages of the Life and Death of the Right Honourable John, Earl of Rochester, Who died the 26th of July, 1680* (1680), A7ʳ.

[6] Burnet, *The Life and Death of Sir Matthew Hale, Kt.*, in Hale's *Contemplations Moral and Divine*, iii. (1696), A2ʳ–A2ᵛ.

more imitable, and do present wisdom and virtue to him, not only in a fair *Idea*; which is often looked on as a piece of the invention or fancy of the writer, but in such plain and familiar instances, as do both direct him better and persuade him more.[7]

The mirror for magistrates has become *speculum populi*, reflecting a refreshingly private image and shedding light on obligations and opportunities shared by an increasingly wide audience. The author of the anonymous manuscript life of Milton (now believed to be Cyriack Skinner) argued that it was 'the duty of every Christian' to celebrate the graces, natural endowments, and acquired habits of 'Persons eminent in thir Generations'.[8] Walton also chose Ecclesiastes as the epigraph for his *Lives*—'These were Honourable Men in their Generations'—and his biographies, like Skinner's, feature men remembered as much for what they wrote in the private of their studies as for the role they played in the turbulent history of their times.

But even if seventeenth-century biographers turned with increasing frequency to the lives of private men, or to the private lives of public men, they left unresolved the central question of how particular or intimate a life they should write. In a powerful statement on the peculiar attributes of 'biographia', Dryden argued that this flexible genre could sustain a 'descent into minute circumstances, and trivial passages of life, which are natural to this way of writing', but unnatural in chronicles and histories:

There you are conducted only into the rooms of state; here you are led into the private Lodgings of the Heroe: you see him in his undress, and are made Familiar with his most private actions and conversations. You may behold a *Scipio* and a *Lelius* gathering Cockle-shells on the shore, *Augustus* playing at bounding stones with Boyes; and *Agesilaus* riding on a Hobby-horse among his Children. The Pageantry of Life is taken away; you see the poor reasonable Animal, as naked as ever nature made him; are made acquainted with his passions and his follies; and find the *Demy-God a Man*.[9]

But contemporary biography rarely probed these recesses, and even Dryden, in his life of Plutarch, was severely limited by the sketchy historical materials within his grasp. In an otherwise intriguing biography, Thomas Sprat hesitated to print Abraham Cowley's private letters to his friends because 'in such Letters the Souls of Men should appear

---

Burnet, *The Life and Death of Sir Matthew Hale, Kt.*, in Hale's *Contemplations Moral and Divine*, iii. (1696), A2.

[8] Darbishire, p. 17. Darbishire's argument that John Phillips is the author of this life has been refuted by William Riley Parker, *Milton: A Biography* (Oxford: Clarendon Press, 1968), xii–xv.

[9] *The Life of Plutarch*, in *The Works of John Dryden*, xvii, ed. Samuel Holt Monk (Berkeley and Los Angeles: Univ. of California Press, 1971), 275.

undress'd: And in that negligent habit, they may be fit to be seen by one or two in a Chamber, but not to go abroad into the Streets'.[10] Although Burnet provided an intimate and moving narrative of the last days of the penitent Rochester, he lamented that he could not *give his Picture with that life and advantage that others may, who knew him when his Parts were more bright and lively*;[11] but if Burnet had actually had access to this knowledge of Rochester as a younger man, his biography would presumably have lacked its distinctive candle-light tone. Similarly, in his life of Matthew Hale, Burnet quickly proceeded from his defence of writing the lives of private men to his announcement that he would draw a veil over Hale's domestic concerns. 'My Design in Writing', he said, 'is to propose a Pattern of Heroick Vertue to the World', and thus he does not even mention Hale's family until he has proceeded halfway through the narrative, leaving a fuller account of Hale's wife and children until the conclusion so that he will not interrupt 'the thread of the Relation'.[12] Burnet's brief description of Hale's extraordinary love of animals provides what is probably the closest glimpse we have of the private character of his ascetic and incorruptible Lord Chief Justice. John Toland went even further in his life of Milton, the last to be published in the seventeenth century: 'I shall not be too minute in relating the ordinary Circumstances of his Life, . . . which are common to him with all other Men.'[13]

Behind these various statements lies not just the pressure of literary decorum but the perpetual enigma of how a person's essential character is to be understood and represented. In spite of Dryden's perceptive tribute to Plutarch and his strong sense of what biography *can* achieve, most seventeenth-century lives foundered on these very issues, for although biography had turned to the depiction of the intriguing individual, these representations of private men were still designed with traditional purposes in mind. (In Thomas Fuller's pithy summary, these were to gain some glory to God, preserve the memory of the dead, instruct and entertain the living, and 'procure some honest profit' for the author.[14]) Among the various biographers who attempted to reconcile these traditional goals with the more innovative analysis of individual character are two writers, Izaak Walton and John Evelyn, whose method I describe as

---

[10] Sprat, *An Account of the Life and Writings of Mr. Abraham Cowley: Written to Mr. M. Clifford*, in *Critical Essays of the Seventeenth Century*, ed. J. E. Spingarn (London: Oxford Univ. Press, 1908), ii. 137. I consider Sprat's life of Cowley in more detail in the second section of this chapter.

[11] Burnet, *Some Passages of the Life and Death Of the Right Honourable John, Earl of Rochester*, A7^r–A7^v.

[12] Burnet, *Life and Death of Sir Matthew Hale*, pp. 5, 94.

[13] Darbishire, p. 83.

[14] *The Worthies of England*, ed. John Freeman (London: Allen and Unwin, 1952), 1–2.

'iconic'. Their iconicism is to be found in static, spatialized, often visualized forms, in their focus on an essential, permanent character (even though it be portrayed in a variety of ways), and in our sense that these biographies are themselves carefully contrived artefacts of devotion, symbolic forms with their own iconographical attributes. Iconicism is therefore closely related to the idealizing instinct in seventeenth-century biographical writing: Walton presents John Donne as an exemplary figure, open to the public gaze; Evelyn's Margaret Blagge is also an exemplary character, but her private life deserves a private memorial, designed for the eyes of her admirers alone. If Walton's portrait functions as a public emblem, Evelyn's retains the personal (and even arcane) iconography of the *impresa*.[15] In both cases, however, this tendency to represent individuals in emblematic terms may also produce uniform characters and stylized forms not unlike those found in earlier biographical modes. Iconicism, in other words, both burdens these biographies with obvious limitations and endows them with the source of their particular power.

i. Walton's *Lives*: 'All Truth and Equal Plainness'

By his own admission, Izaak Walton was a biographer as much by accident as by temperament. In the preface to the collected edition of his *Lives* of 1675, Walton explained how a modest London draper and sempster became the biographer of the dean of St Paul's:

> *by my undertaking to collect some notes for Sir* Henry Wottons *writing the Life of* Dr. Donne, *and by Sir* Henry's *dying before he perform'd it, I became like those men that enter easily into a* Law-sute, *or a* quarrel, *and having begun, cannot make a fair retreat and be quiet, when they desire it.*[16]

Thus, contrary to his original intentions, Walton found himself engaged in writing the life of Donne in 1640 by 'necessity', and that 'begot a like necessity of writing the Life of his and my ever-honored friend, Sir Henry Wotton', eleven years later. The first edition of *The Compleat Angler* followed in 1653, but 'having writ these two lives; I lay quiet twenty years without a thought of either troubling my self or others, by any new ingagement in this kind, for I thought I knew my unfitness'. Walton's biographical slumber was broken in 1665, however, when the Archbishop of Canterbury, Gilbert Selden,

[15] For a discussion of the *impresa*, see below, p. 95.

[16] Walton, *Lives*, p. 5. For the sake of convenience, I quote from this edition, which reprints Walton's final versions of each life; further references are provided in the text. The Scolar Press has reprinted the 1670 edition of the first four lives (Menston, 1971).

asked him to prepare a new life of Richard Hooker, one that would rectify the '*many dangerous mistakes*' to be found in Bishop Gauden's recent biography. Walton, who now held a minor office within the church, both obliged his archbishop and then, in 1670, produced a 'Free-will-offering', a life of George Herbert written '*chiefly to please my self*' (p. 6). Collected editions of these four lives were issued in 1670 and 1675, and in 1678, again prompted by friends in the church, Walton published the life of Bishop Robert Sanderson, written at the age of 84.

Walton's professed aims in these five lives are uniformly conventional. He describes his works as 'well-meant Sacrifices to the Memory of these Worthy men' (p. 4); commemorative and didactic biography of the kind he is writing involves '*an* honour due to the dead, *and* a generous debt due to those that shall live, and succeed us' (p. 7). His subjects are therefore presented as illustrious archetypes, as men who have made their mark in the world, and yet also as men who have nurtured an essential simplicity, a '*harmlesnesse*' he described in *The Compleat Angler* as 'usually found in the Primitive Christians . . .'.[17] He compares Donne with Pico, Pompey, and Achilles, and—more in keeping with his spiritual focus—with Job, Jacob, David, St Paul, and Augustine. He commends the worthy Henry Wotton '*to the imitation of Posterity*' (p. 151). In erecting his own 'humble Monument' to Hooker, he argues that 'he that praises *Richard Hooker*, praises God, who hath given such gifts to men' (p. 220). The life of this pious clergyman '*was visible Rhetorick*' (p. 219); and much the same vision informs his life of Herbert, who 'ought to be a pattern of vertue to all posterity; and especially, to his Brethren of the Clergy' (p. 269). The memory of such men ought to outlive their own lives, he argues, and if he has 'either pleas'd or profited any man, I have attain'd what I design'd when I first undertook' this work, which he characterizes as 'pleasant toyl' (p. 347).

Hand in hand with these traditional aims is Walton's conventional admission of his own artlessness: not a sense of inadequacy, but a confession of unworthiness that persists even as he gains increasing confidence in his own literary abilities. These apologies are especially prominent in his first biography, the life of Donne, where he is resolved that the world should see '*the best plain Picture of the* Authors Life *that my artless Pensil, guided by the hand of truth, could present to it*' (p. 21). He compares himself to Pompey's poor bondman: 'who art thou that alone hast the honour to bury the body of *Pompey* the great? *so*, who am I that do

---

[17] *Compleat Angler*, p. 66. Further references are provided in the text.

thus officiously set the Authors memory on fire?' He concludes, however, by suggesting that at least this artlessness will be of some comfort to the beholder, *'who shall here see the Authors Picture in a natural dress, which ought to beget faith in what is spoken: for he that wants skill to deceive, may safely be trusted'.* But Walton issued similar disclaimers even in his final biographies, pointing out that the life of Sanderson should have been written by 'some person of more Learning and greater Abilities than I can pretend to' (p. 345). His own ambition was simply to write Sanderson's life 'with all truth and equal plainness' (p. 349).

These seemingly modest claims for truth and plainness have provided the focus, however, for much of the criticism devoted to Walton's *Lives* during the past thirty years. For if Walton originally stumbled into biography, it is equally clear that he subsequently pursued it with extraordinary energy, skill, and devotion. Recent scholarship has paid close attention to Walton's tireless reworking of his lives (three revisions of the studies of Donne and Hooker, four of the life of Wotton), his use of sources, his apparently endless polishing of what sometimes became a needlessly elaborate prose, and his methods of shaping his materials into a coherent and unified portrait whose apparent plainness concealed considerable artistry and—as David Novarr and others have shown—substantial manipulation and artfulness.[18] Much less attention, however, has been paid to Walton as a biographical innovator, and especially to his

---

[18] I am indebted at several points to the following discussions of Walton: John Butt, 'Izaak Walton's Methods in Biography', *Essays and Studies*, 19 (1934), 67–84, and *Biography in the Hands of Walton, Johnson, and Boswell* (Los Angeles: Univ. of California, 1966); David Novarr, *The Making of Walton's 'Lives'* (Ithaca: Cornell Univ. Press, 1958); and William H. Epstein, *Recognizing Biography* (Philadelphia: Univ. of Pennsylvania Press, 1988), 13–33. As Butt and Peter Ure point out in their review of Novarr's book (*Modern Language Review*, 54 (1959), 588–91), Novarr may have overstated his case about Walton's 'artfulness'. The issues may be summarized as follows: Novarr argues that Walton moulded his materials to support preconceived, deductive ideas of what his characters were like, always with the intention of stimulating the piety of his readers. Butt, however, argues that this amounts to trying Walton by 20th-cent. standards of biographical accuracy and method rather than by the 17th-cent. biographical traditions in which Walton wrote. Walton, in Butt's view, made use of (or disregarded) whatever materials and biographical devices he needed to represent the essential character of his subject; and in spite of his traditional mode, there was still much room for originality and complexity. In other words, by stressing how carefully Walton manipulated his materials, Novarr has enhanced his image as an artist at the expense of his reputation as an accurate historian (whereas both roles would seem to be necessary for successful biography). R. C. Bald, 'Historical Doubts Respecting Walton's Life of Donne', in *Essays in English Literature from the Renaissance to the Victorian Age*, ed. Millar MacLure and F. W. Watt (Toronto: Univ. of Toronto Press, 1964), 69–84, and John Carey, 'Sixteenth and Seventeenth Century Prose', in *English Poetry and Prose 1540–1674*, ed. Christopher Ricks (London: Sphere, 1970), 417, are considerably less flexible than Novarr, while Francisque Costa, *L'Oeuvre d'Izaak Walton (1593–1683)* (Études Anglaises, 48; Paris: Didier, n.d. [1973]), is even more sympathetic to Walton's method than is Butt. R. E. Bennett, 'Walton's Use of Donne's Letters', *Philological Quarterly*, 16 (1937), 30–4, demonstrates how Walton manipulated his sources, but argues that the total impression that Walton conveys is 'essentially true'. This is close to Butt's conclusions. My own argument in this chapter may be said to support both Butt and Novarr:

imaginative synthesis of the traditional models available to him. In the following pages I therefore consider Walton's experiments with structure and characterization before turning in the next two sections to his handling of narrative and his interest in symbolic form.

When Walton began his career as a biographer, he enjoyed a considerable variety of structural models on which to draw. One of the most traditional of forms was the saint's life, which had thrived both in Latin and Old English, and more recently in Foxe's *Book of Martyrs*. At least two major characteristics of this form—its emphasis on the precocious and holy child and its predilection for dreams and prophecy—were adapted by Walton and prominently featured in his lives of modern saints; but the structural format of the saint's life, with its often monotonous recitation of holy deeds and its usual suppression of genuine drama, had little to offer later biographers.[19] A more appealing alternative, one that Walton followed most faithfully in his life of Donne, could be found in the full biographical narrative that closed with a short epitome or character-sketch. This was a pattern sanctioned by Plutarch, whose 'character' of his subject usually emerged in the 'parallel' that linked one biography with another.[20] Indebted to both the historical narrative and the Theophrastan character, this two-fold pattern continued to retain much of its popularity until late in the eighteenth century, when, as we shall see, Boswell demonstrated that it was no longer necessary.

In the seventeenth century this structural pattern of narrative and epitome was adapted to almost every kind of sustained biography that was not itself a contracted 'character'. Because the dominant narrative section could itself be shaped in a variety of ways, this biographical pattern often overlapped with other structural forms, particularly those developed for political and ecclesiastical biography. The 'life-and-times' format was

for in emphasizing the iconic and emblematic aspects of his lives, I draw attention both to the complex biographical modes in which he wrote and to literary structures that were meant to reinforce preconceived—but not necessarily simplistic—conceptions of character. For a useful bibliography, see Dennis G. Donovan, 'Recent Studies in Burton and Walton', *English Literary Renaissance*, 1 (1971), 294–303.

[19] The nature and influence of the saints' lives have been analysed by Stauffer, pp. 3–22, 91, 118, and Bertram Colgrave, 'The Earliest Saints' Lives Written in England', *Proceedings of the British Academy*, 44 (1958), 37–9; for the precise influence on Walton, see Judith H. Anderson, *Biographical Truth: The Representation of Historical Persons in Tudor–Stuart Writing* (New Haven: Yale Univ. Press, 1984), 65–9, who also draws attention to the portraits in Walton's *Life of Donne* (see pp. 53–5). For the influence on Evelyn, see Bruce Redford, 'Evelyn's *Life of Mrs. Godolphin* and the Hagiographical Tradition', *biography*, 8 (1985), 119–29.

[20] G. W. Bowersock, 'Suetonius in the Eighteenth Century', in *Biography in the 18th Century*, ed. J. D. Browning (New York: Garland, 1980), 28–42, argues that Suetonius had a greater influence than Plutarch on English biography, especially in the development of the contracted character-sketch at the conclusion of a life.

employed in both secular and sacred lives in which the characters were
closely associated with contemporary events. But this is, by its very
nature, a cumbersome and interruptive structure that must balance the
unfolding of an individual life against the broad backdrop of contemporary history, and Walton adopted this pattern with only partial success in
his lives of Hooker and Sanderson. Contemporary events could also be
recounted through the perspective of one major character, and this was an
approach that had already been pursued with great success by biographers
in the sixteenth century. The normal structural pattern consisted of a
rising and falling motif that was traditionally tied to the revolutions of
fortune's wheel. In the hands of the most adept Tudor biographers,
especially George Cavendish and William Roper, this rising and falling
action was accented by a dramatic turn exactly at midpoint in the
narrative, and by a symmetrical ordering in which events in the first half
of the life were carefully balanced against corresponding episodes in the
concluding section.[21]

One of Walton's most perceptive readers, Clayton D. Lein, has
discovered just this kind of symmetrical structure in the life of Herbert, a
biography whose development hinges on Herbert's final decision to enter
the ministry.[22] But this structure is not limited to the life of Herbert;
Walton had already made it the foundation for his representation of
Donne, and he also employed it in a necessarily looser manner in his life of
Wotton, whose ambassadorial career also required recourse to the life-
and-times format. The significance of Walton's adoption of symmetrical
structure, however, does not lie in his indebtedness to Cavendish or
Roper (whose works he may well have known), but in his successful
inversion of a structural pattern that was traditionally devoted to men of
action and historical consequence. In his life of Cardinal Wolsey, for
instance, Cavendish vividly depicts a character whose worldly powers and
acquisitions rise with the king's favour and decline with his displeasure.[23]
In Walton's narratives, however, his subject is characterized as existing in

[21] See Richard Sylvester, 'Cavendish's *Life of Wolsey*: The Artistry of a Tudor Biographer', *Studies in Philology*, 57 (1960), 44–71, and 'Roper's *Life of More*', in *Essential Articles for the Study of Thomas More*, ed. R. S. Sylvester and G. P. Marc'hadour (Hamden, Conn.: Archon, 1977), 189–97; the introduction to *Two Early Tudor Lives*, ed. Richard S. Sylvester and Davis P. Harding (New Haven: Yale Univ. Press, 1962); and Anderson, *Biographical Truth*, pp. 27–51.

[22] 'Art and Structure in Walton's *Life of Mr. George Herbert*', *University of Toronto Quarterly*, 46 (1976–7), 162–76.

[23] This pattern does not emerge as clearly in Roper's life of More, largely because More places so little value on material circumstances. It might be argued, in fact, that Roper's structure is much like Walton's, in which adverse external factors provide the proving-ground for the inherent virtue of these elevated characters.

a kind of static limbo in the first half of the narrative. Walton's hero already possesses the intellectual and spiritual qualities necessary to follow the direction of a 'higher hand', but these talents have not yet been put to use; instead, he must first suffer a number of disappointments that will eventually thwart his secular ambitions.

The climactic point in Waltonian biography therefore inaugurates a *rising* action halfway through the narrative: his heroes must renounce their worldly expectations and accept the higher vocation to which they have been called. But this central episode is never described as a sudden conversion of faith, as a passage from a wicked to a holy life; this is the proper domain of Puritan biography—and especially autobiography. Rather, it is a renunication of one calling and an affirmation of another. Donne and Herbert renounce their secular ambitions and turn to their ministries with a zeal that more than compensates for their prolonged hesitations. Even the worldly Wotton retires from a life of diplomacy to enter holy orders as the provost of Eton. And the characteristic irony in Walton's depiction of these men is that the more they lower themselves— witness the once proud Herbert 'prostrate on the ground before the Altar' of his church in Bemerton—the stronger our sense of a rising movement in their lives (the last shall be first). Even in the biographies of Sanderson and Hooker, which share a different structure, we find this same emphasis on retirement, contemplation, even saintly mortification. It is also the informing vision of *The Compleat Angler*, whose subtitle is 'The Contemplative Man's Recreation' and whose final line introduces Walton's own motto: '*Study to be quiet*' (p. 371). From one point of view, Walton's personal vision—what has been called his 'Anglican quietude'—represents an entrenched, traditional position within a particularly tumultuous age.[24] But from another angle, from the perspective of biographical form, Walton's narratives represent an innovative development, especially in the inverted rhythms that provide them with their triumphal form.[25]

In the life of Donne, for instance, each major event in the first half of Walton's narrative corresponds to a more 'refined' episode following Donne's decision to enter the church. Walton begins with an account of Donne's lineage and early education, his years at Oxford and Cambridge, and his legal studies at Lincoln's Inn. His travels with the Earl of Essex are followed by his years as secretary to the Lord Chancellor; and it is at

---

[24] See Novarr's review of Costa, 'The Anglican Quietude of Izaak Walton', *Études anglaises*, 28 (1975), 314–24.

[25] For a discussion of triumphal form, see Alastair Fowler, *Triumphal Forms: Structural Patterns in Elizabethan Poetry* (Cambridge: Cambridge Univ. Press, 1970).

this time that Donne falls in love with and marries Anne More, which
Walton later characterizes as 'the remarkable error of his life' (p. 60). But
Donne is eventually able to surmount even this predicament, in which he
has greatly displeased his irate father-in-law, been briefly imprisoned with
his friends, and suffered the loss of his position. Once restored to his
former footing with Sir George More, Donne is invited to enter the
priesthood by Thomas Morton, Bishop of Durham, whom Walton
introduces as a pattern of the good priest. But Donne, who had earlier
undertaken a painstaking study of religious doctrine, now hesitates to
accept Morton's sponsorship because of some 'irregularities' in his past
life. Walton conflates several of Donne's letters in order to show us the
'present Condition of his mind and fortune':

*'tis now Spring, and all the pleasures of it displease me; every other tree blossoms, and I
wither: I grow older and not better; my strength diminisheth and my load grows heavier; and
yet, I would fain be or do something; but, that I cannot tell what, is no wonder in this time of
my sadness; for, to chuse is to do . . . I am not a subject good enough for one of my own letters.*
(p. 37)

Walton describes this as 'part of the picture of his narrow fortune, and the
perplexities of his generous mind' (p. 38), and this image of intense
conflict continues to be reflected in the events of the following years. His
embassy to the French government, his prophetic vision of a stillborn
child, his constant search for secular preferment, his hopeful presentation
of the *Pseudo-Martyr* to the king, the Earl of Somerset's efforts to make
him Clerk of the Council—all result in disappointments he must endure
before his own conscience and the ambiguous 'higher hand' (of God, of
the king) enjoin him to embrace the church and make peace with himself.
   Walton characterizes this decision as a triumphal resolution: 'Now the
English Church had gain'd a second St. *Austine*, for, I think, none was so
like him before his Conversion: none so like St. *Ambrose* after it: and if his
youth had the infirmities of the one, this age had the excellencies of the
other; the learning and holiness of both' (pp. 47–8). And it is no less a
triumph for Donne, whom Walton allows to speak for himself: 'and so,
blessed Jesus, I do take the cup of Salvation, and will call upon thy Name,
and will preach thy Gospel' (p. 47). Swift advancement within the church
now replaces his frustrated efforts to win secular preferment; the loss of
his beloved wife recalls many of the passionate torments he had under-
gone when he first married her, but through her death he becomes
'crucified to the world, and all those vanities, those imaginary pleasures that
are daily acted on that restless stage; and they were as perfectly crucified to

him' (p. 51). Now a 'commeasurable grief' takes full possession of him just as 'abundant affection' had while she lived; 'now his very soul was elemented of nothing but sadness'.

In this new and 'most retired and solitary life', Donne dedicates himself with renewed energy to his duties as a man of God. When he is requested by the benchers of Lincoln's Inn to preach before the friends and companions of his youth, he returns to them in a different guise: 'And where he had been a *Saul*, though not to persecute Christianity, or to deride it, yet in his irregular youth to neglect the visible practice of it: there to become a *Paul*, and preach salvation to his beloved brethren' (pp. 52–3). A diplomatic mission abroad similarly enables him to be 'an eye-witness of the health of his most dear and most honoured Mistress the Queen of *Bohemia*, . . . Who, having formerly known him as a Courtier, was much joyed to see him in a Canonical habit, and more glad to be an ear-witness of his excellent and powerful Preaching' (p. 54). Sir George More, once the agent of disaster in his life, now reappears as his son-in-law's debtor and is charitably relieved of his bond. A misunderstanding with the king eventually raises Donne even higher in his sovereign's esteem. (Walton tells us that James 'raised him from his knees with his own *hands*'.) Even his troubling sickness, which inspired those devotions 'in which the Reader may see, the most secret thoughts that then possest his Soul', serves as a parallel with the spiritual conflict we have seen revealed in his letters. Walton's extract of those letters had produced a 'picture of his narrow fortune, and the perplexities of his generous mind' (p. 38); the *Devotions* now reveal 'a *Sacred picture of Spiritual Extasies*', written on his sick bed in imitation of the 'Holy Patriarchs, who were wont to build their Altars in that place, where they had received their blessings' (p. 59).[26] Carefully paired passages such as these—with the implicit growth that lies between them—reinforce a powerful movement towards closure in Walton's narrative, towards a sense of a life fulfilled.

Walton concludes his biography by describing Donne's saintly be-haviour, the delivery of his own funeral sermon, and his final death and burial; but he does not bring his narrative to a close without reminding his readers of the essential structure of Donne's life and of his own biographical monument. Walton describes two portraits of Donne—his 'young, and his now dying Picture'—and associates each with the appropriate stage in Donne's career. I shall return to this remarkable episode in a later section, but it should be clear even now that Walton is

---

[26] Lein, 'Art and Structure in Walton's *Life of Mr. George Herbert*', n. 7, points out that saints were traditionally buried beneath the altar.

experimenting with iconic analogies for the structural patterns he has so carefully drawn. Both the visual and the verbal representations disclose the same moral: '*His great and most blessed change was from a temporal, to a spiritual imployment*: in which he was so happy, that he accounted the former part of his life to be lost. And, the beginning of it to be, from his first entring into *sacred Orders*; and serving his most merciful God at his Altar' (p. 80).

We can see a similar skill in Walton's deft handling of even the minor characters in his lives. It is true, of course, that occasionally Walton introduced brief descriptions of men that were very close to the stock-in-trade of the Theophrastan 'character'; Morton and Bedel are treated in this fashion in the life of Sir Henry Wotton, presumably to swell the narrative section devoted to Wotton's retirement from public office. But in his handling of characters who play a genuine role in his dramas, Walton usually proceeds much more empirically. Throughout his works we in fact find a general aversion to drawing blanket conclusions without substantiating evidence: 'because these things may appear to the Reader to be but Generals, I shall acquaint him with two particular Examples' (p. 123), he writes in his biography of Wotton, and in the life of Hooker he tells us that he will 'enlarge to particulars' (p. 191). Walton's subtle analysis of Sir George More stands as a minor masterpiece of characterization, and deserves its own detailed commentary.

There were conventional procedures for depicting the rash and impetuous man, and Walton was surely familiar with them. Portraits of the angry man often appeared in collections of Theophrastan 'characters' early in the seventeenth century, and we know that Walton had read at least some of Thomas Overbury's (he mentions Overbury's milkmaid in *The Compleat Angler*).[27] Walton's contemporary, Samuel Butler, wrote that the rash man 'has a Fever in his Brain, and therefore is rightly said to be hot-headed. His Reason and his Actions run down Hill, born headlong by his unstaid Will. He has not Patience to consider, and, perhaps, it would not be the better for him if he had; for he is so possest with the first Apprehension of any Thing, that whatsoever comes after loses the Race,

---

[27] *Compleat Angler*, p. 90. Many of Walton's descriptions of fish are presented almost as character-sketches; consider e.g. his analysis of the pike: 'a melancholly, and a bold fish: Melancholly, because he alwies swims or rests himselfe alone, and never swims in sholes, or with company, as *Roach*, and *Dace*, and most other fish do: And bold, because he fears not a shadow, or to see or be seen of any body, as the *Trout* and *Chub*, and all other Fish do' (p. 123). John R. Cooper, *The Art of 'The Compleat Angler'* (Durham, NC: Duke Univ. Press, 1968), argues for a generalized and stylized element throughout Walton's book; he states, for instance, that 'Walton's natural description, even at its most vivid, makes all detail conform to stylized and simplified pastoral forms' (p. 64).

and is prejudged.'[28] A complementary but less graphic approach to these passions or humours could be found in contemporary psychology. In *A Treatise of the Passions and Faculties of the Soule of Man* (1640), a book we know Walton owned, Edward Reynolds devoted two chapters to anger in his analysis of the passions of the mind. Anger, he explained, often causes a 'Precipitancy and impatience of Delay or Attendance on the determination of right reason: which makes it commonly runne away with an halfe or a broken judgement'. There is consequently no other passion that stands in such constant need of moderation, 'being hasty, impetuous, full of Desires, Griefe, Selfe-love, Impatience, which spareth no persons, friends or foes, no things, animate or inanimate, when they fit not our fancy'.[29]

There is nothing in either of these descriptions that is incompatible with Walton's explanation of Sir George More's behaviour when his daughter Anne was suddenly snatched from his home by her passionate husband. Sir George quickly recovered his daughter, managed to have Donne and his friends imprisoned, and then persuaded the Lord Chancellor to dismiss his young and promising secretary; later, when Donne and his father-in-law were finally reconciled, Sir George discovered to his surprise that he was unable to restore Donne to his former employment, thus leaving the young couple virtually penniless. Walton therefore had every justification in characterizing Sir George in brief and conventional terms; but he chose instead to present a more dramatic and intricate portrait of this impetuous man within his luxuriant and supple prose:

It is observed, and most truly, that silence and submission are charming qualities, and work most upon passionate men; and it proved so with Sir *George*; for these, and a general report of Mr. *Donnes* merits, together with his winning behaviour (which when it would intice, had a strange kind of elegant irresistible art) these, and time had so dispassionated Sir *George*, that as the world had approved his Daughters choice, so he also could not but see a more then ordinary merit in his new son: and this at last melted him into so much remorse (for Love and Anger are so like Agues, as to have hot and cold fits; and love in Parents, though it may be quenched, yet is easily rekindled, and expires not, till death denies mankind a natural heat) that he laboured his Sons restauration to his place; using to that end, both his own and his Sisters power to her Lord: but with no success; for his Answer was, *That though he was unfeignedly sorry for what he had done,*

[28] Butler, *Characters*, ed. Charles W. Daves (Cleveland: Case Western Reserve Univ. Press, 1970), 234; see also Butler's character of the inconstant man, p. 243.
[29] Reynolds, *A Treatise of the Passions and Faculties of the Soule of Man*, introd. Margaret Lee Wiley (Gainesville, Fla.: Scholars' Facsimiles and Reprints, 1971), 342–3. For Walton's copy of this book, see Jonquil Bevan, 'Some books from Izaak Walton's Library', *Library*, 6th ser. 2 (1980), 259–63.

yet it was inconsistent with his place and credit, to discharge and readmit servants at the request of passionate petitioners. (p. 30)

Walton's progression in this Ciceronian amble reveals an unexpected subtlety of characterization. He begins with a generalization about passionate men that proves to be perfectly suitable to this particular situation. Having shown how 'silence and submission' have worked their effects on Sir George, he turns once more to general statements on the nature of love and anger, and particularly of the love parents bear their children. Walton then returns to this specific scene by depicting the father's redoubled efforts to procure his son-in-law's restoration, but these particular labours are finally of little consequence to a Lord Chancellor who is himself a man of general principle. The changing focus of Walton's narration is also, of course, analogous to the crucial vacillations in Sir George's behaviour, which Walton wittily emphasizes in his choice of imagery. More first changes from a 'passionate' to a 'dispassionated' man whose anger has 'melted' into remorse. Walton then reverses his terms, demonstrating how parental love, though it may be quenched, is easily rekindled: it 'expires not, till death denies mankind a natural heat'. But even when Sir George pursues his children's interest with a natural warmth, his endeavours will have no effect on those who are unmoved by '*passionate petitioners*'.

Walton's penetrating analysis reveals that Sir George is still essentially the same man, still ruled by his own passions, still impetuous and hasty in his actions. The second half of this lengthy sentence is simply the reverse image of the first, a fitting paradigm for the inconstant man. We can see this same irony at work in Walton's suggestion that Sir George 'could not but see a more then ordinary merit in his new son'. More may indeed have been struck by Donne's inherent worth; he may also, as Walton hints, have been sure to heed what the world had already approved. But it is also the burden of Walton's paragraph that sooner or later Donne's merits must have been noticed by one whose reason continually ran hot and cold. Walton has ultimately characterized Sir George as a prisoner of his own passions, and he has accomplished this by fusing psychological analysis with the development of his larger story. Walton's readers would not have forgotten that it was Donne's own impetuosity and passionate character that precipitated this conflict, nor that its resolution depended upon his 'silence and submission'.

This delicate balance, in which carefully chosen particulars are marshalled in support of Walton's general sense of a man's character, can also be found in his full-length portraits, and especially in his depiction of Herbert and Donne. Walton was normally sparing in his treatment of his characters' appearance; usually, as Francisque Costa has pointed out, he combined visual details with broader psychological remarks.[30] In an interpolated epitome of Sanderson's 'person and temper', for instance, Walton emphasized his hero's 'visible' integrity: 'he was moderately tall; his behaviour had in it much of a plain comliness, and very little (yet enough) of ceremony or courtship; his looks and motion manifested affability and mildness' (p. 397). In miscellaneous notes he made for his life of Donne, he reminded himself to 'make his description that he was 1° for his complexion, then his behaviour, then his stature',[31] and though he altered this order in his final portrait, he nevertheless preserved this close alternation of physical and moral or social characteristics.

Although Walton was bred a draper and sempster, he paid even less attention to another aspect of his characters' appearance—what is now sometimes called the semiotics of dress. But in the one instance in which he did draw attention to a character's clothing, it is interesting to see how skilfully he made it a part of his structural pattern. Walton's usual emphasis on the spiritual and intellectual nature of his subjects indicates that he was largely conditioned, as a biographer, to 'see through clothes' (the phrase is Anne Hollander's), but George Herbert presented a special case.[32] Born into an aristocratic family, Herbert was thought by some, even when he was a student at Cambridge, to keep himself 'at too great a distance with all his inferiours: and his cloaths seem'd to prove, that he put too great a value on his parts and Parentage' (p. 270). In the first half of Walton's narrative, Herbert's clothing serves as a symbolic reminder of his worldly ambitions: should he 'return to the painted pleasures of a Court-life, or betake himself to a study of Divinity, and enter into Sacred Orders?' (p. 277). Ambitious desires, 'and the outward Glory of this World', Walton adds, 'are not easily laid aside'.

Herbert's emotional tumult is finally resolved, however, when he is presented to the living of Bemerton by William Laud, who was then Bishop of London. Walton skilfully suggests how well the bishop had taken the measure of his man by mentioning the speed with which Laud summons his tailor:

---

[30] *L'Oeuvre d'Izaak Walton*, pp. 206–8. Costa points out that Walton does not even describe Wotton, whom he knew quite well, and argues that his portrait of Hooker, whom he did *not* know, is his most successful (p. 209).

[31] *Compleat Walton*, p. 580.

[32] See *Seeing Through Clothes* (New York: Viking, 1978).

And the Bishop did the next day so convince Mr. *Herbert, That the refusal of it was a sin*; that a Taylor was sent for to come speedily from *Salisbury* to *Wilton*, to take measure, and make him Canonical Cloaths, against next day: which the Taylor did; and Mr. *Herbert* being so habited, went with his presentation to the learned Dr. *Davenant* . . . (p. 288)

Thus the once distant Herbert changed 'his sword and silk Cloaths into a Canonical Coat', lowering himself 'in his own eyes' but appearing more 'lovely in the eyes of others' (p. 292). Walton's treatment of Herbert's appearance is only a minor motif in the larger structure of the work, but it is consonant with Herbert's spiritual pilgrimage from the '*empty, imaginary painted Pleasures*' of his secular life to his eventual acceptance of a sacred aesthetic, symbolized by Mary Magdalen's 'Alabaster box *of precious oyntment*', which Walton muses over in his introduction.[33] It is also consistent with Walton's indignation in the second letter of his *Love and Truth*, in which he satirizes clergymen who appear in a 'long, curled, trim *Periwig*, a large *Tippet*, and a silk *Cassock*, or the like vain and costly Cloathing'. This priest's congregation is unlikely to heed his sermons on pride and mortification, even if he speaks the truth, for '*Example* is of greater power to incline men to Vice, than *Precepts* have to persuade to Virtue'.[34] This is one of the lessons Herbert learned in what Walton called his '*almost incredible story*' (p. 288).

ii. Spatial Form and Narrative Threads

Walton's frequent use of symmetrical structure and his fondness for parallel and antithesis in the characterization of his subjects suggest just how far his narratives diverge both from strict chronology—the bare bones of biographical writing—and from the modern norm of linear development, the gradual unfolding of individual character through time. Biography in his hands can be more accurately charted in spatial terms; he is less interested in the steady, incremental illumination of character—one epiphany quickly building upon another—than in broader and more prolonged patterns in which one structural unit must be carefully balanced against all others. In his earliest biography, for instance, we are asked to compare the first half of Donne's career with the second, the portrait of his youth with the likeness of a modern saint posing in his burial shroud; and each of these separate revelations must be read in the

---

[33] See Lein, 'Art and Structure in Walton's *Life of Mr. George Herbert*', for a full discussion of Herbert's fusion of art and religion.
[34] *Compleat Walton*, p. 550.

light of Walton's attempts to provide a summary 'character' at the end of his work.

As students of spatial form continually remind us, narratives constructed in this architectonic manner function as polar opposites of the *Bildungsroman*.[35] In Walton's *Lives* we discover portraits of men whose characters are already developed, even if, as in the case of Herbert and Donne, the directions they will ultimately take—'the many labyrinths and perplexities of a various life'— have not yet been determined. Or, to put this argument another way, it was Walton's habit in his most successful and innovative works to portray men whose lives did not suggest a simple, straightforward narrative. Even in his biography of Wotton, whose career was less adaptable to spatial structure, Walton closed by supplementing (if not quite abandoning) linear development by introducing circular form. Sir Henry, he tells us, often managed in his final years to revisit Bocton, Winchester, and Oxford, the habitations of his youth:

> And thus the Circle of Sir *Henry Wotton*'s Life—(that Circle which began at *Bocton*, and in the *Circumference* thereof, did first touch at *Winchester-School*, then at *Oxford*, and after upon so many remarkable parts and passages in *Christendom*) That *Circle* of his *Life*, was by *Death* thus closed up and compleated, in the seventy and second year of his *Age*, at *Eaton Colledge*, where, according to his Will, he now lies buried. (pp. 150–1)

One of the great difficulties in writing spatial narratives that are not merely collections of fragments lies in the construction of smooth and artful transitions between these various structural blocks. But it is characteristic of Walton that he took little interest in a seamless narrative, that he in fact treated these narrative transitions as opportunities to draw attention to his biographical methods, to what he once called those 'debts' incurred in his contract with the reader. Here is a typical moment, which follows shortly after Herbert has been measured for his canonical clothes:

> I have now Brought him to the Parsonage of Bemerton, and to the thirty sixth Year of his Age, and must stop here, and bespeak the Reader to prepare for an almost incredible story, of the great sanctity of the short remainder of his holy life ... A life, that if it were related by a Pen like his, there would then be no need for this Age to look back into times past for the examples of primitive piety: for they might be all found in the life of George Herbert. But now, alas! who is fit to undertake it! I confess I am not: and am not pleas'd with my self that I must ... my design is ... to assure the Reader, that I have used very great

---

[35] See e.g. David Mickelsen, 'Types of Spatial Structure in Narrative', in *Spatial Form in Narrative*, ed. Jeffrey R. Smitten and Ann Daghistany (Ithaca: Cornell Univ. Press, 1981), 65, 67.

diligence to inform my self, that I might inform him of the truth of what follows; and though I
cannot adorn it with eloquence, yet I will do it with sincerity. (pp. 288–9)

These recurring transitions might actually be thought of as textual
disruptions, but they are crucial to Walton because they mark a change
not only in narrative but often in character itself. Walton emphasizes
Donne's 'conversion', for example, by placing it at the centre of his
biography, as a fulcrum between the two largest structural units in his
work. But he also draws attention to this turning-point, this moment in
Augustinian or Ambrosian typology, by subtly manipulating our sense of
time and point of view. Notice, for instance, how smoothly Walton's
narrative voice modulates from the third to the first person, thus drawing
us even more closely into Donne's moment of personal resolution:

And then, as he had formerly asked God with *Moses, Who am I?* So now being
inspired with an apprehension of Gods particular mercy to him, in the Kings and
other solicitations of him, he came to ask *King Davids* thankful question, *Lord, who
am I, that thou art mindful of me?* So mindful of me, as to lead me for more than
forty years through this wilderness of the many temptations, and various turnings
of a dangerous life: so merciful to me ... And, I now say with the blessed Virgin,
Be it with thy servant as seemeth best in thy sight: and so, *blessed Jesus*, I do take the cup
of Salvation, and will call upon thy Name, and will preach thy Gospel. (p. 47)

Walton is in fact describing the moment in which Donne finally
acknowledges and embraces his essential character, already formed but so
far existing only as untapped potential. Walton closes this transition to the
second half of his narrative by repeatedly reminding us of the 'then-and-
now' structure of his work: 'And now all his studies which had been
occasionally diffused, were all concentred in Divinity. Now he had a new
calling, new thoughts, and a new imployment for his wit and eloquence:
Now all his earthly affections were changed into divine love ... Now he
declared openly, *that when he required a temporal, God gave him a spiritual
blessing.*' Walton's words herald a new series of time, explicitly balanced
against Donne's 'temporal' career and initiating a constant present tense in
Walton's continuing narrative. Everything that follows, including the
epitome that concludes this life, is consistent with Walton's portrayal of
Donne's character at the moment he resolves to serve as a humble '*door-
keeper in the house of God*' (p. 48).

It should be clear, I hope, that the many connecting passages in
Walton's *Lives* are not naïve constructions, even if they occasionally strike
us as awkward or mechanical. Nor are they conventional features that
were forced upon Walton by the decorum of contemporary narrative. As

early as 1668, in Thomas Sprat's *Account of the Life and Writings of Mr. Abraham Cowley*,[36] Walton could have discovered a biographical narrative that, while it was not entirely seamless, was nevertheless unusually free of his own self-conscious stitching. Walton would have found Sprat's portrayal of Cowley to be strikingly congenial to his own taste in illustrious men. Sprat depicted his friend as a man of virtue and learning, as an opponent of religious contention, as a devout Christian who, in his later years, undertook to write 'a Review of the Original Principles of the Primitive Church' (ii. 143). Cowley also appears as a successful diplomat whose greatest ambition was to retire to the country with his quiet muse: 'In his last seven or eight years he was conceal'd in his beloved obscurity, and possess'd that Solitude which from his very childhood he had always most passionately desired.... Some few Friends and Books, a cheerful heart, and innocent conscience were his constant Companions' (ii. 127–8). Like Herbert, whose life Walton would write two years later, Cowley 'employed his Musick to no other use than as his own *David* did towards *Saul*, by singing the Praises of God and of Nature, to drive the evil Spirit out of mens minds'.

Walton would also undoubtedly have been pleased by Sprat's spirited defence of the importance of writing the lives of private men. Sprat concedes that it may perhaps 'be judged that I have spent too many words on a private man and a Scholar, whose life was not remarkable for such a variety of Events as are wont to be the Ornaments of this kind of Relations' (ii. 145). But more profitable instruction 'may be taken from the eminent goodness of men of lower rank'; 'it is from the practice of men equal to our selves that we are more naturally taught how to command our Passions, to direct our Knowledge, and to govern our Actions.' These are words that Johnson would build upon in his study of biography in *Rambler* no. 60, but for the life itself Johnson had little but scorn: Sprat viewed his subject through 'the mist of panegyrick'.[37] Coleridge could only deplore Sprat's refusal to allow his friend to appear undressed in the 'negligent habit' of his private letters: 'What literary man has not regretted the prudery of Spratt in refusing to let his friend Cowley appear in his slippers and dressing gown?'[38] And it must be admitted that Sprat is too

---

[36] I quote from Spingarn's edn., cited above in n. 10; further references are provided in the text. Sprat, who served as the executor of Cowley's estate, published his short life as the preface to Cowley's collected works; a Latin abridgement appeared in the same year.

[37] Here is Johnson's complete verdict: 'his zeal of friendship, or ambition of eloquence, has produced a funeral oration rather than a history: he has given the character, not the life of Cowley; for he writes with so little detail that scarcely any thing is distinctly known, but all is shewn confused and enlarged through the mist of panegyrick' (Johnson, *Lives*, i. 1).

[38] *Biographia Literaria*, ed. J. Shawcross (London: Oxford Univ. Press, 1907), i. 44.

often satisfied in presenting generalizations without corroborative examples; he tells us, for instance, that 'the same men with whom he
[Cowley] was familiar in his Youth were his neerest acquaintance at the
day of his Death', but we are never told who these men are. Sprat's
reticence is unusual in a biographer dedicated to the portrayal of private
men, and incongruous in the historian of the Royal Society.

But Sprat's obvious deficiencies as a biographer may too easily have
prevented his critics from sensing the virtues of this brief life, and in
particular its successful fusion of the various facets of Cowley's character.
Sprat's interest in presenting a lengthy account of Cowley's literary career,
which is unusual in itself, is tied to his conviction that his author can be
seen most clearly in his own works. Early in his narrative he acknowledges that Cowley 'has given the World the best Image of his own mind
in these immortal Monuments of his Wit' (ii. 120). Even in poems that
bear little relation to one another, 'there is still very much of the likeness
and impression of the same mind' at work. In his moral and divine poems,
especially, 'he sat to himself and drew the figure of his own mind' (ii. 133).
What I find significant in Sprat's own portrait of Cowley is his attempt to
demonstrate that the different elements of Cowley's life are essentially of a
piece by devising smooth transitions between the various 'heads' of his
own narrative. Sprat thus begins by interweaving an analysis of Cowley's
character with a chronological presentation of the events in his life;
criticism of his literary works then serves as a bridge linking these early
sections with a full-fledged 'character' in which Sprat considers Cowley's
mind, manners, conversation, speech, and eventually his retirement. And
here, in the most successful of his transitions, Sprat moves gracefully from
a discussion of the projects that Cowley left unfinished in his retirement to
a description of his last days and death, thus marking an elegant return
both to chronology and to the questions of biographical method with
which he first opened his sketch. Having this 'Picture of his life set before
us,' he says, 'we may still keep him alive in our memories, and by this
means we may have some small reparation for our inexpressible loss by his
death' (ii. 146).

Walton would surely have admired the coherence of this portrait—its
ambition to render an individual life in its entirety—but his own methods
in reaching these goals were quite different, as we have seen. Walton made
use of letters and poems whenever they would help him to develop his
picture of a character's mind; he relished the occasional close-up, as in his
charming account of how he spent an hour in conversation with
Sanderson on a cold and rainy evening in London; and he was not afraid

to 'paraphrase and say' what he thought his subjects 'would have said upon the same occasions' (p. 345). But perhaps most distinctive is Walton's compulsive self-consciousness, his tendency to accentuate rather than conceal the seams in his narrative style. We see this in his interpolated or concluding 'characters', in his introductions and codas, and in his numerous digressions, which are explicitly treated *as* digressions from the main narrative: 'But the Reader may think that in this digression, I have already carried him too far from *Eaton-Colledge*, and therefore I shall lead him back as gently, and as orderly as I may to that place, for a further conference concerning Sir *Henry Wotton*' (pp. 139–40). Walton does not even shrink from confessing that some lacunae will appear in his narration by necessity, that he has neither the time nor the materials to treat each episode in his character's life with equal care. Thus in a manoeuvre that is characteristic of spatial narrative, Walton asks his readers to supply their own connections, and to substitute, in effect, an emblematic inscription in Latin for the temporal translation that he himself cannot provide in his life of Wotton:

But for the particulars of these, and many more that I meant to make known, I want a view of some Papers that might inform me, (his late Majesties *Letter Office* having now suffered a strange alienation) and indeed I want time too; for the Printers Press stays for what is written: so that I must haste to bring Sir *Henry Wotton* in an instant from *Venice* to *London*, leaving the Reader to make up what is defective in this place, by the small supplement of the Inscription under his Arms. (p. 126).

This honest acknowledgement of what is 'defective' in his narrative is also related to a phenomenon in the *Lives* that has been characterized as 'Waltonian suspense'.[39] At some point in each of his biographies Walton abandons the chronological narrative of his subject's life and turns instead to a lengthy digression or sustained 'character'. The most elaborate prelude to one of these episodes occurs in the life of Donne:

Reader, This sickness continued long, not only weakening but wearying him so much, that my desire is, he may now take some rest: and that before I speak of his death, thou wilt not think it an impertinent digression to look back with me, upon some observations of his life, which, whilst a gentle slumber gives rest to his spirits, may, I hope, not unfitly exercise thy consideration. (p. 60)

Walton ushers us back more than ten pages later: "*But I return from my long Digression.* We left the Author sick in *Essex* . . .' (p. 73). Almost identical

---

[39] See Stauffer, p. 115.

scenes occur in the lives of Hooker and Sanderson; in his biography of Herbert, Walton asks us to 'leave him in his Study, till I have paid my promis'd account of his excellent Mother, and I will endeavour to make it short' (p. 263).

These are indeed intriguing moments, but they certainly do not constitute narrative 'suspense'. If we take temporary leave of Walton's hero on his deathbed, it is unlikely that we shall be surprised on our return. What we witness in these episodes is in fact a *suspension* of time altogether; instead of increasing our sense of anticipation, of a strong movement forward, Walton actually emphasizes the static nature of his work, fashioning one more iconic unit in his elaborate structure. And it is characteristic that in the one episode in which he does surprise us when we return to the narrative proper—'I should now return to *Boothby Pannel*, where we left Dr. *Hammond* and Dr. *Sanderson* together, but neither can be found there' (p. 389)—he describes this suspension in spatial rather than temporal terms.

These abrupt transitions and prolonged digressions, so different in nature from Sprat's gracefully worded narrative, are none the less consistent with Sprat's ambition to provide his readers with a unified and coherent portrait. But these temporal suspensions also suggest Walton's constant struggle to rescue his characters from the flux of time. In the introduction to his life of Hooker, Walton lamented the '*full Harvest*' of information that was now '*irrevocably lost*' to him; our return to Sanderson's study in Boothby Pannel follows directly upon Walton's remark that the Civil War, which interrupted Sanderson's lectures at Oxford, produced benefits 'so like *time past*, that they are both irrevocably lost'. In his life of Herbert he emphasized his attempts to 'fix' his character in one place:

> We will now by the Readers favour suppose him fixt at *Bemerton*, and grant him to have seen the Church repair'd, and the Chappel belonging to it very decently adorn'd, at his own great charge (which is a real Truth) and having now fixt him there, I shall proceed to give an account of the rest of his behaviour both to his Parishioners, and those many others that knew and convers'd with him. (p. 293)

It is not difficult to see that these experiments provided Walton with one possible refuge from the encroachments of time, one possible solution to the problem of historical representation. In these interpolated episodes and self-conscious transitions, Walton drew attention to his emblematic method by suspending time and accentuating the spatial properties of his narrative; and in one of his biographies, the richly variegated life of

Donne, he reinforced these iconic techniques by drawing analogies with
the visual arts.

iii. Walton's 'Visible Rhetorick'

When Walton described his life of Donne as *'the best plain Picture of the
Authors Life'* and warned his readers that in the ensuing biography they
would find *'the Authors Picture in a natural dress'*, he was in fact speaking in
terms so conventional that they bordered on the formulaic. Numerous
biographies of the seventeenth century opened by suggesting affinities
between verbal and visual portraiture, and many of these parallels were
very casually drawn indeed. Walton himself never attempted to rival the
painter's art by drawing full-fledged portraits of his subjects' appearance,
and his shorter descriptive sketches were, as we have seen, closely linked
with an analysis of moral or social character. But we should neither ignore
Walton's interest in portrait-painting nor underestimate his belief in the
usefulness of this traditional parallel. He described *The Compleat Angler* as
'a picture of my owne disposition', and humorously noted that 'he that
likes not the discourse, should like the pictures of the *Trout* and other fish,
which I may commend, because they concern not my self' (p. 59). Later,
in one of his character-sketches of religious fishermen, Walton referred his
readers to a portrait of Dr Nowell, 'now to be seen, and carefully kept in
Brasennose Colledge . . . in which Picture he is drawn leaning on a Desk with
his Bible before him, and, on one hand of him his *lines*, *hooks*, and other
tackling lying in a round; and on his other hand are his Angle-rods of
several sorts' (p. 205).[40] In the notes on William Hales he prepared for
John Aubrey, he explained the circumstances in which Lady Howe
executed a portrait of Hales in black and white, 'boeth excellently well as
to the curiousness and as well as to the likenes'.[41] In his will he left his son
'all my books, (not yet given) at Furnham Castell and a deske of prints and
pickters'.[42] Most of his biographies, moreover, first appeared with
portraits serving as their frontispieces, and the collected editions of 1670
and 1675 boasted an engraved portrait for each separate life.[43]

[40] The portrait is reproduced by Bevan in Walton, *Compleat Angler*, p. 207.
[41] *Compleat Walton*, p. 596.
[42] *Waltoniana*, ed. Richard Herne Shepherd (1878), n. pag. [4 from end].
[43] For later illustrations of Walton's life of Donne, see Raoul Granqvist, *The Reputation of John
Donne 1779–1873* (Studia Anglistica Upsaliensia, 24; Uppsala: Acta Universitatis Upsaliensis, 1975),
esp. 56–8, where Granqvist discusses Stothard's portraits of Donne, engraved for Bell's *Poets of Great
Britain* (1779). Stothard portrayed Donne in a meditative reverie, as a rake on horseback, and in the
format of the Deanery portrait.

Although Walton chose not to draw explicit parallels between biography and portrait-painting in the last four lives he wrote, he introduced
even more elaborate visual motifs in the revised editions of his life of
Donne. Walton's interest in the iconography of Donne actually had its
origins several years before he became his biographer. He contributed an
elegy to the first edition of Donne's *Poems* in 1633; two years later, in the
second edition, he furnished a short poem that was placed beneath a
portrait representing Donne at the age of 18. The first version of his life of
Donne appeared as a preface to the *LXXX Sermons* of 1640. In dedicating
the second, greatly expanded edition of this biography to Sir Robert Holt
in 1658, he lamented that the beauty of Donne's conversation had not
been preserved 'by the pensil of a *Tytian* or a *Tentoret*',[44] and in the
narrative itself he added an elaborate description of Donne sitting for his
'dying Picture'. Walton finally forged his central contrast between this
painting and the portrait of Donne at 18 in the revised edition of 1675, the
last to appear in his lifetime. Novarr has shown how Walton's portrayal of
Donne became both increasingly detailed and more genuinely hagio-
graphic in the forty-two years that separate his original elegy from the
final version of his life; but it should also be clear that his representation of
Donne also became increasingly iconic, both in its turn toward *ekphrasis*—
the verbal description of visual works—and in its use of portraiture to
accentuate its own emblematic form. Walton draws our attention to these
visual motifs in three related episodes near the conclusion of his biography of Donne. He first describes Donne posing for his portrait on his
deathbed in 1630; he then compares this picture with the portrait of his
youth; finally, in the closing paragraphs of the life, he discusses the
commemorative monument that was later erected in St Paul's.

Walton opens his first episode by explaining that Donne was persuaded
by his physician, Dr Fox, to allow a commemorative portrait to be made
of him, for 'a desire of glory or commendation is rooted in the very nature
of man'. The design of the monument, however, was left to Donne
himself, who had long been a connoisseur of the visual arts:

A Monument being resolved upon, Dr. *Donne* sent for a Carver to make for
him in wood the figure of an *Vrn*, giving him directions for the compass and
height of it; and to bring with it a board of the just height of his body. 'These
being got: then without delay a choice Painter was got to be in a readiness to draw
his Picture, which was taken as followeth. ——Several Charcole-fires being first
made in his large Study, he brought with him into that place his winding-sheet in

---

⁴⁴ Quoted by Novarr, *The Making of Walton's 'Lives'*, pp. 68–9.

his hand, and, having put off all his cloaths, had this sheet put on him, and so tyed with knots at his head and feet, and his hands so placed, as dead bodies are usually fitted to be shrowded and put into their Coffin, or grave. Upon this *Vrn* he thus stood with his eyes shut, and with so much of the sheet turned aside as might shew his lean, pale, and death-like face, which was purposely turned toward the East, from whence he expected the second coming of his and our Saviour Jesus.' In this posture he was drawn at his just height; and when the Picture was fully finished, he caused it to be set by his bed-side, where it continued, and became his hourly object till his death. (p. 78)

Donne bequeathed this portrait to his friend and executor Henry King, who (with the financial assistance of Dr Fox) commissioned Nicholas Stone to create a marble effigy of Donne for St Paul's (Plate 4). The original painting does not appear to have survived, but it was probably used by Martin Droeshout as the model for his engraved portrait of Donne, which appeared as the frontispiece to *Deaths Duell* (Donne's own funeral sermon) in 1632 (Plate 5).[45]

Walton's famous description of this moving, darkly lit scene has provided later biographers with one of the fullest accounts of Donne's final days.[46] It is characteristic of Walton, of course, that he framed this remarkable episode in conventional moral terms. Donne, who shares with all men 'the desire of having our memory to out-live our lives', nevertheless makes of this 'sitting' a moment of intense mortification, stripping himself of his worldly apparel as he poses for his own *memento mori*, which then becomes 'his hourly object' until his death. But in Walton's hands this episode is handled less as an opportunity for *ekphrasis* (the portrait itself is never described) than as a representation of the creative process at work: and it is not the painterly process in which Walton is interested, but Donne's own artistic strategies. Walton appropriately depicts a man who remains a consummate artist even on his deathbed, carefully arranging his urn and winding-sheet, and dictating his own epitaph. Later, when death finally consumes him, Walton tells us that 'he closed his own eyes; and then disposed his hands and body into such a posture as required not the least alteration by those that came to shroud

[45] For an iconography of Donne, see both R. C. Bald, *John Donne: A Life* (New York: Oxford Univ. Press, 1970), who reproduces and comments upon most of the important images, and Geoffrey Keynes, *A Bibliography of Dr. John Donne*, 4th edn. (Oxford: Clarendon Press, 1973), 372–6 and *passim*.

[46] Bald, *John Donne: A Life*, pp. 525–30, makes use of Walton's narrative for this point in Donne's career, although elsewhere he has questioned the veracity of Walton's accounts (see n. 18, above). For a more recent and sceptical view, see Helen Gardner, 'Dean Donne's Monument in St. Paul's', in *Evidence in Literary Scholarship: Essays in Memory of James Marshall Osborn*, ed. René Wellek and Alvaro Ribeiro (Oxford: Clarendon Press, 1979), 29–44.

him' (pp. 81–2). Thus we are allowed to enter a scene of supreme absorption, in which Donne contemplates the image of what he—like us—will soon become.[47] Walton shows us a figure who, in the moment of death, has literally turned himself into a work of art, a visual representation of that temporal movement that most interests any biographer: the point at which man and art absolutely merge.

In the following pages of the life, Walton returns to this haunting image by pairing it with the portrait of Donne as a young man:

> And now, having brought him through the many labyrinths and perplexities of a various life: even to the gates of death and the grave; my desire is, he may rest till I have told my Reader, that I have seen many Pictures of him, in several habits, and at several ages, and in several postures: And I now mention this, because I have seen one Picture of him, drawn by a curious hand at his age of eighteen; with his sword and what other adornments might then suit with the present fashions of youth, and the giddy gayeties of that age: and his Motto then was,
>
> > *How much shall I be chang'd,*
> > *Before I am chang'd.*
>
> And if that young, and his now dying Picture, were at this time set together, every beholder might say, *Lord! How much is Dr.* Donne *already chang'd, before he is chang'd?* And the view of them might give my Reader occasion, to ask himself with some amazement, *Lord! How much may I also, that am now in health be chang'd, before I am chang'd? before this vile, this changeable body shall put off mortality?* and therefore to prepare for it. (pp. 79–80)

Although Walton professes that it is not his primary intention to provide a '*Memento*' for his readers, he has certainly done just that, even at the expense of misconstruing Donne's youthful motto. The proper translation of this Spanish tag ('Antes muerto que mudado') is 'Sooner dead than changed', or, in Sidney's rendering, 'Sooner die than change my state'.[48] A young man's fearless creed—the mark of his own individuality—has thus become a conventional reminder of universal mortality.

But Walton also tells us that these two portraits represent a more crucial change '*from a temporal, to a spiritual imployment*', and they therefore ultimately serve as emblems both of Donne's life and of the symmetrical

[47] See Michael Fried, *Absorption and Theatricality: Painting and Beholder in the Age of Diderot* (Berkeley and Los Angeles: Univ. of California Press, 1980).

[48] For a discussion of the portrait and the motto, see Novarr, *The Making of Walton's 'Lives'*, pp. 118–19 ('Walton turned the comparison of two pictures into a recapitulation of Donne's life. He turned an audacious motto of four words into a testimonial of Donne's inherent religiosity and even into a meditation on man's journey through life'), and Donne, *The Elegies and The Songs and Sonnets*, ed. Helen Gardner (Oxford: Clarendon Press, 1965), 267.

structure of Walton's narrative. Walton had drawn attention to a central pattern in Donne's life as early as his commemorative verses of 1633 (*'such sad Extremities | Can make such men as I write Elegies'*). In the argument of this lengthy poem he began to delineate Donne's progress from a secular to a religious life by comparing his early verses with the divine poetry of his maturity:

> *Did his Youth scatter Poetry, wherein*
> *Lay Loves Philosophy? Was every sin*
> *Pictur'd in his sharp Satyrs? made so foul*
> *That some have fear'd sins shapes, and kept their soul*
> *Safer by reading Verse?*   (p. 88)

Perhaps so, but his real achievements came later: *'But more matur'd: did his rich soul conceive, | And, in harmonious holy numbers weave | A Crown of Sacred Sonnets, fit t'adorn | A dying Martyrs brow'*?[49]

In the 1635 edition of Donne's *Poems*, in which this elegy was reprinted in slightly revised form, Walton's supplementary verses beneath Donne's portrait made this pattern even clearer:

> *This was for youth, Strength, Mirth, and wit that Time*
> *Most count their golden Age; but 'twas not thine.*
> *Thine was thy later yeares, so much refind*
> *From youths Drosse, Mirth & wit; as thy pure mind*

---

[49] Walton later dated this elegy '1631', but this date has been questioned by Novarr, *The Making of Walton's 'Lives'*, pp. 29–30. *Compleat Walton*, pp. 575–7 records Walton's revisions to this poem. It is possible that some of the prefatory matter relating to portraiture in the 1633 edn. prompted Walton to think in visual terms as he prepared his shorter poem for the 1635 edn. and eventually wrote his life of Donne. In 'The Printer to the Understanders', the volume's publisher, John Marriot, wrote that

> a scattered limbe of this Author, hath more amiablenesse in it, in the eye of a discerner, then a whole body of some other; Or, (to expresse him best by himselfe)
> > —*A hand, or eye,*
> > *By Hilyard drawne, is worth a history*
> > *By a worse Painter made.*   (A1ᵛ)

Marriot also included a short poem entitled 'Hexastichon Bibliopolae', in which he refers to the publication of *Deaths Duell* and the frontispiece that depicts Donne's effigy:

> I See in his last preach'd, and printed booke,
> His Picture in a sheet; in *Pauls* I looke,
> And see his Statue in a sheete of stone,
> And sure his body in the grave hath one:
> Those sheetes present him dead, these if you buy,
> You have him living to Eternity.   (A2ᵛ)

Finally, Marriot opens Donne's works with the epistle to 'The Progresse of the Soule', in which Donne states that 'Others at the Porches and Entries of their Buildings set their Armes; I, my picture...' (A3ʳ). These features were also included in the 1635 edn., the first to boast Donne's portrait (and Walton's poem). Walton and Marriot's son (and successor), Richard, were friends as well as professional collaborators; see Jonquil Bevan, 'Izaak Walton and his Publisher', *Library*, 5th ser. 32 (1977), 344–59.

> *Thought (like the Angels) nothing but the Praise*
> *Of thy Creator, in those last, best Dayes.*
> *Witness this Booke, (thy Embleme) which begins*
> *With Love; but endes, with Sighes, & Teares for sinns.*[50]

These intriguing lines, so much more forceful than the limping elegy, represent Walton's original response to William Marshall's engraved portrait of Donne, which shows him clothed in 'the present fashions of youth, and the giddy gayeties of that age' (Plate 6). It is this portrait, believed to have been based on an original by Nicholas Hilliard, the great Elizabethan miniaturist, that Walton later asks us to compare with the picture of Donne in his winding-sheet.[51] But here Walton's vision of Donne is even more extreme than in the life: he denounces this youthful image (*''twas not thine'*) insisting instead on an essential character found only in *'those last, best Dayes'*. And thus Marshall's portrait of Donne cannot serve as a proper emblem; that may be found only in the following poems, which begin with love (in the songs and sonnets) and end with the sighs and tears of his sacred verse. This emphasis is also consistent with the miscellaneous notes he made in preparation for writing the life: 'And his better part is now doing that in heaven which was most of his imployment on earth magnyfying the mercies and making himns and singing them, to that god to whome be glory and honor.'[52]

It is worth noting that the very format of this frontispiece to the *Poems* of 1635 replicates the conventional arrangement of words and images in the popular emblem books of the seventeenth century. The visual image, appearing at the top of the page, was called the emblem; the lines below were called the 'poesie' or, appropriately enough, the 'character'.[53] In this particular case, Walton has actually placed his own verbal icon in opposition to the visual image; in his more sophisticated biography of

---

[50] *Compleat Walton*, p. 578. This emphasis on Donne's progress from secular to divine poetry may also have been influenced by the final lines of Thomas Carew's elegy, which appeared in Donne's *Poems* of 1633:

> *Here lie two flamens, and both those the best:*
> *Apollo's first, at last the true God's priest.*

[51] Dennis Flynn, 'Donne's First Portrait: Some Biographical Clues?', *Bulletin of Research in the Humanities*, 82 (1979), 7–17, argues that the original portrait miniature could have been painted by Oliver.

[52] *Compleat Walton*, p. 579. These preparatory notes regularly vacillate between divine generalizations and reminders to discuss particular aspects of Donne's life; even Walton's rough notes, in other words, represent a form of meditation.

[53] See Rosemary Freeman, *English Emblem Books* (London: Chatto and Windus, 1948; rpt. New York: Octagon, 1966), 37–8, and Hagstrum, p. 97. Walton notes how Donne arranged to have commemorative seals or rings made before he died; his design was a figure of Christ affixed not to a cross but to an anchor, 'the Emblem of hope' (p. 63).

Donne, language and image would be harmoniously fused. If there is in fact a single image that captures Walton's essential vision of Donne, at least as it is portrayed in the concluding character-sketch, it is probably the simple portrait of the frontispiece (Plate 7), which portrays the benign dean of St Paul's. But the burden of Walton's narrative is most successfully represented in those two opposing portraits that form an elegant diptych, an emblematic reminder of the before-and-after nature of Donne's life.

In his essay on 'The Book as Object', Michel Butor has argued that the primary characteristic of 'today's Western book ... is its presentation as a diptych: we always see two pages at once, one opposite the other'.[54] Butor's analogy is perhaps best taken as a provocative metaphor, one that takes on an almost uncanny appropriateness when we consider how beautifully Walton's biography of Donne was first printed in the *LXXX Sermons* of 1640: there Walton's short life was presented in the same imposing format as Donne's own sermons, encased by the printer in an elegant frame and embellished with biblical marginalia (Plate 9). Equally suggestive is Butor's remark that 'the simultaneous presentation of these two panels makes it possible for the material portrayed on them to spread out, to overflow from one to the next, to fill the entire open surface of the book, so that the lines on one side can correspond to those on the other'. Again, if we read Butor figuratively, we can see that he has provided an interesting description of the way in which the two halves of Walton's narrative necessarily overlap and even penetrate each other. It is in fact the tension of Walton's symmetrical structure that provides his portrait of Donne with a sense of dramatic energy. Walton's iconicism is never the product of one static image; in the life of Donne—and even in the early verses on Marshall's portrait—Walton insists on the juxtaposition of emblematic images.

In the final pages of his biography Walton turns once more to the monument Dr Fox commissioned for St Paul's:

he lived to see as lively a representation of his dead Friend, as Marble can express; a Statue indeed so like Dr. *Donne*, that (as his Friend Sir *Henry Wotton* hath expressed himself) *it seems to breath faintly*; *and*, *Posterity shall look upon it as a kind of artificial miracle.* (p. 83)[55]

---

[54] Michel Butor, 'The Book as Object', in *Inventory*, ed. Richard Howard (New York: Simon and Schuster, 1968), 55.

[55] In the original wording (1640), Walton omits Wotton's praise and qualifies 'Marble' by calling it 'dead' (C'). Perhaps Walton's continual revision of his own representation of Donne caused him to appreciate Stone's more fully.

Walton's sense of wonder at the artful *enargeia* of this representation marks a particularly poignant moment in his narrative, especially when we remember that he opened his biography by drawing attention to his own '*artless Pensil*' and '*best Plain Picture*' of Donne. Even in his elegy of 1631, which (like his life of Herbert) he described as a '*Free-will offering*', he grieved that he lacked '*abilities, fit to set forth,* | *A* Monument, *as matchless as his worth*' (p. 84).[56] But in the closing paragraph in his biography Walton also implies that no representation of Donne, not even Nicholas Stone's lively statue, could do more than infuse its subject with faint breath:

> He was earnest and unwearied in the search of knowledge; with which, his vigorous soul is now satisfied, and employed in a continual praise of that God that first breathed it into his active body; that body, which once was a Temple of the Holy Ghost, and is now become a small quantity of Christian dust:
>
> But I shall see it reanimated.

The supreme creator alone can breathe life into men; only death itself will fully revitalize men's souls. And thus portraiture, in Walton's view, performs at best a temporary and imperfect function, standing as a commemorative transition between our lives on earth and that final, reanimating day in which we shall know all men in their essential characters.

iv. Evelyn's Icons of Friendship

In his diary entry for 9 September 1678, John Evelyn brought to an anguished close his description of the final days of Margaret Blagge, who had died in childbirth at the age of 25 only three years after marrying Sidney Godolphin:

> I cannot but say, my very Soule was united to hers, & that this stroake did pierce me to the utmost depth: for never was there a more virtuous, & inviolable friendship, never a more religious, discreete, & admirable creature; beloved of all, admir'd of all, for all the possible perfections of her sex . . . But it is not here, that I pretend to give her *Character*, who have design'd, to consecrete her worthy life to posterity.[57]

True to his design, Evelyn began to write his biography of Margaret Blagge in 1682 or 1683, and his book was finished by 1686; but *The Life of Mrs. Godolphin* was never published during Evelyn's lifetime (it did not appear, in fact, until 1847), and Evelyn's own copy was left among

---

[56] These lines are substantially altered in Walton's revised versions; see *Compleat Walton*, p. 577.
[57] Evelyn, *Diary*, iv. 148–9.

manuscripts he labelled 'Things I would write out fair and reform if I had the leisure'.[58] We can be fairly certain, however, that Evelyn's book had at least two contemporary readers: it was dedicated to Godolphin, who was then Lord High Treasurer of England, and addressed to Lady Silvius (Anne Howard), who was one of Margaret Blagge's closest friends. Both would have been deeply moved by Evelyn's adoring portrait of his spiritual friend, which fused a dramatic narrative with the emotionally charged emblems of a personal iconography.

Evelyn first met Margaret in 1672, when she was a maid-of-honour at the court of Charles II. His attention had been drawn to her by his wife Mary, but Evelyn was reluctant for some time to believe that Margaret, 'or any-body else, in her Court-Circumstances, was Principl'd with such a solid Vertue, and did Cultivate it to that degree'.[59] Evelyn was, by his very nature, wary of the allurements of Whitehall. He once described himself as 'a man of the shade, and one who had convers'd more amongst plants and Books, than in the Circles: I had contracted a certain odd reservedness, which render'd me wholly unfit to converse among the knights of the Carpet, and ye refinéd things of the Antechambers'.[60] And yet it was precisely here that Evelyn discovered someone who shared his own retiring and devout temperament; 'never', his wife said, 'were two people more alike in way and inclination'.[61] Margaret was only 20 when they met, Evelyn 52; but their friendship soon blossomed, based as it was on a common strain of piety and even selflessness. Evelyn managed her affairs during her long engagement to Sidney Godolphin, and even her marriage—which she kept secret from Evelyn for almost a year—did not entirely alter their relationship. When Margaret died, her prostrate husband asked Evelyn to arrange for her funeral and serve as executor of her estate:

having closed the Eyes, & drop'd a teare upon the Cheeke of my blessed Saint, Lovely in death, & like an Angel; I caused her Corps to be embaulmed, & wrap'd in Lead, with a plate of Brasse sothered on it, with an *Inscription* & other Circumstances due to her worth, with as much dilligence & care as my grieved heart would permitt me; being so full of sorrow, & tir'd with it, that retiring home for two dais, I spent it in solitude, & sad reflections.[62]

---

[58] Quoted by Arthur Ponsonby, *John Evelyn* (London: Heinemann, 1933), 252. For a discussion of the composition of the biography, see Evelyn, *Godolphin*, pp. 116–23.

[59] Evelyn, *Godolphin*, p. 19. All quotations from Evelyn's biography are taken from this edn.; further references are provided in the text.

[60] Quoted from Evelyn's *The Legend of the Pearle* by Hiscock, *John Evelyn*, p. 15.

[61] Quoted by Hiscock, *John Evelyn*, p. 22; a variant reading appears on p. 127.

[62] Evelyn, *Diary*, iv. 151.

It is certainly possible, and perhaps even likely, that Evelyn was actually in love with Margaret Blagge, who was widely admired for her wit, charm, and beauty as well as for her extraordinary piety.[63] But even if Evelyn does not fully reveal (or was not even entirely conscious of) the complexity and ambivalence of his own emotions, his *Life of Mrs. Godolphin* apparently does present a faithful portrait of his friend, whom he introduces as 'that Blessed Saint now in Heaven' (p. 7). He offers his book to Lady Silvius as 'a more permanent Record of her perfections' than the 'Image . . . so lively imprinted' in his own heart; but he also confesses, much as Walton invariably did, that there was at least one who knew his subject much better than he did and whose 'pencil could best Delineate' the portrait of this lady. Evelyn refers to her husband, 'who knew her best (and best she Loved)':

If such an Artist as He is, decline the undertaking, for feare that even with all his skill, he should not reach ye Original; how far-short, am I like to fall, who cannot pretend to the meanest of his Talents!

Perhaps Evelyn intended this as a sincere tribute to Godolphin, the shrewd politician whom Charles II praised by observing that 'he is never in the way, and he is never out of the way'.[64] But Evelyn—himself an

---

[63] In Hiscock's view, Evelyn's love for Margaret Blagge turned him into a possessive and emotional tyrant, urging her to renounce Godolphin so that their intense relationship could survive; after her death, he wrote a fraudulent account of their friendship that would present his actions in a virtuous light and in which he could 'recapture' her. (See both *John Evelyn* and *Family Circle*.) Hiscock, who was Librarian of Christ Church College, Oxford, where many of Evelyn's manuscripts had been deposited, drew upon previously unknown or neglected material, especially Evelyn's correspondence with Margaret. These letters do seem to indicate that Evelyn's interest in Margaret was intense enough to displease his wife; but the documents Hiscock quotes (without providing any references in his first volume) do not, in my opinion, provide enough evidence to corroborate his various theories. Hiscock pays little attention to the diary, which often supports *The Life of Mrs. Godolphin*, and he never discusses the crucial question of how significantly Evelyn's religious language (which he judges to be ambiguous and coercive) departs from contemporary rhetorical practice. He is also incapable of seeing Margaret as anything other than a rival to Mary Evelyn, whereas it is clear that Evelyn closely associated her with their children, especially the precocious Richard and Mary, who both died quite young (see Evelyn, *Godolphin*, p. 204, for his comparison of 'Mary & my *Marguerite*'). For a detailed examination of Hiscock's questionable methodology, see E. S. de Beer, 'John Evelyn: Mr. W. G. Hiscock's Account of Him', *Notes and Queries*, 205 (1960), 203–6, 243–8, 284–6; Hiscock's reply follows on 476–7. Hiscock's other critics include Guy Boas, 'John Evelyn, "Virtuoso": In the Light of Recent Research', *Essays by Divers Hands*, xxviii, ed. Angela Thirkell (London: Oxford Univ. Press, 1956), 118; and Jeanne K. Welcher, 'A Survey of the Scholarship on John Evelyn', *Bulletin of the New York Public Library*, 73 (1969), 290, and *John Evelyn* (New York: Twayne, 1972), 89. Hiscock has, however, had considerable influence on other studies of Evelyn: see James Roy King, *Studies in six 17th century writers* (Athens, Ohio: Ohio Univ. Press, 1966), 45–6; Florence Higham, *John Evelyn Esquire: An Anglican layman of the seventeenth Century* (London: SCM, 1968), 80; and Beatrice Saunders, *John Evelyn and His Times* (Oxford: Pergamon, 1970), 112. Another useful bibliography can be found in *Elizabethan Bibliographies Supplements*, xviii, ed. Dennis G. Donovan (London: Nether Press, 1970), 15–32.

[64] Quoted by Hiscock, *John Evelyn*, p. 25.

accomplished writer, and keeper of the great *Kalendarium*—had both the experience and the materials to perform this last service for 'a Dying Friend, for whom I should not have refused even my-selfe to Die'.

In Evelyn's eyes Margaret Blagge was remarkable for an intense spirituality that was unusual in someone so young, and virtually unique in the aristocratic circles in which she lived. His information about her early years was somewhat sketchy, but he was able to corroborate his own sense of her virtue and even her extreme asceticism by quoting from her list of daily reminders:

> In Dressing, I must Consider, how little it signifys to ye Saving of my Soule, and how foolish it is to be Angry about a thing so impertinent: Consider what our B. Savior suffer'd: O Lord *Assist me*!
>
> ....
>
> Now as to Pleasure, they are speaking of *Plays*, and Laughing at devout People: Well, I will Laugh at my selfe for my Impertinencys; that by degrees, I may Come to Wonder why any-body should like me, and divert the Discourse, and talk of God, and Mortality: Avoid those people when I come into the Drawing-roome, especially, among Greate-persons to Divert them: Because no *Raillery* almost, can be Innocent.
>
> ....
>
> Be sure never to talk to the *King* when they speake filthily, tho' I be Laugh'd at: Look gravely: Remembring that of *Micha, There will come a time when the Lord will bind-up his Jewels*. (pp. 14–16)

Evelyn puts similar letters, prayers, and autobiographical fragments to effective use throughout his biography, but his narrative catches dramatic fire only when he records episodes he has witnessed or in which he has played a part: his first meeting with her at Whitehall, her performance as Diana in the royal production of John Crowne's *Calisto*, their reluctant farewell on Dover beach (which bears a striking resemblance to Boswell's parting from Johnson at Harwich), and finally her marriage, pregnancy, and ominous premonitions of death.

At the heart of Evelyn's story stand those scenes in which he and Margaret discuss the meaning of their 'seraphic' friendship or participate in a long and agonizing debate over whether she should embrace a solitary life of devotion and contemplation or pursue a secular role that would enable her to fuse her profound spirituality with the worldly consolations of a husband and family. Margaret clearly needed someone in whom she could confide; she was an orphan, temperamentally isolated from the frivolous court she served, and patiently enduring an engagement protracted by Godolphin's constant ambassadorial trips abroad. And thus when Evelyn one day found her in a particularly solemn mood, she told him that 'she had never a Friend in the World'. Evelyn gently rebuked her by reminding her of Godolphin and of her companions at court, but she was adamant in her reply: 'I would have *realy* a *Friend*, and in *that name* is a greate-deale more than I can Expresse: A *Faithfull Friend*, whom I might trust with all I have, and God knows that's but little' (p. 22). According to his account of this climactic scene, Evelyn then asked her to 'Consider Well what you say, and what you do: For it is such a Trust, and so great an Obligation that you lay upon me, (were I indeede worthy of it) as I ought to Embrace with all imaginable Respect and Acknowledgement, for the greatest mark of your favour, and honor you could do me'. A friend, he told her, 'is the Neerest Relation in Nature', but before he could proceed with his 'Definitions, Complements, and distinctions', she simply asked him to be her friend 'in Earnest', and to look upon her as his own child. Evelyn immediately commemorated this moment by sealing their vows in writing:

And there standing pen & Inke upon the Table, I drew something (in a paper,) like an Altar; with a Book & a Crosse, under-writing,
   Be This the Symbol of Inviolable Friendship:
and presented it to her, with the *Pen*, which she tooke, and subscrib'd: Be it so: *Margarite Blagge* 16 Octo.b. 1672 and then Deliver'd it to me with a Smile. (p. 23)

As Margaret's adviser and spiritual companion, Evelyn had an unparalleled opportunity to observe the intricate workings of an anxious heart. He joined her in prayer, introduced her to the silent communion, and even wrote many of the devotional works that she read when they were apart.[65] 'You have brought your selfe into Bonds', he told her, that 'you can never untie whilst you live: The Title that has Consecrated this Altar, is the Marriage of Soules,—and the Golden Thread that binds the Hearts of all the World.' Friendship, he said, is a relation surpassing those of flesh and blood because it is less material, and he alluded to various works on this topic (presumably those written by his friends Robert Boyle and Jeremy Taylor) with which she was already familiar.[66] And drawing her attention once more to the altar of friendship, he said that 'With this *Symbolum*, You

---

[65] For the silent communion, see Hiscock, *Family Circle*, p. 91; Hiscock quotes extensively from the devotions Evelyn wrote for Margaret.

[66] See Harriet Sampson's discussion of Boyle's *Treatise of Seraphic Love* and Taylor's 'A Discourse of Friendship' in Evelyn, *Godolphin*, pp. xxv–xxxiii; Hiscock, *John Evelyn*, p. 30, also draws on Francis Finch's *Friendship*.

Intitle me to all that you can wth honour, and Religion part with in this World' (p. 24).

It would be natural for Margaret eventually to find these obligations of inviolable friendship as confining as originally they were reassuring. But before she secretly married Godolphin and thus placed her trust more fully in other hands, she shared with Evelyn her most intense and intimate emotions, especially her desire to quit the court and devote herself entirely to religion. Leaving the Restoration court was not an easy affair; both the king and the queen were unwilling to part with such a '*Pearle*'. And when she finally does leave, Evelyn remarks that 'from that moment, I look'd on *White-Hall*, with pitty, not to say, Contempt: What will become, thought I, of *Corinthus* (the Citty of *Luxury*) when the Graces have abandon'd her, whose Piety & Example is so highly necessary to preserve it from Desolation?' (p. 32). He compares her with Astraea emerging from the 'lower World', and then, in a series of biblical parallels, with the imprisoned Israelites 'come out of *Ægypt*, & now in [their] Way to the *Land* of *Promise*', and with Paula and her daughter, who 'quitted the Splendor of a pompous Court, for the *Recesses* of *Bethlehem*, and the *Solitudes* of *Judëa* (pp. 33, 35). Later, in his concluding 'character' of Margaret, he claims that 'if ever it was a *Holy Court*, 'twas when she was the life of it . . . Ô were the Courts of Princes Adornd and furnish'd with such a *Circle of Starrs*! We should call it *Heaven* on *Earth*, *Paradise no longer Lost, and Converse wth Angels*!' (p. 101).

But abandoning a secular life altogether was another matter, and Evelyn vigorously encouraged her not to retire into the countryside with the Dean of Hereford, her spiritual confessor. He understood quite clearly, however, how seriously her loyalties and inclinations were torn, and his presentation of these moments of torment reveals much of the energy and passion of Pope's Eloisa. Evelyn was touched 'in the deepest sense, to see the Conflicts this Excellāt Creature underwent, betweene her *Love* & her *Devotion*; or shall I call them both her *Love*? for so they were' (p. 39). He pictures God and Godolphin as 'two *Rival Lovers*', and quotes from intimate letters in which she beseeches his advice:

'Now (D. Friend) should I *Marry*, & Refuse to go to my Lord; Part unwillingly with *him*, when another so graciously Calls; What, Ô What would become of Me! No, No, I will Remaine my B. *Saviors*. Hee shall be my *Love*, my *Husband*, my *All*: I will keepe my *Virgin*, Present it unto Christ, and not put my-selfe into the Temptation of Loving any Thing in Competition with my God.' (p. 42)

Evelyn finds 'a Spirit & Zeale so extraordinary' in this letter that he compares her with those noble virgins enshrined in the primitive martyrologies. Later, in a curious postscript to his book, he remarks that he has read many famous biographies, but none that furnished the world with a more worthy example. He defies 'all the Tribe of *Legendarys* among the *Theresa's* & Devotas of that *Romantique-Church*, to produce me a Parallel'. Even Xenophon wrote his *Cyropaedia* to display the ideal nature of a prince, but *The Life of Mrs. Godolphin* 'is Written to shew, *not what she should be*, but what *she Realy, was*' (p. 115).

Emotionally charged scenes such as these, usually accompanied by Evelyn's passionate commentary, reveal both his heroine's virtues and the energy and vividness of his own book. But Evelyn had occasional difficulty with events of lesser intensity, and with the local design of his work. He was, in the first place, writing a book that was to serve both as a memoir for Lady Silvius and as a monument for posterity, and this double function sometimes introduced a certain awkwardness in his exposition: ' 'TIS not to Informe y^r L^P of a thing you do not know; but for Methods-Sake, that I Speake Something of the Family of this Lady, which was very honourable' (p. 8). And traditional biographical 'Method' was a problem in itself, especially when it conflicted with his own predilection for generalized statements centred around a highly charged scene. Early in his narrative, for instance, he notes that 'Before I proceede any farther; The Method of Time, & other Circumstances, requires me to say some thing, how I came to be first Acquainted with this Excellent Creature; and by what Tyes of Sacred Friendship, I find my-selfe so highly Oblig'd, to Celebrate her Memory' (p. 18). But his lengthy and enthusiastic description of their first meeting and of their vows at the 'altar of friendship' actually forces Evelyn to jump ahead of his story, which must be properly restored later in the narrative: 'We, Will now then looke upon her, as at *White-hall* onely, whither she came from St *James's*, to waite upon her Matie ... when she was not above Sixteene: I had not then indeed the honour to know her' (pp. 28–9).

Similar limitations appear in Evelyn's concluding 'character' of Margaret, in which we learn little about her that we did not already know from his full and detailed narrative. Evelyn presents an exhaustive account of her charities and concerns for the poor, and even illustrates his point by recalling how she was once mortified to lose £3 at a game of cards when she could have been serving the needy; but these episodes could easily — and perhaps more properly — have been contained in the chronological narrative of her life, and even the generalized virtues he insists upon extolling here owe their credibility to the various materials he has already given dramatic form. In examining the limitations of this final section, however, we may easily overlook the emblematic function Evelyn intended it to serve. His chronological '*Life*' of Mrs Godolphin, he conceded, provided a '*Profile* onely, and wants a World of *Finishing*' (p. 84). He will therefore, 'according to the Usual Method', conclude it with her character, even if his own portrait will barely reach 'the *Out-Stroaks*, and, when I shall have don my *best*, be but an Imperfect *Copy*'. He then carefully separated the character-sketch of Margaret from the preceding narrative and labelled it 'The Picture'.

This parallel between biography and portrait-painting was not an idle metaphor for Evelyn, who was one of the most accomplished connoisseurs of the seventeenth century. He and his wife were both amateur artists, and some of their drawings can still be seen in his ancestral home at Wotton.[67] Evelyn himself sat to Robert Nanteuil, Henrik van der Borcht, Hans van der Bruggen, Robert Walker, his wife Mary, and Sir Godfrey Kneller (twice). He was a collector of engraved portraits, and an adviser to more serious collectors; one evening in 1662 he held the candle and talked about painting with Charles II, whose likeness was being taken for the new coins.[68] Evelyn was in fact an expert on coins and medals, publishing *Numismata* in 1697; he also wrote a book on the art of engraving (*Sculpture*, 1662), and translated Freart's *An Idea of the Perfection of Painting* and several works by Alberti. He took an early interest in perspective and Egyptian hieroglyphics, and was never, he said, completely weaned from his 'extraordinary . . . fansy' for drawing.[69] And thus it was natural for him to open both his diary and his memoir of his early years, *De Vita Propria*, with an intricate physical description of his father:

My Father, named Richard, was of a sanguine complexion, mix'd with a dash of Choler; his haire inclining to light, which (though exceeding thick) became hoary by that time he had attain'd 30 yeares of age; it was somewhat curled towards the extremes; his beard, (which he ware a little picked, as the mode was), of a brownish colour and so continu'd to the last, save that it was somewhat mingled with grey haires about his cheekes; which with his countenance was cleare, and fresh colour'd, his eyes extraordinary quick & piercing, an ample fore head, in

---

[67] Evelyn, *Diary*, i. 39 ('Introduction'). Little attention has been paid to Evelyn either as an amateur artist or as a connoisseur: in addition to the essay by Boas and de Beer's introduction to the diary, see 'Drawings by John Evelyn (1620–1706) in the Manuscript *Elysium Britannium*', *Illustrated London News*, 223 (1953), 779; Hiscock, 'John Evelyn and the Invention of Mezzotint', *Times Literary Supplement*, 10 July 1953, p. 445 (see also pp. 493, 507), and 'John Evelyn's Florentine Cabinet at Christ Church, Oxford', *Connoisseur*, 150 (1962), 221–3.

[68] See Evelyn, *Diary*, iii. 309–10, and my discussion below, p. 126.

[69] Evelyn, *Diary*, ii. 9.

summ, a very well composed visage and manly aspect: For the rest, he was but low of stature, but very strong.[70]

But this remarkably detailed form of portraiture had no place in *The Life of Mrs. Godolphin*, in which Evelyn was completely absorbed in portraying less superficial characteristics. He introduces only one physical description of Margaret Blagge in his narrative, and that is clearly intended to reveal her emotional state as she left the stifling atmosphere of Whitehall for the comparative privacy of Berkeley House:

> I never beheld her more *Orïent*, than she appear'd all this time, and the moment she set foote in the Coach, her Eyes sparkl'd wth joy, and a marvelous Lustur: The Roses of her Cheeks were so fresh, and her Countenance so gay; as if with the rest of her perfections . . . she had Caryed all the Vertues of the Court away with her too, left it desolat. (p. 34)

And thus, even though Evelyn described his 'character' of Margaret as a '*Picture*', the iconicism of his portrait is essentially of a different kind from that found in his depiction of his father. His biographical method here is dictated by the nature of his subject, and he found that Margaret's uncommon virtue—her complete absence of human frailty—posed particularly difficult aesthetic problems. Margaret Blagge's life, like Isaac Barrow's, was so unblemished, so 'altogether *Illustrious*', that it could not properly be expressed 'by *Lights* & *Shades*'.

Evelyn's solution to this dilemma of representation can be found in an emblematic 'character' or 'picture' of Margaret in which chronological time has been completely abolished. And while this is a technique common to all character-sketches, it is especially effective here because of the length and scope of Evelyn's study. Evelyn suspends time and 'fixes' her in place by focusing on the various routines of Margaret's life; he suggests a general pattern, in other words, by describing the smaller patterns of her everyday existence. He begins by recalling 'how she usualy Pass'd the *Day*; for an Instance almost *Inimitable* in the station where she was at *Court*: I will begin with *Sonday*, the *First* of the *Weeke*' (p. 85). His depiction of a typical Sunday then naturally leads him to consider her observance of all holy days—all her feasts and fasts—and to his conclusion that every day 'was a day of Abstinence with her' (p. 90). Even her activities during the week were 'Constant', he tells us; the same regimen and the same saintly behaviour inform her entire life, even following her marriage to Godolphin. And thus Evelyn, himself a deeply methodical

[70] Evelyn, *Diary*, ii. 1–2 (also i. 1).

man, rehearses the invariable routines of her own life to build up a constant, static character of her that will transcend his own time-bound narrative and thus give her life beyond her own untimely death. The result, he admits, is perhaps only an '*Imperfect Draught* of this *Incomparable Lady*' (p. 109), and after all he has said it may still be impossible for us to conceive '*what* she was without Indeavoring to *Imitate*, and *Acquire* those Excellencys, and *Transcendent* Vertues, which made her what she was' (p. 83). But emulation is at the heart not only of his book but of the friendship that drew them together. 'Resemblance is the motive of all affection,' he wrote to his wife Mary: 'Be but like her, and you are perfect, make her like you and she will be so; you both want something of each other, and I of you both, and I hope in God we shall all be the better for one another, and that this threefold cord shall never be broken.'[71]

Although Evelyn drew a clear distinction between his '*Life*' and his '*Picture*' of Margaret Blagge, his attempt to capture her whole and to represent her in emblematic terms can be found in both parts of *The Life of Mrs. Godolphin*. In the central scene of Evelyn's narrative, in which he and Margaret pledge themselves at the altar of friendship, we should remember that Evelyn formalized their vows by drawing an altar on which both inscribed their names. Evelyn's drawing, which survives as part of his manuscript diary, presents a complex cluster of emblematic images (Plate 8). Evelyn described it in his biography as '*the Symbol of Inviolable Friendship*', the '*Symbolum*' that entitled him to all that Margaret could part with in this world (pp. 23–4). T .e most prominent feature in this drawing is the altar itself, which reinforces his many descriptions of her kneeling in prayer at a makeshift oratory she set up in the corner of her room. A human heart is depicted atop the altar, surrounded by the halo of stars he often associated with her: 'AND now Ô *Bright Saint* how does Thou Shine above! What a *Circle of Stars diademe thy Temples*!' (p. 105). On the front of the altar are inscribed the date, her name, and their pledge; his family crest accompanies these words, and a variation of his personal motto has been written below.[72] Margaret's words of presentation ('for my Brouther Euleyn') are placed at the foot of the altar, and beneath these Evelyn added, perhaps at a later time, the five-pointed star known as a pentacle or pentagram.

---

[71] Quoted by Hiscock, *John Evelyn*, p. 127.

[72] Sampson (Evelyn, *Godolphin*, pp. 213–14) points out that the manuscripts of *The Life of Mrs. Godolphin* provide different accounts of who wrote which words on Evelyn's drawing, but she concludes (correctly, I believe) that both the inscriptions on the altar and the line below ('for my Brouther Euleyn') were written by the same hand (i.e., Margaret's); Sampson also believes it is possible that she added the pentacle below (see p. 211).

The pentacle is the symbol Evelyn most frequently used to represent Margaret Blagge in his diary and correspondence; his use of it here, and on the opening and closing pages of his manuscript, suggests his reliance on symbolic forms even in a work completely devoted to the portrayal of character.[73] At the conclusion of his biography, immediately following the inscription he ordered to be engraved on her coffin, he placed a Greek letter between each point of the pentagram—'AGAPE', spiritual love—which is consistent with the heart he placed on top of the altar of friendship. The pentacle traditionally symbolized Christ's five wounds, a fact that was not lost on Evelyn as he compared his young friend with the various 'Devotas' of the Christian martyrologies. But Evelyn's familiarity with this symbol was also based on his knowledge of Egyptian hieroglyphics; he first used it as a kind of personal talisman, writing it inside each of his books and often accompanying it with the motto 'Dominus Providebit'. One of these books, Caussin's *De Symbolica Ægyptiorum Sapientia*, linked this symbol with an ordering providence, defining it as 'Icon indicat Dei Prouidentiâ regi omnia in terris ...'.[74] Evelyn also combined the pentacle with the motto he placed at the beginning and end of his *Life of Mrs. Godolphin*: 'Un Dieu, Un Amy'. The pentacle thus embodied a rich variety of personal and religious sentiments for Evelyn, all of which he associated with his inviolable friend.

In January 1673, in memory of their solemn vows, Evelyn presented Margaret with a five-pointed locket containing sixteen glittering diamonds; in June of that year he commissioned Matthew Dixon to paint Margaret's portrait (Plate 10).[75] Although Evelyn was apparently not completely satisfied with Dixon's work, he decided to keep the painting for himself, first hanging it in his bedchamber and then (perhaps at his wife's request) consigning it to the parlour.[76] The ubiquitous pentacle appears on a funeral urn, which Evelyn tells us Margaret herself chose as part of the background for the portrait: 'she would be drawn in a *Lugubrous Posture*, Sitting on a *Tombstone*, supporting a *Sepulchral-Urne*: Nor was this at all my *Fancy*; but her *Expresse-Desire* & Injunction to the *Artist*: But, to lay no more Stresse on this, How often have I heard her say, she *lov'd to be in the Company of Mourners*, which minded her of her End'

[73] My account of the pentacle is drawn from Evelyn, *Godolphin*, Appendix A (pp. 210–17), and George Ferguson, *Signs and Symbols in Christian Art* (New York: Oxford Univ. Press, 1954), 276 ('popular edn.' (1959), 153).

[74] Quoted by Sampson in Evelyn, *Godolphin*, p. 217.

[75] See Evelyn, *Diary*, iv. 1, 13–14. Dixon's portrait was attributed to Gaspar Netscher in earlier editions of the *Life*: see Geoffrey Keynes, *John Evelyn: A Study in Bibliography and a Bibliography of His Writings*, 2nd edn. (Oxford: Clarendon Press, 1968), 250.

[76] See Hiscock, *John Evelyn*, pp. 64–5, and *Family Circle*, pp. 89–90.

(p. 71). Dixon appropriately portrays Margaret in a meditative reverie, with her head tilted downward and her eyes almost closed; her hair is tied back behind her head, and the few contours of her clothing bear a classical simplicity.

Margaret sat to Matthew Dixon as a favour to Evelyn: 'a most rediculous present, but 'tis at your servis when you pleys . . .'.[77] Evelyn made it clear in an appreciative letter to her that he did not intend to treat the portrait frivolously. He promised never to look upon her image 'without a pure ejeculation on your behalfe; and if you think the reason why I so earnestly desir'd it, to be the putting me in mind of our holy friendship, yr worthy conversation, and to make me more religious, you think which is *True* upon my word'.[78] And then, in a revealing passage, Evelyn told his friend that it was because of the devotional aspect of portraiture that he was 'content to allow of Images, and historical representations; especially, if resembling the persons, and when the Meditation can be abstracted, and without superstition'. Evelyn regarded Margaret's portrait, in other words, as an actual icon, as a religious image before which he could meditate and pray. Reading her letters, contemplating her goodness, casting his eyes on her portrait, Evelyn was put in mind of God and of the divine emotions he and Margaret had shared together at the altar of friendship.

It is clear, moreover, that Evelyn also regarded his *Life of Mrs. Godolphin* as a devotional work, both as an instructive emblem and as an expression of his gratitude and submission to God ('Providentia Providebit'). In a poem he wrote soon after pledging his friendship with Margaret, he carefully associated their vows with Lancelot Andrewes's *Book of Devotions*, one of her favourite texts:

> By *Friendships* sacred Tie combin'd,
> Devoted, and by *Symbol* sign'd;
> With Hand and Seale, & solemn Oath,
> To *Jesu*, we ourselves betroth:
> Witnesse the *Day, Moneth, Yeare, Ring, Vow,*
> This *Book, Crosse, Altar, Heart,* & Thou
> (*Lover of Men*) who dost impart
> Such love, and shed it in our Heart.[79]

The devotions Evelyn himself wrote for her, 'Officium Sanctae & Individuae Trinitatis', bore the symbolic pentacle and his recurring profession of faith both in her and in the God they worshipped ('Un Dieu,

[77] Hiscock, *John Evelyn*, p. 57.   [78] Ibid. 59.   [79] Ibid. 28–9.

Un Amy').[80] But she herself was a sacred text for him; even the slightest contemplation of 'the Life of this Excell[r] Creature', he wrote in his biography, filled him with 'Thoughts above the World' (p. 105). He pictures her as a constant source of inspiration, even as he writes the book that will console him for his loss. She was born, he notes, in 'a moneth & a Yeare, never to be forgotten by me, without a mixture of different Passions', for it was then that Evelyn's favourite son was born, whose premature death he could not recall 'without Emotion' (p. 8). He translated *The Golden Book of St. John Chrysostom concerning the Education of Children* as a consolation for Richard's death, at one point exclaiming that 'My tears mingle so fast with my ink that I must break off and be silent.'[81] Similarly, in *The Life of Mrs. Godolphin*, he concludes his description of her death by remarking that he cannot pass 'the sad *Añiversary* & *lugubrous Period*, without the most *sensible Emotions*, & *Sorrows* that draw *Teares* from my very HEART, whilst I am Reciting it' (p. 79). His biography of Margaret Blagge therefore stands both as emblem and expression, a work of religious devotion and of personal consolation.

Like Walton, however, Evelyn ultimately cherished few illusions about his own attempt at biographical representation. The liveliest impression of his friend's image, he said, was to be found deeply imprinted within him. He told Lady Silvius that it was 'a rare *Artist* indeede, could reach The *Original*, & give those last, & *Living Touches*, which should make it *Breath*'; even Dixon's portrait of Margaret was 'more *lively drawn* upon the *Table of my Heart*' (p. 83). And thus in spite of his labours to capture her 'as *she Realy, was*'—through narrative and picture, through motto and icon— he was resigned to an imperfect pursuit of her essential nature, already translated to that 'happy Shore / Where no dark Night / Obscures the Day'. Breaking into an elegiac ode as he closed his work, he could only celebrate a consolation of a different kind, when 'we in Every Streete / Our *Dearest Friends againe shall Meete*, / And *Friendships more Refin'd & Sweete*, / *And never Loose them more*'.

---

[80] See Ponsonby, *John Evelyn*, p. 262.
[81] Quoted by Boas, 'John Evelyn, "Virtuoso" ', p. 112.

3

Iconic Pictures: Van Dyck and Stuart Portraiture

WHEN John Evelyn described the portrait Matthew Dixon painted of Margaret Blagge in the summer of 1673 (Plate 10), he insisted, as we have seen, that his friend's *'Lugubrous Posture'* and melancholy surroundings had been dictated by the sitter herself.[1] Margaret's pose and the general atmosphere of mourning were not 'at all my *Fancy'*, he wrote, and yet Dixon's portrait suited Evelyn perfectly well as a personal icon in front of which he could himself meditate and pray. Given Margaret's extraordinarily pious character (as Evelyn saw it) and the devotional nature of the biographical narrative he erected as a memorial to her, Dixon's portrait of the future Lady Godolphin must have struck Evelyn as an appropriate emblem of the lovely woman he knew. But to those who knew Margaret Blagge in far different circumstances—as a maid-of-honour in the Restoration court—Dixon's mournful portrait proved to be unsatisfactory. And thus only a year later Lady Berkeley, with whom Margaret lived following her retirement from Whitehall, arranged for her portrait to be painted once again, this time by a more fashionable hand. The painter she chose was Mary Beale, a woman who would eventually make her reputation by painting portraits of Anglican divines, but who had begun her career as a pupil (and copyist) of Sir Peter Lely, the dominant force in portraiture during the reign of Charles II.[2]

Mrs Beale's painting (Plate 11) shares certain formal properties with Dixon's portrait of Margaret, and it is possible, of course, that she was familiar with it. In each painting Margaret is shown seated in an outdoor setting with her left arm resting upon a form of tablature. In the

---

[1] Evelyn, *Godolphin*, p. 71. For my discussion of this work, see above, pp. 62–3.

[2] Mary Beale is identified as the painter of this portrait by Sampson in Evelyn, *Godolphin* (facing p. 52) and by Hiscock, *John Evelyn*, p. 112: 'Lady Berkeley would have something more attractive [than the Dixon portrait]; a challenge to Evelyn let it be: the portrait of a potential wife' (see also Hiscock, *Family Circle*, pp. 96–7). Elizabeth Walsh and Richard Jeffree, 'The Excellent Mrs Mary Beale' (London: Geffrye Museum; Eastbourne: Towner Art Gallery, 1975), no. 39, ascribe this painting to her but note that 'the present painting is reminiscent of her earlier work but the style suggests another hand'. But Beale's close relationship with Lely (he allowed her the rare privilege of watching him paint) should reinforce this traditional attribution. There are two versions, one privately owned and one at Berkeley Castle; I reproduce the second version. For additional information about Mary Beale, see Baker, ii. 34–42, and Elizabeth Walsh, 'Mrs. Mary Beale, Paintress', *Connoisseur*, 131 (1953), 3–8.

background of each painting we find a muted landscape to the left and an architectural or statuary motif to the right. But where Dixon has portrayed her in simple and modest dress, with her hair drawn back and her head slightly tilted forward as if in reverie, Mary Beale has depicted her in attire so elaborate that her left hand must gather the superfluous folds. She wears a large necklace of pearls, and her hair, which is modishly curled, sets off a face that, while not quite inviting, none the less holds us in its forthright gaze. Dixon's effective treatment of her arms, which close in towards each other and thus suggest the separate, isolated space in which she sits, has been replaced by two parallel arms that beckon towards the surface of the picture. Her right hand now holds a sprig of laurel—long associated with love and virtue in the iconography of Italian painting[3]—and Dixon's funeral urn with its pentacle (on the right) has been replaced by a simpler structure whose frieze depicts a small cupid with his bow. Margaret Blagge may have been reluctant to sit for this portrait (there is considerable reserve in her stare), but the painting itself is presumably just what Lady Berkeley had in mind: an elegant image of an official beauty, carefully caught and defined by the conventions of courtly portraiture just as Margaret believed herself to be confined within the conventions of Restoration society.

It is unfortunate, of course, that we have no record of Evelyn's response to this portrait of his maid-of-honour, but we can be confident that it would not have pleased him. Horace Walpole observed that Mary Beale's portraits have 'much nature, but the colouring is heavy and stiff, her usual merit and faults'.[4] We might add that there is a similar stiffness and conventionality in the very *idea* behind a portrait such as this. The pose, the costume, the attitude and air are all consistent with (if not directly borrowed from) the famous set of Windsor beauties painted by Lely a decade earlier, when they were dutifully copied by Mrs Beale.[5] In Lely's *Lady Whitmore*, for instance, we find a similar pose, a similar background, the obligatory pearls, and even a left hand that gathers the excess folds of clothing.[6] Everything that possesses a personal significance in the Dixon portrait, in other words, has been transformed by Mary Beale into the traditional iconography of the court. If we try to look at the Beale

---

[3] See Pope-Hennessy, pp. 218, 226, 240.

[4] *Anecdotes of Painting*, iii. 80 n.

[5] On Beale as a copyist of Lely's beauties, see Baker, who calls her reproductions 'extraordinarily unpleasant' (ii. 35 n.) and characterizes her as 'the last person who should have specialized in women sitters and youths' (ii. 39).

[6] Beckett, *Lely*, no. 564; Millar, *Tudor, Stuart*, no. 265, pl. 112; and Stewart, 'Pin-ups or Virtues?', pl. 1*A*.

portrait through John Evelyn's eyes, we might argue that the painter has forsaken any distinctiveness in her sitter and has instead portrayed her as if she were no different from anyone else (which is, perhaps, exactly how Lady Berkeley and her circle of friends saw her, or at least wished her to be seen).

The problem with this argument lies, of course, in the degree to which portraiture is necessarily governed (or at least limited) by the pressure of convention. Consider, for instance, the mournful attributes in Dixon's portrait of Margaret Blagge. Evelyn attests to the personal nature of the tombstone and the sepulchral urn by pointing out that they were painted according to 'her *Expresse-Desire* & Injunction to the *Artist*' and remarking that 'she *lov'd to be in the Company of Mourners*, which minded her of her End'.[7] For Evelyn, therefore, Dixon's portrait represented Margaret as she saw herself and as she wished herself to be seen by others. But the very features in Dixon's painting that are meant to convey her individuality and thus set her apart from others—the tombstone, the urn, the meditative pose—are themselves stock, conventional elements that can be found in countless paintings with a *vanitas* or *memento mori* theme.[8] In July 1648, for example, Evelyn 'sate for my *Picture* (the same wherein is a *Deaths head*) to Mr. *Walker* that excellent Painter'.[9] The portrait Robert Walker painted of Evelyn (Plate 12) shows him in a conventional, melancholy pose with his right hand supporting his head and his left hand resting upon a skull.[10] Like Margaret Blagge, he is painted in simple, almost negligent dress, and his introspective gaze is consistent with the Greek inscription above his head: 'Repentance is the beginning of Wisdom.'

An even more direct prototype for Dixon's portrait can be found, ironically, in Lely's portrait of the Countess of Rochester, another Windsor beauty painted in the 1660s (Plate 13).[11] The affinities between

---

[7] Evelyn, *Godolphin*, p. 71.

[8] One standard study of this theme is Erwin Panofsky, '*Et in Arcadia Ego:* Poussin and the Elegiac Tradition', in *Meaning in the Visual Arts: Papers in and on Art History* (Garden City, NY: Doubleday, 1955), 295–320.

[9] Evelyn, *Diary*, ii. 541.

[10] Ibid., frontispiece to vol. iii; Waterhouse, pp. 87–8, who calls it 'perhaps the least English-looking portrait painted in Britain during the seventeenth century' and who suggests that it is 'a sort of parody of a typical Italian picture of the "Penitent Magdalen"'; Whinney and Millar, pp. 77–8, pl. 20a, who describe it as 'more purely English in feeling'; Millar, *Age of Charles I*, no. 161; F. Saxl and R. Wittkower, *British Art and the Mediterranean* (London: Oxford Univ. Press, 1948), no. 43; and Geoffrey Keynes, *John Evelyn: A Study in Bibliography with A Bibliography of His Writings*, 2nd edn. (Oxford: Clarendon Press, 1968), pl. 1, who translates the inscription as 'Second thoughts are the beginning of philosophy.'

[11] Beckett, *Lely*, no. 440, pl. 103; Millar, *Tudor, Stuart*, no. 262, pl. 115; Stewart, 'Pin-ups or Virtues?', pl. 7A.

this portrait and Mary Beale's are unmistakable, especially in the pose of the face, in the elaborately draped dress supported by the left hand, and in the right hand that is about to pick a flower. But like Dixon's Margaret Blagge, Lely's countess also leans on a funeral urn, and both the cypress trees in the background and the rose she is about to pluck from the bush are intended to suggest the transitoriness of life.[12] Lely's portrait, in other words, can be seen as a model for the pictures painted by *both* Matthew Dixon *and* Mary Beale. Even Dixon's graceful treatment of Margaret's arms reiterates the standard representation of the Madonna holding her child. Surely Dixon's personal, intimate portrayal of Evelyn's friend is as dependent upon iconographical motifs—is as filled with visual clichés—as is Beale's official, fashionable picture of the queen's maid-of-honour. It might prove difficult, indeed, for us to decide which of the two is the more conventional portrait.

I have compared these two paintings of Margaret Blagge in order to suggest some of the problems inherent in the study of seventeenth-century English portraiture. The particular qualities that I have character-ized as conventional, fashionable, traditional, or iconographical might well be placed within the broader category of the formulaic. Portrait-painting is, of course, notoriously dependent upon formulas and patterns, and much that we deplore in English portraiture (so much sameness in these different likenesses) is a product of the visual formulas developed during the seventeenth century. This is not to say that earlier painting eschewed these patterns; portraiture under the Tudors (and especially under Elizabeth) was certainly more severely limited in both formal and thematic terms. But the arrival of Van Dyck in 1632 clearly marked the beginning of sophisticated (and prolific) studio work in England, and with it the use of assistants, copyists, pattern books, and eventually (in Lely's studio) even the numerical description of standard poses.[13] And while it is true that within a very few years Van Dyck was virtually able to transform English portrait-painting—to open it up, to bring it of age—it is also true that his vision of English society, which was confined to the court and its dominant personalities, had a powerful influence on painting within his own century and well into the next. Ironically, when Interreg-num painters such as Walker searched for models for their Roundhead portraits, they adapted poses developed by Van Dyck, even to the point of placing Cromwell's head on the shoulders of his Cavalier rivals.[14] Several

[12] See Stewart, 'Pin-ups or Virtues?', p. 13.

[13] For discussions of studio practice in the 17th cent., see Cust, pp. 138–9; Waterhouse, pp. 74–5; and Millar, *Lely*, pp. 15–21.

[14] See Waterhouse, p. 88; Whinney and Millar, p. 77; and David Piper, 'The Contemporary Portraits of Oliver Cromwell', *Walpole Society*, 34 (1958), 27–41 (esp. 28–9).

of the revolutionary breakthroughs ascribed to Reynolds and many of the
distinctive painterly qualities we sense in Gainsborough can also be
shown to have their roots in Van Dyck, 'whose works are so frequent in
England,' Walpole noted, 'that the generality of our people can scarce
avoid thinking him their countryman'.[15] The dying Gainsborough is
supposed to have told Reynolds that 'we are all going to Heaven—and
Vandyck is of the company'.[16] Any study of the English portrait in the
seventeenth century, which shares much of the vitality and variety of
contemporary biographical writing, must necessarily focus on Van Dyck
and on the patterns and formulas that are his legacy.

My particular concern in the present chapter is with visual formulas
that I define, in various senses, as iconic.[17] Iconic biography, I have
argued, attempts to endow verbal narratives with visual properties; iconic
texts are usually static in nature, with an emphasis on spatial form and a
tendency to find analogues in paintings and emblems. Biography in the
hands of Walton or Evelyn concentrates on the essential nature of its
subject. Like religious icons, these works are symbolic forms that may
themselves function as artefacts of devotion. Iconicism provides these
texts with considerable vividness and power; but the drive towards
emblematic representation simultaneously serves to encapsulate meaning,
to limit complexity within the portrayal of character.

Much the same is true of visual portraiture when it strives towards or
attempts to incorporate verbal art. Portraits may be described as iconic
not only when they resemble the static, two-dimensional nature of
religious or royal images, but also when they demand to be 'read' in verbal
or literary terms. The common ground of iconic biography and portraiture is the allegorical representation of character, but we can also sense
this interpenetration of forms when portraits attempt to augment visual
properties with verbal cruxes. The addition of the literal to the visual may
enable a portrait to explore broader modes of representation; but, as with
iconic biography, it simultaneously serves to limit that representation
within the confines of its verbal structures.[18] In spite of the personal origin
of Evelyn's iconic devices—the pentacle in the biography of Lady
Godolphin, or the Greek motto he instructed Walker to place within his

---

[15] *Anecdotes of Painting*, ii. 96.
[16] Quoted by Cust, p. 187.
[17] For previous discussions, see above, pp. 18–21, 25–6.
[18] My argument here is complementary to Paulson's: 'As a painting becomes more abstract, its
relationships of colour, form, and texture more emphatic, words fail [to describe] it . . . Conversely,
the higher the level of denotation, the more particular the objects represented (particular as to person,
time, and place, as well as to conventional meanings), the greater its potential for verbalization'
(Paulson, *Emblem*, p. 8). Paulson goes on to argue that visual images are never entirely reducible to
words.

own portrait—both of these iconic portraits tend to accentuate the general rather than the particular: Margaret Blagge is depicted as the embodiment of the divine friend just as Evelyn, in his portrait, is subsumed under a general and highly stylized representation of pious repentance.

In the following pages, I attempt to explore various forms of iconicism in portrait-painting of the seventeenth century. I begin with paintings that actually include verbal forms within their borders, and then turn to portraits whose iconicism is more traditionally rooted in their emulation of religious images. In the final two sections I discuss allegorical portraiture, especially in the work of Van Dyck, and conclude (much as the century does) with portraits that speak for themselves.

i. The Survival of the Literal

Words most often find their way into pictures in the form of titles or painters' signatures. These captions and autographs may have been added long after the painting itself was completed—and they may be fraudulent or inaccurate—but in general we tend to value them as useful introductions to the paintings we behold. In the case of portraiture, titles are especially helpful because they work in concert with the visual image to represent historical characters, many of whose identities would be lost to us without these literal additions. Certain kinds of *tituli*, such as the Lumley *cartellino*, also assist us in identifying the collection to which particular paintings belonged (and for which, in many cases, they were originally commissioned).[19] In the Tudor period especially, titles (and sometimes artists' signatures) were painted on pieces of paper that appear to have accidentally fallen onto the ground, a strategy that both draws attention to their function as words within a larger visual field and also separates them in formal terms from the other images on the canvas.[20] (An interesting compromise can be seen in portraits in which the identity of the sitter is 'engraved' upon a section of stone flooring near the bottom of the painting or 'woven' into the border of an oriental rug.[21]) We can trace a similar motif as late as the 1640s in a portrait of an unknown divine by a painter known to us only as F. How. We can attribute this painting to How because the clergyman he portrays holds a letter in his hand that the

---

[19] For a discussion of the Lumley *cartellino*, see Strong, *English Icon*, pp. 46–7.

[20] There are numerous examples in Strong, *English Icon*; see e.g. nos. 213, 244, 276, 361.

[21] Some of the most ingenious engraved signatures, titles, and inscriptions are to be found in Dutch rather than English painting; see Svetlana Alpers, *The Art of Describing: Dutch Art in the Seventeenth Century* (Chicago: Univ. of Chicago Press, 1983), 172–7.

artist himself has signed.[22] In a portrait such as this, the line between concealing and revealing information is particularly fine; but we can find earlier and later parallels in the signatures of Hans Eworth (who often painted his monogram on the edge of a table) and even Sir Joshua Reynolds (who resolved to go down to posterity on the hem of Mrs Siddons's dress). In general, the tendency has been for titles and signatures to retreat towards the margins—and even onto the backs and frames of canvases—and yet in spite of this movement, the literal remained particularly strong in English painting, especially in portraits of the late sixteenth and early seventeenth centuries.

The kinds of verbal formulas I have been describing so far do not actually intrude upon the visual representation of a painting; their words are not inscribed as integral parts of a composite image. We are able to absorb these verbal elements and thus keep intact the mimetic or realistic integrity of the work. Iconic inscriptions, on the other hand, are part of the representational unity of the paintings in which they are found; they work to help determine the meaning of the portrait as a whole and not just the identity of the artist or sitter. And thus portraits that depend upon iconic inscriptions must be considered as composite forms in which the visual and the verbal elements strive to complement and complete each other. Each kind of representational device acts as a commentary upon its counterpart; and it is possible, of course, that the verbal formula will seek to enhance or even undermine the visual when it speaks about the larger image of which it forms a part.[23] Both of these possibilities can be seen in the medal Quentin Matsys produced in honour of Erasmus in 1519.[24] Matsys portrays the great humanist in profile, with the date carved directly beneath the bust and with a verbal identification of the sitter positioned on each side of his head. Along the edge of the medal (the 'surround') Matsys has inscribed two tags, one in Latin and one in Greek. The Latin inscription pays tribute to the visual likeness the artist has produced by pointing out that it is an *ad vivum* image; the Greek tag, on

---

[22] See Baker, i. 103. There is a similar motif in a portrait of Pope by Richardson, now in the Yale Center for British Art. Alpers treats the theme of letters in Dutch paintings at length in *The Art of Describing*, ch. 5.

[23] For a quite different relationship between word and image in Dutch painting of the 17th cent.— in which verbal inscriptions are treated as an extension of pictorial representation in a painting—see Alpers, *The Art of Describing*, ch. 5: 'Rather than supplying underlying meanings, they give us more to look at' (p. 187). See Mieczysław Wallis, 'Inscriptions in Paintings', *Semiotica*, 9 (1973), 1–28, for a more general overview and for the characterization of inscriptions as semantic enclaves, at odds with the iconic (directly imitative) elements in a painting.

[24] See Pope-Hennessy pp. 92–3 and 314 n. 43.

the other hand, which is written in a less accessible language, warns the beholder that the true portrait of Erasmus is delineated in his works.

In general, however, iconic inscriptions tend to fix rather than qualify visual represenation within a painting. Consider, for example, one of the most frequently cited Tudor portraits, Hans Eworth's *Henry Stuart, Lord Darnley and Charles Stuart, Earl of Lennox*, painted in 1563 (Plate 14).[25] Eworth places these two figures in the immediate foreground of his picture; an unidentified long gallery stretches into the distance behind them (Eworth's monogram is painted on the crossrail of the table). The inscription at the top of the painting amounts to a proclamation: 'THES BE THE SONES OF THE RIGHTE HONERABLES THERLLE OF LENOXE AD THE LADY MAGARETZ GRACE COVNTYES OF LENOXE AD ANGWYSE.' And just as these Stuart ancestors are symbolically introduced at the top of the panel, so their young descendants are verbally identified at the bottom, each with his name and age printed directly beneath his visual image. This careful procedure of blocking out the visual space can also be sensed in Eworth's use of strong verticals (especially in the attenuated figure of the older brother) and horizontals (in the backward thrust of the gallery, its ceiling, and the table). Pevsner has appropriately referred to this portrait as an example of the English perpendicular style,[26] but he fails to point out that the most distinctive clash of verticals and horizontals is not between the two brothers and the room in which they stand but between these two figures and the horizontal inscriptions that frame them both above and below. These inscriptions literally encase the subjects of the painting both in spatial terms and in the sense that they establish their identities and lineage. The temporal perspective has been frozen as well: we are provided with an exact date and with the precise age of each brother at the time the portrait was painted. For similarly determinate signposts in portraiture we would have to turn to Boswell's *Life of Johnson*, in which the format of each opening constantly reminds us both of the year and of Johnson's advancing age.

This spatial, almost architectural use of verbal inscription can also be seen in Eworth's portrait of *Henry VIII* (Plate 15), painted in 1567 but modelled, with only slight revisions, on Holbein's influential fresco in the Privy Chamber (1537).[27] Eworth's king confronts us directly; his feet are

[25] Strong, *English Icon*, no. 39; Millar, *Tudor, Stuart*, no. 56, pl. 34.

[26] Nikolaus Pevsner, *The Englishness of English Art* (1956; rpt. Harmondsworth: Penguin, 1964), 116, pl. 55a.

[27] Strong, *English Icon*, no. 42; cf. Strong, *Tudor and Jacobean*, pl. 309.

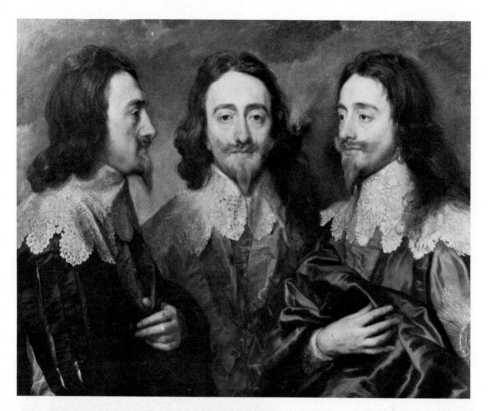

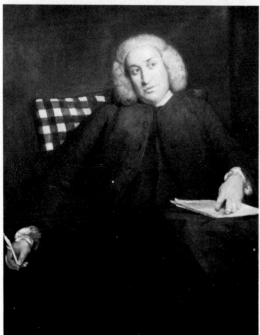

1. (*above*) Sir Anthony Van Dyck, *Charles I in Three Positions*, 1635, Windsor Castle

2. (*left*) Sir Joshua Reynolds, *Samuel Johnson*, 1756–7, National Portrait Gallery, London (restored version)

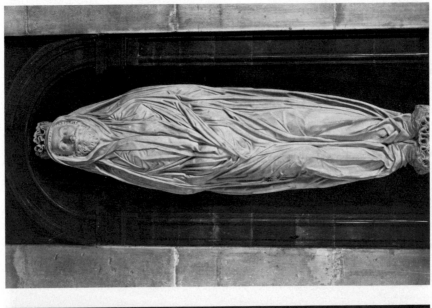

4. Nicholas Stone, *John Donne*, marble effigy in
St Paul's Cathedral

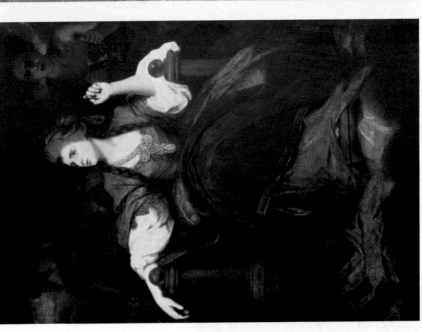

3. Sir Joshua Reynolds, *Mrs Siddons as the Tragic Muse*,
1784, Henry E. Huntington Library and Art Gallery

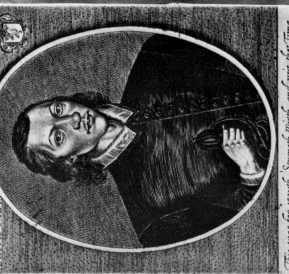

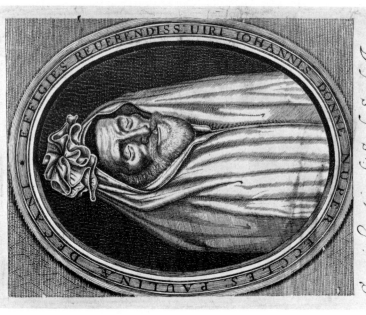

This was for youth, Strength, Mirth, and wit that Time
Most count their golden Age; but t'was not thine.
Thine was thy later yeares, so much refind
From youths Dross, Mirth, & wit, as thy pure mind
Thought (like the Angels) nothing but the Prayse
Of thy Creator, in those last, best Dayes.
Witnes this Booke, (thy Embleme) which begins
With Love; but endes, with Sighes, & Teares for sins.
IZ: WA:

Will: Marshall sculpsit.

6. William Marshall, *John Donne*, frontispiece to Donne's
Poems, 1635

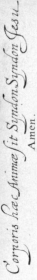

Martin Droeshout sculp. And are to be sould by R R and Ben: Fisher

5. Martin Droeshout, *John Donne*, frontispiece to
Deaths Duell, 1632

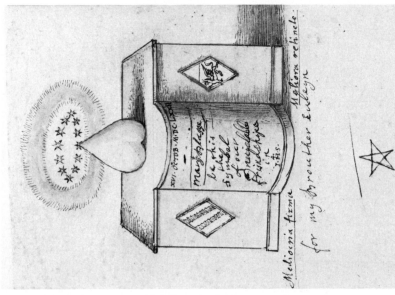

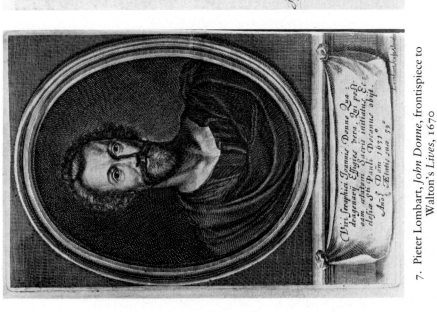

7. Pieter Lombart, *John Donne*, frontispiece to Walton's *Lives*, 1670

8. John Evelyn, 'The Altar of Friendship', a drawing included in his *Diary*, Christ Church, Oxford

as in the midſt of their ſuffering made their bread of ſorrow taſte more pleaſantly then the banquet of fooles.

The recreations of his youth were Poetry, in which he was fo happy, as if nature with all her varieties had been made to exerciſe his great wit, and high fancy. And in thoſe pieces which were careleſly ſcattered in his younger daies (moſt of them being written before the twentieth yeare of his age) it may appeare by his choice Metaphors, that all the Arts joyned to aſſiſt him with their utmoſt skill.

It is a truth, that in his penitentiall yeares, viewing ſome of thoſe pieces looſely ſcattered in his youth, he wiſht they had been abortive, or ſo ſhortliv'd, that he had witneſt their funeralls: But though he was no friend to them, he was not ſo falne out with heavenly Poetry, as to forſake it, no not in his declining age, witneſſed then by many divine Sonnets, and other high, holy, and harmonious compoſures; yea even on his former ſick bed, he wrote this heavenly Hymne, expreſſing the great joy he then had in the aſſurance of Gods mercy to him.

A Hymne to God the Father.

WIlt thou forgive that ſin where I begun,
    Which was my ſin though it were done before?
Wilt thou forgive that ſin through which I run,
    And doe run ſtill, though ſtill I doe deplore?
      When thou haſt done, thou haſt not done,
        For I have more.

Wilt thou forgive that ſin which I have won
    Others to ſin, and made my ſin their dore?
Wilt thou forgive that ſin which I did ſhun
    A yeare or two, but wallowed in, a ſcore?
      When thou haſt done, thou haſt not done,
        For I have more.

I have a ſin of feare, that when I have ſpun
    My laſt thred, I ſhall periſh on the ſhore;
But ſweare by thy ſelfe, that at my death thy Sonne
    Shall ſhine as he ſhines now, and heretofore;
      And, having done that, thou haſt done,
        I feare no more.

And on this (which was his Death-bed) writ another Hymne which bears this Title,

    A Hymne to God my God, in my ſickneſſe.

If theſe fall under the cenſure of a ſoule whoſe too much mixture with earth makes it unfit to judge of theſe high illuminations, let him know, that many devour and learned men have thought the ſoule of this holy

---

in the Kingdome, and favour with the King, (whom his Majeſty knew Doctor *Donne* loved very much) was diſcarded the Court, and preſently after committed to priſon, which begot many rumors in the multitude.

The King ſuffered not the Sunne to ſet, till he had ſearcht out the truth of this report, but ſent preſently for Doctor *Donne*, and required his anſwer to the accuſation: which was ſo ſatisfactory, That the King ſaid he was glad he reſted not under that ſuſpition. Doctor *Donne* profeſted his anſwer was faithfull and free from all Colluſion. And therefore begged of his Majeſty, that he might not riſe (being then kneeling) before he had (as in like caſes he alwayes had from God) ſome aſſurance that he ſtood cleere and faire in his Majeſties opinion. The King with his own hand, did, or offered to raiſe him from his knees, and profeſted he was truly ſatisfied, that he was an honeſt man, and loved him. Preſently his Majeſty called ſome Lords of his Councell into his Chamber, and ſaid with much earneſtneſſe, *My Doctor is an honeſt man*, *And my Lords, I was never more joyed in anything that I have done, then in making him a Divine.*

He was made Deane in the fiftieth yeare of his age; And in the fifty fourth yeare, a dangerous ſickneſſe ſeiſed him, which turned to a ſpotted Feaver, and ended in a Cough, that inclined him to a Conſumption. But God (as *Job* thankfully acknowledgeth) preſerved his ſpirit, keeping his intellectualls as cleere and perfect, as when that ſicknſſe firſt ſeiſed his body. And as his health increaſed, ſo did his thankfulneſſe, teſtified in this booke of Devotions, and applicable to the Emergencies of that ſicknſſe, which booke (being Meditations in this ſicknſſe) he writ on his ſicke bed, herein imitating the holy Patriarchs, who were wont in that place to build their Altars where they had received their bleſsing.

Gen. 12, 7, 8.
Gen. 18, 18.

This ſicknſſe brought him to the gates of death, and he ſaw the grave ſo ready to devoure him, that he calls his recovery ſupernaturall. But God reſtored his health, and continued it untill the fifty-ninth yeare of his life. And then in Auguſt 1630. being with his daughter Miſtris *Harvy* at Abrey-Hatch in Eſſex, he fell into a Feaver, which with the helpe of his conſtant infirmity, (*vapours from the ſpleene*, haſtened him into ſo viſible a Conſumption, that his beholders might ſay (as S. *Paul* of himſelfe) *he dyes daily,* And he might ſay with *Job, My welfare paſſeth away as a cloud; The dayes of affliction have taken hold of me. And weary nights are appointed for me.*

Job. 30. 15.
Job. 7. 3.

This ſicknſſe continued long, not onely weakning, but wearing him ſo much, that my deſire is, he may now take ſome reſt: And that thou judge it no impertinent digreſſion (before I ſpeake of his death) to looke backe with me upon ſome obſervations of his life, which (while a gentle ſlumber ſeiſes him) may (I hope fitly) exerciſe thy Conſideration.

His marriage was the remarkable error of his life, which (though he had a wit apt enough, and very able to maintaine paradoxes, And though his wives competent yeares, and other reaſons might be juſtly urged to moderate a ſevere cenſure; yet he never ſeemed to juſtifie, and doubtleſſe had repented, if (God had not bleſt them with a mutuall, and ſo cordial an affection,

25

---

9. Page from Walton's *Life of Donne* in Donne's LXXX *Sermons*, 1640

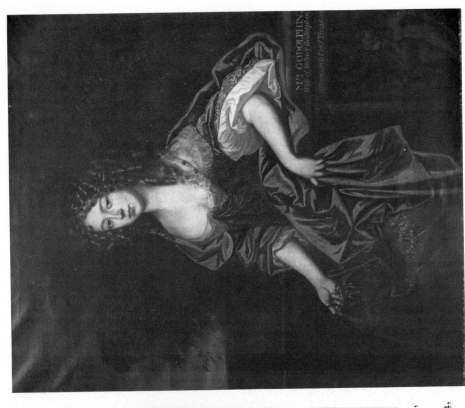

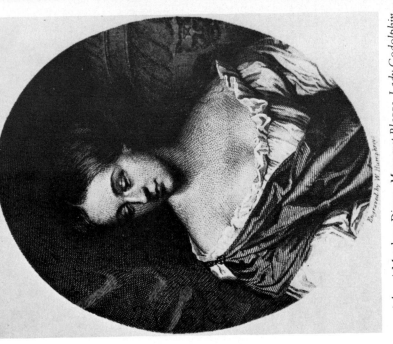

10. (*above*) Matthew Dixon, *Margaret Blagge, Lady Godolphin*, 1673, engraved by W. Humphreys

11. (*right*) Mary Beale, *Margaret Blagge, Lady Godolphin*, 1674, Berkeley Castle

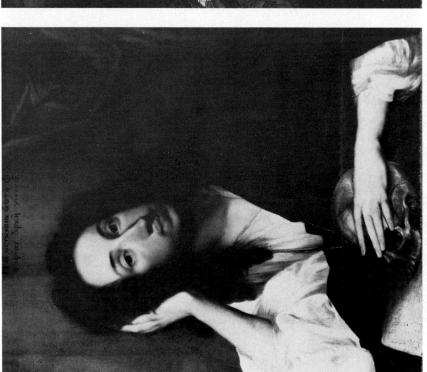

13. Sir Peter Lely, *Henrietta Boyle, Countess of Rochester, c.*1665, Hampton Court

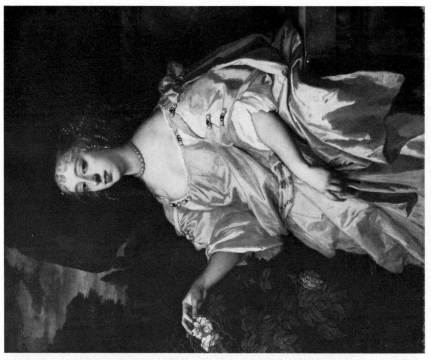

12. Robert Walker, *John Evelyn*, 1648, private collection

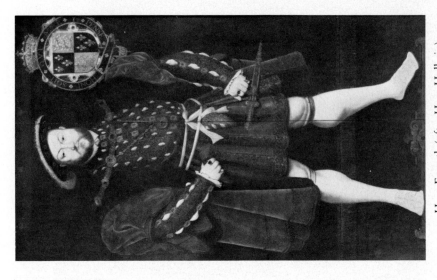

15. Hans Eworth (after Hans Holbein),
Henry VIII, 1567, Trinity College, Cambridge

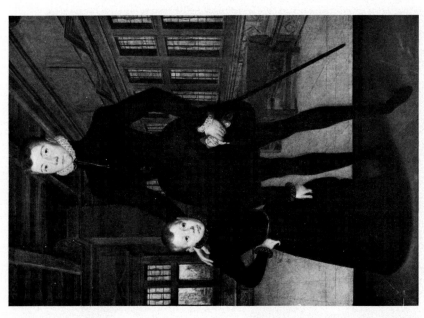

14. Hans Eworth, *Henry Stuart, Lord Darnley and
Charles Stuart, Earl of Lennox*, 1563, Windsor Castle

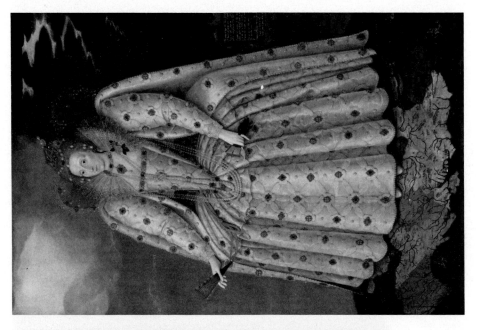

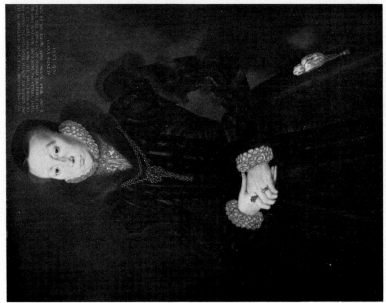

16. (*above*) Hans Eworth, *Joan Thornbury, Mrs Wakeman*, 1566, private collection

17. (*right*) Marcus Gheeraerts, *Elizabeth I* ('Ditchley' portrait), *c.*1592, National Portrait Gallery, London

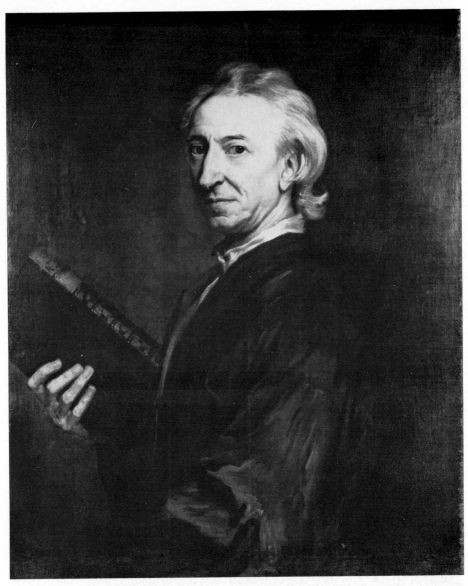

18. Sir Godfrey Kneller, *John Evelyn*, 1689, private collection

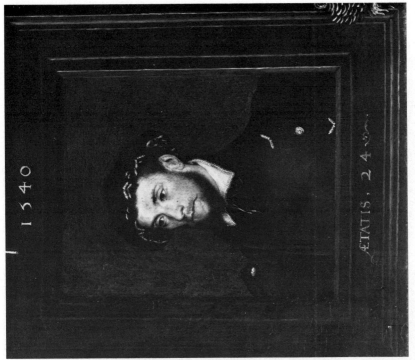

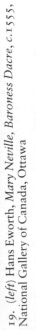

19. (*left*) Hans Eworth, *Mary Neville, Baroness Dacre, c.1555*, National Gallery of Canada, Ottawa

20. (*above*) Detail, Eworth, *Mary Neville, Baroness Dacre*

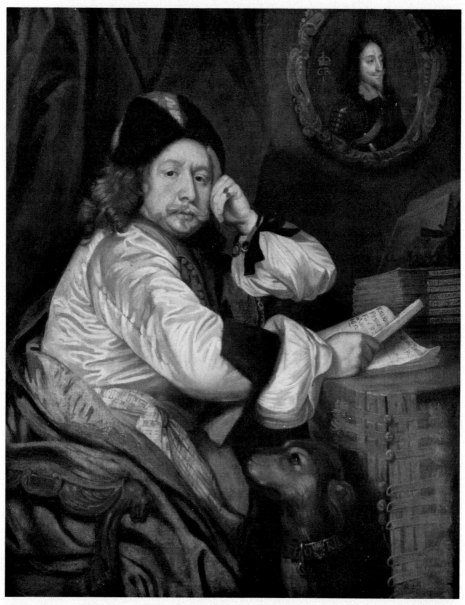

21. William Sheppard, *Sir Thomas Killigrew*, 1650, National Portrait Gallery, London

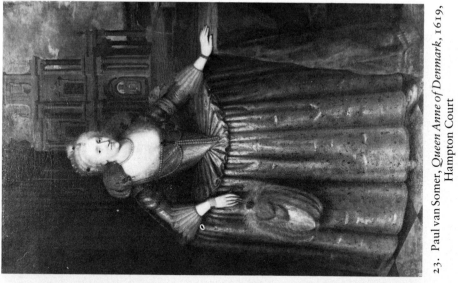

23. Paul van Somer, *Queen Anne of Denmark*, 1619,
Hampton Court

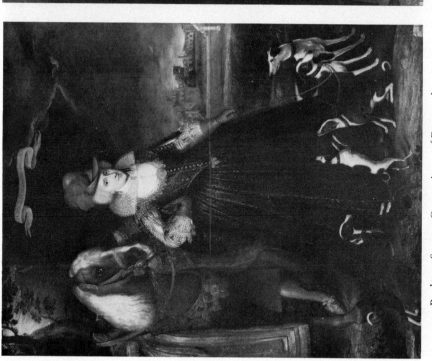

22. Paul van Somer, *Queen Anne of Denmark*, 1617,
Windsor Castle

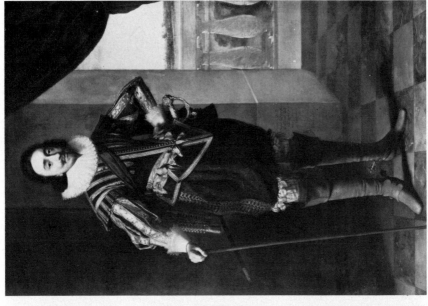

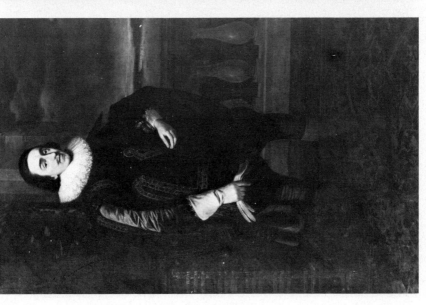

25. Daniel Mytens, *Charles I*, 1628, Windsor Castle

24. Daniel Mytens, *Charles I when Prince of Wales*, 1623, Hampton Court

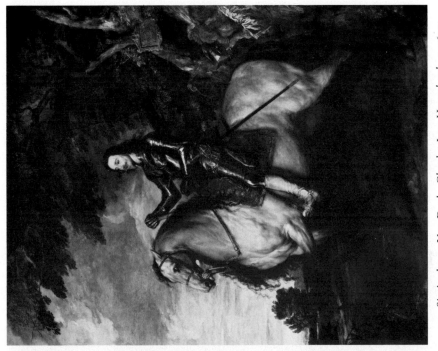

26. Sir Anthony Van Dyck, *Charles I with M. de St Antoine*, 1633, Buckingham Palace

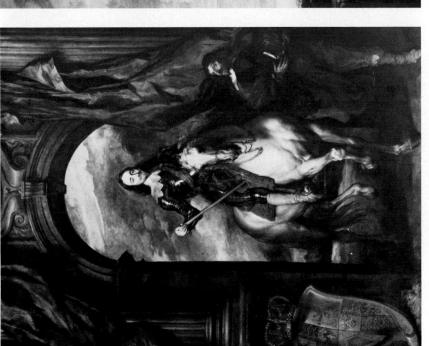

27. Sir Anthony Van Dyck, *Charles I on Horseback*, c.1637, National Gallery, London

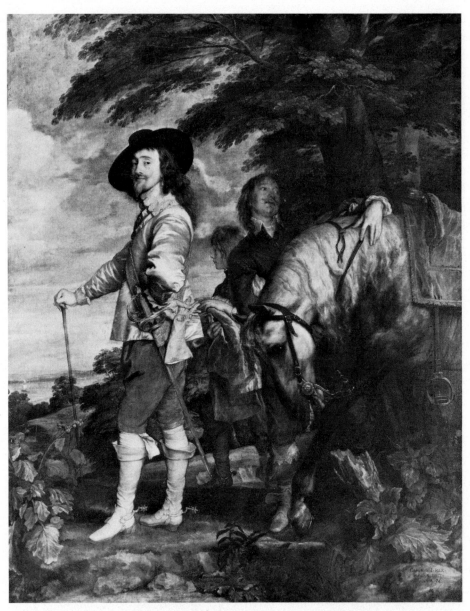

28. Sir Anthony Van Dyck, *Le Roi à la Chasse*, 1635, Louvre

planted firmly apart and his massive arms are painted akimbo. In the background to the right, just beyond Henry's left shoulder, appears the English coat of arms displaying the king's crown and incorporating the royal motto. A large cartouche with an elaborate inscription has been painted directly beneath the massive figure of the king:

EN EXPRESSA VIDES HENRICI REGIS IMAGO

QVAE FVIT OCTAVI MVSIS HOC STRVXIT ASYLVM

MAGNIFICE CVMTER DENOS REGNASSET ET OCTO

ANNOS: QVIS MAIOR REGEM LABOR VLTIMUS ORNET

AN 1546 AET.SVE.51

An inscription as elaborate and detailed as this serves to help define the king, to establish the extent of his royal powers. We are told of his accomplishments, and we learn that he even built the gallery that displays this kind of portrait. The inscribed cartouche, in other words, supports its weighty figure in spatial terms just as it also gives credence to an image of the king ('REGIS IMAGO') that is powerfully depicted in visual terms.

This kind of verbal formula is particularly well suited to the royal icon (as we shall see in greater detail in the next section); but it should at least be noted here that similar inscriptions can be found in English paintings quite late in the seventeenth century. In the portrait of *John, 3rd Lord Lovelace* by Marcellus Lauron (1689), a large urn is inscribed with a lengthy legend describing Lovelace, in part, as 'Capt of ye Band of Gent Pensioners to King William ye third, who came into England on ye fifth day of November 1688, to redeem this Nation from Popery and Slavery'.[28] Here, as in many of Eworth's portraits, personal character has been inextricably tied to public history, and it is the burden of the verbal formula to draw explicit connections while the images themselves remain comparatively mute.

Inscribed pictures such as these approximate a form of *pictura loquens* in which the artists have been able to put words into the mouths of their subjects. In Eworth's portrait of *Joan Thornbury, Mrs Wakeman*, for instance, we encounter a woman dressed in sombre attire, standing, with her hands simply clasped in front of her (Plate 16).[29] Far from being a prepossessing woman, she allows an elaborate inscription to speak for her. The following poem is painted behind and just to the right of her head:

[28] Robert Raines, *Marcellus Laroon* (London: Routledge; New York: Pantheon, 1967), 10, fig. 3. (Marcellus Lauron was the father of Marcellus Laroon.)

[29] Strong, *English Icon*, no. 41; there is also an interesting inscription on her husband's portrait by Eworth, no. 40.

MY CHYLDHODDE PAST THAT BEWTIFIID MY FLESSHE
AND GONNE MY YOUTHE THAT GAVE ME COLOR FRESSHE
Y AM NOW CVM TO THOS RYPE YERIS AT LAST
THAT TELLES ME HOWE MY WONTON DAYS BE PAST
AND THEREFORE FRINDE SO TVRNES THE TYME ME
Y ONS WAS YOVNG AND NOW AM AS YOV SEE.

Below this poem Eworth has painted the date (1566) and the number of her ripe years (only 36). In this portrait the verbal motto makes explicit what the visual image only begins to suggest, and we therefore return to the painted effigy with both an enlarged awareness of what the painter and his sitter have attempted to say and with a natural curiosity about how well the visual image lives up to its literal counterpart. In the case of *Mrs Wakeman*, we cannot but notice her air of quiet resignation (emphasized by the hands), the simple symmetry of her clothing now that her wanton (that is, playful) days are past, and, perhaps most intriguing, the way in which her eyes, which do not quite meet our own, imply a habitual state of detachment. But these are responses culled from our *second* viewing of *Mrs Wakeman*, made only after we have absorbed the painting's explicit verbal communication.

The inscribed poem in Eworth's portrait of Mrs Wakeman does not so much support the visual image as it determines or interprets it. This form of iconicism thrives in the Elizabethan period and survives well into the seventeenth century. The poem in Robert Peake's portrait of *Edward Grimston of Bradfield* (1598) projects a similar theme of *vanitas*, but it also declares that the accompanying figure, perfect in resemblance to the sitter though it may appear to be, is no less transitory than life itself:

> The life that natrures lendes death soone destroi[es]
> and momentaire is that lifes Remembrans
> This seeminge life which pourful art supplieth
> is but a shaddowe, though lifes parfect semblans
> But that trewe life which vertue doth restore
> is life in deede, and lasteth evermore.[30]

Perhaps no closer analogue can be found to Walton's view of portraiture as he expressed it in the conclusion to his life of Donne.

In an earlier painting from this period, George Gower's self-portrait of 1579, the poem painted in the upper right-hand corner of the panel provides a verbal interpretation of a puzzle we first piece together through the iconographical details surrounding the sitter.[31] Gower, who was born

---

[30] Strong, *English Icon*, no. 199; the date has been altered to 1548.
[31] Ibid., no. 113; Waterhouse, p. 34, pl. 20.

a gentleman, staunchly holds a brush and palette in his left hand; the scales in the background inform us that his profession as a painter (signified by the compass) outweighs his gentle breeding (signified by his coat of arms). The inscribed poem augments this personal allegory about the kind of life he has chosen to lead:

> The proof whereof thies Ballance show, and armes my birth displays,
> what Parents bare by iust renowne, my skill mayntenes the prayes
> And them whose vertew, fame and Acts, haue won for me this shield
> I reuerence much wth seruyce eke, and thanks to them do yield.

It is but a short step from this combination of iconic inscription and allegory to the full-fledged *mélange* of Marcus Gheeraerts's 'Ditchley' portrait of Elizabeth I, probably painted in 1592 (Plate 17).[32] In this famous painting, the queen's extraordinarily ornate costume, with its iconographic features, is flanked by two verbal mottoes; she is pictured standing upon an intricately lettered map of England in the exact location of her procession to Ditchley, and the larger historical context in which she appears is illuminated by the lengthy poem painted in the right margin. It is just this kind of iconicism at the turn of the century that so clearly marks the disregard in English portraiture for both Baroque unity and Renaissance principles of perspective.[33]

Iconic inscriptions in Stuart portraiture normally surface in a more personal context. They continue to reinforce emblematic representation, but they are usually confined to the simple motto that is the literary equivalent of the graphic device. Traditionally these two emblematic features had been combined: Matsys's medallion portrait of Erasmus included, on the reverse side, both his motto ('Concede nulli') and Terminus, which he chose as his personal device.[34] Like the medal, the emblematic portrait attempts to reunite the artistic object and the verbal epigram, a combination first found in the engraved inscriptions placed beneath classical statuary.[35] But this reunion of visual *imago* with its accompanying *mot* or posy was also meant to fuse the body (picture) with the soul (word), the sensuous with the intellectual.[36] We can see this

---

[32] The standard sources are Strong, *Portraits*, no. 72, pl. 15; Strong, *English Icon*, no. 285, and Strong, *Tudor and Jacobean*, pl. 207. See also Strong, *Cult of Elizabeth*, p. 154, pl. 74.

[33] See Strong, *Cult of Elizabeth*, pp. 43, 85, 95, and esp. 112; David Piper, 'Tudor and Early Stuart Painting', in *The Genius of British Painting*, ed. Piper (London: Weidenfeld and Nicolson; New York: Morrow, 1975), 85, 102 (Piper provides a brief but shrewd survey of portraiture during this period).

[34] Pope-Hennessy, p. 314, no. 43.

[35] See Hagstrum, pp. 22–3, 96.

[36] One emblem writer (Henri Estienne) even claimed that the device could supersede a painted portrait, which can only represent 'the body and exquisite features of the face, when as a Device exposeth the rare concepts, and gallant resolutions of its Author ...'; see Rosemary Freeman, *English Emblem Books* (London: Chatto and Windus, 1948; rpt. New York: Octagon, 1966), 15.

combination at work if we return to Robert Walker's portait of John Evelyn (Plate 12). Evelyn was (as we have seen) a man of many words and of several mottoes, and in this painting he has induced Walker to incorporate the literal (spiritual and intellectual) elements not only in the Greek motto advising repentance but also in the manuscript placed beneath the skull (the inscription contains part of Seneca's thirtieth epistle). Evelyn's emphasis on the verbal in this portrait marks an interesting reversal of his strategy in *The Life of Mrs. Godolphin*, where he introduced so many symbolic graphic forms (especially the pentacle) to reinforce the pious context of their friendship. We should also note that this painting, like Dixon's portrait of the meditative Margaret Blagge, was devised by Evelyn for iconic, devotional purposes. Originally intended to be a miniature, it was painted to accompany a marriage treatise he had prepared for his youthful wife, who was only 14 years old when Evelyn married her.[37] Its stark denial of the body may strike us as a strange present indeed, but we can at least understand how closely it was tied both to an actual literary work and to the nature of the vows Evelyn considered so sacred.

Walker's unusual portrait of Evelyn should also be compared with those painted of him almost forty years later by Sir Godfrey Kneller, whose reign over English portrait-painting began with Lely's death in 1680. On 8 October 1685 Evelyn noted in his diary that he had had his picture drawn that week 'by the famous Kneller'; four years later, in July 1689, he noted that he 'sat for my Picture to Mr. *Kneller*, for Mr. Pepys late Secretary of the Admiralty, holding my *Sylva* in my right hand: It was upon his long and earnest request; & is plac'd in his Library: nor did Kneller ever paint better & more masterly work' (Plate 18).[38] Evelyn is painted in full profile, with his head turned towards us. He is simply dressed and wears his own hair; his eyes meet ours with an air of quiet confidence. It is appropriate that Secretary Pepys should wish his friend to be portrayed with his influential treatise on forestry in his hand, for Evelyn's call in that work for the reforestation of a depleted countryside eventually enabled England to rebuild its navy. What we may find more significant, however, is the change from a literal to a literary motif in the movement from Walker's portrait to Kneller's. The verbal inscription in Walker's portrait functions as a personal motto; it works to encapsulate

---

[37] Hiscock, *Family Circle*, pp. 20–1.

[38] Evelyn, *Diary*, iv. 479, 644. For the painting, see Evelyn, *Diary*, frontispiece to vol. v; Baker, vol. ii, facing p. 80; Keynes, *John Evelyn: A Study in Bibliography*, p. 30, pl. 8; Killanin, pl. 11; Stewart, *Kneller*, 1983, no. 262*A*, pl. 48*b*.

the character of the sitter. But even though this inscription is consistent with the pose in which Walker has delineated Evelyn, it necessarily remains an addition within the portrait; as an emblematic device, it violates any strict principles of mimetic representation. Evelyn's copy of *Sylva* in Kneller's portrait poses no such problems. Even more than the inscribed quotation from Seneca's *Epistles* in the Walker portrait, it serves as a realistic attribute, a natural extension (in both spatial and thematic terms) of the sitter's personality. And, perhaps just as significantly, it marks a turn away from the denial of this life and towards those accomplishments that distinguish one man from another. Kneller's painting is certainly not the first to portray its subject with one of his own works, but it is characteristic of a renewed concern in English painting with humanistic achievements.

If we return again to Walker's painting of Evelyn, we can see that it functions in one sense, at least, as a double portrait. Walker depicts two heads: one of Evelyn as he appeared to the painter in 1648, and another—the death's head—which is to be construed as an emblem of human frailty and ultimate mortality. Evelyn's right hand supports his own head, whereas his left hand is placed upon the skull. The *memento mori* reminds Evelyn of what he will become; it serves as an emblem of what is on his own mind (and what he wishes his young wife to mind). The skull in Walker's portrait is an actual object, a natural artefact, and it is therefore similar to other forms of iconic representation, especially the portrait painted within another portrait. We most frequently find this combination of images as self-portraits, which reveal the artist at work within his studio; other forms of this genre are rarer, but they, like the other iconic devices I have examined, have strong roots within the Tudor period.

In Hans Eworth's *Mary Neville, Baroness Dacre* (*c.*1555), for example, we find a vigorous woman engaged in work at her writing-desk (Plate 19).[39] She is caught in three-quarter profile; her left hand holds a small book—presumably a devotional work—which has been opened to a particular text; her right hand, which holds a quill pen, pauses above the common-place book in which she writes. On the elaborately decorated wall in the background, in the upper left-hand corner of the panel, is a portrait of Lady Dacre's husband, dated 1540, when he was 24 years old (Plate 20). The portrait is entirely in Eworth's style, but it apparently had no independent existence outside the larger portrait in which it appears (Eworth's work in England cannot be dated earlier than 1549). Lord

[39] Strong, *English Icon*, no. 45 (see also p. 10); Waterhouse, p. 31, pl. 17.

Dacre's pose is almost identical to his wife's, but whereas her eyes are vacant, appearing to stare off into space, his are sharp and keen. We need only one additional detail to pull the elements in this fascinating portrait together: the knowledge that Lord Dacre had been hanged for murder, and that his wife is consequently painted in her widowhood. Eworth thus chooses to capture a precise moment in this portrait. Lady Dacre appears to be caught—to be momentarily suspended—between the work of her left and right hands, as if she had been reading her devotions, and intended to copy them out or write an observation of her own in her commonplace book, but had been interrupted by thoughts of her husband and his fate. Her husband's portrait thus functions as a mirror of her own thoughts; and, like the equivalent devices of verbal inscription, it is carefully positioned near the sitter's head. Amid the clutter of her world, it is the one image marked by distinctness and clarity.

A similar portrait, painted almost one hundred years later (in 1650), represents the playwright Thomas Killigrew when he served as the English king's official resident in Venice (Plate 21).[40] The painter, William Sheppard, depicts the writer at his desk, his body in full profile, his head turned directly towards us and supported by his left hand and arm. His right hand leafs through a bundle of manuscripts that announce his official position and provide the title of the play he is currently writing (apparently *Bellamira her Dream*). Killigrew's name is inscribed on his dog's collar; his table is filled with a large stack of his own works; in the upper right-hand corner of the room hangs a portrait of Charles I, in armour, with a crown and the monogram 'CR' inscribed on the left-hand side. Like Lady Dacre, Thomas Killigrew has been portayed in a moment of reverie. Although he has turned in our direction, his eyes have the same dreamy, far-off expression that we have encountered in Eworth's painting. The object of his thoughts is suggested not only by the portrait of his martyred king, who had been executed the preceding year, but also by his faithful dog, who looks upwards at his master just as Killigrew ruminates upon Charles. Once again we find the portrait within a portrait functioning as an emblem of the sitter's mind; it is the visual equivalent of the literal inscription, and its force within the canvas is to make this representation just as fully iconic as the other paintings we have examined. In both forms of iconic portraiture, meaning has been accentuated or

---

[40] Piper, *Catalogue*, no. 3795 (186–7), pl. 8*h*, and 'The Development of the British Literary Portrait up to Samuel Johnson', *Proceedings of the British Academy*, 54 (1968; pub. 1970), 59–60 (pl. 11), where Piper also points out the motif of devotion in the arrangement of the dog, the sitter, and the royal martyr.

determined by devices external to the expression, costume, pose, or background of the painter's subject.

ii. Icons

The portrait of King Charles within Sheppard's canvas also functions as an icon itself, for it represents a royal image of power that still commands devotion and obedience even after the monarch himself has been deposed. At the bottom of the stack of Killigrew's books appears one volume written by another hand: it is the *Eikon Basilike*, the supposed spiritual autobiography of the royal martyr, published in the year of his death. Killigrew has transplanted both of these royal icons to Venice, which suggests that his thoughts remain very much at home. Sheppard's use of this image of Charles within his portrait thus indicates how powerful a force the idea of the royal icon remained in England halfway through the seventeenth century. The icon functions here, as it had in the Tudor period, as an emblematic form of state portraiture. It projects a public image of the king, and was itself intended to be scattered throughout the realm as a token of the king's pervasive influence and as an instrument of popular devotion.

England's fateful break with the Catholic church had laid the ground-work for this gradual replacement of the religious icon with the secular image of the king, and many of the standard poses we encounter in the feverish portraiture of Elizabeth were modelled on attitudes traditionally assigned to religious figures.[41] Images of the queen were strictly limited to those sanctioned by the pattern books, and in a famous proclamation of 1563 the production of 'debased' images was forbidden until 'some speciall person that shall be by hir allowed shall have first fynished a portraicture thereof, after which fynished, hir Majesty will be content that all other payntors, or grauors . . . shall and maye at ther plesures follow the sayd patron [pattern] or first portraictur'.[42] In the words of Roy Strong, who has almost single-handedly revised our understanding of painting in this period, Elizabethan portraits were designed as images steeped in glory, as icons 'calculated to evoke in the eyes of the beholder those principles for which the Queen and her government stood'.[43] And yet public as this form of portraiture was, important implications also existed for the portrayal of private individuals, especially in the seven-

[41] See e.g. Piper, 'Tudor and Early Stuart Painting', pp. 63, 73.
[42] Quoted by Strong, *Portraits*, p. 5.
[43] Ibid. 34.

teenth century. In the opinion of the miniaturist William Segar, portraits and other 'Monuments' enabled men and women to 'retaine in memory the excellent Actions of such men, as had lived honourably, and died vertuously'.[44] This is a dictum entirely consonant with the principles we have already seen at work in seventeenth-century biography; and, as in biographical writing, it would take several decades before portraiture would fully reach the analysis of individual characters or before the representation of public men would begin to reveal more than a carefully controlled image of their role in the life of the nation.

The essential features of the iconic image can be fleshed out if we return to Eworth's portrait of Henry VIII (Plate 15). We have already seen that the box-like cartouche at the base of this portrait supports the figure of the king just as the inscribed message supports the idea of kingship embodied in Henry's powerful pose. No beholder of this painting can mistake the strength of the man nor the authority of his rule. Like Holbein, Eworth places Henry in a rigid full-frontal position, which thwarts any possibility of three-dimensional characterization. Eworth's depth of portrayal, in other words, is roughly the same in the figure of the king as it is in the words inscribed within the cartouche or in the coat of arms painted in the obscurely demarcated background; all three images are virtually inter-changeable.[45] The frontal positioning within the portrait also produces an atmosphere of confrontation: we cannot avoid the king's piercing stare, and he makes no attempt to avoid ours. This use of the full-frontal figure, adapted from religious painting, also serves as a representation of hierarchy; it reinforces the ritualistic nature of the encounter between monarch and subject. Meyer Schapiro has suggested an interesting interpretation of this position by comparing it with the figure in full profile. The profile face is comparatively detached from the viewer, existing in a space it shares with other profiles on the surface of the canvas. Schapiro characterizes this pose by introducing an analogy with the grammatical form of the third person ('he' and 'she'). The face turned fully towards us, on the other hand, 'corresponds to the role of "I" in speech, with its complementary "you". It seems to exist both for us and for itself in a space virtually continuous with our own, and is therefore appropriate to the figure as symbol or as carrier of a message.'[46] In Eworth's portrait of Henry, as in the later portraits of Elizabeth, the

[44] Quoted by Strong, *English Icon*, p. 29.

[45] On the interchangeability of arms and portraits, see Strong, *Portraits*, p. 39. Segar was both a miniaturist and a heraldist; see Strong, *English Icon*, p. 18.

[46] *Words and Pictures: On the Literal and the Symbolic in the Illustration of a Text* (The Hague and Paris: Mouton, 1973), 39.

message carried by the full-frontal figure is synonomous with the information imparted by the literal inscription and by the emblematic coat of arms. The king confronts us in all his majesty—and in all his pride.

It is generally accepted that one of the first artists to take a significant step in opening up this tightly controlled iconic structure was Paul van Somer, who painted two interesting portraits of Queen Anne of Denmark, consort of James I.[47] In van Somer's portrait of 1617 (Plate 22),[48] the queen still stares directly towards us, and above her head we find an inscribed cartouche in the form of a ribbon with the words 'LA MIA GRANDEZZA DAL ECCELSO' (which Waterhouse suggests is an assertion of the divine right of kings).[49] But she is also portrayed in a specific location (thought to be Oatlands), and engaged in an activity—hunting—that was one of her particular interests. She has descended from her horse and appears to be only momentarily oblivious to the greyhounds that play at her feet. Both the ground-cover in the immediate foreground and the buildings in the background have been painted in careful detail. But against this fresh image of royalty we must place another portrait, painted by van Somer one or two years later, in which a similar face has been placed within a far more iconic frame (Plate 23).[50] In this painting, the stiff horizontal plane at the top of the queen's skirts is accentuated by the table on which she rests her left hand, and the intricate tiers of her dress are reinforced by the architectural columns in the background. The handling of this costumed figure, with its two-dimensional, architectonic structure, is not unlike some of Van Dyck's contemporaneous work for the reigning families of Genoa.[51] It has recently been discovered, however, that this second portrait of Queen Anne is the work of two hands.[52] The head, which is certainly the work of van Somer, is painted on a piece of canvas

---

[47] For an assessment of van Somer, see Waterhouse, pp. 51–3.

[48] Millar, *Tudor, Stuart*, no. 105, pl. 42; Waterhouse, pl. 37.

[49] Waterhouse, p. 53. This was apparently a favourite motto of the queen; it had already been included in John de Critz's portrait of her. See Millar, *Tudor, Stuart*, no. 98.

[50] Millar, *Tudor, Stuart*, no. 106, pl. 44.

[51] The flat, often static features of Van Dyck's work in Genoa can perhaps best be seen in his portrait *La Marchesa Caterina Durazzo*; see Larsen, no. 333 (vol. i, colour pl. 30). Here the shimmering gold embroidery of the marchesa's gown blends into the gold setting in which she stands, especially the fluted column behind her. The two-dimensional character of this painting is also reinforced by the frieze on which she places her right hand. The putto riding the dolphin (above the frieze) will be transformed in Van Dyck's English portraits into an actual child, often functioning within the action of the scene and helping to define the pictorial space. It should also be pointed out that this portrait reveals Van Dyck's early interest in incorporating iconographical motifs in his portraits, a development that is usually associated with his arrival in England; see Erik Larsen, 'Van Dyck's English Period and Cavalier Poetry', *Art Journal*, 31 (1972), 252–60, who calls these allegorical symbols 'hitherto unknown' (p. 253). This portrait might also profitably be compared with the 'beauties' analysed by Stewart, 'Pin-ups or Virtues?'

[52] Millar, *Tudor, Stuart*, i. 81–2.

that has been inset within the larger painting. Even the building in the distance, long thought to be Inigo Jones's St Paul's, has been shown to be an architectural fantasy. But these discoveries only serve to emphasize how strong an influence iconic representation continued to enjoy in the early Stuart period; even work as fresh as van Somer's could still be placed within the static, two-dimensional poses favoured by earlier generations of monarchs and their painters.

Another painter who began to show an increased sense of assurance in the presentation of royal figures is Daniel Mytens, who served as principal painter to Charles until Van Dyck supplanted him in the early 1630s.[53] The growth of Mytens's skills can be gauged by comparing a portrait he painted of Charles in 1623 when he was Prince of Wales (Plate 24) with a remarkably similar painting executed in 1628 after Charles had become king (Plate 25).[54] Not all of the differences between these two portraits can be ascribed to Mytens's development as a painter, of course; we must make allowances for a greater measure of self-confidence in Charles himself, and for changes in his countenance and dress. But the signs of artistic maturity in the second painting are inescapable. In the earlier work, Mytens portrays the prince as awkward and ill at ease; his eyes do not quite meet our own, and his rather ungracefully positioned legs unfortunately resemble inverted versions of the balusters found in the colonnade behind him. In the second painting, on the other hand, the king's legs have been clothed in high boots; his left arm has been drawn akimbo, and his right hand holds the rod of royal office. In general the reworked arms and legs open up the king's stance and invest him with an increased sense of power. His eyes are fuller, his nose has been endowed with a more aristocratic arch, and his new fashion of wearing his moustache and goatee (the style will eventually be called Van Dyckian) helps to give definition to his face. But there is also an irony here that should not be ignored, for if these two portraits reveal Mytens's increasing ability to replace static, two-dimensional poses with more fully modelled forms—to animate his subject, and thus bring him to life—these paintings also document a movement towards more official, public portraiture. The hesitant portrait of Charles as Prince of Wales seems best suited for the private apartments of the royal family, whereas the

---

[53] For interesting comparisons of Mytens's work with Van Dyck's, see Waterhouse, p. 60; Whinney and Millar, p. 71; Millar, 'Painting under the Stuarts', in *The Genius of British Painting*, ed. Piper, p. 120; and Graham Parry, *The Golden Age restor'd: The culture of the Stuart Court, 1603–42* (Manchester: Manchester Univ. Press, 1981), 219–25.

[54] Millar, *Tudor, Stuart*, no. 117, pl. 47, and no. 118, pl. 48.

confident portrait of the king would have served admirably in any public setting.[55]

One of the major distinctions drawn between portraiture in the hands of Van Dyck and Rubens (with whom Van Dyck worked at the time van Somer was painting Queen Anne) centres on Rubens's ability to create more fully rounded, three-dimensional figures; and yet it is precisely this ability that set Van Dyck apart from his rivals when he was coaxed to join the Stuart court in London in 1632. Van Dyck brought with him not only his intimate knowledge of Rubens, but also a detailed appreciation of colouring and soft modelling in Titian (he would eventually own nineteen of his works) and of decorative technique in Veronese. And true to the modern judgement that he was an unusually adaptable painter—with four distinct periods and careers in three different countries—he was soon able to graft his sophisticated skills onto the most fruitful strains of native English painting.[56] He learned from van Somer and Cornelius Johnson; he reworked promising poses developed by Mytens; and he painted *most* of what the king commanded (he balked at adding small perspective scenes to his paintings in the manner of van Steenwyck; Mytens had fewer scruples).[57]

Van Dyck could begin to set his own terms as a painter because of the unusual status he was granted upon his arrival at the English court. He was knighted by the king, given a pension of £200 a year, presented with a gold medal and chain, housed in comfortable quarters in Blackfriars, and even transported to a country residence during the hot summer months. The king arranged for a private stairway to be built on the bank of the Thames near Van Dyck's studio so that he and his royal entourage could visit the painter with ease; and when Van Dyck's domestic arrangements seemed to need attention, Charles even found his painter a wife.[58] No previous artist in England—not even Rubens—had been accorded such

---

[55] Millar in fact points out that the earlier portrait (or a similar version) was painted for the Spanish ambassador.

[56] All modern scholars follow the traditional division of Van Dyck's career into four periods: first Antwerp (1613–21, including his short stay in England in 1620–1); Italian (1621–6); second Antwerp (1626–32); and English (1632–41). Van Dyck's early work has only recently received extended treatment; see, in addition to Cust, Gustav Glück, *The Early Work of Van Dyck* (Vienna: Schroll, n.d.); Leo van Puyvelde, 'The Young Van Dyck', *Burlington Magazine*, 79 (1941), 177–85; Ludwig Baldass, 'Some Notes on the Development of Van Dyck's Portrait Style', *Gazette des Beaux-Arts*, 6th per. 50 (1957), 251–70; Michael Jaffé, *Van Dyck's Antwerp Sketchbook* (London: Macdonald, 1966); John Rupert Martin and Gail Feigenbaum, *Van Dyck as Religious Artist* (Princeton: Princeton Art Museum, 1979); and Alan McNairn, *The Young van Dyck* (Ottawa: National Gallery of Canada, National Museums of Canada, 1980).

[57] See Whinney and Millar, p. 69 n. 2; for examples of van Steenwyck's work, see Millar, *Age of Charles I*, pls. 135–7.

[58] See Cust, pp. 88, 98, 142.

attention, and Van Dyck responded during the following ten years by painting his patron and the Stuart court with great skill and sensitivity. He entertained lavishly at home, often pressing his sitters to stay for dinner so that he could study their countenances under different conditions.[59] He finally lived up to the title facetiously bestowed upon him by his envious detractors in Rome: like Rubens, he became *il pittore cavalieresco*.[60]

Van Dyck's ambitious programme for Stuart portraiture essentially consisted of breaking up the royal icon into a variety of groups and poses, each characterized by grace and subtlety of presentation and by a softer, more silvery handling of texture and colouring. He is said to have painted at least thirty-six portraits of the king and twenty-five of his wife.[61] He portrayed the king in coronation robes and in armour, in the different versions of the order of the garter, on horseback and on foot, with his wife and with their quickly expanding family. He was also very much alive to the nuances of royal portraiture sanctioned in earlier reigns and revived in the poetry of the 1630s. And thus he did not hesitate to embroider his portraits of the king and queen with iconographical allusions to their roles as emperor and consort, hero and lover, melancholy knight and chaste mistress.[62] We therefore find in these paintings not only a reworking of the poses traditionally associated with state portraiture, but also a renewed emphasis on the individual personalities of his subjects and on the domestic happiness they enjoyed until the early years of the following decade. The freshness and versatility of Van Dyck's programme can be seen even in his three experiments with equestrian portraiture, which had been firmly established on the Continent—especially in Titian's influential painting of Charles V—as a form of royal icon that bordered on history painting.[63]

Van Dyck had explored the equestrian portrait long before he settled in England (he painted several versions of Genoese aristocrats on horseback during his sojourn in Italy), and during his English period he continued to paint equestrian portraits of foreign princes during his occasional jour-

---

[59] This is Bellori's account in his life of Van Dyck, published in 1672, which was repeated by William Hookham Carpenter, *Pictorial Notices: Consisting of a Memoir of Sir Anthony Van Dyck* (1844), 32.

[60] Bellori's anecdote is recounted by Carpenter, ibid.

[61] This is Cust's estimate, p. 107.

[62] The fullest account of Van Dyck's allegorical programme is Strong's *Van Dyck: Charles I on Horseback* (New York: Viking, 1972).

[63] Consider Johannes Wilde's characterization of Titian's equestrian portrait of Charles V in *Venetian Art from Bellini to Titian* (Oxford: Clarendon Press, 1974), 252: 'Perhaps it would be more correct to see in it the symbolic representation of an event that altered history.' Van Dyck painted a free interpretation of Rubens's portrait of Charles V at the battle of Mühlburg; see Larsen, no. 401.

neys to the Continent.[64] But his English paintings are really quite different. In his first version of Charles on horseback (Plate 26), Van Dyck portrays the king riding through a triumphal arch; he is dressed in armour, with his right hand firmly holding the royal baton, and his coat of arms is conspicuously displayed in the foreground to the left.[65] He is attended by his riding-master, the Seigneur de St Antoine, who walks beside him holding his shining helmet. There is an interesting relationship suggested here between these two men, for although M. Antoine has served as the king's own instructor (the 'best master' in the art of horsemanship), he is nevertheless depicted in a subordinate position, on foot, his head turned towards *his* master, with an expression of satisfaction and perhaps even awe on his face. Like the king's horse, he advances on his left foot, and the bright scarlet colouring of his garments is echoed in the red riding-blanket, embroidered with gold, on which the king sits.

Van Dyck's introduction of this subsidiary figure—a specific character closely associated with Charles—has enabled the painter to emphasize a sense of grace and assurance in the king and at the same time to structure his painting in spatial terms that work to break up the normally static nature of this kind of portrait. The king placed this painting at the end of his long gallery in St James's, which was already filled with portraits of the Roman emperors by Titian and Giulio Romano.[66] It was only the second work that Van Dyck painted for Charles, and it had a dramatic impact on its viewers, as we can see from a rapturous description by Marie de Medici's secretary, Pierre de la Serre:

At one end of the three-sided gallery there is a portrait of the king in armour and on horseback, by the hand of the Chevalier Van Dheich, and, to tell the truth, his pencil in preserving the majesty of the great monarch has by his industry so animated him, that if the eyes alone are to be believed they could boldly assert that he lived in this portrait, so striking is the appearance.[67]

There is a nice ambiguity here, for we cannot be entirely certain to which eyes de la Serre is referring: his own, or those of the king, painted with such sensitivity by Van Dyck in canvas after canvas? Our witness's general response to this painting, however, is clear. Van Dyck has

---

[64] See e.g. Larsen, nos. 323 and 331 (for the Genovese period) and nos. 787 and 793 for the later period.

[65] Glück, no. 372; Millar, *Tudor, Stuart*, no. 143, pl. 65, who notes other prototypes for this portrait; Larsen, no. 773 (vol. ii, colour pl. 29); Millar, *Van Dyck*, no. 11.

[66] On this point, see also Strong, *Van Dyck: Charles I on Horseback*, p. 25.

[67] Quoted (and translated) by Cust, p. 102; the original French, quoted by Millar, *Tudor, Stuart*, p. 94, is also ambiguous.

preserved the 'majesty of the great monarch' precisely by portraying his personal appearance with such forceful animation, by conveying (as Waller put it) 'not the form alone, and grace, / But act and power of a face'.[68]

A second equestrian portrait, which survives in two versions and is usually entitled *Charles I on Horseback* (Plate 27),[69] is more closely modelled on the imperial motif of Titian's *Charles V* and even on a group of comparatively stiff, native portraits, such as the one of Prince Henry (Charles's older brother) attributed to Isaac Oliver.[70] This painting, which has been examined by Strong in exhaustive detail, portrays the king in virtually the same pose as the earlier portrait, except that here he is viewed from the left side, emerging from a grove of trees. An attendant, his body barely intruding within the right margin of the painting, carries his plumed helmet. The king conspicuously wears the gold medallion of St George around his neck, and an elaborately carved cartouche, proclaiming his title as king of Great Britain, hangs above the attendant's head. And thus even though Van Dyck has positioned Charles here in his most extreme version of the full profile—the third-person 'he' of Schapiro's analogy—the painting itself retains a largely iconic flavour. The royal attributes of power are accentuated by the static nature of the pose; despite the richly painted natural background from which they emerge, both the king and his horse appear to be posing for their formal portraits.

The same is emphatically *not* true of a third equestrian portrait of Charles, which has traditionally been called *Le Roi à la Chasse* (Plate 28).[71] This title, entered in the king's account books, has led to some confusion, for there is no suggestion in the painting itself that this is a hunting-scene. Julius Held, who has analysed the portrait in greatest detail, has been able, however, to show how the scene Van Dyck depicts is related to a number of early seventeenth-century English hunting pictures, especially those that portray a member of the royal family opening the deer's neck at the end of the chase.[72] Held also cites van Somer's portrait of Queen Anne

[68] *The Poems of Edmund Waller*, ed. G. Thorn Drury (1893; rpt. New York: Greenwood, 1968), 44 ('To Vandyck').

[69] See Millar, *Tudor, Stuart*, no. 144, pl. 64, for the version (possibly a *modello*) in the royal collections, and Strong, *Van Dyck: Charles I on Horseback*, for the painting in the National Gallery; Glück, no. 381; Larsen, nos. 827–8 (vol. ii, colour pl. 49).

[70] In addition to Millar and Strong, the following articles also provide background information for this painting: Lionel Cust, 'The Equestrian Portraits of Charles I by Van Dyck', *Burlington Magazine*, 17 (1910), 159–60, and 18 (1911), 202–9; and Margaret R. Toynbee, 'Some Early Portraits of Charles I', *Burlington Magazine*, 91 (1949), 4–9.

[71] Glück, no. 377; Larsen, no. 820 (vol. ii, colour pl. 47).

[72] Julius S. Held, 'Le Roi à la Ciasse', *Art Bulletin*, 40 (1958), 139–49.

with the dogs at her feet, which we have already examined (Plate 22), and to these native prototypes we should add a painting by Mytens of Charles and Henrietta Maria about to depart for the chase, and—the closest model I have been able to find—a portrait by George Geldorp of *William, 2nd Earl Salisbury* (1626), which places its dismounted figure in the foreground, with hat and gloves in hand, while the tiny participants in the hunt stretch out behind him in the distance.[73] Held has also been able to trace Van Dyck's debt to several poses in Rubens, but we cannot help but notice that the figure here also constitutes a dynamic variant of the pose worked out by Mytens in his portrait of the new king (Plate 25).

One of Held's major tasks is to demonstrate how much more complicated a painting this is than Van Dyck's portrait of *Charles I on Horseback*, where the king's horse is employed only as a grand base for the elevation of the ruler. Van Dyck also includes compelling associations of authority in *Charles I à la Chasse*, but there is a new emphasis here on the nobility and superiority of the king; Charles continues to be painted as a monarch, but he is no less portrayed as a gentlemanly courtier, descended from his official perch. I find this to be a convincing argument, and one that can be amplified by a more detailed examination of Van Dyck's careful treatment of both spatial and temporal form. We should notice, in the first place, that even though the king has descended from his horse in this painting, he strikes us in spatial terms as an even more imposing figure. He may be elevated in *Charles I on Horseback*, but, wearing his suit of black armour, he is somewhat diminished as he sits astride his massive mount. In *Charles I à la Chasse*, however, he towers above the horse (now pawing the ground almost as if it were bowing), and his tightly encased appearance has been replaced by what Walpole called 'a most graceful figure in white sattin'.[74] The attendant who reaches for the horse's reins has also been painted as a shorter figure than the king, even though he technically occupies the same space. Each of these variations augments Charles's stature in natural terms; even the conspicuous cartouche in the one portrait is replaced here by a small inscription engraved upon a rock in the lower right-hand corner of the canvas. Too small to be seen except at extremely close range, it appropriately serves more as a title than as an iconic proclamation.

We should also notice that this painting embodies a different sense of movement and time. The two attendants at the centre of the canvas (and even the king's horse) appear to be oblivious to the figure who stands

---

[73] C. H. Collins Baker and W. G. Constable, *English Painting of the Sixteenth and Seventeenth Centuries* (Florence: Pantheon; New York: Harcourt, n.d. [1930]), pl. 43.

[74] *Anecdotes of Painting*, ii. 99.

before them—and to us as well. Although they wait upon the king—by
tending his horse and carrying his cloak—they have been created by the
painter as 'third-person' characters, going about their business with a
complete absence of self-consciousness. They are thus carefully separated
from the figure of the king himself, whose graceful smile, now turned in
our direction, suggests his own consciousness that he, at least, is being
watched. But his is not a static, two-dimensional pose. The placement of
his feet indicates that he has been gazing at the landscape in the distance, a
portion of which we can also see in the left-hand margin of the painting. It
is possible that Van Dyck had a specific scene in mind (Walpole thought it
represented a view of the Isle of Wight[75]). Sir Robert Strange, who
produced a contemporary engraving of Van Dyck's painting, remarked
that 'the local colouring is finely understood' and that the treatment of
landscape throughout the portrait was magnificent: 'There is no empty
space, no naked void left open to fatigue the eye: the whole scene is
clothed with richness and simplicity'.[76] The king, in abandoning the chase,
has turned his attention to the lovely scene surrounding him. He holds the
obligatory cane not as an emblem of royal power but as a simple walking-
stick, and he appears to have been caught by Van Dyck in the process of
surveying—with a connoisseur's eye—the land that he rules. We can sense
a certain stillness at the centre of this painting; all else is vigorous motion
around the king, but he displays a mood of detached serenity. He appears
to us not only as a monarch and as a courtier, but also as a private
individual enjoying the activities that give him pleasure.

I have examined these three related images of Charles at some length in
order to show how Van Dyck can suggest a variety of roles and
perspectives even within the confines of one traditional type of portrait.
Perhaps no single painting of the king captures this insistence on the
possibilities inherent in divergent poses more than the portrait entitled
Charles I in Three Positions (Plate 1).[77] In this painting, as we have already
seen, Van Dyck has been able to break through the severe limitations
placed upon him (in a study intended only to provide Bernini with the
different countenances of the king) by creating a full-fledged portrait in
which the various heads of Charles are both harmoniously fused and yet
distinctly separated.[78] Although the central figure in this composition
shares several of the iconic characteristics we have seen at work in

---

[75] *Anecdotes of Painting*, ii. 99.

[76] Quoted by Cust, p. 105.

[77] Millar, *Tudor, Stuart*, no. 146, pl. 70; Millar, *Age of Charles I*, no. 86 (colour plate); Glück,
no. 389; Larsen, no. 821; Millar, *Van Dyck*, no. 22.

[78] For an earlier discussion of this painting, see above, p. 9.

Eworth's *Henry VIII*, it is nevertheless flanked by other figures that suggest different motifs. In Schapiro's analogy, this portrait embodies not only first-person and third-person poses but also the three-quarter profile that serves as the staple of most secular portraiture. The full frontal rendering may face us directly, but the head in full profile—the pose normally associated with action and narrative—takes yet another study of Charles as its subject of contemplation. If there is a mood of confrontation in this painting, it is dictated as much by introspection as it is by any outward movement towards the picture's beholders. Here, as in the equestrian portraits of the king and in Van Dyck's entire programme for portraiture, no single image is allowed to dominate.

iii. Allegories

Much of Van Dyck's success in establishing a fresh iconography for the Stuart court lay in his ability to enrich his compositions with the refinements of allegory. In frequently adopting an allegorical mode, Van Dyck was in fact reconciling two contrary impulses in European painting, both part of the legacy he inherited at the English court. Allegory was, on the one hand, consistent with the Renaissance insistence on portraying an individual in his or her entirety. The deployment of iconographical attributes enabled the artist to suggest a richly allusive breadth of characterization; portraiture in the wake of Titian was to embody both an essential faithfulness to the decorum of likeness and a more urgent, more idealized fidelity to the strength of the sitter's personality.[79] The effect of allegory in English painting at the turn of the century, on the other hand, was quite different.[80] The combination of allegorical motifs with the static poses and inscribed legends of many Tudor portraits (such as Gheerhaerts's Ditchley portrait of Queen Elizabeth) produced representations that we would call over-determined; these paintings are so saturated with iconic devices that they are unable to suggest the character of the sitter except in hierarchic and formulaic terms. Even when painters such as Eworth attempted to combine natural (that is, comparatively realistic) descriptions with allegorical motifs—as in his unusual portrait of Sir John Luttrell—the two forms of representation remained strangely divorced from each other, carefully separated in terms of proportion and by the

[79] See Pope-Hennessy, chs. 1–3, and Wilde, *Venetian Art from Bellini to Titian*, pp. 224, 228, and *passim*.
[80] The fullest discussions of allegory in Elizabethan painting are Strong, *Cult of Elizabeth*, and Piper, 'Tudor and Early Stuart Painting'.

spatial structure of the work.[81] Van Dyck was not the first painter to reintroduce allegorical motifs in the Stuart period, nor was he as relentless in his pursuit of the iconographical as was a native painter such as William Dobson.[82] But he was responsible for handling allegorical themes with a grace and wit long lacking in English portraiture.

In a motif adapted from Mytens, for instance, Van Dyck depicted the royal couple as they exchanged emblematic tokens of affection (Plate 29).[83] The queen, who was the daughter of Henri IV, presents her husband with a warrior's laurels; the king, who was the son of James I, repays this tribute by offering Henrietta Maria an olive branch.[84] Van Dyck's portrait therefore depicts the union of two individuals and symbolizes, at the same time, the alliance of two royal families, one characterized by war, the other by peace. Similarly, in his portrait of the queen and her dwarf, Sir Jeffery Hudson, Van Dyck both pays tribute to his royal mistress by dressing her in the attributes of Venus and roguishly alludes to the comic exploits of her diminutive knight by suggesting his resemblance to Hercules and Paris.[85] The artist's carefully idealized treatment of the queen is handled with subtlety and grace, and his witty, mock-heroic handling of her dwarf, which diminishes rather than reinforces his courtly virtues, foreshadows the allusive humour of a portrait as late as Reynolds's depiction of *Master Crewe as Henry VIII* (Plate 68).[86]

But the pursuit of allegorical portraiture is fraught with substantial dangers, as Van Dyck must have realized. If a character is to be portrayed 'as' or 'in the guise of' someone else—what Reynolds would eventually call composite portraiture—then the inherent comparison with a mythological or biblical figure must be justified by the strength of the sitter's own position or character. The same is true, of course, when a biographer like Walton devises elaborate parallels between the dean of St Paul's and the saint who gave Donne's church its name. In spite of the element of magic traditionally associated with composite portraiture—in which the person depicted begins to take on these borrowed attributes of power in the minds of his or her beholders—no amount of grace and wit will allow

[81] See Frances A. Yates, 'The Allegorical Portraits of Sir John Luttrell', in *Essays in the History of Art Presented to Rudolph Wittkower*, ed. Douglas Fraser, Howard Hibbard, and Milton J. Lewine (London: Phaidon Press, 1967), 149–59.

[82] Waterhouse, p. 82.

[83] Larsen, nos. 748–9; Glück, no. 374.

[84] See Millar, 'Some Painters and Charles I', *Burlington Magazine*, 104 (1962), 325–30, who also points out that in some of these paintings, including Van Dyck's, the queen is pictured as *enceinte*, thus suggesting a third generation, the fruit of their union.

[85] See Stewart, 'Pin-ups or Virtues?', pp. 17–19.

[86] See Paulson, *Emblem*, p. 88, pl. 43.

this transformation to take place when the parallel cannot be historically grounded.[87] That way lies bathos—and even blasphemy. Consider Collins Baker's response to Lely's portrait of Barbara Villiers and her illegitimate son (or daughter), depicted as the Madonna and child (Lely also painted the mistress of Charles II as Minerva, the Magdalen, and St Barbara): Lely is accused of 'inexcusable stupidity' and of 'pandering to the depravity of his patrons'.[88] Wit this jaded is apparently difficult to redeem, even in the eyes of the painter's most sympathetic admirers.

Lely was on much safer ground when he portrayed the king's niece, Princess Mary, in the guise of Diana (Plate 30).[89] In this lovely portrait, filled with movement and painted in delicate shades of blue, gold, and white, the future queen of England follows the hunt with bow and arrow in hand, her head crowned only with Diana's crescent. Here the implicit parallel is entirely appropriate, for the young Mary was not to marry the Prince of Orange until 1677. It is also probable, in fact, that Lely had even closer associations between the princess and Diana in mind: his painting appears to be connected with the production of John Crowne's *Calisto*, performed at Whitehall in 1675 with the reluctant Margaret Blagge as one of the principal actresses.[90] Crowne's elaborate masque was dedicated to Mary, who played the title-role ('the exact and perfect Character of Chastity, in the person of Calisto'[91]). But even a royal princess could not outshine Margaret Blagge (as Diana), whose extravagant dress, incorporating twenty-four yards of gold brocade, was the central attraction in an entertainment largely devoted to costumes and scenery. Lely's gracious tribute to Mary is thus more richly allusive—and also more appropriate— than may at first appear. He pictures her in the guise of Diana not only because it is a traditional and suitable pose for young, unmarried women, but also because Mary has already played a similar role in front of the same audience that will admire this portrait.

But if it is possible to describe Lely's portrayal of Princess Mary as appropriate, is it also possible to characterize it as distinctive? Does it set her apart from other chaste young women, especially those who played similar parts in Crowne's *Calisto*? Perhaps in superficial terms—in the

---

[87] See Edgar Wind, 'Studies in Allegorical Portraiture: I', *Journal of the Warburg Institute*, 1 (1937–8), 138–62.

[88] Baker, i. 172.

[89] Beckett, *Lely*, no. 104 (called *Jane Kelleway*); Millar, *Tudor, Stuart*, no. 249, pl. 103.

[90] This possible connection, first noted by Stewart, 'Pin-ups or Virtues?', p. 17, strikes me as quite convincing.

[91] Quoted by Eleanore Boswell, *The Restoration Court Stage (1660–1702)* (1932; rpt. New York: Barnes and Noble, 1966), 187, who provides an extensive discussion of Crowne's masque; see also Hiscock, *Family Circle*, p. 97.

sense that the face in this portrait is unlike the faces to be found in other portraits—but not in its essential rendering of character. It would be just as appropriate (perhaps more so) to portray Margaret Blagge in this role, for she was both chaste and, being a few years older than Mary, had even played the part of Diana and worn her splendid attire. The issue I raise here does not merely focus on the problem of iconographical motifs that may eventually strike us as monotonous, although this is often a serious liability of allegorical portraiture. A contemporary of Lely remarked that when the artist painted the Duchess of Cleveland's portrait, 'he put something of Clevelands face as her Languishing Eyes into every one Picture, so that all his pictures had an Air one of another, all Eyes were Sleepy alike. So that Mr Walker ye Painter swore Lilly's Pictures was all Brothers & Sisters.'[92] Much the same kind of charge could be brought against Lely's tireless repetition of iconographical attributes, especially the syringa bushes and St Agnes poses associated with young women about to be married.[93] It remained for Kneller, himself a notorious imitator of Lely's patterns, to add a fresh twist to this motif by naming his illegitimate daughter Agnes and by portraying her in the guise of St Agnes when she was wed (she named her own child Godfrey).[94]

A more difficult problem is posed, however, by the very notion of what it means to characterize a historical figure in allegorical terms. We have already seen, in Van Dyck's portrayal of Charles and Henrietta Maria exchanging tokens of olive branch and laurel, how the introduction of an allegorical motif may suggest a broader and initially unsuspected significance within the portrayal of individual characters. But the more elaborate the allegorical motif becomes—the more it intrudes upon what we call the natural or realistic depiction of character—the more the meaning of the portrait is simultaneously curtailed. This is also true of the other iconic forms I have examined, but it is particularly evident here because of the nature of allegorical figures to be closely identified with only a few essential qualities, pictured in graphic terms as attributes. The characteristics embodied by these figures, moreover, are usually abstract qualities; and because they are abstract and universal, they are by definition shared by a variety of people. Allowance must be made, of course, for the fact that different individuals do actually resemble one another in a number of essential ways. But the nature of allegorical representation, even when it

---

[92] Quoted by Whinney and Millar, p. 174.
[93] See Beckett, *Lely*, pp. 21, 24, and Stewart, 'Pin-ups or Virtues?'
[94] See Stewart, *Kneller* 1971, nos. 6–7; Stewart, *Kneller* 1983, p. 60 n., notes that although she was long called Agnes, the child's name was actually Catherine.

does not fall victim to the dictates of fashion, reinforces the identification of the sitter with only a few dominant, generalized characteristics. Allegorical portraiture may attempt to reveal the qualities that are most distinctive in an individual—Henrietta Maria's beauty and virtue, Princess Mary's chastity—but its method of representation is none the less formulaic and restrictive.[95]

In allegorical portraits, as in images akin to royal icons, the painter may occasionally intend to establish precisely this kind of limited but powerful identification between his subject and a specific, abstract virtue.[96] Evidence survives concerning one painting by Van Dyck in which the quality to be represented is virtue itself. The portrait is *Venetia Stanley, Lady Digby, as Prudence* (Plate 31), painted shortly after this beautiful woman's untimely death at the age of 33.[97] Venetia Stanley's husband, Sir Kenelm Digby, was one of Van Dyck's closest friends; he assisted in inviting the painter to stay permanently in England, and they frequently collaborated in alchemical and astrological studies.[98] Van Dyck painted Digby and his family several times, including an *ad mortem* likeness of his wife in May 1633, two days after she had died. As we shall see in the following chapter, in a discussion of Aubrey's *Brief Lives*, Venetia Digby was celebrated as one of the most beautiful women of her age; but her indiscreet behaviour when she was young (including a long stint as the mistress of the Earl of Dorset) had seriously tarnished her reputation, so much so that even years of devotion to her husband could not entirely repair it. Digby therefore dictated the plan of this painting to Van Dyck as a vindication of his wife's character. In a description that corresponds quite closely to Van Dyck's painting, Digby told Bellori that he conceived of a portrait of Venetia

as Prudence, sitting in a white dress with a coloured wrap and a jewelled girdle. Under her hand are two white doves, and her other arm is encircled by a serpent.

---

[95] Composite portraiture might be seen as a reversal of the process at work in personification, extolled here by William Melmoth: 'To represent natural, moral, or intellectual qualities and affections as persons, and appropriate to them those general emblems by which their powers and properties are usually typified in pagan theology, may be allowed as one of the most pleasing and graceful figures of poetical rhetoric' (quoted by Hagstrum, p. 149). The effect in both forms is quite similar (perhaps often the same), but personification calls for general qualities to be bodied forth in a specific figure, whereas composite portraiture proceeds by enabling a particular person to embody the general and abstract.

[96] This might be thought of as an extreme version of composite portraiture's tendency to classify characters; see Paulson, *Emblem*, pp. 87–8.

[97] Millar, *Tudor, Stuart*, no. 179; Millar, *Age of Charles I*, no. 107; Glück, no. 399; Larsen, no. 743; Millar, *Van Dyck*, no. 9. R. T. Petersson, *Sir Kenelm Digby: The Ornament of England 1603–1665* (London: Cape; Cambridge, Mass.: Harvard Univ. Press, 1956), 102, argues that Van Dyck's *ad mortem* sketch was his last portrait of Venetia, but I agree with Millar, *Tudor, Stuart*, i. 107, that this allegorical painting was meant as a posthumous tribute.

[98] See Petersson, *Sir Kenelm Digby*, pp. 98–100.

Under her feet is a plinth to which are bound, in the guise of slaves, Deceit with two faces; Anger with furious countenance; meagre Envy with her snaky locks; Profane Love, with eyes bound, wings clipped, arrows scattered and torch extinguished; with other naked figures the size of life. Above is a glory of singing Angels, three of them holding the palm and the wreath above the head of Prudence as a symbol of her victory and triumph over the vices; and the epigram, taken from Juvenal, NULLUM NUMEN ABEST SI SIT PRUDENTIA.[99]

Aubrey noted that the painting was hung over the chimney in the queen's drawing-room at Windsor, and Bellori adds that Van Dyck was so pleased with the portrait that he executed a smaller version for himself.[100]

Walpole described this painting as a 'galant compliment' to Lady Digby,[101] but it should be clear that Van Dyck and his collaborator shared the greater ambition of redeeming her character by transforming her image in the eyes of society. The form they chose—composite portraiture—performs this redemptive act by depicting her as the modern embodiment of the ancient concept of Prudentia, thus creating a timeless image that is not contingent upon historical particulars. It is true that Venetia Digby's earlier trials have not been entirely ignored (the torch of profane love has been extinguished), and we may also sense a certain precariousness in the expression of the putto who hands the triumphal wreath to his two colleagues, hovering above her head.[102] But in spite of these touches, Van Dyck's painting still manages to suggest what her husband saw as her essential character, an image entirely consistent with the portrait Digby himself sketched of her in his *Private Memoirs*. Here, in an elaborate autobiographical romance with close affinities to Van Dyck's allegorical painting, Digby has his protagonist, Theagenes, state that 'a wise man should not confine himself to what may be said of the past actions of his wife'. The ideal companion, he declares, should be 'nobly descended, beautiful to please him, well formed to bear children, of a good wit, sweet disposition, endowed with good parts, and love him'.[103] Digby's book represents his own attempt to vindicate his wife's character and his own behaviour, but Van Dyck's portrait seems to have been more effective than this bizarre Arcadian romance. Among his observations in an essay entitled 'The Pictures at Windsor Castle', Hazlitt remarked that it

[99] Quoted by Millar, *Tudor, Stuart*, i. 107. For another description of this allegorical scene, see Petersson, *Sir Kenelm Digby*, pp. 101–2.

[100] *Brief Lives*, i. 232; Bellori is quoted by Carpenter, *Pictorial Notices*, p. 31.

[101] *Anecdotes of Painting*, ii. 102.

[102] For Van Dyck's skill in depicting children, see Waterhouse, *Anthony van Dyck: Suffer Little Children to Come unto Me* (Ottawa: National Gallery of Canada, National Museums of Canada, 1978), 18–20.

[103] Quoted by Petersson, *Sir Kenelm Digby*, pp. 44, 73.

'would be next to impossible to perform an unbecoming action with that portrait hanging in the room. It has an air of nobility about it; a spirit of humanity within it.'[104] If there actually is an element of magic in the transformations that portraiture performs, it seems to lie in the ability of the painter to determine how a person will be remembered once the vestiges of prejudice and infamy have finally disappeared.

There is a potential danger in a collaboration as close as Van Dyck's with Kenelm Digby, for it is possible that the sympathetic artist will follow his patron in the exploration of meanings so private that the interpretation of the portrait will no longer depend upon the conventional iconic sources embedded within it. (It is conceivable, in fact, that the painter may not fully understand the iconographical scheme presented to him by his patron.) The representation of Venetia Digby as Prudence poses no such problems, but there are other important paintings of the period, including Van Dyck's portrait of Sir John Suckling, where the iconic devices have still not been confidently deciphered.[105] The problem is not merely one for latter-day iconographers and iconologists for, as Hagstrum and others have shown, it was often the nature of iconicism in the seventeenth century to strive towards the private, individualized meaning of the device or *impresa*, which was directly at odds with the abstract, generalizing norms of the allegorical emblem.[106]

Some of the problems posed by personal iconography can be seen in a final allegorical painting by Van Dyck, the *Self-portrait with a Sunflower* (Plate 32).[107] In this enigmatic picture, the artist stands with his back to us

---

[104] Quoted by Millar, *Tudor, Stuart*, i. 107.

[105] See Thomas Clayton, 'An Historical Study of the Portraits of Sir John Suckling', *Journal of the Warburg and Courtald Institutes*, 23 (1960), 105–26, and Malcolm Rogers, 'The Meaning of Van Dyck's Portrait of Sir John Suckling', *Burlington Magazine*, 120 (1978), 741–5. Rogers provides the fullest explanation of the motto (taken from Persius) and of the vaguely oriental dress and the use of the Shakespearean folio, with its allusion to *Hamlet* (and thus to Suckling's own works); but his further conjectures about the possible presentation of this portrait to Suckling's lover as an icon to be worshipped are less convincing because they are not supported by any real evidence. Neither Rogers nor Clayton discusses the wild and desolate setting here, which reinforces Suckling's hermit-like isolation and is consistent with the advice of the motto ('Do not seek outside yourself'). More recently, Mark Roskill, 'Van Dyck at the English Court: The Relations of Portraiture and Allegory', *Critical Inquiry*, 14 (1987), 173–99, includes this painting in the group of theatrical, 'masque' portraits that Van Dyck completed after his return to London from Antwerp in 1635; opposed to these paintings, he argues, is another, 'allusive' group that is significantly lacking in 'codified symbolism'.

[106] Hagstrum compares the 17th- and 18th-cent. uses of poetic iconicism: 'The poet of the metaphysical and baroque seventeenth century tended to be emblematic and symbolic, to suggest the world of invisible reality, or to express private, esoteric, and individual meaning. The poet of the neoclassical eighteenth century tended to be pictorial and natural and to suggest, however briefly, the reality of nature and normative human experience' (p. 140). See also ibid. 97–8, and Michael Leslie, 'The Dialogue between Bodies and Souls: Pictures and Poesy in the English Renaissance', *Word and Image*, 1 (1985), 16–30.

[107] Glück, no. 496; Larsen, no. 835; Millar, *Age of Charles I*, no. 92. This painting was engraved by Hollar; see Millar, *Van Dyck*, p. 8.

in three-quarter profile, a pose often adopted in the self-portraits he painted during his stay in England.[108] He stares at us over his right shoulder; his left hand is entangled in the chain presented to him by the king, and his right hand points in the direction of an enormous sunflower. This painting's first commentators, Cust and Waterhouse, interpreted the sunflower as an emblem of royal patronage shining upon the artist, but later critics have found this argument unconvincing. Michael Levey suggested that the portrait 'seems consciously ambiguous, because Van Dyck is possibly the light to which the flower turns',[109] and Robert Wark, the first to take an iconographical approach, showed that Van Dyck, by pointing at the sunflower with his right hand, was establishing an equivalent relationship between himself and the emblematic flower.[110] The sunflower, he demonstrated, was used by early seventeenth-century emblem writers as a symbol of devotion—especially to one's king or lover—and thus it is meant to stand here as an emblem of the artist and not of the master to whom he is devoted. This interpretation was soon corroborated by Bruyn and Emmens, who showed that the sunflower had been employed in a variety of ways in contemporary painting: as an image of the soul devoted to God or of the Virgin devoted to Christ, as a typically English motif suggesting devotion to the king, and as a Dutch emblem for the art of painting itself—for *Pittura*. They concluded that 'the king's favour, the painting seems to argue by means of its unobtrusive symbols, enables the artist to pursue his god-given task, viz. to pay tribute through his art to nature—a tribute which in turn culminates in a handsome eulogy of the King.'[111] The portrait celebrates, in other words, the reciprocal relationship between the artist and the king; Van Dyck depends upon Charles's patronage, and his monarch depends upon the painter's ability to enhance his image.

The issue at stake in each of these approaches to the painting centres on the specific, personal use Van Dyck has made of an emblem that possesses a variety of applications. I believe that the iconographical analysis of this

---

[108] See the (reversed) poses in *Van Dyck and Sir Endymion Porter* (Larsen, no. 836) and in the two self-portraits dating from 1633 (Larsen, nos. 777–8), where Van Dyck also wears his gold chain.

[109] *Painting at Court* (London: Weidenfeld and Nicolson, 1971); 126.

[110] R. A. Wark, 'A Note on Van Dyck's Self-Portrait with a Sunflower', *Burlington Magazine*, 98 (1956), 53–4.

[111] J. Bruyn and J. A. Emmens, 'The Sunflower Again', *Burlington Magazine*, 99 (1957), 96–7. On the other hand, Christopher Brown, *Van Dyck* (London: Phaidon, 1982; Ithaca: Cornell Univ. Press, 1983), 147–9, emphasizes the specifically English association of the sunflower with the relation between subject and monarch both in this self-portrait and in a portrait of Sir Kenelm Digby (with a sunflower). Arguing that 'The flower must possess the same significance in both portraits', Brown concludes that it cannot be interpreted as a symbol of the art of painting.

portrait is sound so far as it goes, but it nevertheless appears to ignore the more direct evidence presented within the painting itself. It should be obvious, of course, that allegory plays a major role in this picture; we might even characterize it as a painting that draws attention to what is missing, to those elements that must be represented in other terms. In addition to Van Dyck's treatment of the sunflower, which suggests the artist's devotion to the king, we should also notice a further implication of the king in the gold chain Van Dyck wears around his neck: the chain was not only an emblem of *Pittura* (in Ripa and other iconographers) and a personal present from Charles, but also a gift that included the king's image. In his biography of Van Dyck, Carpenter revealed that 'the compliment [of knighthood] was further enhanced by the gift of a gold chain, to which was attached the portrait of his royal patron set in brilliants.'[112] Like the gold, emblematic sunflower, the artist's gold chain points in two directions, suppressing an exact image of the king but suggesting a powerful, if unseen, presence.

It is well known that Van Dyck also suppressed any specific image of himself as a painter in his self-portraits; but this painting, I suggest, represents *il pittore cavalieresco* in as close an approximation of this pose as he was willing to condone. He does not portray himself literally as a painter, with brush in hand, nor does he rely solely upon the emblematic motifs of the chain and flower, both associated with *Pittura*; instead he has chosen to suggest his profession through the careful arrangement of his hands, the handling of his pose, and the features of the flower to which he points. We should notice, first of all, that his hands point in two directions: the index finger of his right hand points to the flower, while the corresponding finger of his left hand, carefully distinguished from his remaining fingers by the links of the gold chain, points directly at himself. The equivalence Wark observed in the gesture of the right hand, in other words, is explicitly confirmed in the painting itself by the reciprocal movement of the left. Van Dyck has turned his head in our direction precisely to draw attention to the relationship he has forged. We cannot help but see, moreover, that the artist has represented the sunflower in almost the same proportions as he has painted himself, and the equivalence between these two images is enhanced by the quasi-human figure of the flower, whose right 'arm' (if we may call it that) sports a separate blossom. The sunflower has been drawn, that is, as a parallel figure to the artist, with a metaphorical brush extended from its right hand. And if we

---

[112] Carpenter, *Pictorial Notices*, p. 29; cf. Buckeridge, p. 430.

return to Van Dyck's own pose, we can see that his right hand approaches the flower just as if he were in fact painting it; his left hand, which is more loosely modelled, has been placed where he would normally hold his palette.[113] If there is in fact an element of ambiguity in this painting, it would therefore seem to lie in the object towards which Van Dyck gestures: is it an actual flower, depicted in rather unnatural terms, or is it a canvas that the artist studies within his own studio? The source of light in this painting suggests that either alternative may be true. But even if the sunflower and sky are treated as a symbolic portrait within a portrait, Van Dyck remains no less dignified as a gentleman and as a painter, and the allegorical motifs remain no less allusive in their suggestions of the painter's devotion to his art as well as to his king.

iv. Beyond Iconicism

Iconicism remained an important force in English portraiture throughout the seventeenth century, although the decision to employ iconic structures appears to have become more self-conscious as the century drew to a close. Kneller's standard portraits of William and Mary are quite similar (and presumably deeply indebted) to Van Dyck's models for the early Stuart court. When William returned to England as a glorious peacemaker following the Treaty of Ryswick in 1697, however, a more magnificent and complex scheme was apparently called for, and Kneller responded with a barrage of iconic motifs that were more in the style of Rubens than Van Dyck.[114] Similarly, when Sir James Thornhill worked up a preparatory sketch for a painting of the landing of George I, he annotated his *modello* with arguments against a truthful and unadorned depiction of this important event:

Objections that will arise from the plain reproduction of the King's landing as it was in fact and in the modern way and dress. . . . First of all it was night, which to represent would be hard and ungraceful in picture. No ships appearing, and boats make a small figure. . . . To have their faces and dresses as they really were, difficult. The King's own dress then not graceful, not enough worthy of him to be transmitted to Posterity. There was a vast crowd which to represent would be ugly, and not to represent would be false.[115]

[113] Michael Fried has examined several remarkable variations of this arrangement in 'Painter into Painting: On Courbet's *After Dinner at Ornans* and *Stonebreakers*', *Critical Inquiry*, 8 (1982), 619–43.
[114] See Stewart, 'William III and Sir Godfrey Kneller', *Journal of the Warburg and Courtauld Institutes*, 33 (1970), 330–6.
[115] Quoted by Edgar Wind, 'The Revolution of History Painting', *Journal of the Warburg Institute*, 1 (1938–9), 123.

And so on, with additional comments on whom to depict and in what manner (some of the king's attendants were in disgrace by the time Thornhill completed his task). Hogarth's father-in-law finally chose to abandon all allegorical motifs and to paint the king's landing much as it had occurred, with only a few concessions to what 'it should have been then'. The aesthetic decisions he had to make, however, were reflected throughout English portraiture in this period. We have the anomaly, for example, of Lely seemingly painting his Restoration beauties with one hand while he was creating rugged, fresh, painstakingly naturalistic portraits of the admirals of the British fleet with the other.[116] Even Kneller, years after he had developed the intimate Kit-cat formula, produced a medallion portrait of Pope that is thickly encrusted with iconic devices and allusive motifs.[117] But by this time the fervid pursuit of iconicism was unusual, if not rare. English portraiture had managed to retain its integrity and popularity without benefit of iconic inscriptions and poses, iconographical attributes, or allegorical comparisons.

A tradition of simple, unaffected, but powerful portraiture already existed in England by the time Van Dyck arrived, and it continued to prosper—especially in the provinces—while the Flemish master dominated the artistic world of the court. But Van Dyck himself brought with him a strong taste for intimate portraiture (often beautifully realized in the probing canvases of his second Antwerp period), and while he lived in England he continued to direct the production of a set of head-and-shoulder engravings that has come to be known as his *Iconography*.[118] This unusual project entailed a lengthy collaboration between the artist and two Flemish publishers, Martin van den Enden and Gillis Hendricx. Eventually published by Hendricx as *Centum Icones* in 1645, this group of engraved portrait-heads functioned as a visual biographical dictionary of three types of men eminent in their day: princes and military commanders, statesmen and philosophers, and artists and amateurs (connoisseurs or patrons of the arts). The origin of each engraving was either a full-scale painting or a memorandum sketch (many of them made *ad vivum*, especially of Van Dyck's fellow artists). Van Dyck then proceeded to execute a sketch in black chalk, which served as the prototype for an oil

[116] Lely's 'Flagmen' have been widely admired; see Baker, i. 168–71; Waterhouse, p. 99; and Millar, *Lely*, no. 40, who provides a more cautious judgement.

[117] For extended commentaries on this interesting painting, see Wimsatt, pp. 50-9, and Stewart, *Kneller* 1971, no. 82.

[118] For the *Iconography*, see Cust, pp. 161–73; Arthur M. Hind, *Van Dyck: His Original Etchings and His Iconography* (Boston and New York: Houghton, 1915); *Portrait Etchings of Anthony Van Dyck* (New York: Knoedler, 1934); and Marie Mauquoy-Hendrickx, *L'Iconographie d'Antoine van Dyck: Catalogue Raisonné* (Brussels: Palais des Académies, 1956).

grisaille (in monochrome) produced in his studio; the *grisaille*, in turn, served as the model for the final engraving, which, in fifteen etchings, Van Dyck himself undertook.[119]

Two steps in this elaborate process can be illustrated by Van Dyck's black chalk sketch of Inigo Jones (Plate 33) and by his beautiful etching of the artist Paulus de Vos (Plate 34).[120] The chalk portrait of England's most accomplished architect is as broad in scope as any in the series: Van Dyck sketches Jones to the waist, and even provides him with some manuscript designs, the attributes of his trade. But the artist's focus is clearly on the head itself, and especially on the intensely vigorous, penetrating eyes, whose alertness is set off against the massive and sedentary body. The portrait of Paulus de Vos, on the other hand, in which only the head has been completed, reveals Van Dyck working within an even more restricted space, which is characteristic of many of the fifteen etchings he signed. Everything that the artist wishes to say about his sitters must be communicated through the expression of character in the face alone and through a fresh, open technique of etching whose simplicity makes it all the more forceful. David Piper has aptly characterized the sitters in these portraits as 'aristocrats of sensibility',[121] and it is significant that most of the subjects etched by Van Dyck himself are his fellow artists, and that of the three categories comprised by the *Iconography* as a whole, by far the largest was that devoted to artists and amateurs.[122]

The intensity of these severely restricted portraits, which are not unlike the studio sketches and miniatures produced by Samuel Cooper, can also be glimpsed in more ambitious paintings where character is not established so much by iconic structures as by the careful selection of setting, the sympathetic handling of facial expression, and the imaginative use of pictorial space, especially in portraits that include two figures. William Sheppard's iconic portrait of Thomas Killigrew in Venice (Plate 21) should be compared, for instance, with the portrait Van Dyck painted of Killigrew twelve years earlier, in 1638, shortly after the death of his wife and of his wife's sister (Plate 35).[123] In this double portrait, the playwright

[119] Lely later owned 'thirty-seven sketches on panel for the *Iconography*'; see Millar, *Lely*, p. 25, who presumably refers to the *grisailles*. These preparatory sketches have not always been accepted as Van Dyck's, however; see H. Gerson and E. H. Ter Kuile, *Art and Architecture in Belgium 1600 to 1800* (Harmondsworth: Penguin, 1960), 192, no. 61 (who cite other sources as well).

[120] For *Inigo Jones* see Horst Vey, *Die Zeichnungen Anton Van Dycks* (Brussels: Verlag Arcade, 1962), no. 316; Millar, *Age of Charles I*, no. 45; and Millar, *Van Dyck*, no. 79; for *Paulus de Vos*, Mauquoy-Hendrickx, *L'Iconographie d'Antoine van Dyck*, no. 16. 1.

[121] Piper, 'The Development of the British Literary Portrait up to Samuel Johnson', p. 59.

[122] The breakdown is: princes, 16; statesmen, 12; artists, 52.

[123] Millar, *Tudor, Stuart*, no. 156, pl. 79; Glück, no. 451; Larsen, no. 923.

is seated to the left, his head resting (as in the Sheppard portrait) on his left hand, while his right hand holds a piece of paper on which are drawn two female statuary figures. His companion has been most confidently identified as Lord William Crofts, the brother of Killigrew's wife, who looks up from the blank page in his hand to find that his friend has turned away, lost in thoughts of his own. In Sheppard's painting, the subject of Killigrew's thoughts is revealed through a mixture of iconic modes: the inscribed manuscript and pile of books, the iconic portrait of Charles I, the emblematic motif of the faithful dog, and the inclusion of the *Eikon Basilike*. In Van Dyck's portrait, on the other hand, Killigrew's thoughts are suggested by the black ribbon of mourning he wears on his left sleeve (his wedding ring hangs from the ribbon), the silver cross with his wife's initials, the truncated column in the background (traditionally associated with mortality and fortitude, although it also appears in one of Van Dyck's early self-portraits), the manuscript he holds in his hand, and the presence of his brother-in-law, who shares in his loss and with whom he appears to collaborate on a memorial design and inscription. The sitter's pose and the dreamy-eyed, languorous expression in his eyes are the same in both canvases, but Van Dyck has chosen to explore Killigrew's devotion and mourning in more subtle, less intrusive terms that are much more natural to the scene itself.

Van Dyck's ability to generate dynamic poses involving two figures can be documented in several of the most successful portraits he painted during his English period. Walpole claimed, for example, that the forceful portrait of the Earl of Strafford and his secretary was Van Dyck's masterpiece.[124] Van Dyck's *William Feilding, Earl of Denbigh* (frontispiece) has received considerably less attention than the famous portrait of Strafford, but it just as fully epitomizes Van Dyck's eloquent powers of expression.[125] We do not know a great deal about Denbigh, who seems to have made his fortune by marrying the sister of the Duke of Buckingham. He served as Master of the Great Wardrobe and as an admiral in the navy, and was killed in 1643 during the royalist defence of Birmingham. We also know that in 1631 he sailed on East India Company ships to India and Persia; although he carried letters from Charles I, he travelled as a private citizen, 'apparently simply from curiosity'.[126] Van Dyck painted Denbigh upon his return to England in 1633. He pictures the earl in native dress,

[124] *Anecdotes of Painting*, ii. 104.

[125] Gregory Martin, *National Gallery Catalogues: The Flemish School circa 1600–circa 1900* (London: National Gallery, 1970), no. 5633; Larsen, no. 779 (vol. ii, colour pl. 33); Millar, *Age of Charles I*, no. 97; Millar, *Van Dyck*, no. 16 (colour pl. IV).

[126] *DNB* vi. 1154.

much as he had earlier painted Sir Robert Shirley, who (according to Fuller) 'much affected to appear in foreign vests; and, as if his clothes were his limbs, accounted himself never ready till he had something of the Persian habit about him'.[127] In portraying Shirley in native dress, in other words, Van Dyck has presented him as he normally appeared, even when he held court in Rome as an envoy of the Shah. In painting Denbigh in an Indian costume, on the other hand, Van Dyck has undertaken a more imposing task: the imaginative reconstruction of an Englishman's experience abroad.

Denbigh wears a Hindu or Indian jacket and pyjamas and holds a flintlock fowling-piece in his right hand.[128] Van Dyck has portrayed him in the act of hunting or exploring; his Indian guide is trying, unsuccessfully, to draw his attention to the parrot perched above them in a palm tree.[129] The power of Van Dyck's characterization in this portrait is directly tied to the Indian boy's inability to penetrate the absorbed state in which Denbigh finds himself. Denbigh has stopped dead in his tracks, with his gun lowered, and with his left hand suggestively opening up to the scene that lies before him. The guide's lips, like the parrot's jaws, are slightly parted; but the expression on the boy's face suggests that nothing he or the parrot can say will break this powerful spell. Denbigh is suspended in time just as, in spatial terms, he stands between the English trees on the left (which could have been painted by Gainsborough) and the native Indian tree and mountain scene on the right.[130] What Denbigh himself sees, however, is not disclosed to us; like the native boy, we must read his view in his face. By placing his main figure in the extreme foreground, Van Dyck has in effect opened up the pictorial space in this painting so that Denbigh seemingly inhabits a middle ground: what lies in front of him is just as important as what Van Dyck has depicted in the background.

The relationship between the earl and his guide is also intriguing: Denbigh himself—and not the native boy—is filled with childlike wonder

[127] *The Worthies of England*, ed. John Freeman (London: Allen and Unwin, 1952), 572. For the portrait of Shirley, see Larsen, no. 387 (vol. i, colour pl. 40); Van Dyck also painted his Persian wife (Larsen, no. 388). For earlier portraits in oriental costume, see R. A. Ingrams, 'Rubens and Persia', *Burlington Magazine*, 116 (1974), 190–7.

[128] I am indebted to Martin, *National Gallery Catalogues*, pp. 52–3, for an analysis of Denbigh's costume.

[129] Cecilia Mary Feilding, Countess of Denbigh, *Royalist Father and Roundhead Son* (London: Methuen, 1915), 77, discloses a family tradition that Denbigh had lost his way and is shown being led back to safety by the native boy; but I agree with Martin that this story is not very likely.

[130] For Van Dyck's influence on Gainsborough, see A. M. Hind, 'Van Dyck and English Landscape', *Burlington Magazine*, 51 (1927), 292–7.

as he stares into the distance, and Van Dyck has carefully reinforced this inverse relationship through his schematic use of colour. Denbigh is painted in primary tones of pinkish salmon, with gold stripes on his coat and trousers and with a gold ammunition belt and sword strap criss-crossing his jacket; a small swathe of white fabric is exposed beneath his chest. The Indian guide, on the other hand, is dressed in a gold-coloured coat, and the turban on his head combines this primary colour with equal traces of salmon and white. The gold colour of the rock in the foreground to the left is complemented, moreover, in the opposite corner of the canvas by the three pieces of golden fruit and the salmon-coloured parrot in the palm tree. This intricate structure is accentuated by the carefully designed diagonals in the painting (from lower right to upper left, especially in the earl's legs and gun, the boy's uplifted arm, and the thrust of the trees) and by a triangular motif that links the three observant characters, the fruit in the tree, the three entwined colours, the distinctive shape of the opening in Denbigh's jacket, and even the corresponding silvery tones in his hair and in the cuffs of his two sleeves. It would be possible to cite other paintings—particularly iconic paintings—in which Van Dyck's control of structure is just as impressive, just as sure; but the importance of a painting such as this lies in the artist's ability to dramatize human emotion in direct and natural terms. The gesture of Denbigh's left hand, for instance, had been employed by painters (including Van Dyck) in the representation of St John the Baptist.[131] In this painting, however, Van Dyck has simply adopted it as an appropriate expression of the wonder Denbigh feels as he admires an exotic landscape. Similarly, the intense absorption that characterizes his expression had long served as an integral part of religious painting; but Van Dyck understood, as Titian did before him, that the depiction of this trance-like state was just as suitable to secular portraiture.[132] Here we find neither stock poses nor stale attitudes; the elaborate formulas of iconicism have been subordinated to the dramatic representation of curiosity, wonder, intensity of feeling. Few contemporary portraits could as powerfully illustrate Pope's dictum that passions are the elements of life—and of the vivid portrayal of individual lives.

   A similar portrayal of drama and emotional intensity can be sensed in one of the first important works Lely painted in England, *Charles I with*

---

[131] See Larsen, no. 111. This gesture was also associated with various emotional states, including surprise; see Alastair Smart, 'Dramatic Gesture and Expression in the Age of Hogarth and Reynolds', *Apollo*, 82 (1965), 90–7.

[132] See Wilde, *Venetian Art from Bellini to Titian*, p. 213.

James, Duke of York (Plate 36).[133] This portrait was painted for the Duke of
Northumberland in 1648, a year before the king's execution, when Charles
was held in custody. His younger children, including James, were in
Northumberland's care at Sion House; in July 1647, and later in the same
year, they were allowed to visit their father at Hampton Court. Lely's
composition lacks the dynamic interchange between two characters that
Van Dyck could suggest so well, but the moment he has chosen to capture
possesses a drama of its own. Charles's face is fuller and less animated than
in Van Dyck's portraits, and the look of silent understanding that he
exchanges with his son reinforces the sadness of this occasion. Walpole
remarked that 'the king has none of the melancholy grace which Vandyck
alone, of all his painters, always gave him. It has a sterner countenance,
and expressive of the tempests he has experienced.'[134] The Duke of York
hands his father a small letter-opener or pair of scissors and, like the letter
the king holds in his left hand, the fate of the royal family has already been
sealed.[135]

In Lely's painting, history has finally caught up with the Stuart court. If
we compare this portrait with Van Dyck's depiction of Charles and his
wife exchanging the emblematic olive branch and laurels, we can see how
the motifs of union and renewal have been supplanted by images of
severance and disruption. But if this painting represents what Richard
Lovelace called 'a *clouded Majesty*', it nevertheless represents a pattern of
noble suffering to those who view it. In his poem 'To my Worthy Friend
Mr. Peter Lilly: on that excellent Picture of his Majesty, and the Duke of
Yorke, drawne by him at Hampton-Court', Lovelace praised the 'humble
bravery' and 'griefe triumphant' that break through each line of Lely's
composition. 'Mightiest monarchs by this shaded booke,' he writes, 'May
coppy out their proudest, richest looke', and then, in perhaps the most
significant poetic discussion of a painting in the seventeenth century,
Lovelace analyses the method by which Lely has portrayed the emotional
character of this scene:

> Not as of old, when a rough hand did speake
> A strong Aspect, and a faire face, a weake;
> When only a black beard cried Villaine, and
> By *Hieroglyphicks* we could understand;
> When Chrystall typified in a white spot,
> And the bright Ruby was but one red blot;

---

[133] Millar, *Age of Charles I*, no. 171; Millar, *Lely*, no. 6.

[134] *Anecdotes of Painting*, iii. 292.

[135] Richard Ormond, *The Face of Monarchy: British Royalty Portrayed* (London: Phaidon Press, 1977),
189 (pl. 84), describes the object as a penknife.

Thou dost the things *Orientally* the same,
Not only paintst its colour, but its *Flame*:
Thou sorrow canst designe without a teare,
And with the Man his very *Hope* or *Feare*;
So that th'amazed world shall henceforth finde
None but my *Lilly* ever drew a *Minde*.[136]

Lely would experiment with allegorical modes of portraiture throughout his long career, as we have seen, but Lovelace sensed that in this portrait, at least, he was able to portray the psychology of individual characters precisely by repudiating the stereotypes and '*Hieroglyphicks*' of iconicism.

The existence of this alternative to a highly stylized or idealized form of portrait-painting can also be documented in the increasingly large amount of surviving evidence concerning the accuracy of painted images. Pepys's succinct judgement of Lely's Restoration beauties is perhaps the most famous: 'very good, but not like'. Dryden wrote that Lely 'drew many graceful pictures, but few of them were like and this happen'd to him because he always studied himself more than those who sat to him'. Sitters, moreover, sometimes found their portraits offensive when they finally saw them. The Countess of Sussex considered Van Dyck's portrait of her to be 'very ill-favourede, makes me quite out of love with myselfe, the face is so bige and so fate that it pleases me not at all. It lokes lyke on of the windes puffinge—but truly I think tis lyke the originale.' Dorothy Osborne was the subject of two portraits by Lely, neither of which she thought was entirely faithful to the original; here is her reaction to the second painting:

I cannot tell whither it bee very like mee or not, though tis the best I have ever had drawne for mee, and Mr Lilly will have it that hee never took more pain's to make a good one in his life, and that it was I think that spoiled it: he was condemned for makeing the first hee drew for mee a little worse than I, and in makeing this better hee has made it as unlike as tother.

A single accurate rendering, in other words, would have sufficed; and we can also sense this growing respect for a painter's ability to produce an honest likeness in Evelyn's remark to Pepys that 'Holbein really painted to the life beyond any man this day living.'[137]

---

[136] *The Poems of Richard Lovelace*, ed. C. H. Wilkinson (Oxford: Clarendon Press, 1930, corr. 1953), 57–8; see also Hagstrum's remarks on this poem, pp. 122–3. This poem has recently been placed in its literary (and pictorial) context by Claire Pace, ' "Delineated lives": themes and variations in seventeenth-century poems about portraits', *Word and Image*, 2 (1986), 1–17, and John Hollander, 'The Poetics of *ekphrasis*', *Word and Image*, 4 (1988), 209–17; see also Norman K. Farmer, jun., *Poets and the Visual Arts in Renaissance England* (Austin: Univ. of Texas Press, 1984), 57–8.

[137] These judgements are collected by Piper, *English Face*, pp. 131, 109, 125, 52. Buckeridge (p. 403) notes the languorousness that permeates Lely's portraits.

If English patrons wished to commission paintings 'to the life', they could easily turn to the long line of native artists that stretched from Hayles, Riley, and Richardson to Hudson and Hogarth. But when Evelyn assessed Holbein's talent as a painter, I believe he also meant to pay tribute to the sophistication, vibrancy, and fresh animation that Continental interlopers brought to English portraiture even in his day. These qualities would not be completely absorbed within an English school of portraiture until the young Joshua Reynolds returned from Italy, and this is why the natural outgrowth of this powerful movement beyond iconicism finds its fullest expression at the turn of the century not in the work of Riley and Richardson but in the intimate portraits painted by the ageing Kneller. Kneller's slight enlargement of the dimensions of the standard bust-portrait for his Kit-cat series enabled him to paint his subjects literally 'to the life' while maintaining a concentrated focus on the head, shoulders, and hands alone.[138] This realistic format had important precedents in Raphael, Titian, and Rembrandt (Kneller's early master), but it was now adapted with remarkable simplicity to the portrayal of the members of an English club, named in honour of the publican Christopher Cat's famous mutton pies.

In a variety of poses and with only the barest of attributes, Kneller depicted a group of prominent Englishmen who were linked neither by rank nor by profession, but by their common pursuit of Whig politics and urbane conviviality. The aristocrats in this series are often indistinguishable from the commoners, and Kneller's authors (Dryden and Congreve, for instance) are invariably represented as gentlemen. Although the paintings were initially commissioned by a nobleman, the Duke of Somerset, they were presented to the club's secretary, the publisher Jacob Tonson. Kneller was himself a member of this club, and his splendid portrait of Tonson (Plate 37) epitomizes the warmth and sympathy that he brought to these paintings.[139] Titian's emperors may have hung in splendour at Whitehall—and Kneller's own beauties at Hampton Court—but these paintings were accorded a programme of their own when they were mounted in a special room in Tonson's house at Barn Elms. The patronage of princes would continue, even under the reluctant Georges, but here we can also glimpse patronage of a much more private kind in a

---

[138] For the fullest analysis of Kneller's series, see the appendix to Stewart, *Kneller* 1971, to which I am indebted at several points. For other commentaries see Killanin, pp. 76–83; Piper, *Catalogue*, pp. 398–403; and Harry M. Geduld, *Prince of Publishers: A Study of the Work and Career of Jacob Tonson* (Bloomington: Indiana Univ. Press, 1969), 151–71.

[139] Killanin, p. 77; Stewart, *Kneller* 1971, p. i (colour pl.); Stewart, *Kneller* 1983, no. 753; Waterhouse, p. 142, pl. 118.

collection bestowed upon the 'Prince of Publishers'. Kneller's portraits, unlike their iconic forebears, represent not so much a manifestation of power as an exploration of the mind and character that distinguish successful and powerful individuals from each other. In the finest of these paintings, and in similar pictures that should be associated with his practice here—the portraits of Evelyn, Wren, Newton, and Locke— Kneller can bear the praise that Waller reserved for Van Dyck:

> Strange! that thy hand should not inspire
> The beauty only, but the fire;
> Not the form alone, and grace,
> But act and power of a face.[140]

[140] *The Poems of Edmund Waller*, p. 44.

4

Brief Lives and Miniatures: John Aubrey and Samuel Cooper

WHEN Aubrey wrote to his friend John Ray about the two miniatures that had been stolen from the Ashmolean in 1691, he received this reply from the famous naturalist: 'Your picture done in miniature by Mr Cowper is a thing of great value. I remember so long agoe as I was in Italy, and while he was yet living, any piece of his was highly esteemed there: and for that kind of painting he was esteemed the best artist in Europe.'[1] Cooper's enviable reputation among his contemporaries contrasts sharply with the relative neglect of the prolific Aubrey, who published virtually nothing during his own lifetime. And yet it is precisely Aubrey's habit of collecting biographical materials for others—as well as his natural instinct to work 'in little'—that makes a comparison between these two artists so interesting. Their decision to work outside the mainstream of seventeenth-century biography and portrait-painting enabled them to achieve naturalistic effects that anticipate a much more modern form of portraiture. We discover in the constricted formats of their portraits a fresh sense of *enargeia*, a further movement beyond the iconicism still to be found in the full-scale portraits of their contemporaries.

i. Like Fragments of a Shipwreck

Among the more than 400 biographical entries that make up his *Brief Lives* is an autobiographical sketch intended, Aubrey tells us, 'to be interposed as a sheet of wast paper only in the binding of a booke'.[2] In these miscellaneous jottings Aubrey confides that his 'fancy lay most to geometrie. If ever I had been good for anything, 'twould have been a painter, I could fancy a thing so strongly and had so cleare an idaea of it' (i. 43). Even as a child 'he gave himselfe to drawing and painting'. He regarded himself as a 'pourtraiter' at age 9, progressed from 'plaine

---

[1] Anthony Powell, *John Aubrey and His Friends* (1948; rev. edn., New York: Barnes and Noble, 1964), 217–18.

[2] *Brief Lives*, i. 34. Further references to this edition appear in the text.

outlines' to 'colours', and, having no one to instruct him, 'copied pictures in the parlour in a table book' (i. 36). He noted in his life of Lord Falkland that it was 'Jacob de Valke, who [later] taught me to paint' (i. 152).[3] He sat for his own portrait to Lely, William Faithorne, and David Loggan, as well as to Cooper; he was a friend of Hollar, who made an engraving from one of his sketches. Many of Aubrey's own paintings—most of them landscapes or architectural views associated with his ancestral home at Easton Pierse—have been preserved in the Bodleian Library, and they show a considerable amount of skill and taste.[4] Aubrey also indicated, in one intriguing note, that he had even attempted portraiture—'As Mr. Walter Waller's picture drawne after his death; è contra, I have done severall by the life' (i. 51)—but apparently none of his portraits has survived. Instead we find a variety of sketches and visual motifs among the manuscripts that constitute his *Brief Lives*, and a tendency for Aubrey to talk about his biographical skills in visual terms. He suggested that 'first draughts ought to be rude as those of paynters, for he that in his first essay will be curious in refining will certainly be unhappy in inventing' (i. 20), and he believed that descriptions of complexion, in which he particularly excelled, were 'better expressed with a pencill, than a penne'.[5]

Only a few pages before Aubrey's contention that he 'could fancy a thing so strongly and had so cleare an idaea of it', however, he entered another generalization among his autobiographical remarks: 'my idea very cleer; phansie like a mirrour, pure chrystal water which the least wind does disorder and unsmooth' (i. 37). Here, in characteristically concise and pithy form, are Aubrey's own intimations of the virtues and limitations to be found in his unusual approach to biographical writing. For if it was Aubrey's distinction to be the first English biographer to write with the painter's eye—to pay loving attention to the surfaces of his characters, and to suggest their complexity through the imaginative use of detail—it was also his failing (his 'naeve', or mole, as he would say) to leave behind an enormous mass of manuscripts in which no single biography could stand on its own as a polished representation of his initial 'idaea'. Aubrey preferred to depend upon the narrative and editorial skills of others; he

[3] According to Powell, *John Aubrey and His Friends*, pp. 99–100 n., this was Gerard Valck, an engraver employed by Loggan.

[4] For discussions of Aubrey's connections with painters, see Powell, *John Aubrey and His Friends*, pp. 99–103 and 218 (where he summarizes the different portraits painted of Aubrey), and Hunter, pp. 14, 38–9. Hunter reproduces the largest number of Aubrey's paintings, including several watercolours from his *Designatio de Easton-Piers*; but see also the illustrations in *Brief Lives*, Powell, and Dick.

[5] Quoted by Hunter, p. 38.

likened himself to a whetstone, 'which can make the iron sharp though itself unable to cut',[6] and he called upon one of his collaborators, Richard Blackburne, to serve as his 'Aristarchus' (i. 20). In his own hands, these clear ideas too often became disordered and unsmoothed, and it therefore was (and still is) his editors' task to invest these fragments with the semblance of cohesive form.

Aubrey's inability to 'complete' his work was not limited to the *Brief Lives*; it was, in fact, characteristic of his labours in the many fields— archaeology, astrology, topography, architecture, natural philosophy, folklore, and, above all, antiquarian research—that first brought him to biography. Like much of his work in other areas, his original biographical notes were written to supplement the studies of others. He began by communicating biographical details to Anthony Wood for inclusion in his *Athenae Oxoniensis*. When his friend Thomas Hobbes died in 1679, however, Aubrey felt obliged to write a more sustained biographical account as a commentary on the philosopher's own memoir, written in Latin. Aubrey entitled this manuscript 'Supplementum vitae Thomae Hobbes', but Wood asked him why it should be entitled 'Supplimentum? pray say the life of Thomas Hobbs' (i. 17). Aubrey made the change, but he still relied upon Blackburne to edit his notes and turn the whole into Latin, and he had mixed feelings about the work when it was finally published. He told Wood that it was written in a 'delicate Style', and that it seemed 'as if Mr Hobbes's soule were come into his body'; but he wished that he had been given more credit for his role in this volume, remarking that 'I suffer the grasse to cutt under my feet ... Dr Blackbourne will have all the Glory.'[7] And thus in his later work for Wood, Aubrey concentrated on providing material that was already shaped into rough biographical form, completing at least sixty-six lives in the spring of 1680. But even here Aubrey was to be frustrated, for Wood handled these lives with little discretion and even less care, refused to return important sections (including the index), and brought both himself and Aubrey dangerously close to a prosecution for libel. And thus Aubrey finally deposited his manuscripts in the personal custody of the keeper of the Ashmolean in 1693, with a proviso that Wood was not to be told that they had been placed there.

Aubrey's procedure as he wrote each life has been summarized by his biographer, the novelist Anthony Powell:

---

[6] Quoted by Hunter, p. 63.

[7] Quoted by Hunter, p. 79, who gives a detailed account of the making of this life; see also Powell, *John Aubrey and His Friends*, pp. 178–80.

His method of work was to inscribe the name of the subject of his biography at the top of the page of a folio manuscript book. He would then note below all he could remember of the man's personal appearance and eccentricities, friendships, actions, or writings. If he could not recollect a name, a date, or the title of a book, he left a blank or put a mark of omission. Sometimes he wrote alternative words or phrases (he was for ever pursued by afterthoughts), transposed paragraphs, or added new material. It was not unknown—when the stress of the previous night's good-fellowship lay heavy on his brain—for this additional matter to appear in the wrong place in the text, to be inserted in the margin (so that it is not always clear to whom or to what the words are intended to apply), and even for cognate remarks to be scribbled in the middle of another Life or in a different volume.[8]

Only a few of the lives were written over in a fair hand, and it is therefore not surprising that Aubrey's editors, from Wood to the present day, have had considerable difficulty in arranging his chaotic notes. (Wood unkindly characterized his friend as a 'shiftless person, roving and magotie-headed, and sometimes little better than crased'.[9]) Aubrey himself told Wood that he had, 'according to your desire, putt in writing these minutes of lives tumultuarily, as they occur'd to my thoughts or as occasionally I had information of them' (i. 10). They were the natural fruits of one 'having now not only lived above halfe a centurie of yeares in the world, but have also been much tumbled up and downe in it which hath made me much knowne'. He then described his notes as *'arcana'*, and told Wood that they were not fit to 'lett flie abroad, till about 30 yeares hence; for the author and the persons (like medlars) ought to be first rotten' (i. 12).

Aubrey provided his manuscripts with various titles, each reflecting the miscellaneous character of his biographical work. In addition to *Brief Lives* and 'minutes of lives', he described his entries as 'Skediasmata' (scattered things) and said they were *'Tanquam tabulata naufragii'* (like fragments of a shipwreck). He returned to the metaphor of the shipwreck in his introduction to the *Life of Hobbes*. 'The *recrementa* of so learned a person are valueable', he writes, and thus he will humbly offer both to the present age and to posterity *'tanquam tabulam naufragii*, and as plankes and lighter things swimme, and are preserved, where the more weighty sinke and are lost' (i. 18). Perhaps this analogy had a strong personal significance for Aubrey, whose own career was itself something of a shipwreck: lawsuits, the bottle, and disastrous relations with women were part of his undoing; several generous offers of a new life across the water—in

---

[8] Powell, *John Aubrey and His Friends*, pp. 180–1; see also *Brief Lives*, i. 4.
[9] Quoted by Dick, p. liii.

Maryland, Pennsylvania, New York, Carolina, Jamaica, Tobago, or
Bermuda—remained mere temptations; a list of the '*Accidents of John
Aubrey*' completed his autobiographical memoir, and the final entry
significantly reveals that he had twice been in danger of drowning. But
Aubrey's obsession with the image of the sinking ship is tied, in a more
important sense, to his fear of an entire world of valuable objects—of
culture itself—disappearing forever in the depths of oblivion.

Aubrey saw himself primarily as a collector of human artefacts, devoted
to preserving historical remains that had 'escaped the teeth of time, and
(which is more dangerous) the hands of mistaken Zeale'.[10] In the letter
that accompanied the lives he sent to Wood in 1680, he lamented that
'such minutes had not been taken 100 yeares since or more: for want
thereof many worthy men's names and notions are swallowd-up in
oblivion; as much of these also would, had it not been through your
instigation: and perhaps this is one of the usefullest pieces that I have
scribbeld' (i. 11). He compared the disappearances of 'matters of antiquity'
with the gradual dimming of light at day's end: 'after sun-sett—at which
time, clear; by and by, comes the *crepusculum*; then, totall darkenes' (i. 18).
He complained that men often think that, because they remember
significant events soon after they have occurred, they will never be
forgotten; but it is this misplaced confidence in human memory, and 'want
of registring', that will at last cause these events to be 'drowned in
oblivion'. Even though he was himself 'now inclining to be ancient', he
nevertheless attempted, in all of his pursuits, to rescue antiquities that
would otherwise be 'utterly lost and forgotten'.

Even as a boy Aubrey 'did ever love to converse with old men, as living
histories' (i. 43), and he noted that in his grandfather's day 'the Manuscripts flew about like Butter-flies'.[11] The spectre of these materials
disappearing, especially during the turbulence of the civil wars, haunted
Aubrey throughout his life, and he was therefore anxious to preserve the
documents of others as carefully as he did his own. Near the end of his
entry for Seth Ward, he notes that this Lord Bishop of Salisbury 'studied
the common lawe, and I find this paper, which is his owne handwriting,
amongst his scattered papers which I rescued from being used by the
cooke since his death, which was destinated with other *good papers* and
letters to be put under pies' (ii. 289). He attempted to obtain Edward
Davenant's manuscripts for the library of the Royal Society (i. 201), and
he described with awe and perhaps even covetousness the sumptuous

---

[10] Quoted by Hunter, p. 179.   [11] Quoted by Dick, p. xxxii.

volume in which Sir Kenelm Digby had recorded his family's history: 'a great book, as big as the biggest Church Bible that ever I sawe, and the richliest bound, bossed with silver, engraven with scutchions and crest (an ostrich); it was a curious velame' (i. 228).

Other possible sources—oral tradition in particular—were not always to be trusted, and Aubrey even found it difficult to enlist his own subjects in his campaign for historical accuracy. 'Before I leave this towne,' he wrote in his life of the scientist Robert Hooke, 'I will gett of him a catalogue of what he hath wrote; and as much of his inventions as I can. But they are many hundreds; he believes not fewer than a thousand. 'Tis such a hard matter to get people to doe themselves right' (i. 415). (These difficulties with Hooke must have been especially galling to Aubrey, for Hooke relied upon his friends' efforts to demonstrate that his theory of the earth's motion had been plagiarized by Newton.) Aubrey was also particularly interested in the surviving portraits of his characters, and (like Locke) he wished that painters would inscribe their subjects' names on their canvases so that they could serve as useful documents.[12] And sometimes, of course, portraits provided much of the scanty documentary evidence available to Aubrey. In his life of Sir Edward Coke, he writes that 'he was of wonderfull painstaking, as appears by his writings. . . . He was a very handsome proper man and of a curious complexion, as appears by his picture at the Inner Temple, which his grandson gave them about 1668, at length, in his atturney-generall's fusted gowne' (i. 178–9). He had also seen Sir John Popham's picture: 'he was a huge, heavie, ugly man . . . he lived like a hog' (ii. 159). And he even relied on portraits to make an extended comparison between Hobbes and Galileo: 'They pretty well resembled one another as to their countenances, as by their pictures doeth appear; were both cheerfull and melancholique-sanguine; and had both a consimilitie of fate, to be hated and persecuted by the Ecclesiastiques' (i. 366).

Aubrey was occasionally confronted with too much information, which proved to be equally disquieting. When he first entered the Middle Temple, he was told that Coke had been born 'to 300 *li.* land per annum, and I have heard some of his country say again that he was borne but to 40 *li.* per annum. What shall one beleeve?' (i. 178). But when a fact was clearly established to Aubrey's satisfaction, he stood by it: 'Earl of Corke bought of captaine Horsey *fourtie ploughlands* in Ireland for fourtie pounds. (A. Ettrick assures me, "I say againe fourtie ploughlands")' (i. 115–6).

---

[12] Aubrey made this entry, for instance, in his life of Milton: 'Write his name in red letters on his pictures, with his widowe, to preserve' (ii. 68).

Michael Hunter, who has written the only serious study of Aubrey's antiquarian methods, characterizes his labours on behalf of Anthony Wood as indefatigable, cites his remarkable energy for pursuing accurate information, and quotes from a letter to Wood in which Aubrey declares, with great satisfaction, that 'Chronologie is the prettiest Trap or gin to catch a Lyer in that can be.'[13]

In September 1680, just a few months after Aubrey had sent his first collection of brief lives to his friend in Oxford, he told Wood, in a justifiable moment of pride, that no English works of this kind had ever been 'delivered so faithfully and with so good authority' (i. 3). This was an ambitious claim, but Aubrey could easily point both to the unprecedented minuteness of his entries and to a general policy of inclusiveness that allowed him to collect a much broader range of materials than could be found in previous biography. It was almost inevitable, therefore, that Aubrey should face serious and immediate challenges to both of these revolutionary goals. In the preface to his *Life of Hobbes*, he stated that he did not originally intend to be so minute, but that, once he had set down every particular in his first draft, those friends who read it encouraged him 'to let *all* stand; for though to soome at present it might appeare too triviall; yet hereafter 'twould not be scorned but passe for antiquity' (i. 19). He cited a precedent in Fell's life of Hammond, but his editor, Blackburne, and Blackburne's advisers, Lord John Vaughan and John Dryden, were 'much against Minutiae' and were even willing to falsify details in order to produce 'a better picture'. Aubrey was furious: 'Pox take your orators and poets, they spoile lives & histories': 'A Life, is a short Historie: and *there* minuteness of a famous person is gratefull.'[14]

Aubrey later complained to Wood about the uncertainty to be found in printed histories, which either did not dare to speak plainly because they followed so closely on the heels of truth, or became 'obscure and darke' because their subjects had become 'antiquated' (i. 11). Aubrey promised that he was delivering 'the trueth, and . . . nothing but the trueth', but this, of course, created further problems for his editor, who, in Aubrey's analogy, was to act as confessor to Aubrey's 'poenitent'. In a famous passage, Aubrey told Wood that he was presenting

the naked and plaine trueth, which is here exposed so bare that the very *pudenda* are not covered, and affords many passages that would raise a blush in a young virgin's cheeke. So that after your perusall, I must desire you to make a castration (as Raderus to Martial) and to sowe-on some figge-leaves—i.e., to be my *Index expurgatorius.* (i. 11).

13 Hunter, pp. 74–5.   14 Quoted by Hunter, p. 79.

We can see this principle at work in the *Life of Hobbes*, where Aubrey notes that the philosopher's uncle was a glover by profession: 'Shall I expresse or conceale this (*glover*)? The philosopher would acknowledge it' (i. 324). Much of the contention between Aubrey and Blackburne had in fact focused on a similarly minor detail—Hobbes's service as a page—which the biographer's 'Aristarchus' intended to suppress. Aubrey, on the other hand, envisioned himself as 'Almansar in the Play, that spare neither friend nor Foe, but a religious John Tell-troth'. 'The Doctor [Blackburne] says I am too minute,' he told Wood, 'but a hundred yeares hence that minuteness will be grateful.'[15]

Aubrey was probably not far from the mark when he described himself as 'John Tell-troth', for although there are countless errors in even the briefest of his lives (in some—like Shakespeare's—it is difficult to find anything else), he seems rather to have committed honest mistakes than to have slanted his evidence in one direction or another. It is true that he often wrote about particular characters because they were his good friends, and he even included a list of 'Amici' among his manuscripts. His lives are consequently filled with expressions of his warmth or gratitude towards these close associates, many of whose coffins he helped carry to the grave. But he also managed to maintain a remarkably impartial attitude when he wrote about men whose principles or characters were vehemently opposed to his own. He disparaged a few Puritan politicians by noting that they were of 'Henry Martyn's gang', but when he came to write Martin's own life he paid tribute to the regicide's good humour and quick wit: 'Memorandum when his study was searcht they found lettres to his concubine, which was printed 4to. There is witt and good nature in them' (ii. 47). Milton's politics were also anathema to him—and Wood, in his own biography, would severely attack him on this point—but Aubrey extolled Milton's 'admirable panegyricks' on Cromwell and Fairfax, remarking that 'were they made in commendation of the devill, 'twere all one to me: 'tis the *upsos* that I looke after' (ii. 70).

It is precisely Aubrey's pursuit of 'the *upsos*'—the highest achievements we are capable of performing—that defines his biographical focus. Often the extraordinary in Aubrey's lives is merely the eccentric or the incredible, as in his discussion of 'hard-men' (soldiers who were said to be able to withstand bullets by eating certain herbs); but generally he was drawn by his own curiosity to those who were themselves dedicated to the pursuit of knowledge. Some of his finest lives are of scientists and philosophers, and he even began work on a collection of short

[15] Quoted by Powell, *John Aubrey and His Friends*, p. 182.

biographies that would have represented a virtual history of mathematical studies in England. He was eager to insert a pedigree in his '*Historiola* of our Malmsbury philosopher' because Hobbes, although of 'plebeian descent', was famous for his learning both at home and abroad (i. 322). There is thus a significant levelling effect in the *Brief Lives*, produced both by Aubrey's choice of subjects and by the objectivity of his approach. He quoted General Lambert's remark that 'the best of men are but men at the best', and he told Wood that one could find apt examples of this truth in his own 'rude and hastie collection' (i. 11–12).

ii. Aubrey's 'Pierceing Eye'

The rude and hasty nature of Aubrey's lives has prevented some readers, however, from taking his artistic achievements seriously. In his survey of seventeenth-century biography, Donald Stauffer argues that 'because Aubrey's writings are unfinished notes and to a large extent formless, they are not of major importance in a study of the art of English biography'.[16] Even those who do find a certain aesthetic integrity in Aubrey's works must acknowledge that they are responding in part to the editorial skills of other scholars. Oliver Lawson Dick states that he has 'ruthlessly re-arranged' Aubrey's notes in his edition;[17] and even the more conservative Andrew Clark remarks, in his headnote to the *Life of Hobbes*, that 'considerable re-arrangement has therefore been necessary, but the exact MS. references have been given throughout. Some few notes relating to Hobbes, found in other Aubrey MSS., have here been brought into their natural place' (i. 321). But what constitutes a 'natural place' for us—or for Aubrey's editors—was clearly not natural for Aubrey. Even James Thorpe's prescription for the treatment of manuscript material in this unfinished and unrevised state (he argues that it should be 'presented for study purposes or for tentative consideration rather than as if it were a literary work comparable in status to the "actual" works of the author'),[18] even this suggestion applies only fitfully to Aubrey's lives, which have enjoyed considerable popularity and are, in essence, his 'actual' works even though they were never prepared for the press.

The ambiguous status of Aubrey's lives may well remain a vexed issue, but it does not necessarily support Stauffer's contention that Aubrey's work is not of major importance. I want to argue, in fact, that his lives

---

[16] Stauffer, p. 165.
[17] Dick, p. xviii.
[18] *The Principles of Textual Criticism* (San Marino: Huntington Library, 1972), 187.

represent a significant chapter in the development of English biography precisely *because* they are unfinished and relatively formless. Aubrey's reliance on the synthetic skills of Blackburne and Wood (and later Thomas Tanner) placed him in an unusually protected position, completely free of the rigid decorum of contemporary biography. It is this very lack of restraint that enabled Aubrey to write in more realistic detail than his predecessors and thus furnish us with an even more spontaneous and unguarded record of his times than we find in the diaries of Pepys and Evelyn, which were carefully revised by their authors. How drastically Aubrey would have castrated his observations or covered their pudenda is a moot point, for he enjoyed a privileged status in which these issues were never forced upon him. He notes at one point in the *Life of Hobbes* that 'this is *too low* witt to be published', but he nevertheless allowed his anecdote to stand: 'The witts at Court were wont to bayt him. But he feared none of them, and would make his part good. The king would call him *the beare*: "Here comes the beare to be bayted!" ' (i. 340). And thus we are also told that Bacon was a pederast whose 'Ganimeds' took bribes (i. 71), that Beaumont and Fletcher 'had one wench in the house between them, which they did so admire' (i. 96), and that Sir Philip Sidney's 'salacious' sister, Mary Herbert, Countess of Pembroke, watched the stallions mount the mares from a peep-hole in her house and then 'would act the like sport herselfe with *her* stallions'.[19] And we should remember that in reading Aubrey's *Brief Lives* we are not merely discovering the unbridled curiosity of one isolated individual; his accomplices were everywhere.

Much of the charm and fascination of these fragments lies, moreover, in the sense we have of entering a biographical workshop where we may observe Aubrey as he pieces together his miniature portraits. Consider his well-known entry in the life of Milton: 'He was a spare man. He was scarce so tall as I am—quaere, quot feet I am high: resp., of middle stature' (ii. 67). Aubrey offers us, in other words, a view of the biographical process that often makes up for his failure to provide a polished product. 'He pronounced the letter R (littera canina) very hard', he noted of Milton, and then he entered an additional note a few pages later which indicates that this was something worth following up: 'a certain signe of a satyricall witt—from John Dreyden' (ii. 67). Much of the success of these lives also depends upon this penchant for exactitude and brevity. 'A biography should either be as long as Boswell's or as short as Aubrey's,

---

[19] Dick, p. 138 (suppressed by Clark in his edition).

Lytton Strachey proclaims; the elaborate accretion that characterizes the *Life of Johnson* may be excellent, he adds, 'but, failing that, let us have no half-measures; let us have the pure essentials—a vivid image, on a page or two, without explanations, transitions, commentaries, or padding'.[20]

This is high praise indeed, and it comes from a master of the biographical epitome and from a volume entitled *Portraits in Miniature*. One of the virtues of Aubrey's empirical method is that he does not, like Walton, follow an implicit policy of artistic or didactic selection. But even if it is true that Aubrey is himself the master of the vivid image, supplied without transition or padding, he rarely eschews explanations and commentary. Aubrey's numerous facts and picturesque details work for him so successfully because they manage to suggest a much broader realm of implications; and his ability to bring his characters to life, to intimate so much from so little, must account in large measure for the enthusiasm Anthony Powell and John Fowles have displayed on his behalf.[21] In the preface to his *Wiltshire Antiquities*, he compared his method to that of Pythagoras: just as the Greek philosopher 'did guesse at the vastnesse of Hercules stature by the length of his foote . . . so among these ruines, are Remaynes enough left for a man to give a guesse what noble Buildings &c: were made by the piety, charity, & magnanimity of our forefathers'.[22] And once again he invoked the image of the '*Tabulata Naufragii*', which he chose as the motto for his *Brief Lives*.

Pythagoras began his task of historical reconstruction with Hercules' foot; Aubrey characteristically focuses on his character's face and figure, and especially on the expressive potential of the human eye. Francis Bacon, he writes, 'had a delicate, lively hazel eie; Dr. Harvey told me it was like the eie of a viper' (i. 72). Sir John Denham's eye 'was a kind of light goose-gray, not big; but it had a strange piercingness, not as to shining and glory, but (like a Momus) when he conversed with you he look't into your very thoughts' (i. 220). Ralph Kettell, who was President of Trinity College during Aubrey's years as an undergraduate, 'was a very tall and well growne man. His gowne and surplice and hood being on, he had a terrible gigantique aspect, with his sharp gray eies' (ii. 17). Occasionally, of course, the inferences Aubrey drew from these observations were unwarranted; he noted that 'Ben Johnson had one eie lower than t'other, and bigger, like Clun, the player: perhaps he begott Clun'

[20] *Portraits in Miniature and Other Essays* (New York: Harcourt, 1931), 29.
[21] Powell, in addition to writing a biography of Aubrey, also edited a popular version of the *Brief Lives* (1949); Fowles has recently prepared an edition of Aubrey's *Monumenta Britannica*.
[22] Quoted by Hunter, p. 178.

(ii. 14). But more often than not he was able to use this method of characterization to great effect, as in his incisive description of Hobbes:

> Eie. He had a good eie, and that of a hazell colour, which was full of life and spirit, even to the last. When he was earnest in discourse, there shone (as it were) a bright live-coale within it. He had two kind of looks:—when he laugh't, was witty, and in a merry humour, one could scarce see his eies; by and by, when he was serious and positive, he open'd his eies round (i.e. his eie-lids). He had midling eies, not very big, nor very little. (i. 348–9)

Aubrey's most vivid characterizations are often produced by this careful progression from the superficial to the essential. Samuel Butler was 'of a middle stature, strong sett, high coloured, a head of sorrell haire, a severe and sound judgement: a good fellowe' (i. 136). His description of Hobbes's beard is meant, in fact, to draw attention to the dangers inherent in superficial observations:

> Belowe he was shaved close, except a little tip under his lip. Not but that nature could have afforded a venerable beard ... but being naturally of a cheerfull and pleasant humor, he affected not at all austerity and gravity and to looke severe. ... He desired not the reputation of his wisdome to be taken from the cutt of his beard, but from his reason—Barba non facit philosophum. (i. 348).

In the few pages that Aubrey devotes to Isaac Barrow, he is able to bring him to life—and to show some of the anomalies in his character— far more successfully than Abraham Hill could in his full and spotless biography. Aubrey says of his 'humour when a boy and after:—merry and cheerfull and beloved where ever he came'. The master of his college at Cambridge told him that he was ' "a good boy; 'tis pitty that thou art a cavalier" '. Barrow was strong and stout, 'and feared not any man. He would fight with the butchers' boyes in St. Nicholas' shambles, and be hard enough for any of them' (a feat he repeated with a certain 'Rhadamontade' in Constantinople before he became a divine). Aubrey tells us that his use of opiates, which he acquired in Turkey, eventually killed him when he took his pill 'preposterously' at Mr Wilson's, the saddler. But his habits as a scholar were also extraordinary, and Aubrey reports that he was often so intense in his studies—'so *totus in hoc*'—that he would not know whether his bed was made, his hat was on his head, or his coat was on his back. He was so negligent in his dress that a stranger clapped him on his shoulder in St James's Park and said, ' "Well, goe thy wayes for the veriest scholar that ever I mett with." ' As Barrow lay in the agonies of death, 'the standers-by could heare him say softly "I have seen the glories of the world." ' 'He was a strong man,' Aubrey notes, 'but pale as the candle he studyed by' (i. 88–91).

Aubrey also has great success in his affectionate depiction of Ralph Kettell, President of Trinity, in which he marshals a number of effective anecdotes to corroborate the general opinion that Kettell's 'braine was like a *hasty-pudding, where there was memorie, judgement, and phancy all stirred together*'. If you took Kettell for a fool, you discovered 'great subtilty and reach; *è contra*, if you treated with him as a wise man, you would have mistaken him for a foole' (ii. 19). Aubrey's treatment of women is equally supple, although his own romantic disappointments may have led him to place too much emphasis on their physical charms and deceptive practices. There is a fine psychological twist, for instance, in his short life of Elizabeth Broughton, which opens with her flight from her distinguished family in Herefordshire to set up shop in London ('her price was very deare—a second Thais'), and ends, following her death from the pox, with the observation that her father, perhaps in unwitting expiation, was 'the first that used the improvement of land by soape-ashes when he lived at Bristowe, where they then threw it away' (i. 127–8).

Aubrey's life of Venetia Stanley, mistress of the Earl of Dorset and later wife of Sir Kenelm Digby, is also a short masterpiece in which he fuses external details—concerning her extraordinary beauty, her relations with men, and their various tributes to her—to capture both the glamour and the pathos of one who was almost exclusively known as a handsome woman. She was 'a most beautifull desireable creature', he says, with a delicate and 'sweet-turn'd face . . . a short ovall'. The colour of her cheeks 'was just that of the damask rose, which is neither too hott nor too pale'. And just as these remarks suggest the painter's eye, so Aubrey continues by mentioning the portraits Van Dyck painted of her, the plaster casts Digby made of her hands, face, and feet, and the 'sumptuouse and stately monument' he erected to her memory (and whose gilt bust Aubrey sketched among his notes). But even sensational beauties are soon forgotten:

> About 1676 or 5, as I was walking through Newgate-street, I sawe Dame Venetia's bust standing at a stall at the Golden Crosse, a brasier's shop. I perfectly remembred it, but the fire had gott-off the guilding; but taking notice of it to one that was with me, I could never see it afterwards exposed to the street. They melted it downe. How these curiosities would be quite forgott, did not such idle fellowes as I am putt them downe! (i. 229–32)

Like Pythagoras contemplating the foot of Hercules, Aubrey was thus often able to suggest a fully proportioned character by cultivating the vivid image and suggesting, in his own commentary, its broader significance. There are random and unconnected observations to be found throughout his work, but in his best lives—especially those of Bacon, Barrow, Venetia Digby, Hobbes, Kettle, and Milton—there is ample evidence that he knew where his notes were leading him. There is also a predictable pattern among most of his lives: he will characteristically begin with his subject's family, coat-of-arms, education, and physical appearance, and then work through his or her sayings, writings, habits, last words, death, and commemorative tributes. Aubrey also placed particular emphasis on those personal characteristics that caused a man's career to rise or fall. Colbert, for example, was able to methodize and settle the accounts of his French king: 'This was his rise' (i. 181). Sir Henry Savile was such a great favourite of Queen Elizabeth that there was 'no dealing with him; his naeve was that he was too much inflated with his learning and riches' (ii. 215). Aubrey isolates similar faults in Chillingworth and Raleigh, and it is surely more than coincidental that the biographer who would draw attention to his subjects' 'moles' was the close friend of the painter who (as we shall see) depicted Cromwell 'warts and all'.

Other patterns emerge in Aubrey's lives that are actually at odds with his empirical approach. He was a strong believer in physiognomy, which he said furnished an 'infallible Rule, to discover the Indications of pride, Treachery', and other traits, and thus many of his physical descriptions are closely tied to a broader system of characterization.[23] The same is true of his interest in astrology, which led him to compile a *Collectio Geniturarum* in which he carefully noted the exact birthdates of famous men.[24] Several of his lives—such as his short biography of Erasmus—were literally written around a horoscope, and he noted in his life of the astrologer Henry Isaacson, who ironically met with little luck when he presented his grand *Chronologie* to Charles I, that 'an astrologer would give something to know *that day and hower*. He wanted a good election' (ii. 2).[25] Aubrey was also familiar with the use of emblematic designs, and copied one out of Withers's *Collection of Emblems* to illustrate his own plight: 'A man's spirit

---

[23] Ibid. 127. It should also be noted that, according to the doctrine of traditional physiognomy, the position of moles on the body had astrological correspondences and significances determining character; see e.g. Sir Thomas Browne, *The Garden of Cyrus*, in *The Works of Sir Thomas Browne*, ed. Geoffrey Keynes (Chicago: Univ. of Chicago Press, 1964), i. 207–8.

[24] See *Brief Lives*, i. 21, and Hunter, p. 121.

[25] Hunter includes Erasmus's horoscope as pl. 9; Clark (*Brief Lives*) illustrates Hobbes's in pl. 3. For a discussion of Aubrey's interest in astrology, see Hunter, pp. 117–30.

rises and falls with his fortune: makes me lethargique' (i. 42). He said of William Holder that the biographer who 'would goe about to describe a perfect good man, would drawe this Doctor's character' (i. 405), and he even quoted excerpts from Anthony Walker's formulaic sermon on Mary Rich, Countess of Warwick, entitled 'The Virtuous Woman Found' (i. 116–20).

It therefore appears that in his biographical writings, as in his other works, Aubrey at least tried to forge an uneasy balance between his sometimes indiscriminate love of minutiae and his trust in pseudo-scientific systems. This is the burden of Michael Hunter's careful investigation of Aubrey's historical and scientific interests, but it has also been sympathetically summarized by Strachey, who believed that Aubrey was groping towards a scientific ordering of phenomena in his 'crowded curiosity-shop of a brain'. But even when he fails to organize his materials in a systematic form (as is usually the case), he creates a sense of intimacy and liveliness that enables us to study his characters in their 'negligent habit' and private chambers (the phrase is Sprat's, who would bar the door). And thus we learn how Bacon composed his essays while walking in his garden, or how Hobbes sang to himself in bed at night when he was sure that he could not be heard. Not the least of Aubrey's achievements— and one that is in fact the direct consequence of his rude and hasty method—is his preservation of so much material that otherwise would have been lost. Even when part of this material proves to be apocryphal, we still learn what he was willing to believe and what his contemporaries thought was worth talking about.

When Aubrey revealed in his autobiographical memoir that he should have been a painter, he shrewdly assessed his own abilities but depicted them in somewhat misleading terms. His belief that he 'could fancy a thing so strongly and had so cleare an ideae of it' suggests the ambitious sweep of the full-length canvas, and in his treatise on education he cited the achievements of Titian, Lely, and Van Dyck at the expense of his friend Cooper's art: limning 'is too effeminate. Painting is more masculine and useful.'[26] But these sentiments, if applied to biography, would better suit the '*Out-Stroaks*' and broad contours of Evelyn's *Life of Mrs. Godolphin* or Walton's stylized lives than Aubrey's own scattered remains. In verses 'To his honoured Freinde John Aubrey', George Ent emphasized exactly the same characteristic that Aubrey himself celebrated in other men: 'But cheifly Nature loves, and farre does prye / Into her

---

[26] *Aubrey on Education*, ed. J. E. Stephens (London: Routledge, 1972), 112 (see p. 138 for Aubrey's remarks on Van Dyck and Lely).

secrets with his pierceing Eye'.[27] This is a traditional compliment that presumably was paid to numerous Restoration men and women of learning, but it nevertheless presents an apt description of one who was constantly attempting to pry even the most minuscule of artefacts from nature—and from time. The restricted size of the brief life provided Aubrey with a congenial biographical format in which he could record the images of his 'pierceing Eye' before those clear ideas forever faded from his crowded brain. The retrieval of forgotten things from oblivion, he remarked in his *Wiltshire Antiquities*, 'in some sort resembles the Art of a Conjuror, who makes those walke & appeare that have layen in their graves many hundreds of yeares: and to represent as it were to the eie the places, Customes and Fashions, that were of old Time'.[28] And in his treatise on education he drew special attention to Chaucer's gift for *enargeiac* description, his power 'to possess his readers with a more forcible imagination of seeing (as it were) done before their eyes, which they read, than any other that ever has written in any other tongue'. Chaucer's particular talent (and Aubrey's as well) lay in his ability to present 'the pith and sinews of eloquence and very life itself of all mirth and pleasant writing'.[29]

iii. Cooper and the Paradox of the Miniature

Aubrey's piercing eye, his penchant (in Strachey's words) for the pure essentials, the vivid image, find their closest counterparts in the work of his friend Samuel Cooper, and especially in those unfinished sketches Cooper used as studio patterns for his miniatures.[30] David Piper, who inaugurated the comparison between Aubrey and Cooper, argues that in the painter's 'entranced, minute observation of surface phenomena . . . he was very much of his time; with just that scrupulousness and curiosity did the early fellows of the Royal Society record all strange departures from the norm in the physical world, "warts and all" '.[31] This assessment is quite close to John Murdoch's remark that Cooper's 'stylistic iconography', the unadorned graphic frankness to be found in a portrait sketch

[27] Quoted by Powell, *John Aubrey and His Friends*, p. 16.
[28] Quoted by Hunter, p. 179.
[29] *Aubrey on Education*, p. 57 (he also refers to Dryden and praises Milton in this context).
[30] We might say that Cooper's unfinished sketches bear the same relation to Aubrey's unfinished brief lives as finished miniatures bear to completed and polished character-sketches of the 17th cent. Graham Reynolds, 'Samuel Cooper: Some Hallmarks of his Ability', *Connoisseur*, 147 (Feb. 1961), 17–21, points out that Cooper's unfinished miniatures exist in two groups, the studio models and his late portraits.
[31] *English Face*, p. 118. Another interesting parallel has been suggested by Patricia Fumerton, ' "Secret" Arts: Elizabethan Miniatures and Sonnets', *Representations*, 15 (1986), 57–97.

such as *Thomas Hobbes* (Plate 38), represented a 'Royal Society style' appropriate to the depiction of moral as well as natural philosophers.[32] This emphasis on the genuineness of the image is also tied to the unusually large number of sittings the miniaturist required. Miniatures were therefore expected to be *ad vivum* likenesses, and in the case of a preliminary portrait sketch—such as Cooper's of Hobbes—the distance between the painter and his or her subject was seemingly narrowed even further.

But if there exists a consensus of opinion about the accuracy, relative simplicity, and vividness of the miniature, there is sharp disagreement about how a painter like Cooper achieved these distinctive effects. The argument does not centre on technical skills (for we now have detailed information about how Cooper revolutionized the techniques he inherited from his predecessors), but on our sense of how much of himself he invested in his miniature representations. For Piper, style is normally the man, the artist himself, 'but with Cooper the style is the man he is portraying, and he annihilates himself in his sitter, in this still, yet almost breathing image'.[33] For Murdoch, on the other hand, the lengthy and frequent sittings the miniaturist demanded became, in effect, 'an extended platform for the artist to impress his personality—his *style* in a significantly extended sense—on the client'. Murdoch refers to Pepy's *Diary*, in which Cooper's eight sittings with Mrs Pepys are dutifully recorded, to substantiate his argument that Cooper's contemporaries were less taken by the likenesses he produced than by the artist's skill as a musician, linguist, and conversationalist:

what Cooper was selling was not so much a mere likeness but the magic of genius, the sense of a relationship with a brilliant man and of participation in his creativity. The miniature, enclosed in precious metal and crystal, was the material relic of the moments of its own creation. Its emblematic power came from its actual presence at the moment when, for example, the Lord Protector sat in front of Samuel Cooper, who had conferred on him the special gift of the painter, the privilege of corporeal immortality in the visual dimension.[34]

Contradictions such as these can be found quite frequently in the scholarship on miniatures, and it is my sense that this is so because of the slippery and often paradoxical nature of the miniature itself. Like Aubrey's brief lives, Cooper's paintings raise interesting questions about portraiture in general as well as 'in little'. Cooper is unique in Piper's eyes,

---

[32] Murdoch, in *English Miniature*, p. 109.
[33] Piper, *English Face*, p. 117.
[34] Murdoch, in *English Miniature*, p. 107.

for example, because he disappears as a presence within his own work; he subordinates his own personality within that of his subject's. But how is this significantly different from Van Dyck's depiction of Charles I—or the Earl of Denbigh? If there is a difference, it appears to lie in the restricted size of the image as well as in the suppression of iconic attributes or adherence to a tradition of idealization; there is simply no room here for the artist himself. Conversely, Murdoch contends that Cooper's originality as an artist lies in his personal virtuosity and in the sense of excitement· the painter and his subject share as the painted relic of their relationship emerges before their eyes. But apart from the frequency of the sittings, how does this process differ from the convivial dinners with which Van Dyck supplied his subjects, including the king, when they moored their boats at his studio in Blackfriar's? Like Rubens, Van Dyck was also treated as an equal—or at least as *il pittore cavalieresco*—by his various patrons, and *his* paintings were presumably fired with emblematic power both at the time they were approaching completion as well as later, when they hung in splendour at Whitehall. Again, if there is a distinction to be drawn, it must also involve the question of scale, of the more intensely personal and (as Lévi-Strauss has suggested) the 'qualitatively simplified' element to be found in the reduced format of the miniature.[35]

The smallness of the miniature, however, is only one of several elements that set it apart from painting in large. Even the term itself (from the Latin *minium*) refers to the red-lead technique used in producing these images rather than to their diminutive size.[36] Nor should the miniature be thought of as a specialized form of painting, for its origins lie not in painting itself but in classical medals and medieval manuscript illumination ('limn' is derived from 'illumine').[37] Both sources have left their mark. The medallion portrait dictated the pose of sitters in early miniatures (usually a depiction of the head and shoulders, although Holbein managed to introduce a hand), the occasional preference for the *al'antico* profile, and the roundness of the image. (The oval format, which

[35] Claude Lévi-Strauss, *The Savage Mind* (Chicago: Univ. of Chicago Press, 1970), 23, where he talks about diminutive objects in general. See also Susan Stewart, *On Longing: Narratives of the Miniature, the Gigantic, the Souvenir, the Collection* (Baltimore: The Johns Hopkins Univ. Press, 1984), esp. 125–8.

[36] Murdoch, in *English Miniature*, p. v.

[37] The standard studies, to which I am indebted at several points, are Graham Reynolds, *English Portrait Miniatures* (London: Adam and Charles Black, 1952), ch. 1, and Roy Strong, 'From Manuscript to Miniature', in *English Miniature*, pp. 25–84. Also of use have been Daphne Foskett, *Samuel Cooper 1609–1072* (London: Faber, 1974); Patrick J. Noon, *English Portrait Drawings and Miniatures* (New Haven: Yale Center for British Art, 1979); and two recent books by Roy Strong: *The English Renaissance Miniature* (London: Thames and Hudson, 1983) and *Artists of the Tudor Court: The Portrait Miniature Rediscovered 1520–1620* (London: Victoria and Albert Museum, 1983).

emerged in the late 1570s, allowed a hand and more of the sitter's costume to be included, and thus produced a more informal effect; it was also more compatible with the contemporary jewellery in which it was encased.) The affinity with medallions also strengthened the role of inscriptions in early miniatures; like the medal, the miniature could even be produced with an interlocking image and motto on the reverse side. The subtle textures of the medal influenced the emergence of the miniature as an artistic form that paid particular attention to the shape and contour of the human face, and it was thus natural for Charles II to turn to his royal limner, rather than to his principal painter, when he required a study from which the new coinage could be made. John Evelyn was on hand to hold the candle and record the scene:

Being call'd into his Majesties Closet, when Mr. Cooper (the rare limmer) was crayoning of his face & head, to make the stamps by, for the new *mill'd* mony, now contriving, I had the hounour to hold the Candle whilst it was doing; choosing to do this at night & by candle light, for the better finding out the shadows.[38]

The influence of manuscript illumination on the development of the miniature reinforced several of these classical features, particularly the emphasis on royal images, the smallness of the portrait, and its relation to verbal inscriptions. In the metamorphosis of the miniature from an element in the illumination of manuscripts to a separate artefact, however, the relation between the verbal and visual elements was significantly transformed. In manuscript illumination, the visual image was actually 'inscribed' within the literary work, or consigned to its margins; in either case, the verbal component remained dominant, and the visual element served more or less as an interpretive or exemplary gloss. In the miniature, on the other hand, the visual image has become the centre of focus, and the verbal inscription assumes the secondary role of iconic commentary (as in a medallion portrait encased within a verbal 'surround'). Manuscript illumination also provided the miniature with its distinctive colouring (a combination of water- and body-colour) and the smooth vellum on which it was painted. The miniaturist applied the vellum to a harder surface, usually a playing card, and, if he was also a goldsmith, encased it within a jewel-like setting.[39] Like the illuminator, he would also

---

[38] Evelyn, *Diary*, iii. 309–10. Piper, *English Face*, p. 117, points out that the use of forced light was an unusual technique, dictated by the fact that the likeness was being prepared for the coinage.

[39] For the standard discussion of technique, see Jim Murrell, 'The Craft of the Miniature', in *English Miniature*, pp. 1–24.

occasionally work silver, gold, and jewels into the texture of his work, a procedure that Hilliard, in his *Treatise Concerning the Arte of Limning*, singled out as one of the miniaturist's trade secrets. Jewellery and elaborate costumes could therefore be reproduced within the miniature by employing the very materials with which they were actually made; as Hilliard argued, these techniques 'so enricheth and ennobleth the work that it seemeth to be the thing itself, even the work of God and not of man . . .'.[40] The miniature thus became a more completely imitative object and at the same time an image that was 'precious' not merely because of its diminutive size but because of its status as an expensive and independent work of art.

In the history of the miniature in England, the close association with royal patronage was relatively short-lived. Roy Strong has shown that the miniature had its English origins within the atelier of the Tudor Royal Library during the reigns of Henry VII and Henry VIII, and during the first two-thirds of Elizabeth's reign miniatures were almost exclusively devoted to reproductions of the royal image (only one sixteenth-century locket does not depict the queen).[41] Early miniatures were treated as regal objects, and Elizabeth had a magnificent collection that she stored within the royal bedchamber. Miniatures were therefore very early in their history conceived of as collector's items, often encased in ivory boxes and protected by crystal covers; if, on the other hand, they were worn as lockets, they still contributed to the contemporary cult of majesty. By the end of the century, however, the images became increasingly personal as Hilliard and his successors attempted to augment their salaries by turning to the lesser nobility. Royal connoisseurs like Charles I continued to supply their patronage, and Charles's private collection has been characterized as 'a museum in miniature of the art of limning'.[42] But the cult of the miniature had been much more widely disseminated by this time, so much so that it eventually culminated, as we have seen, in the cult of the private and carefully individuated subject, represented in a simple and direct manner that severed almost all ties with its iconic forebears.

The famous Ditchley portrait of Elizabeth (Plate 17), which I have already invoked as a quintessentially allegorical or iconographic painting, can be usefully compared with the so-called 'Armada' or *Heneage Jewel* of

---

[40] *A Treatise Concerning the Arte of Limning*, ed. R. K. R. Thornton and T. G. S. Cain (Ashington: Mid Northumberland Arts Group/Carcanet, 1981), 62–3. Here and elsewhere I quote from the editors' modernized text.

[41] Strong, in *English Miniature*, pp. 25–52.

[42] Ibid. 84.

Elizabeth fashioned by Hilliard at the turn of the century (Plate 39).[43] This elaborate object comprises four different images: the two external surfaces of the locket depict, on the obverse, a full-profile portrait of the queen modelled in rich gold against a blue enamel ground, and on the reverse a religious image of the Ark of the Reformed Church sailing across a bright blue sea; the inside of the locket cover discloses a red Tudor rose and, balanced against it, an elaborate full-frontal image of the queen painted in Hilliard's richest and most delicate style. Each of these four images bears its own inscription, and all work together in what Strong celebrates as the ideological integration of the Elizabeth miniature.[44]

It is clearly an enormous step from the iconicism of images such as these to the art of Samuel Cooper, but the miniature appears, in fact, to have evolved in this direction even more quickly than painting in large. We can gauge this movement by recalling how strongly iconicism survived in the formal portraits of Van Dyck and Lely—and even of Kneller as well—but a more revealing comparison can be drawn between portraits painted of the same subject by Lely and Cooper. Few Restoration figures were painted as frequently, for instance, as Barbara Villiers, Duchess of Cleveland, and the portraits that survive of her furnish an interesting spectrum along which the work of Lely and Cooper may be gauged. I have already mentioned the various iconographical roles in which Lely depicted the king's mistress: as shepherdess and madonna, as Minerva, Pallas Athena, Mary Magdalen, and St Barbara. Lely also painted her in less elaborate poses, but many of these also involve an iconographical motif when she is represented with head on hand, or holding a symbolic wreath, or in semi-formal state. One central image will have to stand for many: the so-called madonna portrait, a copy of which is in the National Portrait Gallery (Plate 40),[45] in which she is enveloped in rich satiny folds as she gently holds her illegitimate child (variously described as a son or a daughter) with a column, foliage, and vista in the background.

But there also exists a series of chalk drawings, apparently of less interest to Lely's scholarly admirers, which reveals a more direct and intimate interpretation of this Restoration beauty. One of these coloured chalk sketches is clearly associated with the portrait of her as a madonna, and it is interesting to see that within the drawing, which is restricted to an oval format, Lely's perspective is much closer than in the full-sized

---

[43] Strong, in *English Miniature*, colour pl. *9a*.

[44] Ibid. 72–3.

[45] *National Portrait Gallery: Complete Illustrated Catalogue 1856–1979*, comp. K. K. Yung (London: National Portrait Gallery; New York: St Martin's, 1981), 116 (no. 2564); Beckett, *Lely*, no. 110. There is another copy 'after Lely' owned by the Duke of Grafton.

painting, and his focus much narrower: only the duchess and her child are depicted here, and her figure is cut off at the waist.[46] Two other drawings, roughly of the same size (10 × 8 inches), move Cleveland even closer to the surface of the picture. In one sketch she is drawn in three-quarter profile in a hood or cap whose ribbons are tied above her dress (Plate 41);[47] the result is an unusually enigmatic portrait whose indirect, dreamy-eyed pose and enveloping costume conceal as much as they disclose. A third drawing, in which she wears only a pair of pearl-drop earrings, is a close-up depiction of those features that Lely was accused of reproducing in his portraits of virtually every court lady he painted.[48]

Simple and direct as these images are, they merely constitute a middle ground between Lely's allegorical portraits and the even less assuming and more intense miniatures painted by Cooper. Three 'states' of miniatures depicting the Duchess of Cleveland have survived. In the earliest state, we can just begin to see the faint outline of features that Cooper drew upon the ground of the miniature (called the 'carnation').[49] A second work (Plate 42),[50] part of the famous group of unfinished sketches in the Royal Collection, apparently served as a studio pattern from which other miniatures would be painted; it is slightly larger in format than the finished miniature, but still quite a bit smaller than Lely's drawings. Cooper's interpretation of Cleveland's face here is quite unlike what we shall find anywhere else, not just because it is unfinished, or because our focus is so tightly controlled, but chiefly because her face, although not untouched by that languorousness for which she was known, also reveals a gentle sadness and perhaps even vulnerability, so closely are we allowed to scrutinize it. She has let her hair down and parted it somewhat unevenly in the middle; her only ornament is a dark headband that reinforces the smooth oval of her face.

The cumulative effect of such a simple, unfinished image is one of intimacy and perhaps even undress: it is as if Cooper had been admitted to her dressing-room before the paint and ornaments and costume were put on, whereas Lely was constrained to paint the polished beauty only later, when she emerged. This distinction can only be pushed so far, of course, for we have already seen that Lely could capture a more intimate likeness

---

[46] Sotheby sale, 29 Apr. 1971, no. 101; present location unknown. My source is the Yale Center for British Art photograph archive, acc. no. 118211.

[47] British Museum, acc. no. 1876-7-14-34; Laurence Binyon, *Catalogue of Drawings by British Artists* (London: British Museum, 1900), iii. 53.

[48] Whitworth Art Gallery (Manchester), acc. no. D.104.1960; Beckett, *Lely*, nos. 100–9.

[49] Murrell, in *English Miniature*, pl. 14.

[50] Daphne Foskett, *Samuel Cooper and his contemporaries* (London: HMSO, 1974), no. 81.

in chalk, at least, and we cannot disregard the numerous highly finished miniatures that Cooper produced of the duchess, usually with elaborately styled hair, a full complement of jewels, a prominent bust (in profile), and an inviting and at the same time somewhat imperious turn of the head.[51] But Cooper's studio sketch of Barbara Villiers stands as a not extreme example of the simplicity and directness that even a more polished and elaborate miniature is capable of achieving. Like Cooper, most seventeenth-century miniaturists shunned the full-length and the iconic modes, preferring instead to let the part stand for the whole. If iconic art is metonymic, pressing the significant attribute into the service of the entire image, then the miniature may be thought of as synechdochic, in which the significant part—especially the head alone—must stand for the whole. Like Aubrey contemplating the foot of Hercules (or turning his piercing eye on the countenances of his contemporaries), the miniaturist must suggest the entire figure by depicting its most telling features as searchingly as possible; and in the process, he will often isolate what is personally distinctive from what his subject shares with similar men and women.

This movement from the iconic to the more intimate and highly individualized miniature has its parallel in the changing techniques of limning in the seventeenth century, and again it is Cooper who is responsible for the most dramatic of these transformations. Although the miniaturist uses the same brushes as the painter who works on a larger scale, he approaches the construction of the face in a quite different way. Whereas the portrait-painter begins with the central features—the eyes, nose, and mouth—and then works outward towards the contour of the head, miniaturists (with the notable exception of Holbein) reverse this procedure by first designing the silhouette and only then turning to the features within.[52] The result is often a more stereotyped version of the sitter's head, one that proceeds by outline rather than by those elements that most effectively distinguish one face from another. If we add to this the proclivity of the miniaturist for a brush technique (usually stipple) that suggests a smoothly textured surface, we can sense not only the relative polish of a portrait miniature but also its tendency to prettify and flatter its subject. Sir Kenelm Digby noted this effect when he argued that life-size portraits are 'so like as some people think them even the worse for it. The

---

[51] Foskett, *Samuel Cooper and his contemporaries*, no. 95; see also no. 114.
[52] See Murrell, in *English Miniature*, p. 6.

best faces are seldom satisfied with Van Dyck; whereas not the very worst even complained of Hoskins', who was Cooper's uncle and master.[53]

Cooper, however, considerably mitigated this impression of polish and preciousness by handling the brush in a much bolder manner.[54] He in effect opened up the miniature, endowed it with stronger contours and flourishes, by employing a technique that his fellow artists attempted to imitate but could never entirely master; and thus by turning his back on the 'secret' techniques he had inherited, he ironically inaugurated a new style that would, of necessity, retain its own integrity. This fresh style of handling paint also records more of the process of painting itself, a phenomenon we normally associate with oil on canvas, and especially with the brushwork of Titian.[55] Cooper's pioneering style therefore works against the traditionally 'finished' quality of the miniature, instead suggesting the greater freedom and flourish of full-scale oil paintings by Van Dyck and Lely.

It was therefore perhaps inevitable that Cooper should have been 'commonly stiled the Vandyck in little', just as his master, Hoskins, was called the 'Van Dyck in miniature'.[56] These phrases are complimentary and deprecatory at the same time, suggesting the ambiguous status of miniaturists as lesser artists, both because they worked in small and because they were often commissioned to copy original paintings executed in large. Hoskins, for instance, reduced several of Van Dyck's paintings into the compass of the miniature, including the famous double portrait of Charles and Henrietta Maria exchanging the wreath and sprig.[57] Nicholas Dixon copied Lely's portrait of Princess Mary as Diana (Plate 30),[58] and it should be noted that at least one accomplished miniaturist, Richard Gibson, was actually a dwarf (and thus less figuratively a 'Van Dyck in miniature'). Gibson was a close friend of Lely, and it is interesting that in a remarkable (but largely unremarked) series of paintings and sketches, Lely paid his diminutive friend the compliment of portraying him with his wife, in ceremonious poses, in close-up, and even asleep. But Gibson, although he apparently drew upon the painterly techniques he found in Lely, was never as fully engaged in the cult of authenticity as Cooper was, and he established his reputation through

---

[53] Quoted by Piper, *English Face*, p. 124.
[54] See e.g. Murrell, in *English Miniature*, p. 15, and Murdoch, in *English Miniature*, p. 106.
[55] See David Rosand, *Titian* (New York: Abrams, 1978), 9–12.
[56] Buckeridge, p. 364.
[57] Foskett, *Samuel Cooper and his contemporaries*, no. 147.
[58] Ibid., no. 221.

work as a copyist as well as through conventional iconographic pro-
grammes tailored to the noble households in which he worked.[59]

Cooper also appears to have copied Van Dyck's work during his early
career, and it is possible that he developed his own technique by
associating closely with the Flemish master.[60] An early biographer,
Bainbrigge Buckeridge, claimed that he equalled Van Dyck 'in his
beautiful colouring, and agreeable airs of the face, together with that
strength, relievo, and noble spirit; that soft and tender liveliness of the
flesh, which is inimitable'.[61] The forced logic of this praise (Van Dyck
could be imitated, whereas Cooper could not) indicates an important
distinction that should be drawn, however, for later in Cooper's career
full-scale painters would copy *his* works, and not the other way round.[62]
Oliver Cromwell's famous remark, traditionally said to have been delivered to Lely, that the portraitist should 'paint my picture truly like me
& not flatter me at all but remark all these ruffness, pimples, warts &
everything as you see me', is now commonly believed to have been
imparted to Cooper himself, for recent scholarship has shown that Lely's
portrait of the Lord Protector derives from Cooper's original.[63] The
miniaturist's unfinished studio sketches, moreover, which were bequeathed to his wife after his death, were the object of an intense rivalry
between two great collectors, Cosimo III of Tuscany and Charles II,
presumably because these works were thought to represent the artist's
most purely original work (even more so than finished miniatures
produced by the same hand).[64] And Cooper's originality would be valued
not simply because he was an important master in his own right, but
because the early state of these sketches guaranteed the accuracy and
authenticity of images drawn directly from the life.

But accuracy, the authenticity warranted by an *ad vivum* likeness, has
never in itself been the sole or even the most important reason for valuing
works such as Cooper's. The question of scale—of the great compression
to be found within the boundaries of the miniature—is almost always
invoked by those who admire these minute images, and all the more so by
those who marvel at the bold brush-strokes to be glimpsed within

[59] The fullest study of Gibson can be found in Murdoch, in *English Miniature*, pp. 129–35; see also
Foskett, *Samuel Cooper and his contemporaries*, pp. 97–8, 104–7. Two of Lely's paintings are reproduced
in Beckett, *Lely* (nos. 207–8); the portrait of the sleeping dwarf is at Berkeley Castle; the pencil-and-
chalk drawing is in the Ashmolean.

[60] See e.g. Murdoch, in *English Miniature*, pp. 105–6.

[61] Buckeridge, p. 364.

[62] Murdoch, in *English Miniature*, p. 111, calls Cooper the only independent miniaturist.

[63] See Piper, *English Face*, p. 115.

[64] See Murdoch, in *English Miniature*, p. 116.

Cooper's portraits. Pepys was not entirely pleased with the faithfulness of Cooper's miniature of his wife, but whatever misgivings he nurtured were more than counterbalanced by his appreciation of Cooper's artistry:

and thence presently to Mr. Cooper's house to see some of his work; which is all in little, but so excellent, as though I must confess I do think the colouring of the flesh to be a little forced, yet the painting is so extraordinary, as I do never expect to see the like again.[65]

The sense of scale here, to which Pepys returns in other entries in his diary, is closely tied to several additional paradoxes posed by the miniature. We might expect, for instance, that a viewer could assimilate an extremely small image more quickly and easily than its grander counterparts (Van Dyck's equestrian portraits painted for Whitehall, for example). But one of the ironies of the miniature is that it forces us to look minutely and intensely, and thus to admire the artistry that produced it. Similarly, the constriction in size, with its more intense scrutiny of the human face (often viewed at close quarters), actually suggests an augmented importance on behalf of its subject. The narrowed focus of the miniature, which eliminates all that is peripheral, serves to offset any diminishment we might experience through the loss of bulk and context, and the private portrait therefore takes on a significance of its own.

The greatest works in miniature are never simple reductions, moreover, and the exacting brushwork points to a more observant eye—with perhaps different emphases—than we might normally find in visual portraiture. Invoking a photographic analogy, we might say that, as the stops of the camera are closed down, the artist is able to make finer and finer distinctions within his field of vision. But the discriminating powers of an eye this perceptive may also lead to a sense of artistic frustration. As Hilliard noted in a fascinating passage in *The Arte of Limning*, 'How then can the curious drawer watch, and as it were catch those lovely graces, witty smilings, and those stolen glances which suddenly like lightning pass, and another countenance taketh place, except to behold and very well note and conceit to like'?[66] The miniaturist, in other words, is perhaps more intensely aware than other painters of the fluctuations in the human countenance, and of what those fluctuations indicate about the character of the sitter. In advice remarkably close to Aubrey's actual practice, Hilliard suggested that the limner should pay particular attention to the

[65] *The Diary of Samuel Pepys*, ed. Robert Latham and William Matthews, ix (Berkeley and Los Angeles: Univ. of California Press, 1976), 139.
[66] *A Treatise Concerning the Arte of Limning*, pp. 76–8.

sitter's eye, for 'the eye is the life of the picture . . .'. And yet even here, as the miniaturist painfully recognized, an eventual choice would still have to be made. It would remain for his literary counterpart—for the biographer Aubrey in his sketch of Thomas Hobbes, for instance—to capture the fleeting emotions, the elements of life, as they appear and disappear in the twinkling of an eye.

5

Double Agents: Jonathan Richardson and Roger North

ANY study of biography and portrait-painting as sister arts must pay particular attention to those figures who combined both forms of portraiture in their own work or who turned to either artistic medium with comparable skill. But figures such as these are understandably rare, not simply because writing is more widely learned and practised than painting, but because, as we have seen, the impulses that lie behind biography and portrait-painting are often quite different. The painter may create portraits of a highly personal nature—and the miniature is an interesting example of this kind of work—but for the most part the artist toils within a firmly established profession, producing images *of* others *for* others, and often executing them according to contemporary taste. Biographies may also be made to order, and presumably Walton satisfied the tastes of his ecclesiastical patrons; but his lives, no less than Evelyn's biography of Margaret Blagge, are distinctly his own, with a moral and aesthetic vision that others found palatable (and edifying) as well.

We would therefore expect to find a certain amount of tension between works of visual and verbal portraiture produced by the same artist, and this is precisely what we discover in Jonathan Richardson, the first painter within this period to try his hand at both artistic forms. By characterizing Richardson as a double agent, I want to draw attention not only to his career as both painter and writer, but also to that element of subversion that emerges in a comparison of his graphic and literary work. As a double agent, Richardson reveals his divided loyalties as an artist: his conventional practice as a painter of faces is dramatically at odds with his intensely personal and emotionally charged biography of Milton, and with the visual images associated with it. The biographer Roger North, on the other hand, was no more accomplished as a graphic artist than any other writer during this period, but his knowledge of painting, architecture, and music was even more considerable than Evelyn's or Aubrey's. I adduce him as a fellow double agent not only because of his primary career as a Restoration lawyer—or his lively interest in the visual arts—but because of his similar search for a form of portraiture that would give expression to his private vision of family members whose lives were deeply entangled within the public events of their times. Neither Richardson nor North, I want to argue, was finally successful in his attempt to create a fully satisfactory artistic form. Their work becomes more interesting, in fact, when we consolidate each artist's various portraits and examine the combined portraiture towards which both artists were working.

i. Richardson: The Painter as Biographer

Richardson's reputation as a portrait-painter has never fared very well, not even in recent years, when so much sympathetic attention has been directed towards English art of the eighteenth century. Born in 1667, unhappily apprenticed to a scrivener, later trained by John Riley (whose niece he married), Richardson ultimately earned himself a respectable following as a faithful painter of faces.[1] His popularity increased after the deaths of Kneller and Dahl, and like Thomas Hudson—his student and son-in-law—he was responsible for a resurgence of native English portraiture in the opening decades of the century. Horace Walpole believed that his work revealed neither enthusiasm nor servility; it simply captured the good sense of the nation. Reynolds said that Richardson understood his art very well scientifically, but that his manner was cold and hard. Waterhouse wavers between praising a plain, English directness and deploring a solemn, mask-like effect in Richardson's portraits, and this is close to several other recent evaluations, including those of Burke and Piper.[2]

Richardson's real reputation rests with his pen and not with his brush. Walpole, whose portrait Richardson painted in 1734 or 1735, remarked that although he 'wrote with fire and judgment, his paintings owed little to either'.[3] In the 'Life of Dyer', Johnson observed that Richardson was

---

[1] Biographical information concerning Richardson is quite scanty; for the most recent (and accurate) sketch, see Roger Lonsdale, 'Jonathan Richardson's *Morning Thoughts*', in *Augustan Studies: Essays in Honor of Irvin Ehrenpreis*, ed. Douglas Lane Patey and Timothy Keegan (Newark: Univ. of Delaware Press; London and Toronto: Associated University Presses, 1985), 175–94. Lonsdale's essay has enabled me to correct my original article on Richardson in several places.

[2] *Anecdotes of Painting*, iii. 413; Reynolds is quoted by Charles Robert Leslie and Tom Taylor, *Life and Times of Sir Joshua Reynolds* (1865), i. 12–13 n.; Waterhouse, pp. 147–9; Burke, pp. 105–6; and Piper, *English Face*, p. 161. C. H. Collins Baker, in an analysis of Richardson's drawings, perceives 'an artist who begins rather flatly and uninterpretatively, gains bulk and structure, and ends up with a full and forcible style'; see 'Some Drawings by Jonathan Richardson in the Witt Collection', *Connoisseur*, 73 (1925), 195–202. As I suggest later, the difference between Richardson's drawings and oil portraits is more dramatic than in any comparable artist of this period. The drawings I have studied—especially those in the Ashmolean—reveal a vigour and degree of experimentation that is simply not to be found in Richardson's normal work as a portrait-painter.

[3] *Anecdotes of Painting*, iii. 413.

'an artist then of high reputation, but now better known by his books than by his pictures'.[4] In 1715 he published his *Essay on the Theory of Painting*, which later influenced Hogarth and Reynolds; this was followed in 1719 by two more studies, one on *The Whole Art of Criticism in Relation to Painting*, the other on *The Science of a Connoisseur*, a science that Richardson and his son further refined in their account of various art objects in Italy and France, published in 1722. These treatises contain several important, although not always original, formulations of artistic theory and practice, and they helped, in their own way, to elevate the art of portraiture so that it eventually replaced landscape as the second-highest-ranking genre of painting.[5] Richardson also fancied himself a poet, and an unusual volume of poems entitled *Morning Thoughts* was published in 1776, thirty-one years after his death.[6] 'I have from my Infancy Lov'd and Practic'd Painting and Poetry,' he once remarked; 'One I Possess'd as a Wife, the Other I Kept Privately.'[7] Of greater importance, however, is the ambitious project he executed with his son in the early 1730s, which was a lengthy series of explanatory remarks on *Paradise Lost* that included a substantial biography of Milton.

Richardson therefore emerges as an interesting test case for the kinds of questions we might ask about the artist who practises portraiture in two different artistic media. First, how does his biographical work correspond to the theoretical statements he has made about portraiture in his various treatises? Second, how does the successful painter of portraits approach the format of biography? Is he conscious of the similarity between these two forms? More importantly, does he take advantage of the inherent features of biography by manipulating time in a manner that is relatively closed to him in painting? Or, conversely, does he attempt to create visual metaphors or spatial structures drawn from his primary discipline? Finally, does he ever combine the two forms; and if he does, how do they compare with each other? Do the text and the image reveal essentially the same kind of portraiture? I shall try to answer these questions by briefly summarizing Richardson's aesthetic theories and then by turning to his life of Milton and several of his most interesting portraits.

Perhaps the most striking aspect of Richardson's theoretical work is its

[4] Johnson, *Lives*, iii. 343.
[5] For the most extensive analysis of Richardson as a theorist, see Lawrence Lipking, *The Ordering of the Arts in Eighteenth-Century England* (Princeton: Princeton Univ. Press, 1970), 109–26; for the rise of portraiture, see Burke, p. 94.
[6] See Lonsdale, 'Jonathan Richardson's *Morning Thoughts*', and I. A. Williams, 'Two Kinds of Richardsons', *London Mercury*, 7 (1923), 382–8.
[7] *Explanatory Notes and Remarks on Milton's 'Paradise Lost'* (1734), p. clxxviii.

strange divergence from his normal practice as a painter. Whereas his portraits are almost uniformly sober, trustworthy representations of the subjects they represent—Walpole charged that 'he drew nothing well below the head, and was void of imagination'—his treatises constantly emphasize the duty of the artist to create a more imaginative and idealized image of human nature.[8] As a theorist he stands firmly in the Aristotelian tradition of heightened characterization that was still so strong in the late seventeenth and early eighteenth centuries:

> The business of Painting is not only to represent Nature, but to make the Best Choice of it; Nay to Raise, and Improve it from what is Commonly, or even Rarely Seen, to what never Was, or Will be in Fact, tho' we may easily conceive it Might be. As in a good Portrait, from whence we conceive a better Opinion of the Beauty, Good Sense, Breeding, and other Good Qualities of the person than from seeing Themselves, and yet without being able to say in what particular 'tis Unlike: for Nature must be ever in view . . .[9]

Mere flattery, he contends, will never do; but the painter's task is to make what is familiar appear fresh, to represent historical characters in a new light. This ennobling or heightening of character is not restricted to the painter of faces; it is also the prerogative of the poet and the historian. 'Painting', he says, 'is another sort of Writing',[10] and he draws explicit parallels between portraiture and biography: 'A Portrait is a sort of General History of the Life of the Person it represents';[11] to sit for one's picture 'is to have an Abstract of one's Life written, and published, and ourselves thus consign'd over to Honour, or Infamy'.[12] In other remarks he speculates that a portrait illustrates what the historian (the biographer) says 'more expressly, and particularly'.[13] If we read a character-sketch by Clarendon, we will have our knowledge improved by also viewing a picture of the same person by Van Dyck.

---

[8] *Anecdotes of Painting*, iii. 413; Waterhouse (p. 148) disagrees. The question of 'objective' or 'trustworthy representation' is, of course, an extremely difficult issue to resolve, especially when we no longer have a painter's live subjects before us. In addition to accepting contemporary accounts, however, we can also compare Richardson's portraits with others depicting the same subject. Kerslake provides ample material for this kind of study. Kerslake describes a portrait of Dr Richard Mead (pl. 535, NPG 4157) as a 'typical' Richardson, and a comparison of this painting with its companions (pls. 528–38) reveals that Richardson's likeness of Mead is relatively accurate (i.e. it resembles the others) and fairly unambitious (it suppresses body and background to focus on the head, which is consistent with Walpole's remark). Richardson's conventionality can also be seen in an etching of Mead that was apparently meant to counter Arthur Pond's rather impolite version of the doctor, which lacked a wig (see Piper, *English Face*, pp. 164–7).

[9] *The Science of a Connoisseur*, in *Two Treatises* (1719), 13.

[10] Ibid. 17.

[11] *The Whole Art of Criticism*, in *Two Treatises* (1719), 45.

[12] Richardson, *Essay*, pp. 13–14.

[13] Ibid. 10.

Richardson's intense awareness of the objectives common to both verbal and visual art can also be seen in a series of extended remarks on history-painting, the most highly regarded of painterly forms. Richardson suggests that the painter of *istoria* might first sketch his conceptions in written form, embellished with all possible beauty and rhetorical description. Because painting is a sort of writing, he says that it ought to be legible; and thus, paying tribute to Ripa's *Iconologia*, he points out the usefulness of insignia in allegorical paintings. Even in portraiture the introduction of verbal description may prove useful, and he emphasizes the importance of documenting the subject of each canvas.[14] This is a practice he maintained in many of his portraits of literary men, and one that is especially interesting in his representations of Milton and Pope.

Richardson published his *Explanatory Notes and Remarks on Milton's 'Paradise Lost'* in 1734. The biographical section forms a lengthy preface to the commentary proper, which has been described as 'based on a much broader and profounder conception of Milton's poetry' than earlier studies;[15] the biographical account of Milton itself does not add much of significance to previous work.[16] Contemporary reaction to the book was predictably mixed. Hogarth caricatured Richardson senior and junior; Warburton wrote that 'Such a heap of wretched, senseless impertinence, and more senseless vanity I never before saw together.'[17] Walpole, on the other hand, commented that 'again were the good sense, the judicious criticism, and the sentiments that broke forth in this work, forgotten in the singularities that distinguish it'.[18]

Like his portrait-paintings, Richardson's life of Milton initially appears to belie his advocacy of ideal form:

If I can give a more Exact, and a more Just Idea of *Milton*, and of *Paradise Lost* than the Publick has yet had of Either, I am Assur'd it will be Acceptable to all Honest and Ingenuous Minds of What party Soever. This is All I Intend; not a Panegyrick, not to give my Own Sense of What a Man should be, but what This Man Really was. (p. 201)[19]

---

[14] Ibid. 68–9, 74, 111.

[15] Ants Oras, *Milton's Editors and Commentators from Patrick Hume to Henry John Todd (1695–1801): A Study in Critical Views and Methods* (1931; rev. edn., New York: Haskell, 1967), 100; Oras's comparison is chiefly with Bentley's edition.

[16] See William Riley Parker, *Milton: A Biography* (Oxford: Clarendon Press, 1968), p. x, and Darbishire's introduction to *The Early Lives of Milton*.

[17] See *Hogarth's Graphic Works*, ed. Ronald Paulson, rev. edn. (New Haven: Yale Univ. Press, 1970), i. 314–15, and ii., pl. 337; Warburton is quoted by William T. Whitley, *Artists and Their Friends in England 1700–1799* (London and Boston: Medici Society, 1928), i. 99.

[18] *Anecdotes of Painting*, iii. 414.

[19] For convenience, all quotations from Richardson's biography are drawn from Darbishire; further references are provided in the text.

Richardson insists that he will not 'Plead for the Poet, or the Poem, but for Truth', and yet it is clear, even from these opening remarks, that his account of Milton will prove to be a highly polemical one. It is his duty to direct 'Light into What hath Hitherto lain in Obscurity', and to dispel mistakes that have 'Injur'd the Memory of a Deserving Man, Debas'd a Work Worthy of the Highest Estimation', and generally deprived the world of a considerable amount of Horatian 'Pleasure and Advantage'. Although Richardson does not name those who have so unfairly debased Milton's reputation, it is clear that his main target is Anthony Wood, whose deeply unsympathetic portrait of Milton had appeared in *Fasti Oxonienses* in 1691. Wood's personal attack on Milton, coupled with several candid passages in the biographical sketch published by Milton's nephew, Edward Phillips, in 1694, had done much to sour the popular view of the poet in the early eighteenth century; and thus it was from a need to vindicate Milton's character as much as from aesthetic principles that Richardson turned to an idealized portrait in his own life of Milton.[20]

Richardson ennobles or 'raises' Milton's character in a variety of ways, the most predictable of which is a tendency to associate his character of mind with a prominent archetype. Thus Richardson's readers are often asked to picture Milton as an ancient, and to bestow upon him the veneration they have traditionally devoted to classical poets and philosophers:

in fine, He was an Ancient Greek and Roman. a Philosopher, a Divine, a Christian, a Poet.—but there are Readers, who from the Materials I have brought together, will form a Nobler Idea of him than any Words of Mine can give, and Such a One as will Appear in Lustre, though at the same time they Review the Brightest Names of Antiquity. (p. 254)

Near the end of the biography—and this is the kind of posturing that so outraged Richardson's contemporaries—he boasts that he, at least, has been greatly entertained by the picture he has drawn of Milton's mind; it is a portrait, he says, as worthy of our consideration and esteem 'as Most of Those whose Lives are Written by any Ancient or Modern'. Had Milton lived in ancient Rome or Athens, 'what a Lustre would his Name have been Cloath'd with!' (pp. 284–5).[21] Milton's true character as a writer, he

---

[20] For the political background to the literary disputes, see John Robert Moore, 'Milton among the Augustans: The Infernal Council', *Studies in Philology*, 48 (1951), 15–25, and, for a much broader survey, Dustin Griffin, *Regaining Paradise: Milton and the Eighteenth Century* (Cambridge: Cambridge Univ. Press, 1986), *passim*.

[21] Richardson constantly characterizes Milton by invoking images of heat and brightness (see his description of a house on fire, quoted below); his particular emphasis on 'Lustre', however, should

insists at the conclusion of the life, 'is that he is an Ancient, but born two Thousand Years after his Time' (p. 318). And Milton emerges not only as a type of the ancient, but as a type of the poet as well. Although Richardson includes a substantial chronological survey of Milton's entire life, he is in fact chiefly interested in the man who wrote *Paradise Lost*. All of Richardson's careful biographical research and even his intricate textual inquiries are subordinated to this compulsion to delineate not just the mind of the writer but the genius of the author of one specific poem, now so unfortunately 'Debas'd' and forgotten. It is to *this* man that Richardson says he owes 'much of the Happiness of my Life' (p. 218).

Richardson creates this idealized version of the writer through a series of textual strategies. First, because his life of Milton is conceived as a preface to a longer work, we are constantly made aware that we are working towards an elaborate commentary on a specific literary text. Second, Richardson has structured his biography so that his exposition of what he calls the 'Principal Occurrences' of the poet's life actually follows his delineation of Milton's mind. There are very few points in the life where we are not aware of Milton as a writer or of the origin and progess of his principal work. Richardson twice tells us that he is interested in showing us the 'Author of *Paradise Lost*' (pp. 280–1); whatever the biography may tell us about Milton's particular sufferings or triumphs as a young man, as a husband, as a father, it is nevertheless primarily designed to enlarge our understanding of the creation and subsequent history of Milton's great poem. Richardson's emphasis is squarely on the poem— and implicitly on the poet—in the making; it is against this one magnificent achievement that all of Milton's talents and limitations are to be measured. Even the young Milton resolved that '*he would not be frustrated of his hope to write Well hereafter in Laudable things ought Himself to be a true Poem, that is, a Composition and Pattern of the Best and Honourablest things*' (p. 247). This early vision of his future self—of his accomplished self—serves to shape both the life of the poet and the structure of the biographical life that places Milton's poem at its centre.

This passage also points to Richardson's third major strategy, in which he suggests that the prominent features of Milton's character as a man are identical with the central themes of his poetry. One fundamental method of idealizing character is, of course, to associate it with general and

also be associated with the halo-like appearance of the poet's laurels, which I discuss later. Also of interest here is Richardson's insistence that 'there is Somthing in Every Man's whereby he is Known, as by his Voice, Face, Gait *&c.*' (p. 315); in his view, Milton is distinguished by 'a certain Vigour, whether *Versing* or *Prosing*'.

abstract qualities, and Richardson ultimately isolates Milton's 'Piety and Vertue' as those qualities most worthy of our own imitation. Later, when he comments on *Paradise Lost*, he points to these same qualities as the focus of Milton's great epic:

the Moral we are also Directed to, and This the Poet has put into the Mouth of an Angel. Many Moral Reflections are excited throughout the Whole Work, but the Great One is Mark'd Strongly XII. 745 *&c*. PIETY AND VERTUE, ALL COMPRIZ'D IN ONE WORD CHARITY, IS THE ONLY WAY TO HAPPINESS. (p. 317)

In the final analysis, therefore, the man and his work are of the same piece and are conceived by the biographer in the same terms: we read the same lessons in the texture of one man's life and in the text of his greatest poem.

Richardson's idealized portrait of Milton is thus consistent with his theoretical statements in favour of a heightened or ennobling form of portraiture, but it would be a mistake for us to conclude that he provides little beyond a broad abstraction of Milton as a poet in his biography. He begins, in fact, by minutely and sometimes playfully describing Milton's physical appearance, and he is not afraid to mention Milton's deficiencies and limitations. But Richardson's consideration of these possible defects is usually qualified by careful admonitions to the reader. Consider, for instance, his summation of Milton's character at the very close of the life: 'Whatever Spots, or Blemishes appear upon his Judgment in certain Points, let the Charitable Eye look beyond Those on his Immaculate Integrity' (p. 285). Minor failings are constantly to be subsumed under the generally virtuous character of Richardson's subject—much as his blindness was compensated by visionary power denied to 'Common Eyes'—and even when this strategy fails Richardson is able to blunt the edge of hostile criticism by carefully preparing his readers before he proceeds to a discussion of delicate issues. This is a procedure we often discover in Boswell's *Life of Johnson* (especially in the episode in which Boswell must justify Johnson's decision to accept a pension from the king), and Richardson uses it to best effect in his analysis of the two darkest aspects of Milton's personal life: his disastrous first marriage and views on divorce and, later, his tyrannical treatment of his two daughters. Richardson skilfully structures this part of his narrative by placing it between a general discussion of Milton's mind and an equally broad analysis of his religious character; and the effect, of course, is that popular rumours of any particular 'Blemishes' in Milton's private life—even if they are actually valid—cannot overturn the general representation of Milton's character that the biographer has already developed.

Richardson also calls upon Milton to defend himself, usually by quoting lengthy passages from Milton's poetry and prose; and thus as we work through Richardson's text we not only read a great deal about Milton, but actually read a considerable amount of his work as well (a practice all the more unusual because the biography is merely a preface to the lengthy commentary on the poems). Richardson often recedes from his role as a mediating figure, preferring instead to have us experience Milton's mind as directly as possible. And yet there are occasions, as in his discussion of Milton's treatment of his daughters, when he cannot call upon the poet to stand as his own advocate. In situations such as these Richardson often abandons his normal celebration of Milton as a unique character—as the best of men—and instead emphasizes his common humanity, the flawed but aspiring nature that he shares with all mankind: 'in Judging of a particular Man, let us Consider him as an Individual of the Species, as a Rational Creature, not as of any Particular Country, or as having had his small Portion of Being in whatsoever Point of the Vast Circle of Eternity. We all judge Thus when we Read *Plutarch*; Reading Mee alters not the Case in That' (p. 214). Richardson therefore wants it both ways: although he will normally extol Milton's character as a type or exemplar of refined human nature, he will nevertheless stress Milton's similarity with the species whenever certain problems—certain 'Spots, or Blemishes' in his portrait—cannot be overlooked.

Richardson's characteristic choice of diction in describing Milton's character—his repeated use of terms such as spots and blemishes, and his request that we train our charitable eyes to look beyond these superficial defects—suggests, of course, that his approach to biography is often pictorial in nature. He takes pleasure, for instance, in extolling Milton as a painter: not as a writer actually interested in art ('He does not appear to have Much Regarded what was done with the Pencil'), but as a poet capable of producing exquisite pictures in 'L'Allegro' and 'Il Penseroso' (p. 212). He even boasts that Milton's pictures in *Paradise Lost* 'are more Sublimely Great, Divine and Lovely than *Homer's*, or *Virgil's* or those of Any Other Poet, or of All the Poets, Ancient, or Modern' (p. 328).[22] And Richardson is himself interested in creating pictorial images of Milton; we relish the glimpse we are offered of the poet sitting 'in a Grey Coarse Cloath Coat at the Door of his House, near *Bun-hill* Fields Without

---

[22] Peter M. Briggs, 'The Jonathan Richardsons as Milton Critics', *Studies in Eighteenth-Century Culture*, 9 (1979), 115–30, provides an accurate assessment of Richardson's interest in Milton's pictorialism, particularly the painter's sense that visual metaphor functioned in Milton as a form of spiritual transcendence beyond the physical.

Moorgate, in Warm Sunny Weather to Enjoy the Fresh Air' (p. 203), as well as a later picture of him dictating the verses of *Paradise Lost* as 'he Sat leaning Backward Obliquely in an Easy Chair, with his Leg flung over the Elbow of it' (p. 291). But these descriptions are no more frequent than the visual images Richardson occasionally employs to delineate Milton's creativity or cast of mind. He describes Milton's essential 'Odour of Sanctity', for example, by noting that, even in the heat of the most virulent polemical battles, ' 'tis seen Breaking forth in his most Furious Disputes, 'tis seen even There; as I once saw the Sunbeams Wreathing amongst the Flames and Smoak and Horror of a House on Fire' (p. 252). And he gauges the reputation of *Paradise Lost* by suggesting that 'This Poem, this *Waste Paper*, (like an Acorn Hid and Lost) has, by its Inherent Life, and a Little Cultivation, Sprung Out of the Earth, Lifted up its Head and Spread its Branches, a Noble Oak' (p. 297).

For the most part, however, pictorialism enters Richardson's biography less in its local texture than in specific analogies with the art of portrait-painting. This helps in part to explain the general structure of the book, which abandons any sustained narrative in favour of a more schematic and spatial arrangement of discrete topics:

Concerning *Milton*, I will First of All, as well as I am Able, Show you his Person; Then his Mind; Afterwards You shall be Acquainted with the Principal Occurrences of his Life; his Provision for Maintenance; and Lastly, I will Consider the General Character of his Life, as to Happiness, by Comparing in very few Words his Sufferings and Enjoyments. (p. 201)

Richardson therefore begins with Milton's external appearance before delving more deeply into his distinctive character as a man and as a writer; and at each stage in this process Richardson draws explicit parallels between his own task as a biographer and his work as a portrait-painter. Here is the analogy he draws as he introduces his discussion of Milton's religious life:

As in making a Portrait, the Complexion and each particular Feature may have been Carefully enough Observ'd and Imitated, but still what is Most Important remains; the Air, the Mind, the Grace, the Dignity, the Capacity, the Vertue, Goodness, *&c.* (p. 231)

If these are not found in the subject of his biography, then it will prove to be an 'Insipid, a Bad Picture'. And he assures us that he will employ the same faithfulness in finishing his portrait of Milton's general character as he has already adhered to in his depiction of Milton's physical appearance.

Later Richardson tells us that his picture of the mind of Milton has been drawn chiefly by the poet himself, although he has 'put it together'; and because it may be too large for the eye to take in clearly in one viewing, he will 'Contract it' for us (p. 254), thereby providing what is essentially a short character-sketch in the tradition of seventeenth-century histori-ography.

There are other important parallels that Richardson points to between biography and portrait-painting, including, in his detailed discussion of textual problems in *Paradise Lost*, his equation of the improvement of Milton's text with a flattering, 'puffed' form of portraiture (pp. 309–10). But perhaps the most interesting parallel lies in the portrait of Milton that Richardson engraved as the frontispiece for his biography. Richardson tells us that his etching has been taken from a crayon drawing in his possession made by Robert White. According to Richardson, this is the portrait that so excited Milton's daughter Deborah when she first saw it: ' 'tis my Father, 'tis my Dear Father! I see him! 'tis Him! and then She put her Hands to several Parts of Her Face, 'tis the very Man!' (p. 229). I find this a particularly intriguing reaction, largely because Deborah appears to quote directly from Aristotle's influential explanation of why visual and verbal portraits affect us so strongly: they bring before us 'the very man'.[23] (In a later etching, Richardson would in fact inscribe Aristotle's 'OΥΤΟΣ ΕΚΕΙΝΟΣ' beneath a portrait-head.[24]) Robert White's crayon drawing was probably not, however, drawn directly from the life; it was probably taken from the so-called Bayfordbury portrait of Milton, generally attributed to William Faithorne (Plate 43).[25] Richardson's engraving is therefore a direct descendant of this famous portrait, but his own representation of Milton is not without an important and characteristic modification (Plate 44).

Richardson draws our attention to this engraving at the very beginning of the biography when he describes Milton's voice, complexion, and hair. He introduces this image as the representation of 'the Face of him who *Wrote Paradise Lost*, the Face We Chiefly desire to be Acquainted with' (p. 202). By this I think Richardson means two different but related things. In the first place, he wants to portray Milton at the exact time when he

---

[23] *Poetics*, iv. 5.

[24] Wimsatt, p. 196 (pl. 48. 1).

[25] For discussions of these portraits, see Darbishire, p. 344; Parker, *Milton: A Biography*, pp. 1135–6; and John Rupert Martin, *The Portrait of John Milton at Princeton and its Place in Milton Iconography* (Princeton: Princeton University Library, 1961), and 'The Milton Portrait: Some Addenda', *Princeton University Library Chronicle*, 24 (1963), 168–73.

wrote *Paradise Lost*. Because he believes that Robert White's crayon drawing was finished shortly before Milton's death, he has added 'a little more Vigour' to his own print; Milton must be imagined as one who had been fair and 'Fresh Colour'd'. In his engraving and in the text of his biography, Richardson is therefore eager to reanimate and heighten White's drawing of Milton in old age so that we may view the more vigorous face of the writer at the zenith of his literary career.

But this is not all that the final engraving suggests, for if it attempts to portray Milton at a specific moment in his life, it also presents an idealized image of Milton as poet; and this, I think, is the face with which Richardson chiefly desires to acquaint us. Richardson tells us, for instance, that Milton was 'Blind, Infirm, and 52 Years Old' when he wrote *Paradise Lost*, which he persisted in completing despite 'Ill health, Blindness; Uneasy in his Mind, no doubt, on Occasion of the publick Affairs, and of his Own' (pp. 275, 289). But the engraved portrait shows a relatively composed and even youthful face, with a slight smile playing about his lips. And the crown of laurels, moreover, is not in the original painting; he has added it, he tells us in a somewhat enigmatic remark, because of the justification provided in lines from Milton's *Mansus* (which he appends beneath the bust), 'not what Otherwise would have been Imagin'd. All the World has given it him long since' (p. 202). Richardson thus conceives of Milton as the true successor of Virgil, Dante, and Petrarch; only those who prate about pride or ambition, he argues, will deny Milton the tribute he deserves. And like his biography of Milton, Richardson's engraved head of the poet strives to mediate between an honest, faithful representation of its subject—'the very man'—and a more idealized or ennobling conception of character or mind. Richardson's engraved frontispiece may well achieve a harmonious marriage of these often conflicting forces, but the text itself, the numerous treatises on pictorial theory, and the bulk of Richardson's other portraits of literary men reveal that the idealizing impulse was by far the stronger of the two.

Milton was a compelling force in Richardson's life, but perhaps of equal importance to him was his relationship with the most prominent poet of his age. This intriguing relationship—between sister arts, between brother artists—has recently been examined by Morris Brownell in his study of *Alexander Pope & the Arts of Georgian England*, and it is a necessary focus of much of Wimsatt's lengthy catalogue of the portraits of Pope. Richardson himself believed that his paintings and drawings of Pope were among his very best works. In an essay entitled 'Masters in Portraits' he wrote of himself that '*Richardson* etched several heads for Mr. Pope and others of his friends, they were slight, but spirited; Mr. Pope's profile is the best.'[26] Of central importance here is the relation between Richardson's portrait of Milton and his series of portraits of Pope, at least nine of which show Pope laureated, and many of which portray him in ancient dress.[27] This iconographical representation of the poet was actually begun by Kneller—and of course it was actively encouraged by Pope himself, who consigned the ivy to the critics and reserved the bays for the bards—but it was left to Richardson to suggest an even more radical vision in which separate likenesses would be blended together to form a composite portrait of the type of the poet.

In a pencil sketch dated 25 March 1738 (Plate 45), Richardson has attempted to merge his earlier, separate portraits of Milton and Pope. The result is a medallion portrait in which Pope's features and the full profile that normally characterizes his portraits have been combined with Milton's hair—even down to the detail of the locks falling on each brow. The inscription beneath the collar identifies Milton (in Greek), and the insignia, which Richardson had championed in his theoretical work, reads 'A. Pope, as Milton'. An even more daring experiment followed in the same year (Plate 46). In this etching of three heads we find (on the right) separate portraits of Milton and Pope, both executed in full profile; at the left appears a third head, laureated, and drawn in three-quarter profile (an intriguing compromise between the full profile usually associated with portraits of Pope and the full frontal model associated with those of Milton). In this composite portrait Richardson has not merely substituted Pope's features in place of Milton's, but has actually combined their features so that the resulting 'likeness', if we can continue to use that term, represents neither of these two figures. The portrait instead represents Richardson's notion of what the ideal poet would look like: surely he can be visualized by coalescing the images of the two greatest poets of the age, for Dryden had already suggested that Homer and Virgil had been merged in Milton:

> Three poets in three distant ages born,
> Greece, Italy, and England did adorn:
> The first in loftiness of thought surpast,
> The next in majesty; in both the last.
> The force of Nature could no further go,
> To make a third she join'd the former two.[28]

---

[26] *The Works of Jonathan Richardson*, 'new edition' (1792), 265–6.

[27] See Wimsatt, pls. 9. 1, 19(1), 23a, 26a, 27, 35, 36, 37(1), 54 (in 9.1 there is simply a green branch in the lower left-hand corner). Richardson wrote on the bottom of 23a: 'Your Friend but gives the Bay you had before, / Friendship wou'd fain, but Friendship Can no more.'

[28] Quoted, with Johnson's Latin translation, by Piozzi, *Anecdote* pp. 84–5.

Richardson, moreover, provides an ideal portrait in the literal sense that
he attempts to create a visual *idea* of the poet, an image that stands as only
an extreme of the kind of improvement he suggests in *The Science of a
Connoisseur*: to move from what is commonly or rarely seen 'to what never
Was, or will be in Fact, tho' we may easily *conceive* it Might be' (my
emphasis).[29] As he pointed out elsewhere, 'There are many Single Heads
which are Historical, and may be apply'd to several Stories';[30] and it is
interesting to note in this context that when De Quincey first came across
Richardson's engraved portrait of Milton, he thought that it was a
remarkably true likeness of Wordsworth.[31]

This idealized form of portraiture, moreover, was not restricted to
Richardson's depictions of Milton and Pope. He also experimented with
likenesses of Pope dressed in Chaucerian garb, and he dared, in one self-
portrait sketch at least, to portray himself with the same attendant crown
of bays (Plate 47). Richardson, we should remember, thought of himself
as a poet, and in his private fancies—in this pencil sketch and in some
verses he wrote on the recto—he represented himself in this great poetic
train:

> Yes Pope, yes Milton I am Bayes'd you see.
> But Why—go ask my Oracle, not Me:
> Shee, not Severe is Beautyfull, & Wise,
> She Thus Commanded me, & Thus it is.
> May you enjoy your plenitude of Fame!
> While Shee with Smiles embellishes my Name
> I ask not Your Applause, nor Censure Fear,
> I am Pope, Milton, Virgil, Homer Here.[32]

It is probably fair to say that Richardson lived at least as fully and perhaps
more richly in the literary worlds he celebrated than in his own formal
practice as a portraitist.[33] He saw himself as yet another descendant in this

[29] *The Science of a Connoisseur*, in *Two Treatises* (1719), 13.

[30] *The Whole Art of Criticism*, in *Two Treatises* (1719), 46; Richardson's examples are heads of boys
drawn by Parmeggiano and Leonardo, which he imagines as angels rejoicing at the birth of Christ. Cf.
his comment in *The Science of a Connoisseur* on the idea of an 'epitome': 'However Different we are from
Our Selves; Or One Man is from Another, Every Man is an Epitome of the Whole species' (p. 119).

[31] *Recollections of the Lakes and the Lake Poets*, ed. David Wright (Harmondsworth: Penguin, 1970),
140–1; De Quincey's comment was first pointed out by Darbishire, p. 344.

[32] Quoted by Wimsatt, p. 157; Lonsdale, 'Jonathan Richardson's *Morning Thoughts*', p. 182,
provides an interesting context for this fragment by linking it—and especially the 'Oracle' mentioned
here—to a Mrs Knapp, with whom Richardson enjoyed a brief friendship after his wife's death.

[33] An ambitious (and personal) approach to portraiture can also be found in six group portraits,
formerly in the collection of Karl Freund, in which Richardson celebrates the most prominent
scientists, sculptors, authors, musicians, painters, and architects of the early 18th cent. (Richardson
includes himself among the painters). For a description, see Horace Townsend, *The Ante Room of a
Georgian Library* (New York: privately printed, 1917).

distinguished lineage, and it was in fact his work on Milton's *Paradise Lost* that brought Richardson and his own son so closely together.

Richardson drew attention to the collaborative nature of his *Explanatory Notes and Remarks* in an infamous passage near the conclusion of his biographical narrative. Here Richardson playfully explains how he has been able to comment on Milton's classical learning even though he, as a portrait-painter, possesses formal knowledge of neither Greek nor Latin: 'I have them because a Part of Me Possesses them to Whom I can recur at Pleasure, just as I have a Hand when I would Write or Paint, Feet to Walk, and Eyes to See.' His son, he explains, is his learning:

as I am That to Him which He has Not; We make One Man; and Such a Compound Man (what Sort of One Soever He is whom We make) May Probably, produce what no Single Man Can. When therefore I, in my Own Person talk of Things which in my Separate Capacity I am known to be a Stranger to, let Me be Understood as the Complicated *Richardson*. (pp. 312–13)

We have already seen this form of authorial collaboration in Richardson's frequent injunctions to Milton to speak for himself; what also emerges from this passage is Richardson's conception of a 'Compound Man', the biographical equivalent of his composite profiles of Milton and Pope. But what sets an actual, historical character apart from an ideal character is, of course, each man's inability to fuse these disparate qualities within himself. Richardson perceives this weakness even in Milton, whom he gently criticizes for his excessive severity as a father and husband: 'He should Thus as it were Set up Another Person within Himself, and let Him make Proper Abatements to his Own Laws of Perfection' (p. 225).

Richardson celebrated his relationship with his own son—whom he named after himself, portrayed in countless drawings, and referred to as his 'Telescope'—in an unusual painting discovered by John Kerslake thirty years ago (Plate 48).[34] Here the biographer, on the left, and his son, in the centre, are allowed to stand in the presence of Milton himself, depicted, of course, in the format of the Bayfordbury portrait. Like the combined portraits of Milton and Pope, this painting may strike us as merely odd or whimsical; to his contemporaries, had they seen it, it must have seemed downright grotesque. But in these unusual experiments and in his unorthodox biography of Milton, Richardson was at last able to strive towards that idealized and exalted notion of character about which

[34] See J. F. Kerslake, 'The Richardsons and the Cult of Milton', *Burlington Magazine*, 99 (1957), 23–4, who also offers several acute observations on the relationship between Richardson's *Explanatory Notes* and his work as a painter; and Piper, *Image of the Poet*, 66–72, who sees this painting as a 'secular restatement of the donor portrait' and who emphasizes Richardson's affirmation here of the equal status that should be given to the painter as well as the poet.

he speculated so often in his theoretical works and which he was largely unable to achieve in his ordinary practice as a portraitist. The portrait-painter's most difficult task, he wrote in his first treatise on painting, is to raise character in a justifiable manner: 'Life would be an Insipid thing indeed if we never saw, or had Ideas of any thing but what we Commonly see.'[35]

ii. North: A Life of 'Perpetual Observation'

Like Richardson, Roger North was a biographer by impulse—perhaps even obsession—rather than by design. Like Boswell, whom he forshadows in so many ways, he was a lawyer whose fame now rests on the ambitious literary work of his later years, when he wrote at length about himself and about those 'near friends' to whom he had become 'a shadow'.[36] He chose as his subjects those three elder brothers whose concerns had in fact sharply overshadowed his own. Of his eldest brother, Charles, who inherited the family's modest estate as the fifth Lord North, Roger has little to say, simply noting at one point that 'We had, at that time, the misfortune of an elder brother's importunity, who was not contented that any of our common concerns should pass quietly and smooth . . .' (ii. 172). The other members of this family were left to shift for themselves, pursuing these 'common concerns' with uncommon industry and preserving unusually close fraternal ties. The most illustrious, Francis, later Lord Guilford, Roger repeatedly refers to as their 'best brother', the 'sheet anchor' of their lives, the 'bond to the fagot: he kept us together and was as a common father to us' (iii. 141). Francis was one of the most successful lawyers and judges during the Restoration period, rising to become Solicitor-General, Attorney-General, Lord Chief Justice of the Common Pleas, and finally Lord Keeper of the Great Seal. Whatever success Roger had as a lawyer he ascribed to the training and preferment he received from Francis. A third brother, Dudley, followed a naturally restless temperament by becoming a wealthy merchant in Smyrna and Constantinople; when he returned to England, he served as a Sheriff of London, Commissioner of the Customs, and a Commissioner of the Treasury; he was knighted in 1682. Roger and Dudley were particularly close, and it has recently been shown that Roger assisted his brother

---

[35] Richardson, *Essay*, p. 183; cf. Reynolds, *Discourses*, p. 244: 'the object and intention of all the Arts is to supply the natural imperfection of things, and often to gratify the mind by realising and embodying what never existed but in the imagination.'

[36] North, *Lives*, i. 400. Further references to this edition (for the lives of Francis, Dudley, and Roger) appear in the text.

in writing and revising his influential *Discourses on Trade* (1691).[37] A fourth brother, John, served as Roger's tutor at Cambridge and eventually became Professor of Greek and Master of Trinity.[38]

But Roger's own accomplishments, even as a lawyer, were not meagre. He flourished under the benign influence of his best brother, becoming King's Counsel, solicitor to James II when he was still Duke of York, and finally Attorney-General to James's Queen Mary. As a non-juror he was forced to abandon his career in the early 1690s, but his earnings as a lawyer enabled him to buy and improve an estate in Norfolk (where he eventually married, and raised his own family) and to satisfy his need to explore an impressive range of personal interests—and to write about them. Retirement agreed very well with Roger North. He continued to pursue his lifelong interest in music, eventually becoming 'without question the most important native writer in English on the subject of the "science" of music'.[39] His interest in architecture, which had earlier led to his design of the new gate for the Middle Temple and to a friendship with Sir Christopher Wren, later culminated in the 'metamorfosis' of his own estate, Rougham, and in meticulous plans and descriptions of these improvements. His treatise on building has recently been characterized as 'probably the most detailed account of the planning and building of a seventeenth-century house in English architectural literature' and 'the most entertaining treatise on its subject in the English language'.[40] Similar essays were written on perspective, Hobbes's theory of government, legal education, etymology, the barometer, and numerous moral and social subjects.[41]

By the time of his death in 1734, however (the year in which Richardson published his life of Milton), few of North's works had appeared in print, the best known being an essay on fishponds.[42] The burden of preparing his manuscripts for the press fell to his second son, Montagu, who published the massive *Examen*, a Tory rebuttal of Kennett White's Whig

[37] See William Letwin, 'The Authorship of Sir Dudley North's *Discourses on Trade*', *Economica*, 18, no. 69 (Feb. 1951), 35–56.

[38] A fifth brother, Montagu, assisted Dudley North in his career as a merchant.

[39] Jamie Croy Kassler, *The Science of Music in Britain, 1714–1830: A Catalogue of Writings, Lectures and Inventions* (New York: Garland, 1979), ii. 800. See also *Roger North on Music*, ed. John Wilson (London: Novello, 1959), p. xxv.

[40] *Of Building: Roger North's Writings on Architecture*, ed. Howard Colvin and John Newman (Oxford: Clarendon Press, 1981), pp. xv–xvi.

[41] Several of these essays are printed by F. J. M. Korsten, *Roger North (1651–1734) Virtuoso and Essayist: A Study of His Life and Ideas, Followed by an Annotated Edition of a Selection of His Unpublished Essays* (Amsterdam: APA–Holland Univ. Press, 1981).

[42] For the most detailed account of North's publishing history, see Korsten, *Roger North*, pp. 24–5. All of North's works were published anonymously.

interpretation of Restoration politics, in 1740, the life of Francis in 1742, and the lives of Dudley and John in 1744. An autobiographical sketch, entitled *Notes of Mee*, was printed in 1887, and the essays on music and architecture have had to wait even longer for publication. The 'General Preface' to the *Lives of the Norths*, in which he clearly justifies his reputation as the most important biographical theorist before Johnson, was not published in its entirety until 1984.

North's pronouncements on the art of biography crystallize many of the attitudes that were slowly emerging during the seventeenth century, and which we have glimpsed in writers as diverse as Walton and Aubrey. The history of private lives, he argues, is much more beneficial than that of nations and public figures, for it addresses our 'own proper concerns'.[43] He asks us to turn to the 'emergent concerns of human life, to be gathered from the patterns of private men, who have at their great risk proved divers ways of living, and it may be have found out the best at last, and possibly suffered by their mistakes' (p. 64). He praises several seventeenth-century biographers, including Walton, because in their works 'we find the man at home as well as abroad'.[44] If public figures are to be depicted, their private characters should also be revealed: 'What signifies it to us how many battles Alexander fought? It were more to the purpose to say how often he was drunk, and then we might from the ill consequences to him incline to be sober' (p. 63). There is thus a moral focus in proper life-writing, but it should proceed from lively examples of virtue *and* vice, 'fit to be depicted in the strongest colours', and not merely from panegyric or the venom of personal prejudice (p. 64). A biographer must be accurate and he must be impartial; but at the same time he must know his subjects well, must be 'in almost continual conversation or converse' with them, 'and so attached to the very persons, that little of importance in their whole lives could escape their notice'. Such a relationship between the biographer and his subject, in which they 'live almost at bed and board together, and communicate to each other their most recondite thoughts and designs' (p. 80), is in fact an accurate description of North's relations with his own three brothers, with each of whom he lived at some period in his life. And this unusual degree of intimacy will allow the biographer to substantiate his generalizations with examples, anecdotes, scraps of conversation, extracts from his subject's written works, entries in his journals, and other 'monuments' of the self. 'Friends may, but things will

[43] Millard, p. 51. All quotations from the 'General Preface' or the *Life of Dr. John North* are taken from this edition, with references provided in the text.
[44] BL Add. MS 32525, fos. 14ʳ–14ᵛ; quoted by Korsten, *Roger North*, p. 95.

not prevaricate or falsify,' North cautions his readers, 'and no description can come up to the force and expression of them' (p. 80).

Additional theoretical statements about biography, some of which are even more impressive in their relative modernity, are carefully couched in terms of their parallels with portrait-painting. It would be fair to say, in fact, that no biographer made more consistent use of the parallel between these two arts than North, whose knowledge of painting was almost as substantial as his understanding of music and architecture. Sir Peter Lely was a close friend of his brother Francis, with whom he traded portraits for legal advice. When Lely died, Roger became his chief executor—and later his son's guardian—and even lived in his former house. His highly successful handling of the sale of Lely's effects—including his paintings, sketches, books, and famous collection of pictures and prints—drew considerable attention at the time and became the focus of the final chapter of Roger's autobiography. As part of his duties, North kept a careful tabulation of 10,000 items in Lely's estate, each entry carefully noted and described by one who was as much a connoisseur as he was a lawyer. He was also proficient at drawing: his architectural designs reveal a competent draughtsman, 'well able to envisage a complicated building in all its dimensions'.[45] More creative exercises, however, seemed to fall beyond his reach:

I have endeavoured, but for want of early practice under a good instruction, could not attain the art of designing figures as painters do, and left off all attempt towards it, saving an antique head, festoons, capitals, and such common decorations of architecture; but for the regular part of the design, so as to give the true profile in proportion all manner of ways, none were readier than myself nor more exact. (iii. 63)

North's comments on art reveal that he had read widely in contemporary theory, especially Richardson's treatises; he was also a persistent collector, boasting at least 200 paintings when he settled at Rougham.[46]

At least one of the parallels North draws between biography and portrait-painting points to the potential superficiality of both arts. In condemning 'the many sketches or profiles of great men's lives' that commonly pretend to be 'synoptical, or *multum in parvo*', North suggests that we may 'walk in a gallery, and extract as fair an account from the air of their countenances or the cut of their whiskers'.[47] But this is a form of biography that North, with his preference for the exhaustive and the detailed, could neither praise nor practise. His own version of biography,

---

[45] *Of Building*, p. 155.   [46] See Korsten, *Roger North*, pp. 26, 88–9.   [47] Millard, p. 63.

with its focus on the inner life of its subject, will necessarily lead to an examination of what might otherwise be considered trivial or irrelevant. In his *Life of Francis North*, he states that 'a life should be a picture; which cannot be good if the peculiar features whereby the subject is distinguished from all others are left out' (i. 100). This emphasis on the uniqueness as well as the typical (and therefore imitable) nature of his subject—which seemingly combines the focus of an Aubrey with that of a Walton—dictates that 'scars and blemishes as well as beauties ought to be expressed; otherwise it is but an outline filled up with lilies and roses'. Later in the same biography, when forced once again to defend his treatment of minutiae, North remarks that he fancies himself a 'picture-drawer',

aiming to give the same image to a spectator as I have of the thing itself which I desire should here be represented. As, for instance a tree, in the picture whereof the leaves and minor branches are very small and confused, and give the artist more pain to describe than the solid trunk and greater branches. But if these small things were left out it would make but a sorry picture of a tree. History is as it were, the portrait or lineament and not a bare index or catalogue of things done; and without the how and the why all history is jejune and unprofitable. (i. 327)

This insistence on realistic representation must, however, be set off against North's awareness that no form of portraiture can capture the full complexity or entire truth about a man. In his 'General Preface' he admits that 'all history of one sort or other is like painting, never exactly true; that which comes nearest is best . . .' (p. 77). Some biographers, he writes in *The Life of Dr. John North*, have written lives based entirely on 'formal remains' and traditional hearsay: 'So painters copy from obscure draughts half obliterated, whereof no member, much less the entire resemblance, is to be found' (p. 94). But conscientious biography, even if it is never exactly true, may nevertheless animate these mortal remains, especially if it is pursued with a creative flair. And thus North authorizes the use of techniques that are normally 'brought to adorn fiction . . . that is, choice of words, charming periods, invention of figures, interspersion of sentences, and facetious expressions'.[48] These are the elements of art that lend colour, vividness, drama, *enargeia* to the depiction of individual lives.

In his portraits of famous men, North is therefore careful to augment his even-handed treatment of their characters by introducing a physical description. His portrayal of Chief Justice Saunders is among his most successful:

[48] Millard, pp. 59–60.

As to his person, he was very corpulent and beastly; a mere lump of morbid flesh. He used to say, 'by his troggs,' (such a humorous way of talking he affected) 'none could say he wanted issue of his body for he had nine in his back.' He was a fetid mass that offended his neighbours at the bar in the sharpest degree. Those whose ill fortune it was to stand near him were confessors, and, in summertime, almost martyrs. This hateful decay of his carcase came upon him by continual sottishness; for, to say nothing of brandy, he was seldom without a pot of ale at his nose or near him. (i. 294)

North makes Saunders come to life by forcing us to see, hear, and smell him. The biographer invents his own figures (confessors, martyrs), interpolates his own running commentary in the middle of Saunders's sentence, and allows us to relish his subject's own facetious expressions. And when he later turns to a more general interpretation of Saunders's character, he draws upon this portrait once more by emphasizing how other features of this extraordinary man easily compensated for his lump of morbid flesh: 'He had nothing of rigid or austere in him. If any near him at the bar, grumbled at his stench, he ever converted the complaint into content and laughing with the abundance of his wit' (i. 295).

In his biography of John North, Roger muses several times on the possible discrepancy between a man's physical appearance and his essential, underlying character.

His temperature of body and austere course of life were ill matched, and his complexion agreed with neither. For his face was always tincted with a fresh colour, and his looks vegete and sanguine, and as some used to jest, his features were scandalous, as showing rather a *madame en travestie* than a bookworm. (p. 139)

This florid complexion was noticeable even when John was young, and in describing the young scholar North introduces an interesting account of how his portrait was painted by a Mr Blemwell, who 'was allowed of by Lely to have had a very good judgment in the art of picture, but his performances were not equal to his skill' (p. 100). The biographer appeals to this portrait (Plate 49), then in his possession, 'for demonstration of what I have alleged concerning his grave disposition. The countenance is modest and composed, and copied from pure nature, wherein nothing is owing to the painter, for it was very like him' (p. 100). And having introduced this painting as corroborative evidence in his own account, North then reverses his strategy by suggesting that 'this short relation'—

his own portrait of John—'may serve to interpret the bizarre posture and habit expressed in that picture' (pp. 100–1).[49]

North particularly values this painting because his brother would never sit for another one—not even to Lely. This early portrait thus serves as an appropriate introduction to a motif that pervades Roger's reading of John's life: his unusual modesty, his insistence on leaving behind him as few traces of his personal existence as possible, his tendency 'to hold all within himself till he was entirely satisfied that no slip or oversight might give disadvantage to his cause or himself, lest any less guarded words or expressions should escape him' (p. 138). Much to Roger's dismay, there-fore, John consigned all but one of his manuscripts 'in lumps as innocent martyrs to the fire' (p. 134). No official or private portraits could be commissioned for his college or his family, 'And what was very odd,' Roger adds, 'he would not leave the print in his bed where he had lain remain undefaced' (p. 138). As a memorial in the ante-chapel at Trinity he allowed 'nothing significant but *J. N.* upon a small stone over him. He was desirous that if he could not leave somewhat behind him worthy to be remembered, of which (as I have shown) he never was satisfied, not to be remembered at all' (p. 161).

Roger's history of his brother's life thus serves as a particularly poignant example of the confrontation that may emerge between a recalcitrant subject and an eager biographer, especially one who, like Aubrey, treasured up what he could salvage from the remains of past time. And it is characteristic of North that when he meditated upon the pleasures of a contemplative and observant life, he often associated these qualities with the 'science of picture', of which a complete understanding flows from 'perpetual observation, instruction, and variety of experience; and an artist's whole life is little enough for gathering a competent qualification to warrant his judgment' (i. 392). Francis North had a 'good taste of picture' but, Roger adds, 'was a minor critic till his acquaintance and association with Sir Peter Lely was embraced; and then he began to see how little he understood of the matter' (i. 392, 393). Similarly, in his *Notes of Mee*, North excuses Lely's lack of business sense by reflecting on 'how arts and business are like contraries, and will not consist *in eodem subjecto*'. Art, he argues, 'fills a man's life and thought, and he can no more endure business than a man of business can endure the minute phantasms of an artist' (iii. 190).

What then are we to make of Roger's own life, of his own career as a double agent, in which a successful stint at court and at the bar was

[49] Part of this line is missing in Millard.

succeeded by a retirement of over forty-five years in which he turned most of his energies to music, architecture, landscape gardening, writing, and contemplating those paintings by Lely that he would not 'change for some I had seen of Vandyke, no, barring relation' (iii. 190)? The answer, I suggest, lies in North's ability to bridge the gap between business and art by drawing upon the experiences of his early years—his rigorous legal training, his knowledge of men's characters under stress, his 'eye and ear witness' to turbulent times and to the fluctuating careers of public men— when he himself retired to a life of private pleasures and imaginative reconstructions. The pattern of his own life, in other words, influenced not only his preference for personal history, or the private history of public characters, but also forced North to look critically at how various men reconciled their public responsibilities or desire for fame with their domestic happiness and peace of mind. It is not simply that North preferred private histories because they afforded his readers with useful models for instruction. In his view, the personal lives of his subjects were valuable because it was precisely there—retired to their studies, or drawing-rooms, or gardens—that they lived their lives most fully.

We therefore often notice an excited and expansive note in North's prose when he can reveal his subject in his private character. He can barely wait to bring his brother Dudley home from Constantinople, and then, after Dudley's various public commissions, to secure him in the 'pure privacy' of his family and familiar surroundings:

> But now we have our merchant, sheriff, alderman, commissioner, &c. at home with us, a private person divested of all his mantlings; and we may converse freely with him in his family and by himself without clashing at all against any concern of the public. (ii. 234)

Here, North argues, it may be possible to 'show the best side of his character', which he then skilfully does by recounting the warm and bantering and playful times he shared in his brother's house. Retirement also agreed well with Sir Dudley, who, 'scraping a stick or turning a piece of wood', was 'incomparably better pleased than he had been in all the stages of his life before' (ii. 245). It is a mortifying speculation, Roger continues, that of all the employments of this man's life, only this innocent pastime is 'really worth taking up'. And yet the slavery of our nature is such that this manner of life must be despised, 'and all the rest with the attendant evils of vexation, disappointments, dangers, loss of health, disgraces, envy and what not of torment, be admitted'. And for those, like the Lord Keeper, who cannot divest themselves of their heavy responsibilities, the occasional retreat will still provide consolation: 'O what a difference between his own family, friends, and relations, and the court!' (i. 349).

There is naturally a tendency in this view of human life to value public achievements only so far as they are consonant with private satisfaction and happiness, and these North specifically associates with a life that is not 'spun out in pain, want, misery, contempt, and sorrow' (iii. 150).[50] The central word for this condition in North's vocabulary is 'ease': ease from physical pain, financial pressures, mental strife; an ease of the spirit and of the imagination. Some of North's liveliest writing is devoted to the description of public events of which he was an eyewitness—the death of Charles II, the burning of the Middle Temple, the delivery of the Great Seal—but episodes of a far more serene nature, depicting his intense personal contentment, also etch themselves upon our memories. Consider, for example, this verbal picture of a supper upon an island in the Tyne:

In short, all circumstances taken together, the cool of the evening, the verdant flat of the island with wood dispersed upon it and water curling about us, view of the hills on both sides of the river, the good appetites, best provisions, and a world of merry stories of the Scots (which by the way makes a great part of the wit in those parts), made the place very agreeable, where every one walked after his fancy and all were pleased. (i. 175)

Or the marvellous narrative describing Dudley's return to London, when, in a reversal of their normal roles, Roger played the part of *cicerone* to his older brother, who marvelled at the sights: 'I, like an old dame with a young damsel, by conducting him had the pleasure of seeing them over again myself' (ii. 237). Or this nostalgic sketch of a day upon the water:

And thus, passing alternately from one entertainment to another, we sat out eight whole hours and scarce knew what time was past. For the day proved cool, the gale brisk, air clear, and no inconvenience to molest us, nor wants to trouble our thoughts, neither business to importune, nor formalities to tease us; so that we came nearer to a perfection of life there than I was ever sensible of otherwise. (iii. 32)

North implies (and most of his readers would surely agree) that scenes such as these occur too infrequently in our lives, and when they do they tend to be clustered in one's youth or old age. These are demarcations to

---

[50] For a highly critical treatment of North's values, see T. A. Birrell, 'Roger North and Political Morality in the Later Stuart Period', *Scrutiny*, 17 (1951), 282–98, who stresses North's rejection of social obligations and consequent cynicism and despair (p. 297).

which North repeatedly draws our attention, often by commenting on the different 'epochs' in his subject's life. He normally associates each '*epocha*' with a stage of development or accomplishment. The biography of Lord Guilford is thus constructed in terms of the four stages in Francis's legal career.[51] We discover an epoch or crisis in Dudley's life when he resolves never to become indebted again, when he leaves Smyrna for Constantinople, when he returns to London, and when he retires. John, who proceeds by easy degrees within the church and university, must nevertheless face the trauma of governing his spirited colleagues. Roger's own epochs are also clearly marked: the moment at which he began 'to have a sense of myself', and thus of his difference from other young boys; his arrival in London; the rebuilding of the Middle Temple; his appointment as King's Counsel; or, most vividly, 'my first flight in practice, . . . under my brother, which was a crisis like the loss of a maidenhead . . .' (iii. 90). Roger's greatest crisis, however, remained the death of his best brother, 'and with him all my life, hope, and joys' (iii. 188). North in fact approaches this event in the very terms Freud was to use to describe a man's response to the death of his father: 'But after his death I was turned up to shift in the world as well as I could; and this I make another great crisis of my life, for from henceforward all my actions were both really and in appearance my own' (iii. 194).

North also sees these various crises as forming part of a larger pattern in his subject's life. In the 'General Preface' he wishes that biographers would delineate 'in lively examples the precipitous steps and dangerous meanders of youth, the difficulties of riper years, and the fondness of old age, and where one may see distinctly the early application of some persons to proper employments, with the eventual prosperities attending them, as by what small beginnings they advanced to great estates, with the methods and true causes of it stated' (p. 64). These are moral grounds, of course, for examining the stages in a man's life with such care, but North is also intrigued by the early influences that help determine an individual's character. Like Boswell, he sometimes views the child as the man in miniature: John appears to us as a scholar almost from birth, and Dudley is early headstrong and precipitous. But we find, at the same time, a more complex speculation on North's part on how the accidental experiences of youth emerge much later in the actions of mature men. Thus he ruminates on how his own lack of clearheadedness—even as he writes—may have

---

[51] For a recent commentary on structure and characterization in this biography, see Hamilton E. Cochrane, 'The Man of Law in Eighteenth-Century Biography: The *Life of Francis North*', *Studies in Eighteenth-Century Culture*, 16 (1986), 139–48.

been caused by childhood diseases, or, more astutely, on how his early assimilation of royalist discourse, 'though not much minded by me, might sink and make an impression so as to determine my early inclination, and that goes a great way in the future conduct of life'. 'Such little accidents,' he writes, 'when placed on men that come forwarder in the world than I could pretend to, have great influence in the great revolutions and troubles of the world' (iii. 19).

The sense of development that North discovers in men's lives is also open to an eventual reversal. He is troubled, for instance, by a sudden change in character during the Lord Keeper's final sickness. 'All that was peculiarly good in his humour left him. He concerned himself strangely about his economy and the abuses of it', treating his family as if they were 'inmates' in his house (i. 349–50). A similar reversal assailed his brother John after he had partially recovered from a severe illness. In Lytton Strachey's amused retelling of the story, 'He, who had been so noted for his austerities, now tossed off, with wild exhilaration, glass after glass of the strongest sherry; the dry ascetic had become a convert to the golden gospel of *la dive bouteille*.'[52] North shares Strachey's sense of irony in this metamorphosis, but he nevertheless argues that even though a man may lose 'his judgment of true values, and relapse into a sort of puerility . . . his moral character, that is will to good or evil, remain[s] unaltered' (p. 155). He also believes that these reversals have been caused by the heavy and, in his mind, unnecessary burdens of public life. Thus the passing of the Great Seal to his brother Francis marks the culmination of his brilliant career as a lawyer, 'but, in truth (and as his lordship understood) it was the decadence of all the joy and comfort of his life; and, instead of a felicity, as commonly reputed, it was a disease like a consumption which rendered him heartless and dispirited, till death came which only could complete his cure' (i. 253). A similar moral is reserved for Chief Justice Saunders, and for John when he is appointed Master of Trinity: 'But after this preferment, than which nothing could have more nicely suited his desires, he fell under such gnawing cares and anxieties that he had small joy of his life; and it was really shortened thereby . . .' (ii. 299).

These stages of growth and decline are reinforced by North's preference for natural, organic metaphors. He refers to himself as 'a plant of a slow growth, and when mature but slight wood, and of a fleshy fruit' (iii. 103). Francis, on the other hand, flourished as a young lawyer: 'In the

---

[52] 'The Life, Illness, and Death of Dr. North', in *Portraits in Miniature and Other Essays* (New York: Harcourt, 1931), 39.

process of this stage of his lordship's life, his condition was like that of a plant set in a proper soil, growing up from small beginnings into expanded employment; so much that one would think it scarce possible for one man to find time to dispatch the affairs of it' (i. 121). Dudley, the tenacious merchant, would brook no nonsense in his fellow traders; he was 'a thorn in the sides of the foolish and malicious . . . a creature that had sharp claws and scaly sides' (ii. 40). Francis and his enemy Lord Sunderland were like animals that, 'out of a contrariety of their natures, have a mutual antipathy and can scarce bear the sight of each other'. Sunderland's speeches against him were 'as venomous as the deadly nightshade . . .' (i. 304). John, 'like a flourishing fruit tree, blossomed fairly, and then underwent a fatal blight that destroyed fruit and tree altogether . . .' (p. 127). Later Roger describes him as a 'high-flying fowl with one wing cut. The creature offers to fly, and knows no cause why he should not, but always comes with a side-turn down to the ground' (p. 156).[53]

North's emphasis on epochs and crises, patterns of development and reversal, metaphors of growth and decline, is ultimately tied to his understanding of men's essential characteristics and their capacity to improve them. Of Saunders he says that 'He was born but not bred a gentleman, for his mind had an extraordinary candour, but his low and precarious beginnings led him into a sordid way of living . . .' (iii. 91). In reviewing his own abilities (and thinking of Demosthenes with the stones in his mouth), he offers the more general observation that 'a man's faculties may be mended, but not made, by industry and practice' (iii. 23). Here, in one of the most important passages in North's entire works, he once again invokes a parallel with portraiture: a man's nature, like 'a statue or picture, may receive a polishing or neatness from the statuary or painter. But if the draught of the figure be naught, all the labour will not mend it; and at last, however finished, it shall be but a lame piece.' Industry and art alone will not do; a man's talents must be evident before they can be nourished. Contemplating his own 'incurable confusion', North finds himself contented not to 'drudge to meliorate a bad plant, which might perhaps be so determined very much by laziness, of which my schoolmaster so long since accused me' (iii. 23). Providence, and the love of his three brothers, he concludes, have provided him with whatever happiness and success he has enjoyed.

---

[53] Millard (p. 33) points out North's use of bird imagery throughout this biography.

iii. North and Biographical Form

However much he may have thought of himself as a bad plant or lame piece, North's considerable skill and industry as a biographer, if not as a lawyer, can hardly be underestimated. But even as we continue to admire his obvious virtues as a private historian—his racy, colloquial language, vivid character-sketches, and narrative skills; his sense of the shape of men's lives; his reliance on the hard bedrock of 'fact'—we must also examine his struggles with the method and form of biographical writing. If we consider each of the lives separately, we can see how carefully North adjusted his narrative to the materials at his disposal as well as to the kind of life he was writing. But an analysis of the four lives together (and of the *Examen* as well) reveals an extraordinary amount of repetition and cross-reference, which tends to vitiate the force of individual parts and of the ambitious project as a whole. I want to suggest that the very scope of North's biographical enterprise presented him with unusual problems, and that these difficulties with scale and coherence are related to dilemmas he faced in the local texture of his work.

North left behind a staggering collection of unpublished manuscripts when he died in 1734.[54] Sixty-eight manuscript volumes are devoted to his writings on miscellaneous subjects, many of which have not yet been published. Thirty additional volumes contain his biographical works. These manuscripts reveal that North was a constant and meticulous reviser: the *Life of Francis North* exists in six versions, each a reworking of its predecessor; there are four versions of the life of John, two of the biography of Dudley, four of the 'General Preface', and one of the *Notes of Mee*. The manuscript evidence also suggests that North wrote and revised these lives over a long period of time, and that he usually worked on them concurrently (sometimes having three or four in hand at once). *The Life of Francis North* was primarily written during the years 1710–18, but North toiled at this particular biography for thirty or forty years. The final version consists of the life in four manuscript volumes, with six additional volumes containing selections from Francis's own writings. When Montagu North published the biography in 1742, however, he understandably omitted the six-volume supplement and, less forgivably, pruned his father's own work, often omitting his most caustic and salacious observations.

The biographies in their published form constantly suggest that North

---

[54] My account is based on P. T. Millard, 'The Chronology of Roger North's Main Works', *Review of English Studies*, n.s. 24 (1973), 283–94, and on his recent edition, pp. 38–42.

intended each of these narratives to represent part of a larger design—much as the actual lives of these brothers did—and in the 'General Preface' he announced that he would begin with John and end with Francis, 'and so as I rise in the eldership, I shall also advance in the dignity of the subject' (p. 82). There are numerous cross-references from one biography to another, and even the historical *Examen* is invoked as a general background against which these private lives must be viewed. Thus in the *Life of Sir Dudley North* Roger remarks that he

shall not here give any account of this plot of Oates's, nor of the monster brought forth by it, called *Ignoramus*; nor of the troubles about choosing sheriffs of London and Middlesex, because a particular account is given of all these in the Examen, and the Life of this gentleman's best brother, the Lord Keeper North. It may be found also in the same Life, how this gentleman was persuaded to hold sheriff; I shall therefore omit that also, and proceed to some particulars, not so exactly related there. (ii. 181)[55]

In many places, however, North repeats episodes in which more than one of his brothers were involved, especially if the event is important in his own life as well. These retellings of the same story are often similar to his method of manuscript revision, in which successive versions tend to become fuller and more dramatically rendered.[56] But North also recasts these passages so that they are consistent with the tone and perspective of the particular life he is writing. Here are his two versions of the Lord Keeper's arrival home with the Great Seal, the first from his autobiography, the second from the *Life of Francis North*.

And so it fell out, that after the death of Nottingham he came home one evening with his load in the coach—the Great Seal. And after the stir was over, and we came to ourselves, and fell to discourse as usual, I perceived him full of passion up to the brim, to a degree as to hinder even his utterance, and at last to fly out in terms of passion and concern, that men should think him worthy that charge and withal so weak as to be imposed upon as they attempted to do. When a man's heart is full a small thing will heat and inflame it. The *crepa cuore* was, to be removed from a quiet honourable station in the law, which was a. b. c. to him, with profit enough, to a post of first ministry in the State, full of trouble, form, noise, and danger; in no sort agreeable with his temper, nor very profitable. (iii. 163)

---

[55] Millard (p. 29) notes that North included brief sketches of Francis and Dudley in the *Examen*, 'further proof that North started out with a complete concept of his subject in his mind'.

[56] See Millard, 'The Chronology of Roger North's Main Works', and James L. Clifford, 'Roger North and the Art of Biography', in *Restoration and Eighteenth-Century Literature: Essays in Honor of Alan Dugald McKillop*, ed. Carroll Camden (Chicago: Univ. of Chicago Press, 1963), 275–85.

The evening when he went upon this errand to Whitehall, some of us stayed in expectation of his coming home, which was not near ten; little doubting the change that was to happen. At last he came with more splutter than ordinary, divers persons (for honour) waiting upon him and others attending to wish him joy, and a rabble of officers, that belonged to the seal completing the crowd which filled his little house. His lordship by dispatching these incumbrances, got himself clear as fast as he could; and then I alone stayed with him. He took a turn or two in his dining-room and said nothing; by which I perceived his spirits were very much roiled; therefore I kept silence also expecting what would follow. There was no need of asking what news, when the purse with the great seal lay upon the table. At last his lordship's discourses and actions discovered that he was in a very great passion, such as may be termed agony; of which I never saw in him any like appearance since I first knew him. He had kept it in long; and, after he was free it broke out with greater force: and accordingly he made use of me to ease his mind upon. (i. 255–6)

It is probable that the first passage, from the autobiography, was also written first, although North continued to tinker with both works for some time. It is certainly more straightforward, both in its presentation of Francis's arrival and in its explanation of the reasons for his 'passion and concern'. The language is colloquial and energetic—'after the stir was over', 'up to the brim', 'to fly out', 'a. b. c. to him'—and his analysis of Francis's character is perhaps even more penetrating: 'When a man's heart is full a small thing will heat and inflame it.' The reasons for his brother's anger are also clearer here, for we learn that Francis is distressed not only by his shabby treatment over a pension but also by the certain decline in his income as he takes on even greater responsibilities. The second version is appropriately more dignified—specifying the 'incumbrances' that honoured him—and more dramatic in its use of suspense. We are not immediately told about 'the load in the coach', nor do we as quickly discover the causes of the Lord Keeper's 'agony', which is the focus of Roger's real narrative skill in this passage. At the same time, we find North aggrandizing his own presence here in a fashion that is unnecessary in the autobiography. 'I alone stayed with him', he tells us, so that Francis could make 'use of me' to ease his mind.

Like Boswell, North may have referred to his autobiographical writings as he wrote his more ambitious works; this would explain much of the repetition as well as the increased drama and grandeur in the longer narratives. In his autobiography, for instance, North presents a full character-sketch of Chief Justice Hale that includes an attack on Gilbert Burnet's biography ('Burnet has pretended to write his life, but wanted both information and understanding for such an undertaking'), a balanced judgement of Hale's virtues and failings, a Plutarchian 'collation' with the character of Saunders, and a last-minute reminder that Hale was a great admirer of Pomponius Atticus (iii. 93–102). In the sketch of Hale in the *Life of Francis North*, the attack on Burnet and the collation with Saunders have been omitted, the comparison with Atticus has been worked into a more integrated view of Hale's character, and the episode closes with a highly synoptic judgement of this complex man. Similarly, the character of Saunders in the biography of Francis becomes more detailed than in the autobiography, includes the famous description of Saunders's corpulent and redolent body, speculates more discreetly on the judge's relations with the couple he lived with, and emphasizes the manner in which he rose by dint of his own hard labour. But at the same time this extended narrative makes much less of the pattern of Saunder's life, in which 'preferment was an honour fatal to him; for from great labour, sweat, toil, and vulgar diet, he came to ease, plenty, and of the best, which he could not forbear, being luxurious in eating and drinking' (iii. 92).

While it is natural to assume a considerable amount of repetition between North's autobiography and the lives of his three brothers— works that he may never have intended to publish together—this alone does not explain the repetition that runs throughout the biographies themselves. North was, in fact, noticeably afraid of repeating himself too often in his narratives. In the biography of Francis, he writes that he 'must not enlarge upon these subjects here, lest I anticipate the proper place of them or, what is worse, repeat when I come there' (i. 143). But he was even more worried that he might forget to record everything that he knew about a subject. In writing of his legal apprenticeship, he confesses that 'I could never, though dealing in things of perfect familiarity to my mind, relate without omissions and oversights of considerable articles' (iii. 22). And after explaining the four-fold structure of his biography of the Lord Keeper, he remarks that, 'in this method, I hope to evacuate my mind of every matter and thing I know and can remember materially concerning his lordship' (i. 14–15). Similarly, in the 'General Preface', he notes that he will attempt to 'rectify want of art by *copia* of matter . . .' (p. 81).

This desire for fullness and accuracy—even at the possible cost of redundancy—is also tied to North's determination to reveal his subjects in every possible light, from every possible perspective (the private as well as the public, the harsh as well as the favourable). North thus makes use of an unprecedented variety of material in his work, including Dudley's account of his journey to the Middle East and his letters home to his brothers, and Francis's spiritual memoranda, which he called his '*speculums*'. These moral reminders are particularly interesting because they provided Francis—and thereby Roger's readers—with a means of peering within: 'as a man looks in a mirror in order to be acquainted with his outside; so by looking upon what was written in these papers, he might see his inside and have a thorough knowledge of the inner-man, his excellencies, and imperfections' (i. 419–20 n.). North also quotes extensively from the Lord Keeper's notes, often interpreting and amplifying them at great length. These notes are especially valuable, he argues, because they 'were the result of his thoughts and researches upon affairs then in agitation abroad and are like painters' first scratches, which commonly have more spirit than their more finished pieces . . .' (i. 15). By inserting these extracts, North believes that he will be able to provide both an 'interior and exterior' view of one 'great man's life and entire character'.

Materials such as these are invaluable to the biographer who wishes to convince his audience of the validity of his own interpretations, but they are rarely as engaging as the personal memories upon which the writer's own understanding is based. Sometimes, of course, these materials simply do not exist. In the troublesome case of John North, for example, Roger cautions that it will be difficult to 'retrieve' his character 'because he took express care that nothing real should remain whereby in after times he might be remembered, and my memory is now the repository of most that may be recovered of him' (pp. 94–5). And because so little is known, North will forsake the chronological format of his other biographies. As in his autobiography, which is structured in terms of the major interests as well as events in his life, North will here 'proceed in a style of familiar conversation, and as one engaged to answer such questions concerning our doctor as may be obviously demanded'. But even in the other lives chronology may pose a problem: not because the precise dates are missing, but because the narrative itself may take a different direction. In the *Life of Francis North*, Roger states at one point that he does not observe 'any order of time in the mention of these passages, nor do I intend it more in those that follow', because each of these events falls within the general epoch of Francis's life when he was a judge of the common law (i. 140). Only occasionally does his narrative fall silent because he cannot, for instance, account for the precise methods by which Dudley amassed his fortune (ii. 72) or remember the lively conversations he overheard when he and John visited the famous Dr Fell at Oxford (p. 119).

A more noticeable inconsistency emerges when North must decide how he is to present himself in his brother's narratives. Normally his solution is a graceful vacillation between objective, third-person narration and the more personal and vivid accounts written in the first person. The anomalies occur when North refers to *himself* in the third person, as in this passage from the life of the Lord Keeper: 'His Lordship having taken that advanced post, [designed] to benefit a relation (the honourable Roger North,) who was a student in the law and kept him company . . . And that young gentleman instantly went to work . . .' (i. 95). Sometimes he does not actually name himself: 'While the doctor lived in Jesus College and was fellow, he had but one solitary pupil, and that youth discovered to him an inclination to know what the mathematics were' (p. 130). And in at least one instance North refers to himself in the first and third persons at the same time: 'But these are remote instances; I ought to come nearer home and take an account of his benevolence to his paternal relations. His youngest brother (the honourable Roger North) was designed by his father for the civil law . . .' (i. 399). North may have believed that this form of presentation was appropriate when he depicted himself in a dependent situation (as Francis's beneficiary, or as John's pupil), but it nevertheless remains an awkward device in an otherwise smooth and assured narrative.

These local difficulties, often caused by a disparity in perspective, are ultimately tied to the general problem North encountered in designing his work, in envisioning it as a whole. The separate lives are carefully—painstakingly—revised and recast, and numerous passages in each of them are brilliantly executed. But any comprehensive reading of the works—even in their sometimes drastically pruned editions—reveals considerable tediousness, inconsistency, and occasional redundancy.[57] We should remember that North was particularly interested in the questions of perspective and method, that he wrote essays on these subjects. In his treatise on building, he speculated that there was a certain architectural habit that involved 'conceiving in your mind things not existent but *in potentia*; and comparing them with your occasions, and your scituation; and after bringing them to a more permanent idea, by draught, so as to take further deliberation, alteration and amendment'.[58]

---

[57] Millard (pp. 27–8) talks about North's 'prolixity' and his open and sometimes uncontrolled form.
[58] *Of Building*, p. 4.

But whereas North may well have been adept at this kind of visual conceptualizing, he suffered limitations in his verbal formulations. Speaking in his autobiography of his natural 'confusion and disorder of thought', he notes that he 'was ever pleased to be writing somewhat or other, and striving at method and clearness, but could not attain so as to perfect any one design' (iii. 21). And then, in a fascinating passage that reflects his early philosophical interests, he confesses that his 'great aim hath been at a system of nature, upon the Cartesian or rather mechanical principles, believing all the common phenomena of nature might be resolved into them . . .'.[59] But all that he gained was 'a discovery that I did not understand so much as I thought I did, and that my style (if it might be called such) was unnatural, affected, and obscure'. Writing itself, however, was never a problem for the mature biographer: 'enough is past of writing to shew it is not uneasy, but a pleasure to sit, as I now do, passing the pen from side to side of the paper' (iii. 198). The problem lay, rather, in ordering the whole and in bringing it to completion. North may have felt reluctant to bring his work to a close because it would also draw an end to his extended conversation with his brothers. Or he may have taken to heart the distinction between drawings and paintings that he elaborated in his description of Lely's efforts: 'These drawings are observed to have more of the spirit and force of art than finished paintings, for they come from either flow of fancy or depth of study, whereas all this or great part is wiped out with the pencil [brush], and acquires somewhat more heavy, than is in the drawings' (iii. 202). Perhaps a further analogy can be drawn from North's description of the pains he took to rework the codicils in Francis's will: 'and all these he would put into my hands and I should frame them all into one entire form of a will which he would publish, and the others should be revoked' (i. 350). In his own works, however, these codicils were never revoked, and it fell to his heir to put North's remains in order.

The solution I am suggesting, of course, is that the separate biographies be recast 'into one entire form', into family history or group portraiture. North's most sensitive commentator, John Morris, has argued that his autobiography consists 'not only of the manuscript modestly entitled *Notes of Mee*, but also of his biographies of his brothers. Roger North's *Lives* and his autobiography are really one work', to which we might wish to add the *Examen* as well.[60] It is probable that such a radical rethinking of

    [59] North included a lengthy digression on Descartes in his *Life of Dr. John North*; see Millard, pp. 41–2, who summarizes its contents but does not reprint it in his edition.
    [60] John N. Morris, *Versions of the Self: Studies in English Autobiography from John Bunyan to John Stuart Mill* (New York: Basic Books, 1966), 42.

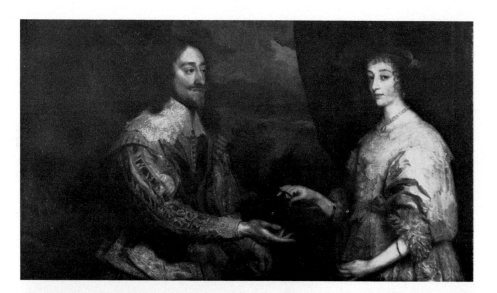

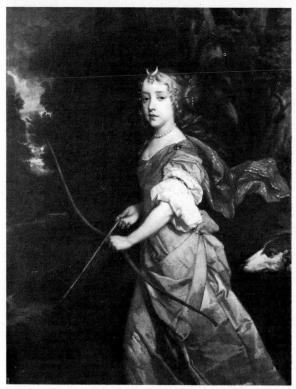

29. (*above*) Sir Anthony Van
Dyck, *Charles I and Henrietta
Maria*, *c*.1632, private
collection

30. (*left*) Sir Peter Lely,
Princess Mary as Diana,
c.1672, Kensington Palace

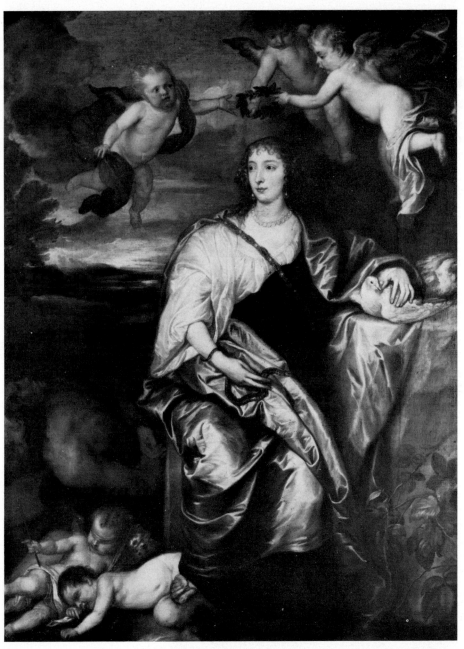

31. Sir Anthony Van Dyck, *Venetia Stanley, Lady Digby, as Prudence*, c.1633,
Windsor Castle

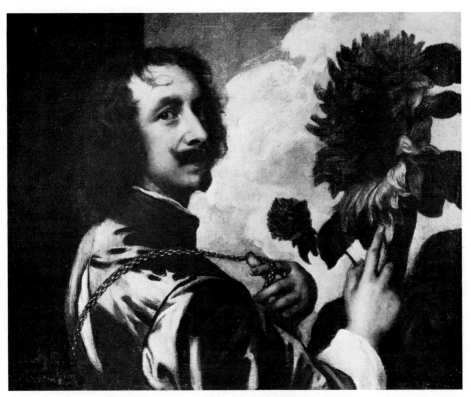

32. Sir Anthony Van Dyck, *Self-portrait with a Sunflower*, 1633, Duke of Westminster, Eaton Hall

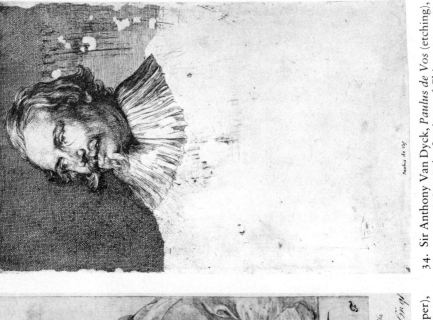

34. Sir Anthony Van Dyck, *Paulus de Vos* (etching),
   c.1628–36, Art Institute of Chicago

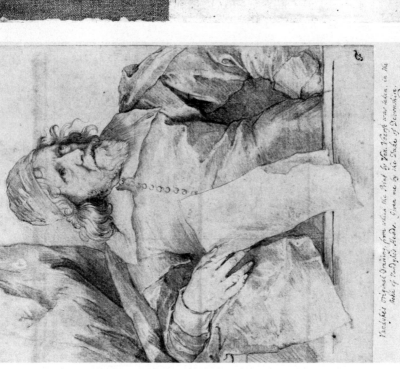

33. Sir Anthony Van Dyck, *Inigo Jones* (black chalk on paper),
   c.1630, Devonshire Collection, Chatsworth

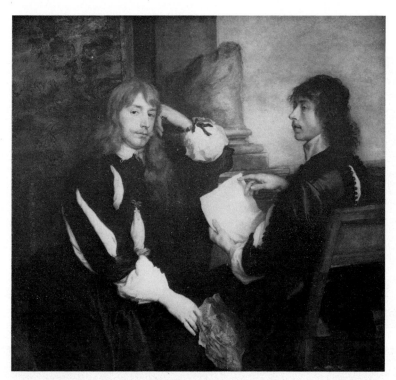

35. Sir Anthony Van Dyck, *Sir Thomas Killigrew and (?) Lord William Crofts*, 1638, Windsor Castle

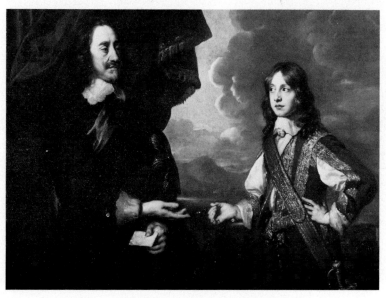

36. Sir Peter Lely, *Charles I with James, Duke of York*, 1647, Duke of Northumberland

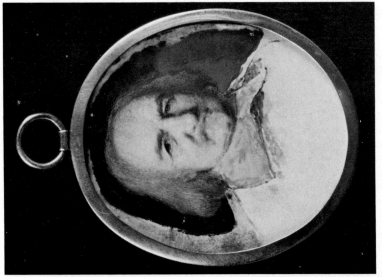

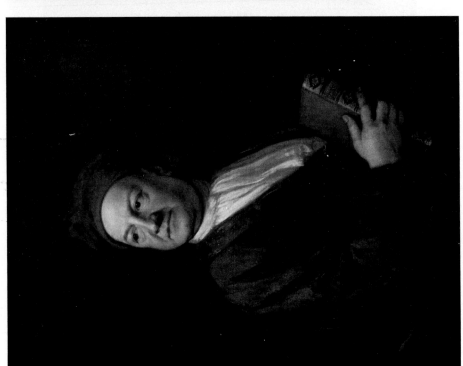

37. (left) Sir Godfrey Kneller, *Jacob Tonson*, 1717, National Portrait Gallery, London

38. (above) Samuel Cooper, *Thomas Hobbes* (watercolour sketch on vellum), c.1660, Cleveland Museum of Art

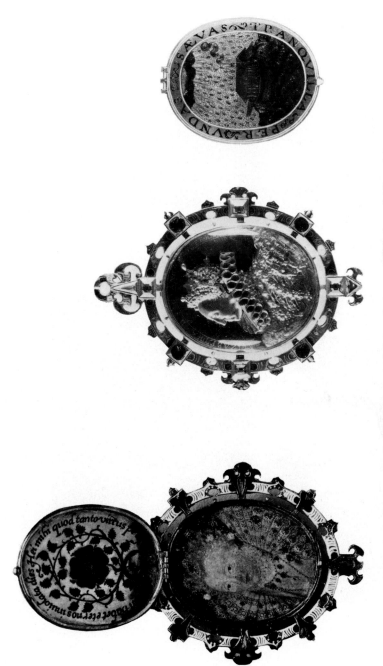

39. Nicholas Hilliard, *Heneage* ('*Armada*') *Jewel*, c.1600, Victoria and Albert Museum

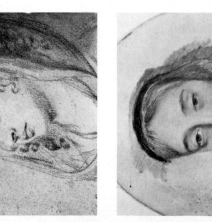

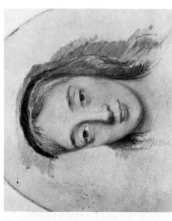

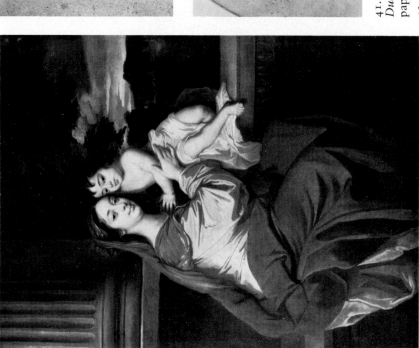

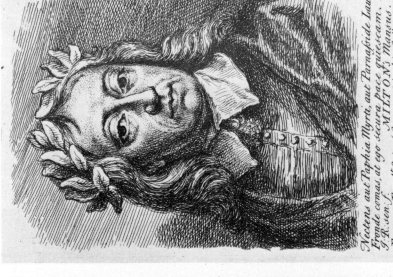

Nectens aut Paphia Myrti, aut Parnasside lauri
Fronde comas, at ego secura pace quiescam.
J.R. sen.f.   MILTONS Mansus.
From an Excell:Orig:/(Crayons) in his Collection.

44. Jonathan Richardson, engraved frontispiece to his *Explanatory Notes and Remarks on 'Paradise Lost'*, 1734

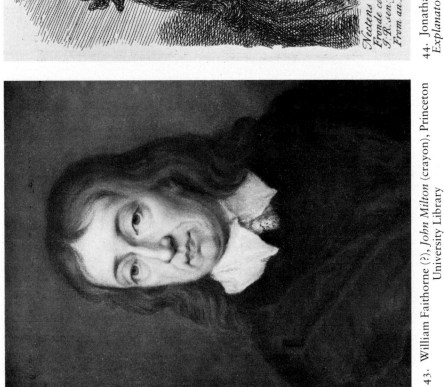

43. William Faithorne (?), *John Milton* (crayon), Princeton University Library

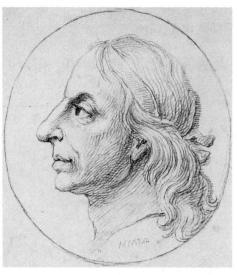

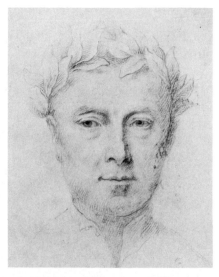

45. Jonathan Richardson, *A. Pope, as Milton* (pencil on vellum), 1738, Cornell University Library

47. Jonathan Richardson, *Self-portrait* (pencil on vellum), Cornell University Library

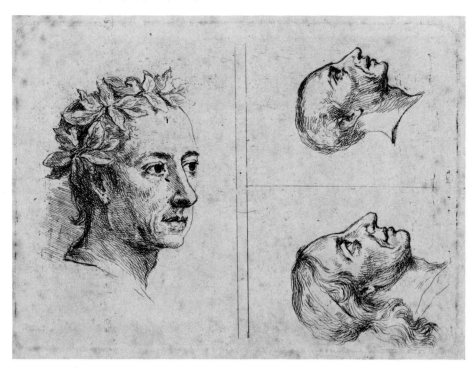

46. Jonathan Richardson, composite portrait of Milton and Pope (etching), 1738, British Museum

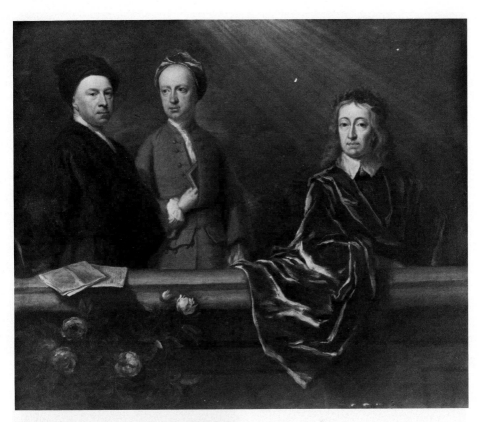

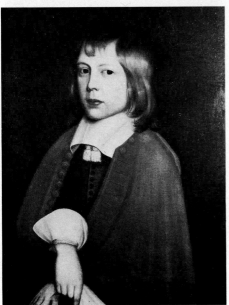

48. (*above*) Jonathan Richardson,
*The Richardsons with Milton, c.*1734,
Lt.-Col. Sir Walter Bromley-Davenport,
Capesthorne Hall

49. (*left*) Blemwell, *John North as a
Child*, Mrs Roger North, Rougham

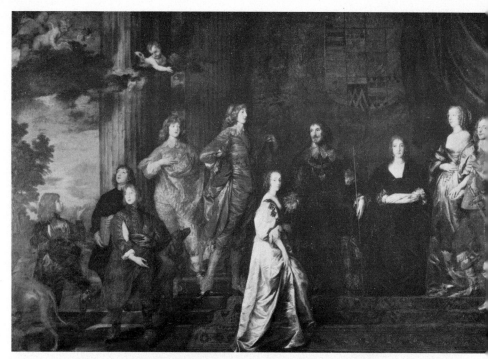

50. Sir Anthony Van Dyck, *The Earl of Pembroke and His Family*, 1635, Wilton House

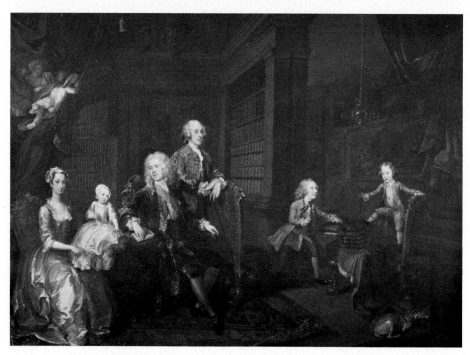

51. William Hogarth, *The Cholmondeley Family*, 1732, private collection

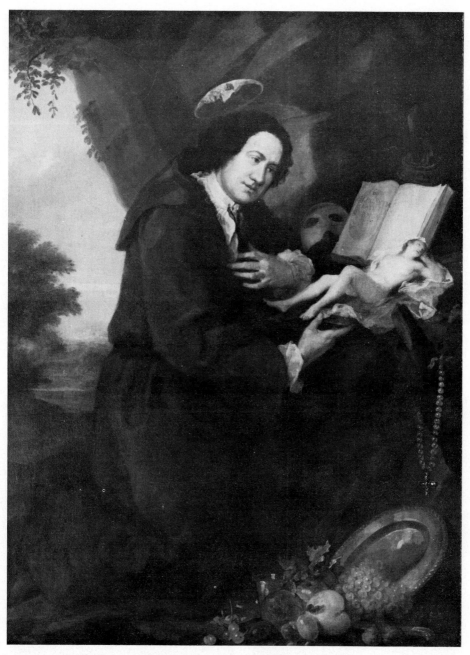

52. William Hogarth, *Sir Francis Dashwood at His Devotions*, c.1755, the Rt. Hon. the Viscount Boyne

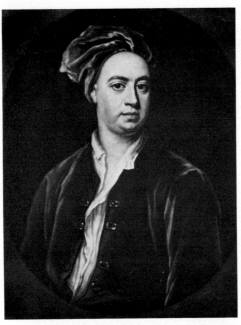

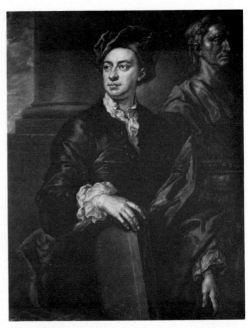

53. Jonathan Richardson, *Martin Folkes*, 1718 (now lost), engraved by John Smith, 1719

54. John Vanderbank, *Martin Folkes*, 1736, Hillington Hall (in 1909), engraved by John Faber, 1737

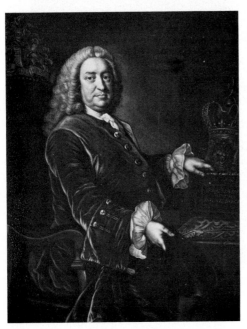

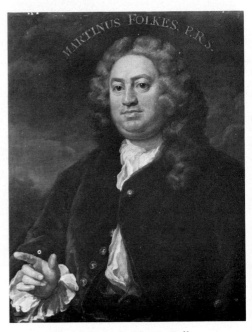

55. Thomas Hudson, *Martin Folkes*, n.d., Hillington Hall (in 1909), engraved by James McArdell, n.d.

56. William Hogarth, *Martin Folkes*, 1741, Royal Society, London

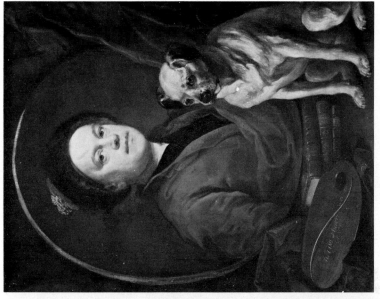
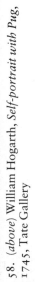

58. (*above*) William Hogarth, *Self-portrait with Pug*, 1745, Tate Gallery

57. (*left*) William Hogarth, *The MacKinnon Children*, 1740s, National Gallery, Dublin

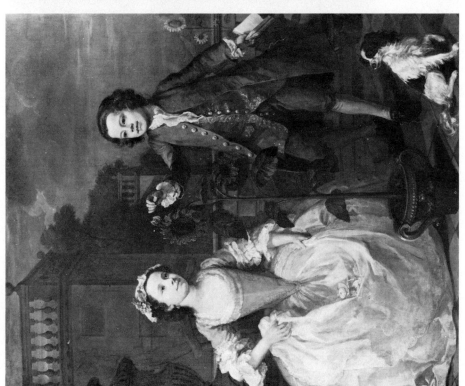

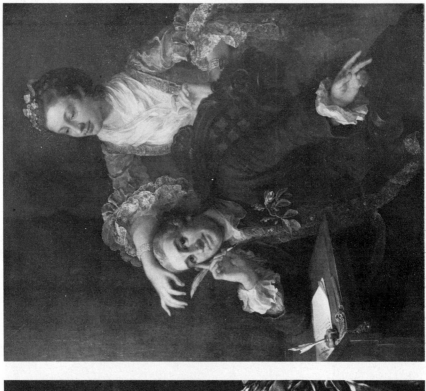

60. William Hogarth, *David Garrick and His Wife*, 1757,
Windsor Castle

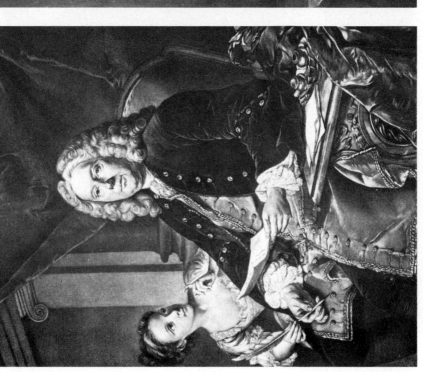

59. J. B. Van Loo, *Colley Cibber and His Daughter*, c.1740
(now lost), engraved by Edward Fisher, 1758

biographical form was not within North's capabilities, even though the lives, as they now stand, represent a rough approximation of the scope and materials that would be required. And it is possible that group portraiture of this kind might conflict with North's strong views on the importance of unity and variety in art. In a comparison of literature, painting, and architecture in his treatise on building, North specified that writers and architects, like painters, must 'not have a clutter, but some principall thing, at first view eminently cheif, to which all the other figures must relate'.[61] 'So 2 pictures in one is unlike nature,' he argues, 'for wee cannot look at 2 things at once.' And yet the doctrine of unity must not exclude variety; 'artists must find out such as will divert, and not devide, and that is the consummate height of art.' North might reasonably have argued that, in a single, synthetic narrative, individual character and accomplishments would be slighted and the central focus of the work would remain obscure. But North does have a central, common subject in mind in each separate biography as well as in the lives as a whole: the 'General Preface' closes with a concise history of his entire family's lineage; each brother is portrayed *as* a brother; and the entire project issues from one brother's desire to bring his family together again. The narrative challenges to North would have been considerable, but no other form of composition could have paid greater tribute to his own deeply seated belief in the importance of his own family and in the public benefits of private history.

[61] *Of Building*, p. 56.

6

Hogarth's Dilemma

IT is surely one of the ironies—and, as I have suggested, one of the weaknesses—of Roger North's biographical work that, despite the high value he placed on family relations, he rarely drew his brothers together for a group portrait. There was, of course, no existing biographical form on which North could have drawn, and it is also understandable that he modelled his lives of his brothers on his own experiences with them, experiences that were to a large extent separate from each other. His brother John was closest to him while Roger was still his pupil; Francis helped him to advance at the bar; whereas Dudley, with whom Roger enjoyed his most festive relationship, shared with Roger in high-spirited forays about London and in relaxed, intimate interludes with Dudley's family in the country. But if North had chosen to draw these often diverse strands together, he would have found an analogous form of portraiture emerging in England during the years of his retirement. The 'conversation', a group portrait depicting family members or close friends engaged in a common activity, was imported from the Continent by Philippe Mercier, a Frenchman whose polished work was soon absorbed by the more traditionally middle-class character of native English (and Dutch) painting.[1] English conversation pieces might be thought of as informal, less aristocratic versions of the majestic group portraits Van Dyck painted of the royal family. Smaller in format, the conversations are also more intimate and lively in their design, replacing the stately baroque compositions of Van Dyck and Kneller with a rococo emphasis on variety and motion.

This transformation in group portraiture emerges vividly in a comparison of Van Dyck's portrayal of *The Earl of Pembroke and His Family* (Plate 50) with William Hogarth's conversation piece of 1732, *The Cholmondeley Family* (Plate 51).[2] It would be possible, of course, to cite examples of Van Dyck's work that are not as grandly designed and coloured as this

---

[1] For the most recent—and freshest—surveys of the conversation piece, see Paulson, *Hogarth*, i. 196–226, and Paulson, *Emblem*, ch. 8.

[2] For Van Dyck's painting, see Larsen, no. 825 (vol. ii, colour pls. 44–5), and Sidney, 16th Earl of Pembroke, *A Catalogue of the Paintings and Drawings in the Collection at Wilton House* (London: Phaidon Press, 1968), no. 158 (Pembroke provides a helpful description of each sitter). For Hogarth's, see Beckett, *Hogarth*, pl. 55; Baldini and Mandel, no. 62; and Paulson, *Hogarth*, pl. 109.

particular painting, especially those involving the depiction of very young children; but most of his group portraits convey a similar suggestion of dignity and hierarchy. The entire canvas, one of the largest Van Dyck painted, is bathed in rich hues of red and gold. The Earl and his Countess, the only figures seated in this picture, are almost austerely clothed in black, whereas the other figures, carefully placed in arrangements that suggest their position within the family, are elegantly contraposed in colours of red, silver, gold, and brown. As in many of the group portraits painted during Van Dyck's stay in Genoa, the figures in this painting look neither at each other nor at a common object. The only exception is the group of three young boys in the lower left-hand corner of the painting, where one of the Duke's sons watches his brother observe the putti flying overhead, trailing clouds of baroque glory. The three cherubs on the left—representing children who died in infancy—are balanced by the heavy drapery on the right edge of the canvas, while the mighty columns are flanked by the imposing family crest, which hangs directly above Pembroke and his second wife. The effect throughout this impressive portrait is one of harmony and order, but the careful orchestration of the figures and motif prevents any possibility of interaction among the various characters Van Dyck depicts.

Van Dyck's portrayal of the Pembroke family functions not only as a group but also as a state portrait, not unlike those he painted for the royal family. Hogarth was offered, or at least attempted to win, a similar commission for himself in the early 1730s, and his ultimate failure to receive the royal family's support led directly to his decision to try his hand at alternative forms of portraiture—and patronage.[3] His conversation piece of the Cholmondeley family is characteristic of much of the group portraiture upon which he first built his reputation. Lord Malpas, later the third Earl of Cholmondeley, is seated near the centre of the canvas; his wife, like Lady Pembroke, is seated beside him. Malpas, who has apparently just put down a book he has been reading, looks directly at his wife and child, an infant girl perched on a table between them. His legs are crossed in an informal and relaxed gesture, but his attention will soon be violently drawn to the other actors in this domestic drama—his two energetic young sons—one of whom is precariously attempting to scale a stack of books that has been placed on a table in the other corner of the room.

Humorous sub-plots such as this one, which engages our attention just

---

[3] See Paulson, *Hogarth*, i. 312–18.

as it soon will the father's, recur throughout Hogarth's portraits as a firm
but gentle warning about the fragility and transience of youth. The sub-
plot has a more direct function here, however, for the boys' mother (or, in
some accounts, their infant sister) has been painted posthumously in this
portrait.[4] This would explain the comparative stiffness and disengagement
of Lady Malpas's figure and, as Ronald Paulson suggests, its smaller size
as well.[5] Like Van Dyck's angels, the two putti that hover above her head
serve as iconic reminders, but they are entangled here in an actual
arrangement of drapery and cord, and the dog in the lower right-hand
corner of the canvas has, unlike Van Dyck's attentive canines, turned his
back on his family's activities (perhaps after rumpling up the oriental rug
on the floor). Hogarth, with his lifelong interest in the theatre, has of
course staged this composition as carefully as Van Dyck ever did; but
between the curtains that mark the boundaries of our vision he has also
attempted to provide us with a glimpse of the drama inherent in this
family's life, even leading our eyes into further interiors filled with the
books and paintings they owned.

Conversation pieces like that painted of the Cholmondeley family
occupied much of Hogarth's practice during the 1730s. As he put it in his
fragmentary and often enigmatic *Autobiographical Notes*, these paintings of
subjects in conversation with each other 'had some novelty' and 'succeeded for a few years', but although they 'gave more scope to fancy' than
common portraiture did, they also required a 'kind of drudgery' and were
not extremely lucrative.[6] It was thus a natural step—although one that
Hogarth continued to fight against much of his life—to safeguard his
security as a painter by turning to individual portraits. This was clearly a
painful choice, one that he thought of as professionally demeaning, as we
shall see. But it did not mean that he turned his back on what he had
already learned as a painter of men and women in relation to each other;
his experience as a painter of conversation pieces emerges, in fact, in many
of his most successful portraits. We can sense it in his interest in painting

---

[4] See Gowing, pl. 42, for the traditional interpretation of the putti signifying the death of Lady
Cholmondeley, and Paulson, *The Art of Hogarth* (London: Phaidon Press, 1975), pl. 19, for the
association of the putti with her dead children. Frederick Antal, *Hogarth and His Place in European Art*
(London: Routledge, 1962), who is often more interested in the affinities between Hogarth and his
predecessors than in Hogarth's adaptations, notes that, as in some of Van Dyck's and Lely's
compositions, 'genuinely baroque angels hover over the principal group or play with the tassels of the
(van Dyck) curtains' (pp. 37–8). Antal cites several French sources for this painting, as well as Van
Dyck's *Charles I and Family*.

[5] Paulson, *Hogarth*, i. 305.

[6] The *Autobiographical Notes* are printed in Hogarth, *Analysis*; my reference here is to p. 202 (further
references are provided in the text).

members of the same family, especially families that he knew well himself;
in his careful discriminations between different generations; in his handling of two figures within a portrait or, in a single likeness, his ability to
relate the character portrayed to his or her surroundings. As he remarked
in *The Analysis of Beauty* 'the art of composing well is the art of varying
well', and we can sense his struggle to realize this principle in even the
simplest of his compositions.[7] It is precisely this combination of
Hogarth's interest in human drama and his insistence on the variety of
visual forms that enabled him to combat what he clearly saw as the twin
vices of contemporary portraiture: its merely mechanical nature, whose
drudgery drained the very life from its subject, and the alternative
temptation for the painter to flatter and idealize the sitter far beyond what
nature could justify. In this chapter I want to explore, in greater detail
than previous critics, Hogarth's ambivalent commentary on the art of
portraiture, and then examine how successful he was in adapting traditional forms and motifs in his own paintings.

i. The Reluctant Face-painter

We do not immediately think of Hogarth as a portrait-painter, and neither
did his contemporaries. They either celebrated or attacked him as the
painter and engraver of satiric progresses, a form of moral history that he
created with the publication of *A Harlot's Progress* in 1732. Hogarth, on
the other hand, nourished higher ambitions, hoping to play a latter-day
Van Dyck to Sir James Thornhill's Rubens. Like Van Dyck, however, he
was disappointed in his quest for major religious commissions and was
forced to rely instead on what he could do best within the existing artistic
market-place. In 1733 he placed a 'Van Dyck's Head' as the sign above his
studio door, and he turned increasingly towards portraiture from 1738 to
1743 and then again in 1757, when he announced that he would 'employ
the rest of his Time in PORTRAIT PAINTING chiefly', and boasted that he
could complete a full portrait from four 15-minute sittings.[8] It should not
surprise us, then, that the most recent catalogue of his paintings lists well
over 100 individual and group portraits, nor that Hogarth's portraiture
and his other work as an artist interpenetrate each other at almost every

---

[7] Hogarth, *Analysis*, p. 57 (further references are provided in the text). Hogarth's *Analysis* has
recently been 'deconstructed' by Peter de Bolla, 'Criticism's Place', *The Eighteenth Century: Theory and
Interpretation*, 25 (1984), 199–214.
[8] Quoted by David Bindman, *Hogarth* (New York and Toronto: Oxford Univ. Press, 1981), 193.

turn in his career.[9] We have already seen how his individual portraits
emerged from his experiments with the conversation piece, and we can see
similar relations between his portraits and his progresses, especially in
those episodes that contain recognizable characters. Hogarth's first
biographer, John Nichols, noted that the artist enjoyed pointing out these
figures to the men and women who visited his studio, asking them to
guess which of their contemporaries he had portrayed. All of his satirical
characters were portraits, Nichols argued, although he was subsequently
forced to differentiate between these characters and the figures in
Hogarth's 'real portraits'.[10] But what makes these figures comparable, of
course, is Hogarth's keen delight in human nature—no matter where it
occurs—and in the representation of character, two interests that he
shared with Henry Fielding, who celebrated his friend's achievements in
Joseph Andrews and *Tom Jones*.[11]

Hogarth's remarks in *The Analysis of Beauty* reveal that he thought as
carefully about portraiture as he did about the artistic genres he believed
to be superior to mere 'face-painting'. In a rejected passage, for instance,
he praises Rubens for his adherence to the serpentine line of beauty and
then muses upon the work of his pupil:

> Vandike his scholar perhaps for fear of running into what he might think gross
> in his masters manner, Imitated Nature just as it chanc'd to present itself, and
> having an exact Eye produced excessive true imitations of it with great delicacy
> and Simplicity, but when Nature flag'd he was Tame not having principles which
> might have raised his Ideas, however grace often appears in his best works[.]
> (p. 169)

The 'principles' Hogarth has in mind here are formal ones, related to the
lines of beauty and grace and to the structural qualities—variety, simplicity, utility—that he extols in his treatise. But even in this formal
analysis, Hogarth quickly comes to grips with the problem of the direct
imitation of nature, particularly when the subject itself appears to be
deficient.

In other comments he focuses on the human face, agreeing with most of
his contemporaries that it serves as 'the index of the mind'. 'It is
reasonable', he writes, 'to believe that aspect to be a true and legibile

[9] See Baldini and Mandel, as well as Beckett, *Hogarth*, pp. 39–62.

[10] J. Nichols, *Biographical Anecdotes of William Hogarth; and a Catalogue of His Works Chronologically Arranged; with Occasional Remarks* (1781), 14–15.

[11] See Robert Etheridge Moore, *Hogarth's Literary Relationships* (Minneapolis: Univ. of Minnesota Press, 1948), 107–61, and Martin C. Battestin, 'Pictures of Fielding', *Eighteenth-Century Studies*, 17 (1983–4), 1–13.

representation of the mind, which gives every one the same idea at first sight; and is afterwards confirm'd in fact,' as in the case of 'a down-right idiot' (p. 136). But it is also characteristic of Hogarth that these observations are merely the starting-point for his meditation on human countenances, 'no two [of which] have been so exactly alike, but that the usual and common discernment of the eye would discover a difference between them . . .' (p. 134). Unlike the rest of the body, the face constantly engages our curiosity because the 'vast variety of changing circumstances keeps the eye and the mind in constant play, in following the numberless turns of expression it is capable of' (p. 53). But children's faces, he remarks, express very little (a surprising observation from someone so skilled in portraying them sympathetically), and a hypocrite 'may so manage his muscles, by teaching them to contradict his heart, that little of his mind can be gather'd from his countenance . . .' (p. 137). The hypocrite, he concedes, lies entirely outside the power of the pencil, unless some 'adjoining circumstance'—an action that belies his behaviour—is included as part of the portrayal.

The character of most men, Hogarth argues, will in some measure be written upon their faces by the time they reach 40, and in an intriguing passage later in the *Analysis* he describes the gradual or dramatic changes that take place with each passing decade:

what further havock time continues to make after the age of fifty, is too remarkable to need describing: the strokes and cuts he then lays on are plain enough; however, in spite of all his malice, those lineaments that have once been elegant, retain their flowing turns in venerable age, leaving to the last a comely piece of ruins. (p. 145)

But lest we think that he places too much emphasis on 'outward shew, like a physiognomist', he also warns us that many different causes produce the same kinds of movements and appearances of our features: 'the old adage, fronti nulla fides, will ever stand its ground upon the whole; and for very wise reasons nature hath thought fit it should' (pp. 137–8). This unsparingly balanced analysis of the physical features of the face, with its empirical understanding of what can be veiled as well as disclosed, eventually leads to an even bleaker concession: that nature has strangely 'afforded us so many lines and shapes to indicate the deficiencies and blemishes of the mind, whilst there are none at all that point out the perfections of it beyond the appearance of common sense and placidity' (p. 141). This, it seems to me, is Hogarth's acknowledgement of the naturalist's central dilemma. In a genre dedicated to the commemoration

and celebration of individuals, how does the portrait-painter successfully—and honestly—suggest generous qualities of character and mind?
'All that the ancient sculptors could do,' he relentlessly argues, 'notwithstanding their enthusiastic endeavours to raise the characters of their
deities to aspects of sagacity above human, was to give them features of
beauty' (p. 142). A Richardsonian connoisseur may style these achievements 'a divine idea, inconceivably great, and above nature', but all the
sculptor has been able to add is an ample beard or prominent brow. In an
observation that foreshadows Reynolds's complaint to Boswell in his
character-sketch of Johnson, Hogarth concludes that 'Deportment,
words, and actions, must speak the good, the wise, the witty, the humane,
the generous, the merciful, and the brave' (p. 141).[12] But these are
elements that properly belong to the sister art of biography, or to the
theatre, or to the serial form of Hogarth's visual narratives.

It should not be surprising, therefore, that the ambivalence Hogarth
already felt as he surveyed a field he closely associated with drudgery, with
the merely mechanical reproduction of likenesses, should be compounded
by his knowledge that the vital enterprise of portraiture—which was to
reveal character in an honest and convincing manner—presented inherent
problems of its own. Hogarth summarized his misgivings about portraiture as a profession in the manuscript of his 'Apology for Painters':

Portrait painting is the chief branch ⟨of the art⟩ by which a man can promise
himself a tolerable lively hood and the only one by which a money lover ⟨can⟩
get a fortune. and a man of very middling Talents may easily succeed in it more of
artifices and the address of a mercer is required than of their genious. their patern
is before them an exact external eye and much practice with very little speculation
are sufficient to make and excellent face painter. Yet they strut especially if by the
assistance of a drapery painter and cry how we apples swim.[13]

When he judged the success of his own work in this field, moreover, he
was usually constrained to place it within this professional context. In his
autobiographical notes he remarked that portraiture requires a 'constant
practise to be reddy at taking a likeness' and that 'the life must not be
strictly followd'. His own portraits therefore received the same reception
as Rembrandt's did, extolled by some as 'Nature itself' but damned by

---

[12] Cf. Gainsborough: 'Had a picture Voice, Action, etc. to make itself known ... but only a face,
confined to one View, and not a muscle to move to say here I am, falls very hard upon the poor
Painter who perhaps is not within a mile of the truth in painting the Face only.' Quoted by Nadia
Tscherny, 'Likeness in Early Romantic Portraiture', *Art Journal*, 46 (1987), 197.

[13] Michael Kitson, 'Hogarth's "Apology for Painters" ', *Walpole Society*, 41 (1966–8), 100 (words in
angle brackets were added later by Hogarth; further references to this edition are provided in the text).

others as 'exicrable' (p. 212). Even when he described the creation of his greatest portrait, *Captain Coram*, in which he successfully blended the traditional elements of monumental portraiture with the individual character and middle-class appearance of his sitter, he wrote from the perspective of one who knew that his best work would not be appreciated even by his fellow painters. Provoked by colleagues at the St Martin's Lane Academy who were seemingly cowed by the success of Van Loo, Hogarth 'set about this mighty portrait, and found it no more difficult than I thought it . . .'. But even though he was convinced that he could paint a portrait as well as Van Dyck, his 'Brothers' at the Academy refused to acknowledge that this kind of artistry lay within the reach of a native painter: 'we will never allow it' (p. 217).

Hogarth quite naturally consoled himself by boasting of the prices his most ambitious paintings fetched, and by remarking how strange it was that his portrait of Captain Coram in the Foundling Hospital had stood 'the test of twenty years as the best Portrait in the place notwithstanding all the first portrait painters in the Kingdom had exerted their talents to vie with it' (pp. 212–13). But these defensive statements unfortunately find their counterpart in his troubled commentary on the aesthetic issues involved in creating successful portraits. In his almost obsessive interest in the distinctions between character and caricature, for instance, he betrays his constant fear that some of his own works will be dismissed as witty squibs in the manner of the Carracci. This deep distrust of minimalist portraiture, in which a subject is pared down with a few strokes of the pen, should be seen in relation to his corresponding hostility towards sublime or idealized portraits, which tend to flatter sitters by glossing over their deficient features or by embedding them in an incongruous context.

Both of these extremes are forms of exaggeration; character, in Hogarth's view, lies somewhere near the middle of this spectrum, neither too simplified nor too heavily made over. And yet this is where the serious painter's greatest challenges lie, not merely because he is largely bereft of the 'Deportment, words, and actions' that underwrite painting's sister arts, but because the very nature of this middle ground poses certain contradictions. In his autobiographical notes he complains that 'Painters and writers speak and writers never mention, in the historical way of any intermediate species of subjects for painting between the sublime and the grotesque. We will therefore compare subject[s] for painting with those of the stage.—' (p. 212). But this passage characteristically, and perhaps understandably, breaks off at this point. Similarly, in the 'Apology for

Painters', he states that 'the best statues ⟨which are very few⟩ have something [in] them superior to what is but rarely seen in nature but at the same time also something always inferior' (pp. 85–6). The first half of this sentence is vintage Richardson; the second half, however, poignantly captures Hogarth's distrust of the idealizing impulse. Both of the extremes of contemporary portraiture—the sublime and the grotesque—were clearly available for the moralist and satirist in Hogarth to draw upon; but both were anathema to the empirical portrait-painter, who was as devoted to faithful representation as he was to the painstaking accumulation of those nuances that separate one individual from another.

ii. The Painter as Pragmatist

It would be difficult to find an English painter who has been charged with inconsistency by his modern critics as often as Hogarth has. Scholars have pointed to the discrepancy between his theories about centralized formal structure and his actual practice as a rococo artist, the realism within his *œuvre* and the seemingly contradictory formalist approach of the *Analysis*, his dislike of caricature and visual shorthand and his own experiments with them, his spirited repudiation of much Continental art and his easy absorption of those influences into his own paintings, and his contradictory statements about the value of preliminary sketches for his work.[14] When we turn to his portraits, however, we may detect certain tensions, but rarely any contradictions; he appears never to have proposed any principles about portraiture with which he could not later live.

The tensions that emerge in his work are those we would expect to find in an eclectic artist with somewhat divided allegiances. Sir James Thornhill, after all, was his father-in-law as well as his master, and yet there was much in the work of England's last prominent baroque artist that could not be assimilated into contemporary portrait-painting. Hogarth was looked upon, and quite rightfully so, as a supremely literary artist. In the 'Apology for Painters' he echoed Richardson by claiming that 'Drawing and painting are only a much more complicated kind of writing' (p. 106), and in a frequently quoted passage in the *Autobiographical Notes* he stated that 'my Picture was my Stage and men and women my actors who were

---

[14] See, in the following order, Robert R. Wark, 'Hogarth's Narrative Method in Practice and Theory', in *England in the Restoration and Early Eighteenth Century*, ed. H. T. Swedenberg, jun. (Berkeley and Los Angeles: Univ. of California Press, 1972), 161–72; Hogarth, *Analysis*, p. liii; Devin Burnell, 'The Good, the True and the Comical: Problems Occasioned by Hogarth's *The Bench*', *Art Quarterly*, n.s. 1. 2 (1978), 17–46; Antal, *Hogarth and His Place in European Art*, *passim*; and A. P. Oppé, *The Drawings of William Hogarth* (New York: Phaidon Press, 1948), 12–13.

by Mean of certain Actions and express[ions] to Exhibit a dumb shew'
(p. 209). Principles such as these, when translated into visual practice,
naturally led critics like Lamb (and Hazlitt after him) to praise Hogarth
for his narrative gifts: 'Other pictures we look at,—his prints we read.'[15]
But how could this literary approach, in which a heavily encrusted image
or series of images demanded its own textual exegesis, be squared with the
demands of naturalism? Lamb's remark must be placed next to that of
Richard and Samuel Redgrave, who began their Victorian survey of
English painting by celebrating Hogarth as 'the man wanted; the reformer
the art needed; one who was determined not to follow, but to lead; one
who had formed his art upon the observation of nature only ....'.[16]
Hogarth, they concluded, treated men and women as human beings, 'and
felt that the commonest phase of existing society might be rendered
pictorially interesting' (p. 26). In short, how are we to reconcile the
century's most literary artist, endowed with his rich inheritance of
allegorical stock, with the century's greatest naturalist, the iconoclast who
bristled at most received tradition? The answer, I propose, lies in
Hogarth's empirical and pragmatic approach to portraiture, and especially
in his ability to translate the burden of iconic motifs into the inherent
drama of private lives.

There are, of course, exceptions to this rule. His depictions of Lord
Lovat, John Wilkes, and Charles Churchill, intended for popular
audiences, are difficult to distinguish from the grotesqueries of caricature.
Conversely, two unusual moral portraits, intended for private audiences,
are overtly emblematic. His portrait of *Frank Matthew Schutz Being Sick*, a
subject commissioned by Schutz's bride, strangely combines the graphic
realism of the central action, as Schutz lurches out of bed, with a symbolic
lyre (the songs of his youth) now hung upon the wall and two admonitory
quotations from Horace reminding him that his days of revelling are
over.[17] The second portrait, whose overt morality is much less certain,
depicts *Sir Francis Dashwood at His Devotions* (Plate 52).[18] Dashwood was
the central figure in the group of rakes and epicures known as the Monks

---

[15] Lamb, 'On the Genius and Character of Hogarth', in *The Works of Charles and Mary Lamb*, ed.
E. V. Lucas (London: Methuen, 1912), i. 82; Hazlitt, 'British Institution: Hogarth, Wilson, Etc.', in
Complete Works, ed. P. P. Howe (London and Toronto: Dent, 1933), xviii. 22. There is a short but
perceptive study of Hogarth's ambivalent response to the emblematic tradition he inherited as an
engraver in Derek Jarrett, *The Ingenious Mr Hogarth* (London: Michael Joseph, 1976), ch. 2.
[16] Richard and Samuel Redgrave, *A Century of British Painters* (1866), ed. Ruthven Todd (1947; rpt.
Ithaca: Cornell Univ. Press, 1981), 20 (see also pp. 22, 26).
[17] Gowing, pl. 190; Baldini and Mandel, no. 197; Paulson, *Hogarth*, pl. 270.
[18] Beckett, *Hogarth*, pl. 191; Baldini and Mandel, no. 181; Gowing (who notes the face in the halo),
pl. 125; Paulson, *Hogarth*, pl. 269.

of Medmenham. Hogarth had been on friendly terms with him for some
time, although he never, apparently, entered fully into the Medmenham
brotherhood. Hogarth pictures his friend, dressed in his monkish habit, as
he worships the goddess Venus in a travesty of Catholic ritual. Dashwood
leers so intently at the erotic icon before him that he neglects, at least for
the moment, the sybaritic objects in his grotto: a mask to be worn during
his intrigues, a book containing Latin sermons, a rosary of rich pearls, and
a silver salver that cannot quite contain the fruits and wine of the reveller's
repast. This witty composite portrait of Sir Francis as Saint Francis is not
only filled with icons but is in a sense *about* icons, about the nature of our
worship and the fetishes we place before us. Dashwood's voyeuristic
tendencies, moreover, are reinforced by the profile of Lord Sandwich, a
fellow monk, caught in the arc of Sir Francis's halo. The extent of our
own participation in this ceremony is uncertain; Dashwood's pleasures,
like his goddess's unveiled attributes, are never fully disclosed to us. We
are confronted by a painting that would have humoured its owners and
satisfied its critics, and Hogarth's own perspective is presumably an
amused combination of these two views.

In most of Hogarth's work as a portrait-painter, however, these iconic
motifs are either divested of their traditional significance or disappear
entirely, especially in the early 1740s, when he painted the great individual
portraits of Coram, Manning, Hoadly, and Folkes. The antiquarian
Martin Folkes provides a particularly interesting case, for the earlier
likenesses of him represents the entire lineage of English painters between
Richardson and Hogarth. An early portrait by Richardson (1718), reproduced here in the engraving by John Smith (Plate 53), depicts Folkes
roughly in the format of Kneller's contemporary Kit-cat series; the only
major alterations are the oval surround and the exclusion of the obligatory
elbow and hand.[19] Richardson's presentation is informal, even unbut-
toned, but it lacks—perhaps as the face of the young Folkes also did—the
penetration and visual interest that Richardson captured in a pen-and-ink
drawing later in his career. A second major painting, shown here in an
engraving by John Faber after John Vanderbank (1737), represents
Folkes within far more imposing surroundings (Plate 54).[20] Vanderbank
has formally posed his sitter between a massive column in the background
and a railing in front; a bust of Newton in the background to the right
serves to remind us of Folkes's position as vice-president of the Royal
Society, and in fact the folds of classical drapery on Newton's shoulders

---

[19] Kerslake, pl. 201.   [20] Ibid., pl. 202.

appear almost to blend into the voluminous robe that encloses Folkes's left arm and the entire front of his body. His right hand gracefully secures the top of a large folio volume, presumably his *Tables of English Gold Coins*, published in 1736. Both the book and his pose should remind us of Kneller's portraits of Dryden or Tonson (Plate 37), but the bust, column, and classical costuming clearly distinguish this as a far more formal and iconographical portrait.

A similar image, shown here in an engraving by James McArdell (Plate 55), was painted by Thomas Hudson following Folkes's ascension to the presidency of the Royal Society.[21] Folkes is now seated in the elaborately carved presidential chair, and he holds up the book containing the statutes of the society with his left hand; his right hand, seemingly bereft of any other significant activity, simply holds his hat. Hudson has clearly attempted to produce as august and impressive a portrait of Folkes as possible, but the only focus of human interest here, the sitter's head, is dwarfed as much by his grand surroundings as by his own stout frame. When Hogarth painted Folkes in 1741, he banished the personal and official attributes that had embellished earlier portraits of this antiquarian, and instead focused solely on his sitter's face and body (Plate 56).[22] There is nothing in this portrait that explicitly tells us who Martin Folkes was or what he accomplished; the inscription at the top of the canvas was added later, by a different hand. We must mount any interpretation, instead, on the natural visual image that Hogarth presents to us, noting the open face with its steady gaze, the cocked right hand, which is literally about to assist Folkes in making a point, and perhaps above all the fresh and free handling of paint, especially in the flesh tones, which energizes this figure even though the massive body is painted in repose. In fact by emphasizing Folke's own physical stature, by moving him as close to the surface of the picture as he can, Hogarth has endowed Folkes with a presence far more vivid and impressive than that to be found in the more stately portraits by his predecessors.

In other types of portraits, particularly those of children, allegorical motifs often play at least a subdued role in determining meaning within Hogarth's paintings. In *The Graham Children*, for instance, it has often been pointed out that the exuberance and complacency of the various children that Hogarth so lovingly depicts are subtly undermined by the image of Time's scythe in the background to the left and by the greedy cat

---

[21] Ibid., pl. 203.
[22] Beckett, *Hogarth*, pl. 133; Baldini and Mandel, no. 134; Paulson, *Hogarth*, pl. 168; Kerslake, pl. 206.

that is about to attack the youngster's songbird. Paulson makes a similar
case for *The MacKinnon Children* (Plate 57):

The symbolism again has to do with the children's future—with fleeting time,
lost beauty, and lost innocence. The girl has been collecting fallen petals in her
apron and the boy is reaching out for a butterfly poised on the sunflower, an
emblem of transient beauty that appears in so many Dutch flower pictures. And,
of course, the potted sunflower in the foreground, big as a tree and flanked by the
two children with their attention on the butterfly, is the real center of the picture,
endowing it with ironic overtones of Adam and Eve, their Tree of Knowledge
(unpotted), and their lost Garden of Eden.[23]

This is a persuasive argument, and yet it does not take full account of all
the details and possible iconic connotations within the painting. It is true,
for instance, that the sunflower is located in the centre of the picture space,
and Paulson might have strengthened his argument by noting that its
russet colour matches the hue of the young boy's coat (an additional
sunflower, painted yellow, is casually placed on another part of the
terrace). But the flower is not as large as a tree and it does not dominate
our attention—nor that of the children reaching out to it. The boy,
moreover, has been reading a book; knowledge is already at his fingertips.
    The allegorical significance of the flower is also problematic here, for as
we have already seen in the case of Van Dyck's *Self-portrait with a Sunflower*
(Plate 32), the meaning of this motif, in Dutch emblems as well as English,
was connected exclusively with devotion. We might therefore argue that
Hogarth has attempted to dramatize the devotion this young brother and
sister share for each other, or the devotion their parents share for the
children whose portraits they have commissioned. By having each child
focus on a common object—the butterfly atop the sunflower—Hogarth
has in fact been able to display the emotion these children feel far less
sentimentally than if he had portrayed them looking directly at each other.
The qualities of energy and suspense are so vivid here that even the family
dog has turned in their direction, sensing that something is afoot. The
elusive butterfly, I would argue, is the real centre of this painting, for it
coalesces all of the other images into one principal action, captured at one
specific moment. The butterfly certainly symbolizes transient beauty and
the passing of time, but it is also the means by which the particular vitality
and beauty of this young couple can best be shown. And Hogarth, who

---

[23] Paulson, *Hogarth*, i. 459 (pl. 179; also reproduced in colour as the frontispiece to vol. i); see also
Baldini and Mandel, no. 2°D. In a more recent book, *The Art of Hogarth* (London: Phaidon Press,
1975), pl. 69, Paulson interprets the sunflower as an emblem of devotion, but does not attempt to
reconcile this view of the painting with the one he had proposed in *Hogarth* in 1971.

noted how difficult it was to find distinct expressions in children's faces, is necessarily in the same predicament as the sitters he paints: he too must reach out, attempting to capture a fleeting moment before it passes forever. This is what portrait-painting, even more than its sister art, is able to accomplish; and this is one of the reasons—in Hogarth's view, the most important reason—why parents commission portraits of their children.

I want to suggest, in other words, that it is often difficult to determine meaning even within relatively conventional paintings that make use of stock allegorical motifs and that may be generically related to other canvases painted at the same time. In *The MacKinnon Children*, for example, the principal allegorical motif may be read in at least two different ways and, more importantly, the very vitality of the central figures, their dynamic poses, and the sympathy with which they have been painted work against or at least complicate too narrow an iconographical response. A similar argument can be made about portraits that have traditionally been praised for their forthright honesty and naturalness, perhaps none more so than Hogarth's famous *Self-portrait with Pug* of 1745 (Plate 58).[24] Here is how the brothers Redgrave introduce this painting:

It shows a different school of art to that of the periwigged worthies of his predecessors—an honest, homely, matter-of-fact Englishman; not the least idealized; his short nose a little inclined to turn up; his round open face, his clear blue eye and rather firmly closed lips, are characteristic of one who might be a warm friend or a bitter enemy, and who did not shirk what he saw in his glass as he wrought to display himself for posterity. (p. 21)

Even his dog, they later point out, is 'no sleek spaniel or slim greyhound, but a bandy-legged black-nosed pug, not without some similarity to his master'. The only naturalistic detail the Redgraves fail to mention, in fact, is the prominent scar that Hogarth scrupulously records above his right eye.

The major difficulty with this approach is that it places all of its weight on the honest representation of Hogarth's countenance, while neglecting the obvious artifice of the painting, which is, among other things, a portrait within a portrait, and which relies for much of its meaning not only on the relation of the painter to his dog but on the relations that unify

---

[24] Beckett, *Hogarth*, pl. 155; Baldini and Mandel, no. 160 (colour pl. 48); Paulson, *Hogarth*, pl. 190; Gowing, pl. 135; Kerslake, pl. 391. Robin Simon, *The Portrait in Britain and America* (Oxford: Phaidon Press; Boston: G. K. Hall, 1987), 92 (fig. 82), suggests that the motif of a painted canvas with an ancillary figure may derive from Houbraken's engraving of the Countess of Arundel (1743). For a brief analysis of this portrait in the context of Hogarth's presentation of his satirical persona, see Joel Blair, 'Hogarth's Apologia', *The Eighteenth Century: Theory and Interpretation*, 25 (1984), 263–74.

all of the diverse objects in this picture. David Bindman, for instance, has
noted the inherent paradox created here by the play between the painted
portrait, with its accompaniment of baroque drapery, and Hogarth's real,
demotic dog; and Paulson has similarly pointed out that in this self-
portrait, unlike his others, Hogarth has presented himself as a work of art
and thereby ascribed a more objective status to the elements that surround
his painted image.[25] We should also notice that each of the objects
Hogarth pictures here has its counterpart in iconic painting of the
seventeenth century: the faithful dog, the portrait within a portrait, the
stack of books, the elaborate and somewhat extraneous drapery, even the
inscription on the painter's palette. Hogarth's palette—which is in turn an
iconographical attribute itself—contains yet another figure, the line of
beauty, which may be thought of as a version of *impresa*, of personal or
arcane allegory, for Hogarth had not yet written the theoretical treatise
that would explain its qualities: 'The bait soon took; and no Egyptian
hierogliphic ever amused more than it did for a time, painters and
sculptors came to me to know the meaning of it, being as much puzzled
with it as other people, till it came to have some explanation . . .' (*Analysis*,
p. 10).

   And yet with all of its iconographical freight, this is not a painting that
can be read in a conventional way. It is true that we identify the
faithfulness of the painter's dog with his own faithfulness of presentation,
that his image literally rests (as does his palette) upon the English literary
tradition (the volumes are labelled 'Shakespeare', 'Milton', and 'Swift'),
and that the inscription suggests an aesthetic programme that Hogarth
would soon disclose. But each of these objects is simultaneously subordinate—both physically and thematically—to the figure of Hogarth himself
who, unlike his dog Trump (who is painted in three-quarter profile),
stares directly at us. Unsettled by his defiant gaze, we may find ourselves
peering more comfortably at the figures below, but his own countenance
continues to dominate the painting; the carefully chosen clutter that
surrounds him is simply representative of those qualities that have made
him what he is. Against the argument that Hogarth has painted himself as
a work of art while depicting the other figures as actual, 'demotic' objects,
we must also argue that Hogarth's portrayal of himself is the only aspect
of the painting that does not share some iconic significance. The portrait-
within-a-portrait motif, for example, partially breaks down as we notice
how the red sweep of Hogarth's costume flows up to meet the sweep of

---

[25] Bindman, *Hogarth*, p. 151; Paulson, *Hogarth*, ii. 4.

green drapery in the right-hand corner of the canvas, an optical illusion all the more intriguing because the point of merger is hidden behind the head of the ambiguous dog, both demotic pup and iconographical attribute. Even the process of composition betrays this tension between realistic and iconographic qualities, for Hogarth apparently began painting a conventional studio portrait, with the palette placed roughly in the same position, and only later reworked these images into the painting we know today, with his faithful Trump a late addition.[26]

One final portrait, also heavily reworked by Hogarth, reveals the wit and intelligence with which he was able to adapt a conventional format to the specific situation of his sitters. His portrait of *David Garrick and His Wife* is based, as Antal first pointed out, on a painting of *Colley Cibber and His Daughter* by the detested J. B. Van Loo (Plate 59).[27] In this picture the fashionable and elegant Frenchman has revised the traditional depiction of the man of letters in a moment of meditative reverie by introducing the figure of the daughter as a literal muse, gently fingering her father's quill pen and staring with unquestioning features as he struggles to find the correct words for his new play. Cibber's left arm rests upon an elaborately wrought side-table that supports a double inkstand; the obligatory column and drapes are displayed in the background. This portrait dates from the late 1730s, just a few years before Cibber would publish his autobiographical *Apology* and subsequently find himself parodied as the alleged author of Fielding's *Shamela*. The combination of Hogarth's friendship with Fielding and Garrick and his animosity towards Van Loo would therefore seem to have made this portrait a perfect target for Hogarthian subversion—especially when we recall that Van Loo had painted Garrick as well—but the portrait of Garrick that Hogarth finally painted seems to have pleased neither the sitters nor the painter himself (Plate 60).[28]

The first contemporary account of this picture reveals a firm sense of what Hogarth was trying to accomplish. In a letter of 21 April 1757 to

---

[26] See Gowing, p. 58 (pl. 135).

[27] F. Antal, 'Hogarth and his Borrowings', *Art Bulletin*, 29 (1947), 36–48 (n. 31), and *Hogarth and His Place in European Art*, p. 70. The female figure is possibly Cibber's granddaughter, Jenny; see Helene Koon, *Colley Cibber: A Biography* (Lexington: Univ. Press of Kentucky, 1986), 147 and 214 n. 83 (where Koon mistakenly says that the portrait is in the National Gallery, London; it is now lost).

[28] Beckett, *Hogarth*, no. 187; Millar, *Tudor, Stuart*, no. 560, pl. 211; Baldini and Mandel, no. 188 (colour pl. 63); Gowing, pl. 200; and *Thirty Different Likenesses: David Garrick in Portrait and Performance* (exhibition catalogue, Buxton Museum and Art Gallery, 1981), no. 11. 1. Van Loo's portrait of Garrick also shows him in a retiring pose, holding his quill pen; see George Winchester Stone, jun., and George M. Kahrl, *David Garrick: A Critical Biography* (Carbondale and Edwardsville: Southern Illinois Univ. Press, 1979), 48.

Joseph Warton, John Hoadly, the bishop's son, notes that Hogarth has begun to paint portraits again and that 'He has almost finished a most noble one of our sprightly friend David Garrick and his Wife: they are a fine contrast. David is sitting at a table, smilingly thoughtful over an epilogue . . . his head supported by his writing-hand; and Madam is archly enough stealing away his pen unseen behind. It is not so much fancy as to be affected or ridiculous and yet enough to raise it from the formal inanity of a mere Portrait.'[29] John Nichols, however, in his biography of Hogarth, wrote that the painting 'confers no honour on the painter or the persons represented'. He observes that the portrait was unpaid for by the time Hogarth died, that Garrick did not approve of it, and that Hogarth consequently painted out the actor's eyes. As to the figures of the two sitters, Nichols argues that 'He has certainly missed the character of our late *Roscius's* contenance while undisturbed by passion', and that the elegance of his wife's form understandably evaded the efforts of a painter who excelled more in the depiction of '*la basse nature*'.[30] These are harsh strictures, but the *pentimenti* in the portrait bear out Nichols's belief that Hogarth found this a difficult canvas to paint: Oliver Millar confirms that there are traces of erasure in the left eye, and states that a more elaborate background was painted over at the time Hogarth's widow presented the portrait to Mrs Garrick.[31] In the painting's present condition, the only props that remain in addition to the prologue Garrick is writing for Samuel Foote's comedy *Taste* are a dimly perceived copy of Shakespeare's works and a pillar vaguely painted behind it.

The unfinished and somewhat sketchy condition of the portrait should not blind us, however, to its considerable wit and charm. Hogarth has depicted his friend in a traditional pose of poetic reverie, with the index finger of his right hand touching his temple and with his left hand extended, awaiting the arrival of the muse. But the character who appears is not the dutiful daughter of Van Loo's portrait but the actor's mischievous wife, about to snatch his pen from his hand and thus disrupt his serious meditation. We relish the dramatic irony in this scene all the more, in fact, because Hogarth has drawn upon his personal knowledge of his sitter. Garrick's wife, Eva Maria Veigel, has been able to enter silently into her husband's study not only because he is deeply rapt in his poetic reverie but because she had formerly been a famous dancer in the London

---

[29] Quoted by Millar, *Tudor, Stuart*, i. 185.

[30] Nichols, *Biographical Anecdotes*, pp. 12–13.

[31] Oliver Millar, ' "Garrick and his Wife by William Hogarth" ', *Burlington Magazine*, 104 (1962), 347; also see Millar, *Tudor, Stuart*, pl. 560.

theatre (her stage name was 'La Violette'). Garrick, on the other hand, was best known for the variety of emotions he could express with his mobile face and naturalistic gestures, especially his representation of surprise, which Hogarth had captured a decade earlier in his portrait of *Garrick as Richard III*. Here he is about to be surprised again, in a moment of domestic drama that echoes the fleeting moments of Hogarth's conversation pieces and re-creates, now in a more intimate environment, the qualities of characterization that Garrick was best known for in his public triumphs. According to one famous anecdote, Hogarth is said to have had difficulty painting this portrait precisely because Garrick consciously (or perhaps unconsciously) altered his countenance as he sat for his friend.[32] Like the *Self-portrait with Pug* and *The MacKinnon Children*, this painting also suggests the problematical nature of representation itself.

By choosing Van Loo's portrait as the type to be parodied in his own creation, Hogarth was in effect formulating a double-edged ratio between these two paintings: just as Cibber's reputation as an actor was eclipsed by the young Garrick, so Van Loo's vogue as a fashionable portrait-painter will eventually be supplanted by Hogarth's own achievements. The formal and somewhat pompous style of Van Loo's portrait, moreover, has its counterpart in the outdated, bombastic acting style that Cibber and his generation had practised for so long on the London stage. The more naturalistic and informal method of acting introduced by Macklin and then triumphantly popularized by Garrick, on the other hand, finds its appropriate analogue in Hogarth's more realistic and intimate style of painting.[33] Hogarth appears to be claiming, in effect, that greatness of character need not be suggested solely in solemn and stately compositions; it is a mark of Garrick's stature, in fact, that he can be portrayed in such a playful manner. Nor, of course, does the domestic drama Hogarth has chosen to depict lessen our sense of the affection Garrick and his wife share for each other: the sprig pinned to his breast balances the flowers woven into her hair, and she, in turn, wears a miniature portrait on her left wrist, the blue of its dress mirroring the colour of his coat. The moment Hogarth has chosen to portray, moreover, is cleverly tied to our anticipation of what will happen next. After Garrick's surprise has faded, which choice will he make between his two mistresses: will he return to his muse or be tempted away by his wife?

[32] This anecdote is recorded by Paulson, *Hogarth*, ii. 344, and n. 57.
[33] On changes in 18th-cent. acting styles, see Paulson, *Hogarth*, ii. 24-7, who surprisingly makes little use of this portrait to substantiate his points.

The pregnancy of the moment Hogarth dramatizes here already anticipates two scenes in which Reynolds will choose to portray Garrick. In *Garrick between Tragedy and Comedy* (Plate 61), the actor, like Hercules at the crossroads, will have to choose between the two figues that pull him in opposing directions; and, as Paulson has suggested, the greatest tribute Reynolds can pay Garrick is to show that such an accomplished actor *cannot* choose between the two roles he loves equally well.[34] In a later and less well-known portrait by Reynolds (Plate 62), in which Garrick and his wife are seated in a rural setting, the actor awaits his wife's response to a passage he has just read to her, a reversal of the situation in Hogarth's portrait in which Eva Maria is about to provoke a reaction from her husband.[35] In Reynolds's painting, an older Garrick looks up at his wife, awaiting her verdict, while she, like the musing husband in Hogarth's picture, is caught up in a moment of meditative silence. Although Reynolds always nurtured ambivalent feelings about Hogarth's achievements as a painter, he surely sensed Hogarth's ability to create dramatic portraits in which conventional motifs could be subverted or mixed, and in which the problem of representation would itself emerge as part of the painter's focus. It is in this, as much as in his emphasis on the interest and even heroism of middle-class lives, his preference for the informal and the intimate, and his empirical approach to the character of each sitter he painted, that Hogarth continues to press his claims upon us not just as an innovator, but as a particularly modern artist.

[34] Paulson, *Emblem*, p. 80.

[35] This painting is a recent acquisition of the National Portrait Gallery. It has been reproduced by Stone and Kahrl, *David Garrick*, p. 466.

7

Biography at Mid-century:
Acts of Complicated Virtue

LATE on the night of 20 November 1727, a young and impoverished writer, having spent the evening carousing with his friends, entered Robinson's Coffee-house, near Charing Cross, where one of his companions demanded a room for the night. Within a few minutes lightning seems to have struck Richard Savage for the second time in his life, and his world was once again turned upside-down: a brief scuffle with a company of men and women about to leave the adjoining room left one of them, James Sinclair, dead, and a maid in the house wounded. Savage and his friends were soon brought to trial and found guilty of murder; only the intercession of the Countess of Hertford with the Queen led to Savage's pardon and reprieve, and even the Countess faced considerable difficulties, for she was petitioning on behalf of someone who had already made a controversial reputation for himself by claiming that he was an 'injured nobleman', the illegitimate son of the Countess of Macclesfield and the Earl Rivers. Some time later, after he had obtained his liberty, Savage accidentally met the 'Woman of the Town' who had testified so severely against him at his trial:

She informed him, that she was in Distress, and, with a Degree of Confidence not easily attainable, desired him to relieve her. He, instead of insulting her Misery, and taking Pleasure in the Calamities of one who had brought his Life into Danger, reproved her gently for her Perjury, and changing the only Guinea that he had, divided it equally between her and himself.[1]

This well-known description of Richard Savage's behaviour was published in 1744 by Samuel Johnson, who commended his friend's benevolent gesture by proclaiming that in some ages it 'would have made a Saint, and perhaps in others a Hero, and which, without any hyperbolical Encomiums, must be allowed to be an Instance of uncommon Generosity, an Act of complicated Virtue . . .' (p. 40). By 'complicated' Johnson means 'compounded', for he quickly proceeds to tell us that Savage 'at once relieved the Poor, corrected the Vicious, and forgave an

---

[1] Johnson, *Savage*, p. 40. Further references are provided in the text.

Enemy; . . . at once remitted the strongest Provocations, and exercised the most ardent Charity'. But Savage's act is complicated in the modern sense of the word as well, for virtually every action that Savage ever took reveals the deeply seated ambiguities within his complex character.[2] In the following paragraphs, moreover, Johnson directly confronts these paradoxes by drawing our attention to the fact that 'Compassion was indeed the distinguishing Quality of *Savage*', and then by immediately qualifying this judgement by reporting that 'when his Heart was not softened by the Sight of Misery, he was sometimes obstinate in his Resentment, and did not quickly lose the Remembrance of an Injury.'

In choosing to write a life of Savage—and by presenting the notorious materials of his friend's life in a sympathetic but even-handed way— Johnson was in effect creating a paradigm that would influence most of the major biographical texts written in the following half-century.[3] This is not to suggest, however, that Johnson maintained a detached attitude towards his subject; far from it. Savage was Johnson's companion while they were both young writers struggling to make their reputations in London. Johnson had a keen sense of Savage's virtues, and he is a strong advocate on his friend's behalf. But Johnson was also painfully aware of Savage's shortcomings, and if he punctuates his narrative with a personal outburst against the apparently motiveless malignity of Savage's mother at one point, he is equally capable of balancing this later in the text with a similar cry against Savage's propensity to bite the many hands that fed him.[4] In writing the *Life of Savage* Johnson was tackling a 'mixed' character if ever there was one. In articulating an attitude that was neither scathing nor panegyrical, Johnson was himself committing an act of complicated virtue; in choosing to analyse such a problematical subject, he was creating a biography significantly different from the work of his most important predecessors—Walton, Evelyn, Richardson, and North—and even from his own biographical experiments earlier in his career.[5] In this

[2] Robert W. Uphaus, 'The "Equipoise" of Johnson's *Life of Savage*', *Studies in Burke and His Time*, 17 (1976), 46, interprets 'complicated' to mean 'entangled': 'at the very moment Savage is entangled and joined with the woman, the reader as well becomes entangled with this passage' and must enter into Savage's circumstances. I find this less convincing than Uphaus's observation that Savage and the prostitute share a psychological understanding of each other.

[3] Virginia Spencer Davidson, 'Johnson's *Life of Savage*: The Transformation of a Genre', *Studies in Biography*, ed. Daniel Aaron (Harvard English Studies, 8; Cambridge, Mass.: Harvard Univ. Press, 1978), 72, sees Johnson taking a 'genetic' leap beyond his commemorative or defamatory predecessors by insisting on biography's mimetic qualities. But surely Aubrey—and perhaps even North—are more insistently realistic than Johnson.

[4] See pp. 38, 132.

[5] Most of Johnson's early lives are discriminating but admiring assessments of men of achievement, especially those of Boerhaave and Barretier. He is clearly at odds with his subject in the *Life of*

chapter I want to gauge the pressure of Johnson's theory and practice on two of his closest friends, Mrs Piozzi and Oliver Goldsmith, before returning to the *Life of Savage* and to the difficult problems it continues to raise.

i. Mrs Piozzi's *Anecdotes*: Biography as Conversation

Of Johnson's biographical heirs it might be said that Hester Lynch Thrale Piozzi learned the least from his example and yet owed him the greatest debt, for the deep impression Johnson printed on her mind not only occasioned her first major attempt as an author but also provided her with a broader perspective on her life, one that allowed her to envisage herself as a successful writer as well as a devoted wife and mother. In her autobiographical sketch of 1778, she noted that her friendship with Johnson 'began opening my Eyes to my odd kind of Life', a life in which she had created a personal identity largely in terms of her service to others: to her husband, Henry Thrale, to their children, and to a mother she continued to idolize.[6] When her husband, a prosperous brewer normally unsympathetic to her intellectual pursuits, presented her with several bound commonplace books entitled *Thraliana*, it was natural for her to choose the imposing Johnson as the focus for much of her miscellaneous writing, and even to supplement these volumes with other blank books in which she, as well as her family and guests, wrote down all they could remember of what Johnson had said. Even her one great act of independence—her decision, as a widow, to marry the Italian singer she loved so much—was by its very nature a renunciation of the strict forms of behaviour that her family and her closest friend themselves embodied. It is not surprising, then, that her contribution to eighteenth-century biography, *The Anecdotes of the Late Samuel Johnson*, was read by her

Cheynel (1751); perhaps his only 'mixed' or ordinary subject is Edward Cave, whose life he wrote in 1754. These works have been collected by J. D. Fleeman, *Early Biographical Writings of Dr Johnson* (Westmead: Gregg International, 1973).

  [6] *Thraliana*, i. 309. Further references are provided in the text. For discussions of Mrs Piozzi's relations with her family (and with Johnson), see Patricia Meyer Spacks, 'Scrapbook of a Self: Mrs. Piozzi's Late Journals', *Harvard Library Bulletin*, 18 (1970), 221–47, and *The Female Imagination* (New York: Knopf, 1975), 198–207; Martine Watson Brownley, 'Eighteenth-Century Women's Images and Roles: The Case of Hester Thrale Piozzi', *biography* 3 (1979), 65–76, and ' "Under the Dominion of *Some* Woman": The Friendship of Samuel Johnson and Hester Thrale', in *Mothering the Mind: Twelve Studies of Writers and Their Silent Partners*, ed. Ruth Perry and M. W. Brownley (New York and London: Holmes and Meier, 1984), 64–79; and John C. Riely, 'Johnson's Years with Mrs. Thrale: Facts and Problems', *Bulletin of the John Rylands Library*, 57 (1974), 196–212, and 'Johnson and Mrs. Thrale: The Beginning and the End', in *Johnson and His Age*, ed. James Engel (Harvard English Studies, 12; Cambridge, Mass.: Harvard Univ. Press, 1984), 55–81.

contemporaries and continues to be interpreted as a vindication of her own conduct as well as an ambivalent portrait of the friend she was forced to renounce in order to ensure her own happiness.

The book Mrs Piozzi presented to the public in 1786 has been widely read and rarely praised. It was written in Italy, shortly following Johnson's death, under unfavourable circumstances. Afflicted by bouts of ill health, she noted in her text that 'a fever which has preyed on me while I wrote [these sheets] over for the press, will perhaps lessen my power of doing well the first, and probably the last work I should ever have thought of presenting to the Public.'[7] Living abroad, she was bereft of many of those friends who could augment her cache of Johnsonian stories, many of which were offered instead to Boswell or to Sir John Hawkins, Johnson's executor and official biographer; she was thus forced to rely, instead, on her volumes of *Thraliana* and her 'papers apart' devoted to Johnson. She was also racing against time. Several short sketches of Johnson had already appeared, and the more ambitious works advertised by Boswell and Hawkins could easily swamp her slighter book. So many biographies were in fact promised that she speculated in the opening pages of her text that 'all the readers would, on this singular occasion, be the writers of his life' (p. 61). She was also keenly aware that the anecdotes she told were already well known, a fact she had acknowledged earlier in a conversation with Johnson himself: 'I doubt not but this story will be told by many of his biographers, and said so to him when he told it me on the 18th of July 1773' (p. 70). But in spite of her obvious inexperience and limited point of view, she also knew that she had a unique portrait of Johnson to offer to the reading public—and even to many of Johnson's friends, especially those who were male—for she had lived on an intimate footing with him for eighteen years and had a more thorough knowledge than anyone else of both his playfulness and his debilitating melancholia. Perhaps Johnson acknowledged as much when he exhorted her to 'rescue me out of all their hands My dear, & do it *yourself*', a passage that follows directly upon her tantalizing comments in *Thraliana* in which she mentions her attempts 'to conceal his fancied Insanity' (ii. 625).[8]

It should not surprise us that contemporary response to the *Anecdotes* was quite spirited. A reading public still hungry for more Johnsoniana

[7] Piozzi, *Anecdotes*, p. 134. Further references are provided in the text.
[8] The standard study of Mrs Thrale's knowledge of Johnson's illness is Katharine C. Balderston, 'Johnson's Vile Melancholy', in *The Age of Johnson*, ed. Frederick W. Hilles (New Haven: Yale Univ. Press, 1949), 3–14, but see also W. Jackson Bate, *Samuel Johnson* (New York: Harcourt, 1977), 371–89.

bought up the entire first edition of 1,000 copies by nightfall of the day on which the book was published. Boswell read it avidly, if with derision; he would not be badly stung, however, until he read her second literary effort, the edition of Johnson's letters in which it became clear that Johnson had indeed loved Mrs Piozzi more than he had Boswell.[9] Sir Horace Walpole, a more objective observer of both the author and her subject, summed up much of the blue-stocking reaction when he concluded that it was 'wretched; a high-varnished preface to a heap of rubbish, in a very vulgar style, and too void of method even for such a farrago. . . . Her panegyric is loud in praise of her hero; and almost every fact she relates disgraces him.'[10] As Mrs Piozzi's biographer, James Clifford, has pointed out, much of the strong revulsion in this response can be attributed to an uneasiness with what Hannah More called 'This new-fashioned biography', which 'seems to value itself upon perpetuating every thing that is injurious and detracting'.[11] In this sense, at least, Mrs Piozzi was substantially faithful to the Johnsonian principles of veracity and minute observation of character, even at the expense of an unblemished portrait of her friend.

But there is more in Walpole's responses than a mere dislike—strong as it may have been—for distressing verisimilitude; he also objected to Mrs Piozzi's contradictory statements about Johnson, and to her want of method. The charge of inconsistency was repeated at the time by Mrs Chapone and more recently by Clifford, who notes that the text is filled with contradictions about Johnson's character and who concludes that her divided purpose in the *Anecdotes*, 'to justify her treatment of Johnson, and to achieve fame as one of his biographers', ultimately injured the quality of her work.[12] W. K. Wimsatt has been even more critical, arguing that the work is 'grotesque, even shocking', that the anecdotes are presented in a 'random order', and that Mrs Piozzi creates 'no coherent Johnson of her own'.[13] Katharine Balderston, on the other hand, has attempted to show how hard Mrs Piozzi laboured to soften her transitions and provide continuity and coherence to limited sections of the book, but the only real champion the *Anecdotes* has had is Donald Stauffer, who finds

---

[9] See Mary Hyde, *The Impossible Friendship: Boswell and Mrs. Thrale* (Cambridge, Mass.: Harvard Univ. Press, 1972), 129–30.

[10] Quoted by James L. Clifford, *Hester Lynch Piozzi (Mrs. Thrale)*, 2nd edn. (Oxford: Clarendon Press, 1952, rpt. and corr., 1968), 265.

[11] Quoted ibid. 265–6.

[12] Ibid. 265, 267.

[13] 'Images of Samuel Johnson', *ELH* 41 (1974), 359–74; I quote from pp. 364, 366, and 367. In a later note (p. 368) Wimsatt softened his position, but apparently did not feel it necessary to revise what he had already written.

it 'artistic in its absolute concentration on Johnson and its unhesitating conception, well integrated, of his character', a judgement that Stauffer does not—and cannot—support.[14] This is not to say, however, that the *Anecdotes* is actually 'void of method', as Walpole suggested. I want to argue, instead, that an understanding of Mrs Piozzi's method lay quite close to hand, and that it was in fact Walpole who unwittingly put his finger on it.

Three years later, in a comment on Mrs Piozzi's travel narrative (her *Observations and Reflections made in the Course of a Journey through France, Italy, and Germany*), Walpole wrote to a friend that 'her friends plead that she piques herself on writing as she talks: methinks, then, she should talk as she would write'.[15] Walpole's witticism found an uncanny echo in a response to the same book by one of Mrs Piozzi's friends, Leonard Chappelow: 'to read twenty pages and hear Mrs. Piozzi's talk for twenty minutes is the same thing.'[16] These judgements were meant to be critical, but the parallel drawn here between conversation and writing is not only at the heart of Mrs Piozzi's literary 'method' but also crucial to her understanding of Johnson's character. Conversation meant a great deal to her—at times, perhaps, everything to her—during her long lifetime.[17] When she was a young wife, saddled with numerous children, a demanding mother, and a large house to run, conversation remained one of the few avenues of intelligent discourse that were open to her. During her second marriage, when she was increasingly sensitive to the linguistic difficulties that sophisticated talk posed for foreigners, she published her *British Synonymy*, a book that attempted to regulate the choice of words in familiar conversation (we might think of it as a shorter, more refined version of Johnson's *Dictionary*).[18] And during her middle years, when she

[14] See Balderston's introduction to *Thraliana*, pp. xviii–xxviii, and Donald A. Stauffer, *The Art of Biography in Eighteenth Century England* (Princeton: Princeton Univ. Press, 1941), i. 407. For the most recent—and most admiring—assessment of the *Anecdotes*, see William McCarthy, *Hester Thrale Piozzi: Portrait of a Literary Woman* (Chapel Hill: Univ. of North Carolina Press, 1985), ch. 4: 'It is tempting to suggest that had Boswell never written we might have known Johnson better from the beginning, for the light Piozzi sheds on him, although less brilliant than Boswell's, is often shed upon more relevant places' (p. 126). Claims such as these are rather too sweeping, but McCarthy does isolate several interesting aspects of the *Anecdotes*, especially Mrs Piozzi's perspective as a mother and her anticipation of some of Boswell's more finely honed techniques.

[15] Quoted by Clifford, *Hester Lynch Piozzi*, pp. 343–4.

[16] Quoted by Hyde, *The Impossible Friendship*, pp. 139–40.

[17] Her other outlets were in her letters and marginalia. We should remember that epistolary writing was often called 'talking on paper' in the 18th cent. For an interesting perspective, see Keith Stewart, 'Towards Defining an Aesthetic for the Familiar Letter in Eighteenth-Century England', *Prose Studies*, 5 (1982), 179–92. For an assessment of her other outlet, see Morris R. Brownell, 'Hester Lynch Piozzi's Marginalia', *Eighteenth-Century Life*, 3 (1977), 97–100.

[18] I take my description from her subtitle; for an analysis of the work, see Clifford, *Hester Lynch Piozzi*, pp. 366–74.

enjoyed her reputation as the lively hostess of Streatham Park, she lived much of the time with the greatest talker of her age. It was therefore natural for her to portray Johnson in the role in which she knew him best: as a spirited but demanding conversationalist, as a living book, as a stern but sympathetic moralist whose presence was a source of knowledge and wisdom as well as admonition and even fear.

This conception of the force of Johnson's character is not unique, of course; we can also find it in Boswell's work, although perhaps more strongly in the journals than in the recollected *Life*. But Boswell knew Johnson as an author before he knew him as a friend and conversationalist, and his justly celebrated retention and reanimation of Johnson's talk were skilfully fused with his dramatic approach to narrative and his close attention to Johnson's letters and published works. Mrs Piozzi essayed a much less ambitious task, concentrating solely on the last twenty years of his life, and relegating their correspondence to separate volumes that would have to be published later. Johnson's work as a writer is usually treated in a peripheral manner. If she can provide a personal connection, she will supply it; but most of her attention is devoted to the impromptus and other ephemeral productions that only she could save from oblivion.[19] Chronology plays little part in her design: she dutifully follows Johnson's progress from Lichfield to London, but the bulk of her 'narrative', if such a term can be used to describe it, follows the twists and turns of her Johnsonian musings. More than anything else, her book represents a compendium of Johnson's opinions—opinions derived from his own stories and from stories told about him—but always opinions spun in the intricate threads of talk.

Her justification for writing in this unusual and highly subjective manner lay in her own conception of Johnson's character, which she carefully if somewhat repetitively develops in her text. Near the beginning of the *Anecdotes* she claims that 'To recollect . . . and to repeat the sayings of Dr. Johnson, is almost all that can be done by the writers of his life,' for

his life, at least since my acquaintance with him, consisted in little else than talking, when he was not absolutely employed in some serious piece of work; and whatever work he did, seemed so much below his powers of performance, that he appeared the idlest of all human beings; ever musing till he was called out to converse, and conversing till the fatigue of his friends, or the promptitude of his

[19] In this sense, at least, Johnson's fugitive pieces are like his conversation, and must be recorded— and then published—if they are to survive. I think that this explains, at least in part, Mrs Piozzi's deep interest in these minor pieces; another explanation is that they were often written for her, or to her, or in her presence.

own temper to take offence, consigned him back again to silent meditation. (pp. 67–8)

Johnson had other interests, to be sure, but when, for example, his chemical experiments necessarily came to an end, he was 'thus reduced to the pleasures of conversation merely: and what wonder that he should have an avidity for the sole delight he was able to enjoy?' (p. 139). He would therefore have tea made at 2 in the morning in order to detain his companions even further into the night, and prefer winter to summer and carriages to the open air because carriages and bad weather allowed his company fewer means of escape.

'Talk beyond that which is necessary to the purposes of actual business is a kind of game', Mrs Piozzi argues (p. 74), and in her circle of friends no one played that game better than Johnson. She portrays Johnson as 'a very talking man' and 'a tremendous converser' in what she calls 'the talking world'; 'few people ventured to try their skill against an antagonist with whom contention was so hopeless' (pp. 129, 122, 128). She writes that 'Promptitude of thought indeed, and quickness of expression, were among the peculiar felicities of Johnson: his notions rose up like the dragon's teeth sowed by Cadmus all ready clothed, and in bright armour too, fit for immediate battle' (p. 128). But if he talked for victory, as Boswell was to argue, he also talked for the common good:

He did not wish to confound, but to inform his auditors; and though he did not appear to solicit benevolence, he always wished to retain authority, and leave his company impressed with the idea, that it was his to teach in this world, and theirs to learn. (p. 120)

But even this sentence betrays some of the ambivalence she felt towards one who 'always wished to retain authority', especially when he turned his wrath on her, as he occasionally did.

Mrs Piozzi responded to Johnson's rebukes and harshness of manner in two strikingly different ways, and we must understand both of her reactions if we wish to account for the contradictions at the heart of her work. She believed, on the one hand, that Johnson's severe treatment of even his closest friends could be justified because his judgements were so often true. In a remarkable passage in which she portrays him as a kind of living book, she discriminates between the effects that written and oral reprimands have upon us:

It is easy to observe, that the justice of such sentences made them offensive; but we must be careful how we condemn a man for saying what we know to be true, only because it *is* so. I hope that the reason our hearts rebelled a little against his severity, was chiefly because it came from a living mouth.—Books were invented to take off the odium of immediate superiority, and soften the rigour of duties prescribed by the teachers and censors of human kind—setting at least those who are acknowledged wiser than ourselves at a distance. When we recollect however, that for this very reason *they* are seldom consulted and little obeyed, how much cause shall his contemporaries have to rejoice that their living Johnson forced them to feel the reproofs due to vice and folly . . . (p. 89)

Johnson must be accommodated and admired because he embodies the cautionary wisdom we normally find only in books and tailors it to the situation at hand, even at the price of domestic harmony. His oral (and oracular) authority is so great in Mrs Piozzi's eyes that she includes among her anecdotes the amusing story of how Johnson was accosted by two gentlemen who wanted to know how to pronounce the adjective 'irreparable'. After offering an answer, Johnson told his companions that they should ' "better consult my Dictionary than me, for that was the result of more thought than you will now give me time for." No, no, replied the gentleman gaily, the book I have no certainty at all of; but here is the *author*' (p. 136).[20] Mrs Piozzi characterizes this as a 'strange thing', but it reinforces, if only unintentionally, her belief in Johnson's personal authority, whether he be holding forth in her parlour or walking along the Strand.

This was one response, but it was not the only one. Like many of her friends, Mrs Piozzi smarted from Johnson's astringent judgements and often brutish behaviour. She tells us at one point that she would like to conclude her book by showing her zeal for her friend and thereby leading others to emulate his goodness; but she must also offer this caveat, which represents a strikingly different moral to her story: 'but seeing the necessity of making even virtue and learning such as *his* agreeable, . . . all should be warned against such coarseness of manners, as drove even from *him* those who loved, honoured and esteemed him' (p. 134). This is one of the principal points of her book, and it must be set against her repeated submission to Johnson's personal authority. But it was not, I think, Johnson's coarseness of manners that led her to paint this often unflattering portrait of her friend, so much as her own decision to desert him (and virtually her entire family) by marrying Gabriel Piozzi. This major act of disruption in her life, with its attendant pain and guilt, compelled her to

---

[20] Cf. an anecdote by William Seward in *Johnsonian Miscellanies*, ed. George Birkbeck Hill (1897), ii. 310, where Johnson is asked to introduce a woman to a writer: ' "Dearest Madam," replied he, "you had better let it alone; the best part of every author is in general to be found in his book." '

see the rugged and uncouth side of a character that others had complained about for some time.

In her narrative, however, there are no serious disruptions—only artful transitions. Like the patriarch or squire in one of Hogarth's conversation pieces, Johnson serves as the central focus in the composition, drawing the other figures together and holding them in a harmonious relationship. Occasionally Johnson's abrupt behaviour will endanger this delicate balance—like the gaping couloir that appears in Hogarth's early conversations—but in the *Anecdotes* Mrs Piozzi holds authority in her own hands; domestic harmony always triumphs.[21] Like an extended conversation her narrative expands and contracts, digresses and repeats itself as it circles round her major figure, but it remains in perpetual motion, an ideal version of the *conversazione*, the intimate gathering referred to in England as an 'at home'.[22] By a sleight of hand, Mrs Piozzi gently manœuvres our attention from one aspect of Johnson's character to another, often with such subtlety that any prescriptive judgement is lost amid the wealth of anecdotal nuance.

The most extraordinary example of this association of ideas occurs shortly after Mrs Piozzi considers Johnson's relations with her mother, the other dominant force in her life. Although these two forceful characters did not always please each other, Mrs Piozzi is thankful that they existed on such amiable terms during her mother's final illness. Johnson, she says, 'acknowledged himself improved by her piety, and astonished at her fortitude, and hung over her bed with the affection of a parent, and the reverence of a son'. And then, in prose so much at variance with her own loose and colloquial style, she rounds off her portrait of her mother in a sentence worthy of Johnson himself:

Nor did it give me less pleasure to see her sweet mind cleared of all its latent prejudices, and left at liberty to admire and applaud that force of thought and versatility of genius, that comprehensive soul and benevolent heart which attracted and commanded veneration from all, but inspired peculiar sensations of delight mixed with reverence in those who, like her, had the opportunity to observe these qualities, stimulated by gratitude, and actuated by friendship. (p. 103)

Johnson and Mrs Salusbury merge in this passage just as harmoniously as Mrs Piozzi had often wished they would in life, an assurance that

---

[21] For a discussion of the couloir, see Paulson, *Hogarth*, i. 217–18.

[22] The *OED* notes the association between the *conversazione* and the 'at home' as early as 1787, just a year after the *Anecdotes* was published.

stimulates her to think next about how frequently Johnson laboured to resolve her husband's perplexities of mind. She then prints Johnson's Latin epitaph on her mother's monument, followed by Arthur Murphy's English rendering, which had not yet been published. This leads, however, to 'The following epitaph on Mr. Thrale, who has now a monument close by her's in Streatham church' (p. 104), a transition she thought natural, perhaps, because it continued her discussion of the epitaphs Johnson wrote for his friends, but which is none the less startling in its treatment of her first husband, of whose illness and death we have heard nothing. She then proceeds to tell us that Johnson wrote only one other engraved inscription, for Goldsmith, although he also wrote a four-line epitaph on Hogarth; and thoughts of Hogarth draw her back to her own youth, when the artist was 'very earnest that I should obtain the acquaintance, and if possible the friendship of Dr. Johnson, whose conversation was to the talk of other men, like Titian's painting compared to Hudson's, he said . . .' (p. 106). By this point, of course, we have been transported back to Mrs Piozzi's favourite subject. Not even her mother's death—let alone her husband's—will disrupt the fluid continuity of her narrative; their difficulties and even their deaths afford yet another opportunity for her to reveal Johnson's friendship and his conversational powers.

Like Mrs Piozzi's narrative, it is natural for conversations to repeat and even contradict themselves, and I find it intriguing that many of the repetitive or inconsistent passages in her book focus on the value of 'stories' and on Johnson's scruples about story-telling. Consider, for instance, the following excerpt on Johnson's 'rigid attention to veracity', which will be repeated almost word for word later in her text:

'a story (says he) is a specimen of human manners, and derives its sole value from its truth. When Foote has told me something, I dismiss it from my mind like a passing shadow: when Reynolds tells me something, I consider myself as possessed of an idea the more.' (p. 98; cf. p. 159)

A little later, however, she tells us that Johnson did not 'much delight in that kind of conversation which consists in telling stories', and she quotes him at length on this subject:

'every body (said he) tells stories of me, and I tell stories of nobody. I do not recollect (added he), that I have ever told *you*, that have been always favourites, above three stories; but I hope I do not play the Old Fool, and force people to hear uninteresting narratives, only because I once was diverted with them myself.' He was however no enemy to that sort of talk from the famous Mr.

Foote, 'whose happiness of manner in relating was such (he said) as subdued arrogance and roused stupidity: *His* stories were truly like those of Biron in Love's Labour Lost, so *very* attractive.' (pp. 118–19)

Inconsistencies cannot both be right but, as Imlac reminds us, when they are attributed to man, they may both be true. It is possible that Mrs Piozzi has quoted Johnson accurately two—or even three—times here, but it is also the burden of Johnson's commentary on story-telling that the embellishment and polish with which anecdotes are told may easily undermine or obscure their truthfulness, which is the sole reason for valuing them in the first place.[23]

Mrs Piozzi encountered a similar dilemma when she attempted to reconcile Johnson's benign actions with his verbal rebukes. When she relates 'various instances of contemptuous behavior' to those who do not know Johnson well, she is afraid that her readers will 'cry out against his pride and his severity'. And yet she tells us that she has been as careful as possible

to tell them, that all he did was gentle, if all he said was rough. Had I given anecdotes of his actions instead of his words, we should I am sure have had nothing on record but acts of virtue differently modified, as different occasions called that virtue forth: and among all the nine biographical essays or perform-ances which I have heard will at last be written about dear Dr. Johnson, no mean or wretched, no wicked or even slightly culpable action will I trust be found, to produce and put in the scale against a life of seventy years, spent in the uniform practice of every moral excellence and every Christian perfection . . . (p. 133)

If she wanted to write a panegryic rather than a biography, she would have 'told his deeds only, not his words', for Johnson appeared to her, like Socrates and Pascal, as 'an excepted being' (p. 134). Other friends knew him longer, and in different circumstances; she knew him only through the world of talk, a world in which his brusqueness, high-handedness, and inconsistencies were bound to emerge. No one, she tells us, was so careful 'to maintain the ceremonies of life', and she quotes Johnson's famous remark to her husband that while it was true 'that he had never sought to please till past thirty years old, considering the matter as hopeless, he had been always studious not to make enemies, by apparent preference of himself'. No sooner had this 'curious conversa-

---

[23] Perhaps there is confusion here simply because Mrs Piozzi did not edit her manuscript as carefully as she should have done; it is possible that Johnson could praise Foote's delivery and yet remember little of what he had said. Mrs Piozzi quoted Johnson on Foote as a story-teller under the heading of 'Fascination' in *British Synonymy*; see Clifford, *Hester Lynch Piozzi*, pp. 371–2. The same conversation was recorded by Boswell; see *Life*, iii. 69–70.

tion' ended, however, than Johnson abruptly contradicted these genteel principles by refusing to pay his compliments to a visitor on horseback: ' 'Tis Mr. Ch—lm—ley, says my husband;—"Well, Sir! and what if it is Mr. Ch—ml—ley" says the other sternly, just lifting his eyes a moment from his book, and returning to it again with renewed avidity' (p. 145).

Passages such as these clearly had an alarming effect on Mrs Piozzi's readers: some berated her for her audacity, others for her carelessness and inaccuracy. To Boswell, in particular, the *Anecdotes* reinforced an opinion he had shared with Johnson years earlier. In a journal entry for 7 April 1778, he wrote: 'We talked of Mrs. Thrale's laxity of narrative, inattention to truth, and he said, "I'm as much vexed at the ease with which she hears it mentioned to her as at the thing itself. I told her, 'Madam, you are contented to hear every day said to you what the highest of mankind have died rather than bear.' You know, Sir, the highest of mankind have died rather than bear to be told they tell a lie." '[24] Boswell's response to the book itself was more complex. He objected to the anecdote about Cholmondeley, for instance, because Johnson had not only later told her that he was 'utterly unconscious' of the story but had also apologized to their friend.[25] Boswell deleted in revised proof a statement that he had inserted in the manuscript of the *Life of Johnson*: 'Her *double picture* occurs here again . . . she can without remorse give a hideous caricature of *Him* to whom she was under the greatest obligations . . .'. This *'double picture'* refers to a suggestion Edmond Malone had included earlier in the manuscript, that Mrs Piozzi extolled Johnson as a 'Guide Philosopher and Freind', but belittled him when he appeared as 'the indignant upbraider of Signora Piozzi'.[26]

Whether she was prompted by a sense of personal vindication or by a Johnsonian conviction to tell the truth—or by both—her portrait of Johnson nevertheless manages to convey much of his complexity and vitality, even if it occasionally belittles or trivializes him, for the conversational mode in which she chose to write prevented a static conception from emerging. In one of the few surviving fragments from her commonplace books devoted to Johnson, she noted that 'These Anecdotes are put down in a wild way just as I received or could catch 'em from Mr. Johnsons Conversation, but I mean one day or another to digest and place

---

[24] *Boswell in Extremes: 1776–1778*, ed. Charles McC. Weis and Frederick A. Pottle (London: Heinemann; New York: McGraw-Hill, 1970), 246–7. This quotation was reprinted in the *Life*; see my discussion below, p. 277.

[25] See Hyde, *The Impossible Friendship*, pp. 159–60.

[26] Quoted by Hyde, ibid. 160, 159.

them in some order.'[27] It is part of the virtue and charm of her published
work that her editorial tasks did not entirely destroy the spontaneity and
vivacious personal voice that we find in her journals. She was also quite
scrupulous in revising and recombining her original sources; when she
did make a change, it was often an attempt to soften her depiction of
Johnson's behaviour, even at the price of directing Johnson's wrath at
herself rather than at others.[28] Even what Boswell called her double
portrait of Johnson had emerged earlier in the unusual classification of her
friends' virtues that she drew up in her journal in July 1778, long before
her break with Johnson. There, on a scale of 0 to 20, she rated Johnson
extremely highly in the categories of religion, morality, scholarship,
general knowledge, wit, and humour; but in three other columns—
devoted to person and voice, manner, and good humour—she awarded
him flat noughts, noting below that 'with regard to these People I really
think they are very fairly rated: those that have os have none of ye Quality
mentioned' (*Thraliana*, i. 329–30).[29]

This unusual system of evaluating her family's and friends' personal
characteristics is especially intriguing because it mirrors, in its compart-
mentalization of a personality, the structure of the *Anecdotes* itself, in
which a consideration of one particular quality inevitably leads to a
discussion of others related to it. She had much difficulty, however, in
trying to convey a more contracted and essential portrait of Johnson, and
it is significant that in her attempts to provide such a synthetic figure she
almost invariably had recourse to visual motifs, with their representation
of fixed or delimited meaning. These visual metaphors also appear when
she acknowledges the particular difficulties she must face in re-creating
Johnson's character through the limited resources available to her. Here is
the most famous of her parallels, embedded in a particularly rich passage
that repeats many of the themes with which we are already familiar:

I saw Mr. Johnson in none but a tranquil uniform state, passing the evening of

[27] Quoted in *Thraliana*, i, p. xix. It is interesting to note that in the following lines Mrs Piozzi talks
about 'digesting' her anecdotes by using an example that Walton had already made use of in his *Life of
Donne* (see above, pp. 27–8): 'as the poor Egyptian gather'd up the relicks of a broken Boat and
burning them by himself upon the Beach said he was forming a Funeral Pile in honour of the great
Pompey—may it be long before that day comes'.

[28] See Balderston's introduction to *Thraliana*, esp. i, pp. xxii–xxv, and Frederick A. Pottle and
Charles H. Bennett, 'Boswell and Mrs. Piozzi', *Modern Philology*, 39 (1942), 421–30. For an interesting
example of Mrs Piozzi's softening of her portrait of Johnson, compare her *Anecdotes*, pp. 94–5, with
Thraliana, i. 165, 185.

[29] Mrs Piozzi based her system, she says, on Joseph Spence's *Crito* (1752); she could also have
found an example in Jonathan Richardson's tabulation of the perfections (and imperfections) of artists
in *The Science of a Connoisseur*. Spacks points out that the criteria for men and women are significantly
different; see 'Scrapbook of a Self: Mrs. Piozzi's Late Journals', p. 229.

his life among friends, who loved, honoured, and admired him: I saw none of the things he did, except such acts of charity as have been often mentioned in this book, and such writings as are universally known. What he said is all I can relate; and from what he said, those who think it worth while to read these Anecdotes, must be contented to gather his character. Mine is a mere *candle-light* picture of his latter days, where every thing falls in dark shadow except the face, the index of the mind; but even that is seen unfavourably, and with a paleness beyond what nature gave it. (p. 141)

Once again she emphasizes her limited perspective and draws a distinction between Johnson's actions and his words. Hers is presumably a *'candle-light'* picture because it is drawn during 'the evening' of his days, not during the full blaze of his career, and yet the figure of the candle and its attendant shadow also reinforces the sense we have throughout the narrative that we are being offered an intimate view. Those who read this narrative, moreover, must 'gather' his character; her readers must necessarily be active interpreters, synthesizing his character from the hundreds of stories in which it is dispersed. But the portrait she provides is also a close-up, focusing on the face alone, which is not only the conventional 'index of the mind' but also the medium through which Johnson's conversation emerges. And even the face itself, she admits in an ambiguous slip, is seen 'unfavourably', by which she means only to say that her talents are perhaps not equal to her task.

Visual analogies such as this *'candle-light* picture of his latter days' occur regularly throughout her narrative. She opens her book by suggesting that a preface, 'like the portico before a house, should be contrived, so as to catch, but not detain the attention of those who desire admission to the family within, or [desire] to leave to look over the collection of pictures made by one whose opportunities of obtaining them we know to have been not unfrequent' (p. 59). She does indeed introduce us to the family within, and at the very close of her anecdotes, immediately preceding her turn to a 'character' proper of Johnson, she even draws our attention to the collection of portraits her husband commissioned Reynolds to paint of their family and friends, and of the verse portraits she wrote to accompany them.[30] Other metaphors, however, are more self-deprecating. She is aware that she 'cannot give each expression of Dr. Johnson with all its force or all its neatness', but at the same time she knows that 'To endeavour at adorning, or adding, or softening, or meliorating such anecdotes, by any tricks my inexperienced pen could play, would be

---

[30] There appears to be no detailed study of this collection of library portraits, but see Hyde, *The Impossible Friendship*, p. 18, and *Johnsonian Miscellanies*, i. 342 n. 3.

weakness indeed; worse than the Frenchman who presides over the porcelain manufactory at Seve, to whom when some Greek vases were given him as models, he lamented *la tristesse de telles formes*; and endeavoured to assist them by clusters of flowers, while flying Cupids served for the handles of urns originally intended to contain the ashes of the dead' (pp. 148–9). Elsewhere she claims that 'The cork model of Paris is not more despicable as a resemblance of a great city, than this book, *levior cortice*, as a specimen of Johnson's character', and then compares her narrative to 'a piece of motley Mosaic work' (p. 140). Each of these visual metaphors tells us something interesting about how Mrs Piozzi conceived of her own work, but the comparison with a multi-coloured mosaic is perhaps the most telling because it is consistent with our own experience of reading her book, especially of sifting its numerous fragments. But how is this dispersed narrative, this breathless conversation, to end? Deprived of chronology, we are spared the disruption of a death. Instead she introduces Reynolds's own image of Johnson, and supplements the library portrait with her 'character' in verse. Such a sketch, she concedes, 'will for the most part be found imperfect as a character', presumably because a poetical synopsis is necessarily too contracted a portrait of her friend. She will therefore close with a prose 'character' as well, although even here she again insists that she will not 'complete, but . . . conclude these Anecdotes of the best and wisest man that ever came within the reach of my personal acquaintance . . .' (p. 157). Her verse portrait is consistent with the 'double picture' in her narrative that so annoyed both Boswell and Malone; like Ulysses, Johnson is pictured looking down with a contemptuous frown on the 'wit and worth' of his comrades:

> We suffer from JOHNSON, contented to find
> That some notice we gain from so noble a mind;
> And pardon our hurts, since so often we've found
> The balm of instruction pour'd into the wound.

The prose 'character' that concludes—but cannot complete—her book was, like the poetical sketch, completed years before she contemplated publishing her anecdotes and was written originally for Johnson himself: 'One Evening as I was giving my Tongue Liberty to praise Mr Johnson to his Face; a favour he would not often allow me he said in high good humour; come! you shall draw up my Character your own Way, & shew it me; that I may see what you will say of me when I am gone. at Night I wrote as follows—' (*Thraliana*, i. 205). Like Boswell when he was confronted by the problem of concluding his own biography of Johnson, Mrs Piozzi returned to a contracted 'character' she had already written, and which in her case Johnson had already praised. The sketch as it appears in the *Anecdotes* is virtually the same as the one she wrote in 1777; even her comments on 'a roughness in his manner which subdued the saucy, and terrified the meek' had appeared in her earlier version. But it was an arbitrary and conventional ending to her spirited narrative, as her comments on 'concluding' and 'completing' suggest she realized. Boswell's closing character-sketch in the *Life* must have struck him (as it does us) as superfluous and even reductive after the thousands of detailed episodes through which he had led his readers; Mrs Piozzi's is equally disappointing because it differs so little from what precedes it and yet lacks the liveliness of her conversational imagination. It repeats the well-known categories and opinions, adding little to what we have already 'gathered'. Her conception of Johnson's mind, for example, is once again synonymous with her response to his conversation: 'no language but that he used could have expressed its contents; and so ponderous was his language, that sentiments less lofty and less solid than his were, would have been encumbered, not adorned by it' (p. 158).

When she returns to this subject, however, in the final sentence of her book, she finally severs this almost inevitable association of his mind with his talk and turns instead to an extended analogy with the natural world. Johnson's mind is stored with such a variety of knowledge that it resembles, she says, a 'royal pleasure-ground' in which every plant flourishes in the full perfection of its powers,

and where, though lofty woods and falling cataracts first caught the eye, and fixed the earliest attention of beholders, yet neither the trim parterre nor the pleasing shrubbery, nor even the antiquated ever-greens, were denied a place in some fit corner of the happy valley. (p. 160)

It is a daring and somewhat strange metaphor, fusing the organic with the artful, the sublime with the picturesque; and it is as ambitious and as moving as her attempt during Johnson's lifetime to domesticate him within her own family circle, to provide him with his own pleasure-ground at Streatham. At the same time, her reliance on a grand, stable image is at odds with the free play and variegated mosaic of her own narrative; she is most distinctive and original as a biographer when she does not strive to adapt her familiar style and visual imagination to the moral landscape of Johnson's mind. Johnson, of course, never saw the

Anecdote as a whole, but he told Mrs Piozzi that her 'character' of him 'was a very fine Piece of Writing'.[31]

ii. Goldsmith's *Nash*: Biography as Romance

'And who will be my biographer?' Johnson asked Mrs Piozzi in the summer of 1773. Without hesitation she replied that Goldsmith 'will do it best among us', an answer that did not entirely please her friend: 'The dog would write best to be sure, replied he; but his particular malice towards me, and general disregard for truth, would make the book useless to all, and injurious to my character.'[32] Johnson, moreover, knew at least three months earlier that the more sympathetic Boswell was already entertaining a 'constant plan' to write his life, for Boswell had taken the occasion of Johnson's condemnation of Goldsmith's *Life of Parnell* to propose this project to him:

> He said, 'Goldsmith's Life of Parnell is poor; not that it is poorly written, but that he had poor materials; for nobody can write the life of a man, but those who have eat and drunk and lived in social intercourse with him.'
>
> I said, that if it were not troublesome and presuming too much, I would request him to tell me all the little circumstances of his life ... He did not disapprove of my curiosity as to these particulars; but said, 'They'll come out by degrees as we talk together.'[33]

And this is of course one of the great virtues of Boswell's *Life*—and part of its originality—that his portrait of Johnson emerges as much by the slow accretion of episode and fact as by overt generalization. But Mrs Piozzi was not entirely mistaken when she praised Goldsmith's own biographical gifts; as for his prejudice, she assured Johnson, 'we should all fasten upon him, and force him to do you justice ...'.[34] Johnson himself would later condense the *Life of Parnell* in his *Lives of the English Poets*, in which he paid tribute to Goldsmith's 'variety of powers' and 'felicity of performance', and he must have known, from Goldsmith's many published comments, that his friend was, at least in *theory*, fully impregnated by Johnson's biographical '*æther*'. In addition to writing short sketches of Walpole, Boyle, Voltaire, and Parnell, Goldsmith had abridged several volumes of Plutarch's *Lives*, opening the preface to his edition by arguing that biography has always 'been considered as the most useful manner of writing, not only from the pleasure it affords the imagination, but from

[31] *Thraliana*, i. 208.
[32] Piozzi, *Anecdotes*, p. 70; see also *Thraliana*, i. 173.
[33] Boswell, *Life*, ii. 166.
[34] Piozzi, *Anecdotes*, p. 70.

the instruction it artfully and unexpectedly conveys to the understanding', and concluding it by quoting *Rambler* no. 60 in its entirety.[35] But Goldsmith died ten years before Johnson—thus allaying his friend's fears—and his reputation as a biographer therefore rests almost entirely on his *Life of Richard Nash, Esq.*, published in 1762.[36] Almost all twentieth-century criticism of the *Life of Nash* has focused on two central issues. How, in the first place, are we to interpret the tone of Goldsmith's biography? Is the narrator's attitude towards his slight subject (Nash was the master of ceremonies at Bath) understanding and sympathetic, or is it heavily ironic, as Robert Hopkins and others have recently argued?[37] Is Goldsmith a 'cool biographer, unbiassed by resentment or regard', as he describes himself near the conclusion of his text, or does he consistently damn his hero with sarcasm and faint praise?[38] How seriously are we to take Goldsmith when, in the skilfully balanced sentences that were the hallmark of his style, he tells us that we shall probably find nothing in Nash 'either truly great, or strongly vicious', that 'To set him up, as some do, for a pattern of imitation, is wrong, since all his virtues received a tincture from the neighbouring folly; to denounce peculiar judgments against him, is equally unjust, as his faults raise rather our mirth than our detestation' (iii. 378)?

A second issue, which I believe is related to the first, concerns the nature of Goldsmith's sources. Modern scholars have discovered that at least two of the anecdotes Goldsmith includes in his narrative are not unique to *The Life of Nash*. The story of Colonel M——, for instance, in which this character is finally united with his lover when she sees him appear upon the stage, bears a close resemblance to the experience of George Primrose in *The Vicar of Wakefield*. It is not clear, however, as

---

[35] Goldsmith, *Works*, v. 226. For Goldsmith's other debts to Johnson, see Joseph E. Brown, 'Goldsmith and Johnson on Biography', *Modern Language Notes*, 42 (1927), 168–71, and Friedman's footnotes to the text of *The Life of Nash* in Goldsmith, *Works*, iii.

[36] On Goldsmith's other biographical projects, see R. W. Seitz, 'Goldsmith's Lives of the Fathers', *Modern Philology*, 26 (1929), 295–305, and 'Goldsmith and the "English Lives"', ibid. 28 (1931), 329–36.

[37] See Robert H. Hopkins, *The True Genius of Oliver Goldsmith* (Baltimore: The Johns Hopkins Univ. Press, 1969), 152–65, who sees Nash as a paradoxical symbol of corrupt aristocratic taste. Almost all subsequent criticism on Goldsmith has been forced to respond to Hopkins's ironic reading of this—and other—texts. His closest ally is Richard J. Jaarsma, 'Biography as Tragedy: Fictive Skill in Oliver Goldsmith's *The Life of Richard Nash, Esq.*', *Journal of Narrative Technique*, 1 (1971), 15–29. Both Hopkins and Jaarsma are reacting to the earlier view—embraced by such critics as Stauffer, Wardle, and Quintana—that the *Life* is sympathetic as well as critical, a view that, as my following argument makes clear, I share as well. For an intelligent refutation of Hopkins's argument, see John A. Dussinger, 'Philanthropy and the Selfish Reader in Goldsmith's *Life of Nash*', *Studies in Burke and His Time*, 19 (1978), 197–207. Samuel H. Woods, jun., provides a useful overview of this and other controversies in 'The Goldsmith "Problem"', ibid. 47–60.

[38] Goldsmith, *Works*, iii. 378. Further references are provided in the text.

Arthur Friedman points out in his edition, 'whether Goldsmith is heightening the story in the *Life* with an incident he had invented or whether the passage in the *Vicar* is based upon a supposedly true incident that he heard of while collecting material about Nash', for Goldsmith wrote both books at roughly the same time.[39] Similarly, at an earlier point in the *Life*, Goldsmith shows the young Nash to be so generous and yet so constitutionally short of funds that he would cheerfully lend money to his friends while refusing to pay the debts he had himself contracted, a paradox Goldsmith had noted three years earlier in *The Bee* and which has sources in at least two other writers, Mariveau and Justus Van Effen.[40] We are also led to suspect that even some of the written materials quoted in the text were penned by Goldsmith himself, particularly a long letter on the evils of the gaming-table that may have been included in order to lengthen the volume for the printer.[41]

But even as Goldsmith's scholars have unearthed these problematical borrowings and interpolations, they have curiously refrained from speculating on what significance they may have for the biography as a whole. Because biography is principally distinguished from fiction by its complex relation to fact—to the greater or lesser memorials of the dead that form the bedrock of personal history—knowledge of how a biographer shapes his or her materials is normally crucial to our understanding of private prejudices as well as one's conception of how human lives should be portrayed. In writing the *Life of Nash* Goldsmith had, for once in his brief career as a biographer, no paucity of original and secondary materials on which to draw. Beau Nash was a well-known figure, the 'King of Bath', and he had lived a long life. Nash's executor is said to have given the author 'all the Papers found in the Custody of Mr. *Nash*, which any ways respected his Life, and were thought interesting to the Publick' (iii. 287), and Goldsmith also borrowed heavily from the second edition of John Wood's *Essay towards a Description of Bath*, both for biographical information and for a first-hand account of how Bath had been transformed from a provincial retreat for the diseased to a fashionable resort beckoning the

[39] Ibid. iii. 324 n. 2; earlier noted by Morris Golden, 'Another Manufactured Anecdote in *The Life of Richard Nash?*', *Notes and Queries*, 202 (1958), 20–1.

[40] See Arthur Sherbo, 'A Manufactured Anecdote in Goldsmith's *Life of Richard Nash*', *Modern Language Notes*, 70 (1955), 20–2, and Sven Bäckman, 'The Real Origin of One of the "Manufactured Anecdotes" in Goldsmith's *Life of Nash*', *Modern Philology*, 72 (1975), 277–9.

[41] See Oliver W. Ferguson, 'The Materials of History: Goldsmith's *Life of Nash*', *PMLA*, 80 (1965), 372–85, esp. 381 ff. Ferguson argues that the manuscript of the *Life* may originally have been shorter than the published version, and that the material subsequently added to it may have been even more extensive than what was finally printed in the text.

polite, the improvident, and the reckless.[42] In short, Goldsmith had both the resources and the subject matter he needed to produce an immensely popular—and perhaps even scandalous—narrative, one filled with tales of the famous and the notorious. No wonder, then, that he emphasized his own truthfulness (and even his alleged acquaintance with Nash) as often as possible, claiming in the advertisement to the book that his account was 'genuine, and not the Work of Imagination, as Biographical Writings too frequently are' (iii. 287). Were he 'upon the present occasion to hold the pen of a novelist,' he later writes, 'I could recount some amours, in which he was successful. I could fill a volume with little anecdotes, which contain neither pleasure nor instruction . . . But such adventures are easily written, and as easily atchieved' (iii. 321).

But here, I want to argue, even as Goldsmith tells us what he will and will not disclose, we can begin to detect the actual relation between the biographer and his sources and thus the structural characteristics of his narrative as a whole. With a substantial amount of potentially salacious material at his disposal, Goldsmith in fact thwarts the vicarious satisfaction of his audience by concealing the identities of most of his fashionable characters and by placing their examples in the context of what is essentially a moral tale. Even his focus on Richard Nash, with all of his peculiarities, is intended to illustrate general truths that apply to each of us: 'The great and the little, as they have the same senses, and the same affections, generally present the same picture to the hand of the draughtsman . . .' (iii. 290). Goldsmith draws the portrait of 'one, who was just such a man as probably you or I may be, but with this difference, that he never performed an action which the world did not know, or ever formed a wish which he did not take pains to divulge' (iii. 291). He therefore draws a veil over Nash's 'amours' not simply because they would 'gratify the pruriency of folly', but also because they would fail to distinguish him from other scheming lovers. He is at pains throughout his narrative to show that, despite Nash's fame, this *'little king of a little people'* is much like everyone else—neither better nor actually worse—that his character is sharply divided between warm generosity on the one hand and manifest imprudence on the other, and that both of these qualities necessarily precipitate his early success and eventual demise. Goldsmith's narrative is therefore permeated by the sure hand of causality and by an archetypal presentation of character.

[42] See Arthur Friedman, 'Goldsmith and Wood', *Times Literary Supplement* (2 Nov. 1956), 649, and the notes to his edition.

One of his critics has argued that Goldsmith the historian was plainly at war with Goldsmith the novelist in the *Life*, but I believe the reverse to be true: whenever he can, Goldsmith moulds his episodes and manipulates his sources according to the dictates of fiction.[43] At one point he notes that the story he has just related also appears 'in a celebrated romance [*Roderick Random*]; I only repeat it here to have an opportunity of observing, that it actually happened' (iii. 357). And the parallel between history and romance cuts both ways, for it enables Goldsmith not only to enrich his particularized narrative with familiar motifs, but also to give the archetypal pattern he draws upon a local habitation and a name. This is not to say that his tale is untrue; on the contrary, it is one of his closest approximations to that general truth Johnson had extolled even in his discussion of biographical writing.

Consider, for example, Nash's circuitous journey to the world of Bath. It was Nash's good fortune to stumble upon the one role in life in which he could succeed—as an *arbiter elegantiarum*, the servant (and master) of polite society—but his success did not come easily; his early life was strewn with failure. Of Nash's parentage and education Goldsmith tells us little, for he owed 'so little of his advancement to either' (iii. 292). His father's 'name and circumstances were so little known, that Doctor *Cheyne* used frequently to say that *Nash* had no father', and the Duchess of Marlborough compared him to Gil Blas, 'who was ashamed of his father'. These jests enable Goldsmith to introduce Nash's witty and polite reply ('I seldom mention my father in company, not because I have any reason to be ashamed of him; but because he has some reason to be ashamed of me'), but they also, at the very opening of the narrative, suggest the archetypal nature of the main character, the traditional 'orphan' of romance who must make his way in the world alone. Born into a world in which one's birth is almost everything, Nash will quickly squander the opportunities his family affords him, eventually making himself over, not so much by renouncing his imprudence as by learning to regulate himself and thereby earning the right to regulate others.

His short career at Oxford is a disaster, largely because he falls prey to the temptations posed to all inexperienced young men:

A mind strongly turned to pleasure, *always* is first seen at the university . . . In the neighbourhood of *every* university there are girls who with some beauty, some coquettry, and little fortune, lie upon the watch for *every* raw amorous youth,

---

[43] Clara M. Kirk, *Oliver Goldsmith* (New York: Twayne, 1967), 177. Later, however, she concludes that Goldsmith's interest in the historical truth of these anecdotes 'was secondary to his interest in them as the source of romances with a moral meaning' (p. 178).

more inclined to make love than to study. Our Heroe was quickly caught, and went through *all* the mazes and adventures of a college intrigue, before he was seventeen ... (iii. 292–3; my emphasis)

His military career is just as brief: 'the life of a soldier is more pleasing to the spectator at a distance than to the person who makes the experiment. Mr. *Nash* soon found that a red coat alone would never succeed, that the company of the fair sex is not to be procured without expence ...' (iii. 293–4). And thus he turns to the inns of court, where the fate awaiting the improvidence of young men-about-town is averted only by his services as the master of ceremonies at an entertainment for King William. On this occasion Nash reveals such a 'spirit of regularity' and attention to trifling but pleasing detail that the delighted king offers him a knighthood. Although Nash chooses to refuse the knighthood, which he could ill afford to support, this moment marks a turning-point in his life as he—and others—recognize the true nature of his gifts. It is as if Freud's family romance had come true: the child of obscure birth dreams that he is actually of royal blood, and eventually the king recognizes his kinship in a public ceremony. 'In the populous city where he resided, to be known was almost synonimous with being in the road to fortune', Goldsmith remarks (iii. 295), but it is only after virtually losing his resuscitated reputation in London that he finally follows the road to Bath.

Like the hero of myth and romance, Nash establishes his authority (and thereby confirms his identity) by resolving a crisis as he enters the city. An English physician, convinced that the waters were not effective, had recently threatened to '*cast a toad into the spring*':

In this situation of things it was, that Mr. *Nash* first came into that city, and hearing the threat of this Physician, he humorously assured the people that if they would give him leave, he would charm away the poison of the Doctor's toad, as they usually charmed the venom of the Tarantula, by music. He therefore was immediately empowered to set up the force of a band of music, against the poison of the Doctor's reptile; the company very sensibly encreased, *Nash* triumphed, and the sovereignty of the city was decreed to him by every rank of people. (iii. 300–1)

As master of ceremonies, Nash played an important role in the city's development—restraining the violent, encouraging public works, laying down his 'Rules' for polite behaviour—but he remained a gambler even though he was too 'constitutionally passionate and generous' to be successful at it (iii. 313). His sovereignty was challenged only when it was discovered that he was not only a gamester but a silent partner in one of the city's gambling concerns: 'This is the greatest blot in his life, and this it is hoped will find pardon' (iii. 315). This revelation left him financially insecure and his reputation blemished, 'declining from his former favour and esteem, the just consequence of his quitting, tho' but ever so little, the paths of honour', but Goldsmith is willing to balance these failings by revealing 'those brighter parts of his life and character, which gained the affection of his friends, the esteem of the corporation which he assisted, and may possibly attract the attention of posterity' (iii. 320).

We consequently learn of his generosity and humanity, especially in the interpolated tales of Colonel M—— and Miss Sylvia S——, the latter a woman of intelligence and virtue whose associations in Bath nevertheless lead to her ultimate downfall. Like Nash himself, the heroine of Gold-smith's embedded tale suffers from imprudence, 'putting herself into the circumstances of the object whose wants she supplied' (iii. 325). Finally deciding to leave a life 'in which she could see no corner for comfort', she reads the story of Olympia in *Orlando Furioso* and hangs herself with a girdle made of silver thread. 'Thus ended', Goldsmith remarks, 'a female wit, a toast, and a gamester; loved, admired, and forsaken' (iii. 330). 'Formed for the delight of society, fallen by imprudence into an object of pity', she is the perfect complement to Nash, the 'beau of three genera-tions' whose vanity prompts him to accept the flattery of his inferiors now that he has lost the caresses of 'the great'. Finally appearing as the mere remnant of a man, haunting the places where his honour died, Nash nevertheless pursues his former pleasures even though he is now too old to enjoy them. The monarch who once admonished his subjects is now the recipient of their own distressed concern, until he is taught at last to know 'that a man of pleasure leads the most unpleasant life in the world' (iii. 379).

The very equilibrium of this final phrase, like the many carefully balanced periods throughout Goldsmith's text, is consistent with his even-handed judgement of Nash as a man who confused pleasure with happiness and ceremony with virtue, who knew that '*nothing debases human nature so much as pride*', but who could apply this wisdom to others far more easily than he could to himself (iii. 356). This sense of symmetry also extends to the structure of the narrative as a whole, which is carefully divided into two sections, the first relating Nash's precarious rise to fame and the contemporary resurgence of Bath, and the second devoted to his decline and old age, the pathetic memorials raised in his honour, and the miscellaneous attacks mounted against the vice of gambling.[44] Midpoint

[44] There is a mixture of materials and judgements on each side of this turning-point, of course: in the first half of the narrative we learn of Nash's stake in the gambling establishment, in the second we are told of his virtuous domestic life and of the more harmless foibles of his character.

in the narrative we learn that Nash is at 'the meridian of his glory' and that he has arrived 'at such a pitch of authority, that I really believe *Alexander* was no greater at *Persepolis*' (iii. 344). Once again Goldsmith's judgement is two-edged, for he simultaneously pays tribute to Nash's personal achievements and belittles both the provincial monarch and the little kingdom he rules. To add to his honours, Goldsmith continues, a full-length portrait of Nash by William Hoare was hung in Wiltshire's Ballroom, placed between the busts of Newton and Pope (Plate 63).[45] But even this monument is quickly undermined by the 'severe, but witty epigram' Goldsmith attributes to Chesterfield:

> Immortal *Newton* never spoke
> > More truth than here you'll find;
> Nor *Pope* himself e'er pen'd a joke
> > Severer on mankind.
>
> This picture placed these busts between,
> > Gives satire its full strength;
> *Wisdom* and *Wit* are little seen,
> > But *Folly* at full length.
>
> (iii. 344)

Another portrait was hung in the Pump Room, showing Nash with a plan of Bath Hospital in his hand (Plate 64),[46] but here too Goldsmith qualifies the tribute due to a 'great man' by ironically noting that he also had 'his levee, his flatterers, his buffoons, his good-natured creatures, and even his dedicators' (iii. 345).[47]

Goldsmith's skilful introduction of these two portraits halfway through the biography is somewhat surprising, for elsewhere in his narrative he rarely draws parallels between these sister arts. In the preface he states that his readers will have to be satisfied with 'a genuine and candid recital' of the details of Nash's life rather than 'a romantic history filled with warm pictures and fanciful adventures ...' (iii. 288), and near the conclusion of the book he dismisses an elegy in Nash's memory by remarking that 'The reader sees in what alluring colours Mr. *Nash*'s character is drawn; but he must consider, that an intimate friend held the pencil ...' (iii. 372).

---

[45] Probably Kerslake, pl. 563 (ii. 191–2), although this portrait is not a full-length. An engraving of Hoare's painting served as the frontispiece to *The Life of Nash*.

[46] Probably Kerslake, pl. 560 (artist unknown); it now belongs to the Borough of Royal Tunbridge Wells.

[47] In his commentary on this passage, as elsewhere, Jaarsma provides a more capacious reading of the ironies in the text than Hopkins; his major point is that the greatness of the book lies not so much in its theme as in 'a species of near-symbolism that forms the structural framework of the *Life*' (p. 18), an entirely tragic structure in which Nash is shown to have been destroyed by society (p. 19). I believe that Goldsmith, however, is more concerned with the internal rather than the external causes of Nash's personal tragedy.

Analogies as casual as these suggest that the parallel between biography and portrait-painting had become an unconscious (and perhaps unimportant) staple of the biographical enterprise in the eighteenth century, and yet Goldsmith's strategic deployment of Nash's portraits—and of the other monuments raised in honour of the city's royal visitors—would not have been out of place in a biography written by one of Goldsmith's seventeenth-century predecessors.[48] Like Walton in his *Life of Donne*, Goldsmith employs these visual motifs at a significant turning point in his narrative in order to accentuate the rising and falling action of his subject's life. But unlike Walton, Goldsmith actually reverts to the older *de casibus* tradition of the sixteenth century, pointing his moral not by celebrating his hero's ultimate salvation but by chronicling, with both irony and sympathy, his inevitable fall from social as well as moral grace.

Goldsmith's biography therefore represents a modern mock-heroic version of *The Mirror for Magistrates* in which Nash, like Johnson's Wolsey in 'The Vanity of Human Wishes', finally falls prey to his own weaknesses, and none more so than the promptings of human pride. And like Johnson, whom he had extolled in his preface to Plutarch's *Lives* for 'his great knowledge of the human mind' and his ability to see, 'as it were, at one view, every thing that can be said on any subject' (v. 227), Goldsmith is not satisfied to point his moral at Nash alone. The traditional characteristics of his narrative—with its triumphal form and motifs drawn from romance—implicate each of us, Goldsmith's readers as well as his subjects, for 'whether the heroe or the clown be the subject of the memoir, it is only man that appears with all his native minuteness about him, for nothing very great was ever yet formed from the little materials of humanity' (iii. 290).[49] And though the author may claim that his work requires 'scarce any other art, than that of arranging the materials in their natural order' (iii. 288), it is the very ordering of the archetypal episodes in Nash's life that gives Goldsmith's narrative its own power and authority. As he noted in the opening line of his text, 'History owes its excellence more to the writer's manner than the materials of which it is composed' (iii. 290).

---

[48] Goldsmith approaches the 'meridian' of Nash's glory by describing the monumental obelisks Nash and others raised in honour of visits by the royal family; see iii. 341–3.

[49] The relation between Nash and the reader is made most forcefully by Dussinger, who shows how Goldsmith thwarts any superior response on the reader's part by broadening his satire to encompass all of us. Unlike Hopkins, Dussinger realizes that the satirical and ironic elements in Goldsmith's text would have little significance if they were aimed only at the poor figures of Nash and his close associates.

iii. Johnson's *Savage*: Biography as Redemption

A month after Goldsmith published his *Life of Nash*, the *Monthly Review* dismissed its hero as 'A trivial subject, treated for the most part in a lively, ingenious, and entertaining manner. Mr. Samuel Johnson's admirable Life of Savage seems to have been chosen as the model of this perform-ance.'[50] The similarities between these two biographies are indeed strik-ing, even if Johnson enjoyed a much more complex and intriguing subject (the *Critical Review* complained that Goldsmith had tortured himself 'to give substance to inanity'[51]). Like Goldsmith, Johnson warned his readers that he was presenting a history, not a 'Novel filled with romantic Adventures, and imaginary Amours'.[52] Like Johnson, Goldsmith depicted a hero whose compassion often outstripped his prudence: 'He had pity for every creature's distress, but wanted prudence in the application of his benefits. He had generosity for the wretched in the highest degree, at a time when his creditors complained of his justice' (iii. 295–6), a characteristic that should remind us of Savage's 'Act of complicated Virtue', in which he shared his last guinea with the witness for his prosecution. Nash even plays a minor role in Johnson's narrative when he is introduced as one of Savage's benefactors during his imprison-ment in Bristol, an event that Goldsmith, interestingly enough, fails to mention.

These two biographies are even more closely related, however, in their choice of subject—the self-made man whose career has led to notoriety as well as to fame—and in their determination to present the complexities of their hero's character. Critics have justly described the 'equipoise' of Johnson's text, the manner in which he, like Goldsmith after him, deftly modulates a voice that ranges from satire to sympathy.[53] We can see this quite clearly, for example, in the paradox Johnson skilfully presents of the intelligent man who is a keen observer of contemporary manners and human foibles, and yet virtually blind to similar failings in his own character. Above all else, Johnson states in his concluding sketch, 'The Knowledge of Life was indeed his chief Attainment' (p. 136), a judgement carefully documented throughout Johnson's narrative. The structure of

---

[50] Quoted in Goldsmith, *Works*, iii. 282–3.

[51] Quoted in ibid. 282.

[52] *Gentleman's Magazine*, 13 (Aug. 1743), 416.

[53] See, in addition to the article by Uphaus (n. 2, above), Martin W. Maner, 'Satire and Sympathy in Johnson's *Life of Savage*', *Genre*, 8 (1975), 107–18, and Tracy's introduction to Johnson, *Savage*, p. xviii. William Vesterman, 'Johnson and *The Life of Savage*', *ELH* 36 (1969), 659–78, offers a perceptive treatment of Johnson's style.

Savage's *Wanderer* may be irregular, its design obscure, and its plan perplexed, for instance, but 'It was never denied to abound with strong Representations of Nature, and just Observations upon Life' (p. 53). Turning to another poem, Johnson praises Savage's 'Proficiency in the important and extensive Study of human Life, and the Tenderness with which he recounts' human miseries (p. 94). Savage, moreover, had 'perhaps a more numerous Acquaintance than any Man ever before attained, there being scarcely any Person eminent on any Account to whom he was not known, or whose Character he was not in some degree able to delineate' (p. 104). Savage took 'all Opportunities of conversing familiarly with those who were most conspicuous at that Time, for their Power, or their Influence; he watched their looser Moments, and examined their domestic Behaviour, with that Acuteness which Nature had given him . . .' (p. 64).

Passages such as these occur so frequently in the narrative that Johnson leads us to suspect that Savage would have made a splendid biographer himself. Years later, in the *Life of Addison*, Johnson would in effect summarize the biographer's task as he mused, like John Aubrey, on the fate of personal history: 'Lives can only be written from personal knowledge, which is growing every day less, and in a short time is lost for ever. What is known can seldom be immediately told, and when it might be told it is no longer known. The delicate features of the mind, the nice discriminations of character, and the minute peculiarities of conduct are soon obliterated . . .'[54] As early as 1744 he had sensed these qualities in Savage himself, 'for as he never suffered any Scene to pass before his Eyes without Notice, he had treasured in his Mind all the different Combinations of Passions, and the innumerable Mixtures of Vice and Virtue, which distinguish one Character from another; and as his Conception was strong, his Expressions were clear, he easily received Impressions from Objects, and very forcibly transmitted them to others' (p. 45). But Savage was much more inclined to impart this knowledge of life to others than to put it to use in his own life. 'For the acquisition of Knowledge,' Johnson notes, 'he was indeed far better qualified than for that of Riches,' which were always to be enjoyed 'in some distant Period of his Life' (p. 102). He had the 'peculiar Felicity, that his Attention never deserted him; he was present to every Object, and regardful of the most trifling Occurences'. But this was coupled with his 'Art of escaping from his own Reflections and accomodating himself to every new Scene' (p. 136). Other maxims were 'treasured up in his Mind, rather for Shew than Use, and operated

---

[54] Johnson, *Lives*, ii. 116. Further references are provided in the text.

very little upon his Conduct, however elegantly he might sometimes explain, or however forcibly he might inculcate them' (p. 67).

This, in Johnson's view, is the paradox at the heart of Savage's character—his refusal to reflect on how he, too, is implicated in the follies and crimes he can so easily observe in others—and it is Johnson's task in his biography to trace Savage's tangled motives and often unpardonable behaviour with both sympathy and candour. Many of his carefully balanced judgements display the economy and bite of the epigram:

... if his Miseries were sometimes the Consequence of his Faults, he ought not yet to be wholly excluded from Compassion, because his Faults were very often the Effects of his Misfortunes. (p. 52)

It was his peculiar Happiness, that he scarcely ever found a Stranger, whom he did not leave a Friend; but it must likewise be added that he had not often a Friend long, without obliging him to become a Stranger. (p. 60)

Such were the Life and Death of *Richard Savage*, a Man equally distinguished by his Virtues and Vices, and at once remarkable for his Weaknesses and Abilities. (p. 135)

Passages such as these must surely have echoed in Goldsmith's mind as he wrote about Richard Nash—a man of pleasure leading the most unpleasant life in the world—and Goldsmith would certainly have sensed the larger structural patterns in Johnson's narrative as well: Savage's long struggle for success; the 'Golden Part' of his life, when he enjoyed the patronage of Lord Tyrconnel; his inevitable fall from grace and eventual exile to Bristol; and finally the divided judgement implicit in the closing paragraphs of Johnson's character-sketch, in which we are warned of the effects of imprudence, negligence, and irregularity, and yet simultaneously asked to suspend our judgement about a man whose 'Condition' is so very different from our own.[55]

Johnson reinforces this sense of balance in his text by carefully pairing characters against each other and by suggesting alternative choices in life. The Countess of Macclesfield, for instance, finds her counterfoil in the Countess of Hertford, who saves Savage from the gallows: 'It is by no Means necessary to aggravate the Enormity of this Woman's Conduct, by placing it in Opposition to that of the Countess of *Hertford*; no one can fail to observe how much more amiable it is to relieve, than to oppress, and to rescue Innocence from Destruction, than to destroy without an Injury' (p. 39). The Queen accepts Savage's tribute as her 'volunteer laureate', but

---

[55] On the divisions within the narrative, see John A. Dussinger, *The Discourse of the Mind in Eighteenth-Century Fiction* (The Hague and Paris: Mouton, 1974), 128 and 143–5.

Mrs Oldfield 'had formerly given him the same Allowance with much more heroic Intention; she had no other View than to enable him to prosecute his Studies, and to set himself above the Want of Assistance, and was contented with doing good without stipulating for Encomiums' (p. 79).

These pairings are most significant when they involve Savage himself, and this in part explains why Johnson takes such care in creating his portrait of Sir Richard Steele, who is not only Savage's first patron, but also an unfortunate example of the hazards of improvidence. Johnson's editor, Clarence Tracy, has characterized two anecdotes about Steele's debts as 'amusing but irrelevant';[56] but at this early point in the narrative no example could be more relevant to the impressionable Savage than that of Steele, a man of letters from whom he 'was not likely to learn Prudence or Frugality . . .' (p. 15). Savage is also taken up by the actor Wilks, who extends a generous hand to another unfortunate creature, a Mr Smith, educated in Ireland and now—like Savage—forced to make his fortune by writing a tragedy for the London stage. In a long footnote we learn that Smith had originally intended to enter the church, but had been hindered by 'an Impediment in his Pronunciation'; his dramatic offering was successful enough, however, to enable him to pursue the study of medicine in Leyden, and with the recommendation of Boerhaave he eventually became one of the chief physicians at the Russian court (p. 17). Here, subtly embedded in the text and completely neglected by Johnson's readers, is an intriguing parallel to Savage's own desperate situation. Both young men suffer from an original 'Impediment' that forces them to pursue a different course of life; both turn to the stage and are assisted by the same benevolent man; both even share the same name, for Savage was known as Richard Smith until he discovered who his actual parents were.[57] Dr Smith, however, pursued both his dramatic and his new career with 'Diligence', and 'prosecuted his Design [to study physic] with so much Diligence and Success' that he earned the praise of Boerhaave, whose life Johnson had published in 1739.

Diligence, of course, was not one of Savage's virtues. Always impetuous, ever eager to shine, he is later captured in a brilliantly condensed sketch of those motivations that were so transparent to others and yet so hidden from him:

It was always Mr. *Savage*'s Desire to be distinguished, and when any Controversy became popular, he never wanted some Reason for engaging in it

---

[56] Johnson, *Savage*, p. 16 n.   [57] Ibid. 5 n.

with Ardour, and appearing at the Head of the Party which he had chosen. As he was never celebrated for his Prudence, he had no sooner taken his Side, and informed himself of the chief Topics of the Dispute, than he took all Opportunities of asserting and propagating his Principles, without much Regard to his own Interest, or any other visible Design than that of drawing upon himself the Attention of Mankind. (p. 83)

The economy and circular progression of this passage should remind us of a similar description of a rash and impetuous man, Sir George More in Walton's *Life of Donne*. Like Walton, whom he greatly admired, Johnson is able to reveal much of the essential nature of his subject in a few brisk lines: Savage yearns to be distinguished, enters controversies with ardour but without reason, insists on asserting his own pre-eminence while simultaneously neglecting his own interest, and pursues no design other than ensuring that he is noticed. We must realize, moreover, that Savage courts public notice—even notoriety—as emotional compensation for the personal recognition he believes he has been denied. This is Savage's 'Condition', and it is against this backdrop of human misery that Johnson always asks us to draw our conclusions about his friend's behaviour.

Savage's misfortunes are indeed so unusual and so frequent that Johnson is moved to summarize them late in his narrative (p. 109). By this point most of Savage's troubles are clearly of his own making, but Johnson never allows us to forget that this is a man on whom fortune has rarely smiled. By the time Savage discovers who his parents actually are, he has already lost both his father and the financial allowance the Earl Rivers had settled on him. His mother not only refuses to recognize and assist him, but attempts to have him transported to the colonies and even murdered. Savage therefore sues for redress to other members of the aristocracy, seeking patrons, as William Epstein has suggested, in recompense for the parents he has lost.[58] As a thoroughly disenfranchised member of the society he seeks to enter, he is no less an outcast than the prostitute who testifies against him; like the pathetic hero of one of his early pamphlets, he too is an *Author to be Let*, forced to sell his talents to the highest bidder. Savage's original decision to renounce his life 'at the Awl' as a shoemaker's apprentice is soon shown to have spawned a lifetime of unhappiness: 'nor was it perhaps any great Advantage to him,' Johnson notes, 'that an unexpected Discovery determined him to quit his Occupation' (p. 10).

Savage's unexpected discovery should remind us of the romance motifs

---

[58] *Recognizing Biography* (Philadelphia: Univ. of Pennsylvania Press, 1987), 60–4.

we have already noticed in Goldsmith's biography of Nash, who eventually emerges as '*the little king of a little people*'. In the *Lives of the English Poets*, Johnson speculates that Prior was 'perhaps willing enough to leave his birth unsettled, in hope, like Don Quixote, that the historian of his actions might find him some illustrious alliance' (ii. 180). In Savage's case, the childish wish of the family romance actually comes true, but with the ironical twist that he finds himself 'exposed' and 'abandoned' (terms also drawn from folklore and romance), a natural child suffering the indifference of an unnatural mother. Although Savage adopts his father's name, he cannot claim his title as the Earl Rivers, a predicament that may have unconsciously echoed in Johnson's mind when he described his friend as 'doomed to Poverty and Obscurity, and launched upon the Ocean of Life . . .' (p. 6). In an autobiographical preface that Johnson subjoined to his narrative, Savage explicitly laments the fact that he is 'No-body . . . *nominally*, No-body's Son at all . . .' (p. 27).[59]

Alienated from the society that produced him, Savage is forced, in his own words, to live by his 'wits'; having no profession, Johnson adds, he 'became, by Necessity, an Author' (p. 12). Like Smith, the alter-ego of Johnson's interpolated anecdote, Savage becomes a writer because he is fit for little else, a sad comment on what Paul Fussell has called Johnson's sense of the sacrament of literature.[60] But Savage also becomes a writer 'by Necessity' because he must 'author' himself, must establish his identity through his autobiographical writings and thereby create a reputation that reflects his inherent abilities. Authorship, however, entails perils of its own: 'Volumes have been written only to enumerate the Miseries of the Learned, and relate their unhappy Lives, and untimely Deaths', and it is to these 'mournful Narratives' that Johnson adds Savage's own unhappy tale (p. 4). Savage writes—as well as lives—from hand to mouth, as Johnson's famous portrait reminds us:

> During a considerable Part of the Time, in which he was employed upon this Performance [the tragedy *Sir Thomas Overbury*], he was without Lodging, and often without Meat; nor had he any other Conveniences for Study than the Fields or the Streets allowed him, there he used to walk and form his Speeches, and afterwards step into a Shop, beg for a few Moments the Use of the Pen and Ink, and write down what he had composed upon Paper which he had picked up by Accident. (p. 21)

---

[59] Hogarth would later oppose his sketches of 'Mr Nobody' and 'Mr Somebody' in *Hogarth's Peregrination*, ed. Charles Mitchell (Oxford: Clarendon Press, 1952), pls. 1, 9; see intro., pp. xxiv–xxxi.

[60] *Samuel Johnson and the Life of Writing* (New York: Harcourt, 1971), chs. 4 and 9.

When his play is finally performed he must suffer the disgrace of acting in it himself, a fact that he later attempts to hide, just as he will suppress his authorship of a controversial pamphlet. Even his 'autobiography' is written by someone else, his friend and patron Aaron Hill, who, unlike Savage, is 'an Author of an established Character' (p. 23). His eventual degradation is so severe that he is parodied in a farce as the pathetic figure of the impoverished poet (p. 100), and he ends his days singing freely only in his prison cage, ' "sometimes indeed in the plaintive Notes of the Nightingale; but, at others, in the chearful Strains of the Lark.———" ' (p. 125).

Richard Savage finally fails in his attempt to author himself. Completely abandoned by the aristocracy as well as by his putative family, he enjoys only the patronage of his fellow writers—Steele, Wilks, Hill, and later Pope—and then only intermittently and with the complications that attend all of his personal relationships. Finally, Epstein has argued, Savage must be authored by Johnson, who, by inverting the traditional relation between biographical patron and client, himself assumes responsibility for Savage's reputation.[61] Perhaps we might more properly say that Johnson ultimately *authorizes* Savage's account of himself. He attempts to authenticate Savage's claims about his own identity, and, as Savage's ultimate character-witness, strives to present his private life and professional reputation in as full but sympathetic a light as possible, something that Savage could not accomplish for himself. Johnson's biography is therefore an act of personal redemption—an attempt to salvage his friend's name from disgrace and even obscurity—as well as a broader moral tale that implicates all of us who ponder Savage's tortured character and sad career. The figure he re-creates, Johnson's Savage, is more cohesive, more easily understood, and perhaps more convincing than the historical character Johnson knew. By enlisting his own authority on Savage's behalf, Johnson has been able to create a text that is more unified and compelling than the texture of Savage's own life.

iv. Coda

And this, it seems, is precisely why Johnson's subject and text have remained so controversial: the very unity and seamlessness of Johnson's narrative have made his readers suspicious, not so much of his motives, which are clear enough, but of his own ability to distinguish 'the nice

---

[61] *Recognizing Biography*, pp. 68–9.

discriminations of character'. Consider the dilemma of James Boswell, who opened his biography of Johnson by extolling him as an author 'who excelled all mankind in writing the lives of others' (i. 25), but who soon found himself spending page after page disputing many of the facts and conclusions in the *Life of Savage*. In Frank Brady's words, the book 'offers a glorious tangle of theoretical problems',[62] and I therefore want to conclude my discussion of Johnson as a biographer not simply by reaffirming the profound influence he had on his contemporaries—nor by emphasizing the balance and unified vision of his text—but instead by opening up his narrative to questions of a more speculative nature. The *Life of Savage* remains a compelling story not just because of the answers it provides, but also because of the practical and theoretical questions it continues to force us to raise.

The first question we must ask ourselves is whether Johnson provided an accurate account of Savage. Boswell thought that Johnson did not. Faced with the choice of believing Savage or his alleged mother, Boswell chose to side with the Countess of Macclesfield: 'for the honour of human nature, we should be glad to find the shocking tale not true' (i. 170). In Boswell's view, it is less plausible—less inconsistent with what we know of 'human nature'—that the Countess actually repudiated a child she knew to be her own than that Savage was himself guilty of duplicity. Many of us will certainly agree with his assessment, but many will also balk at the alternative he offers: that 'the person who then assumed the name of Richard Savage was an impostor, being in reality the son of the shoemaker, under whose wife's care Lady Macclesfield's child was placed; that after the death of the real Richard Savage, he attempted to personate him; and that the fraud being known to Lady Macclesfield, he was therefore repulsed by her with just resentment' (i. 172). Boswell believes that there are strong circumstances in support of this argument—that Savage was what was known at the time as a 'supposititious' child, a changeling—but his conclusion does not tally with the facts we now have, nor is the either/or logic of his argument very convincing. It is possible that Savage was indeed the child of the Countess and that she was simply convinced that he was an imposter; and it is perhaps even more likely that Savage was a self-deluded rather than a conscious impersonator, and that the Countess regarded him as such.

The crucial point, in any case, is not really Savage's identity, for even

---

[62] 'The Strategies of Biography and Some Eighteenth-Century Examples', in *Literary Theory and Structure: Essays in Honor of William K. Wimsatt*, ed. Frank Brady, John Palmer, and Martin Price (New Haven: Yale Univ. Press, 1973), 252.

Clarence Tracy, his modern biographer, has not been able to resolve this murky issue.[63] As Boswell put it, 'the world must vibrate in a state of uncertainty as to what was the truth' (i. 174). It is more a question of Johnson's credulity, and it is here that Boswell strikes his most telling blow: 'Johnson's partiality for Savage made him entertain no doubt of his story, however extraordinary and improbable. It never occurred to him to question his being the son of the Countess of Macclesfield, of whose unrelenting barbarity he so loudly complained, and the particulars of which are related in so strong and affecting a manner in Johnson's life of him' (i. 169–70). The *Life of Savage* is unusual because it violates principles we have come to value in Johnson's other biographical texts: an instinctual scepticism concerning suspicious sources and contested information, an eagerness to consider all possible explanations for even the smallest acts of human behaviour, and an extreme caution in drawing conclusions when little can be confidently concluded.[64] In the *Life of Cowley* he would note that 'actions are visible, though motives are secret' (i. 15) and then add, in the *Life of Dryden*, that 'enquiries into the heart are not for man . . .' (i. 378). These admissions should not suggest that Johnson did not himself endeavour to pry into the human heart; the *Lives* are filled with his examinations of hidden motives. But we can sense an increasing self-consciousness in Johnson's later biographical work as he sifts through the materials at his disposal and comments on the uncertainty of historical knowledge.

It is therefore surprising to see how often the *Life of Savage* is cited as the embodiment of Johnson's biographical principles. It could be argued, of course, that Johnson knew Savage better than most of the men whose lives he wrote, that he possessed printed sources, that he made ample use of Savage's own literary works, that he asked his readers to exercise their own act of sympathetic imagination so that they would place themselves in the 'condition of him whose fortune' they contemplate, and that he examined both the virtuous and the more despicable aspects of Savage's character before drawing together the moral threads of his tale. But there are severe limitations here as well. Johnson's familiarity with Savage appears to have allowed him to suspend his normal scepticism when he addresses the most important episodes in Savage's life. His sources were often inaccurate, and he apparently did not realize that Savage had

[63] See *The Artificial Bastard: A Biography of Richard Savage* (Cambridge, Mass.: Harvard Univ. Press, 1953).

[64] See the two standard studies of Johnson as a biographer, Lawrence Lipking, *The Ordering of the Arts in the Eighteenth Century* (Princeton: Princeton Univ. Press, 1970), 452 and *passim*, and Robert Folkenflik, *Samuel Johnson, Biographer* (Ithaca: Cornell Univ. Press, 1978), 74.

corrected many facts himself in a letter to Elizabeth Carter.[65] Johnson's chronology was therefore confused at several crucial points in his narrative, especially when he attempted to reconcile various incidents in Savage's life with the publication of his literary works.

It is therefore somewhat problematical to argue, as several scholars have, that in writing the *Life of Savage* Johnson was actually inventing 'critical biography'.[66] It is true, for example, that Johnson considers Savage's poetry in some detail, and that he quotes it at great length (although less so in each subsequent edition).[67] And it is also true that Johnson integrates his analysis of Savage's poetry with his discussion of Savage's life far more fully than in his other major biographies. But he does so in order to emphasize the disparity between Savage's poetry and his life: the integration of criticism and narrative is one of convenience and necessity; it does not embody the harmonious unity that we find in his lives of Milton, Addison, and Pope.[68] Savage's literary productions are rarely praised for their structural or stylistic virtues; Johnson values them for their moral sentiments, and quotes from them in support of personal qualities that he would otherwise have difficulty establishing.[69] By stating that Savage is an author 'by Necessity', Johnson also suggests that he is a writer by accident. Savage's life provides ample material for the biographer interested in charting the miseries of the literary profession, but Johnson has little opportunity to speculate on the poet's calling, which will emerge as one of the central motifs in the *Lives*.

We might more profitably direct our attention to that other crucial turning-point in Johnson's text, the moment when Savage is struck by lightning for the first time. Once he learned who his real parents were,

He was now no longer satisfied with the Employment which had been allotted

[65] Johnson, *Savage*, p. xii.

[66] See Bate, *Samuel Johnson*, p. 223. Lipking, *The Ordering of the Arts*, p. 413, makes a similar claim, but also shows how a poetic vocation 'can lend grace to a life otherwise of small fortune, like that of Savage, and sometimes confer even a limited kind of secular redemption' (p. 457). Fussell, *Samuel Johnson and the Life of Writing*, pp. 254–5, sees *Savage* as the immediate thematic original of the *Lives* but not their formal paradigm. Leopold Damrosch, jun., *The Uses of Johnson's Criticism* (Charlottesville: Univ. Press of Virginia, 1976), 132, argues that *Savage* 'is the biography of a man who happens to be a writer, much as the subject of the *Life of Boerhaave* is a man who happens to be a physician and theologian', but Boerhaave—unlike Savage—had a genuine calling; he chose his own vocation.

[67] See Benjamin Boyce, 'Johnson's *Life of Savage* and Its Literary Background', *Studies in Philology*, 53 (1956), 576–98, who also compares the events in Savage's life with those of a similar 'injured nobleman' as well as with Defoe's *Roxana*.

[68] See Lipking, *The Ordering of the Arts*, pp. 438–9 and 445; Brady, 'The Strategies of Biography', pp. 248–50; and James L. Battersby, 'Patterns of Significant Action in the "Life of Addison"', *Genre*, 2 (1969), 28–42.

[69] This has also been noticed by David E. Schwalm, 'Johnson's *Life of Savage*: Biography as Argument', *biography*, 8 (1985), 137–8.

him, but thought he had a Right to share the Affluence of his Mother, and therefore without Scruple applied to her as her Son, and made use of Every Art to awaken her Tenderness, and attract her Regard. (p. 11)

This smooth transition passes over a number of intriguing issues in silence. What is it like for someone to discover who he really is? What effect does this discovery have on the way Savage conceives of his 'self'? How difficult a transition will he undergo as he is essentially transformed from a 'No-body' to someone with vastly different notions, not just about his nominal identity but also about the qualities he has inherited? According to Johnson, Savage was not dissatisfied with his previous existence until he learned about his real mother and father; how does he suddenly grow into this new sense of himself? This moment of acute psychological awareness, in which one contemplates the mystery of one's identity and the unfolding of one's life, is the natural territory of modern biography, and we can already see its emergence in Boswell's journals and Gibbon's musings among the ruins of Rome. Perhaps, as Johnson was later to argue in his essay on autobiography, these matters can never be fully known at second-hand. In the *Life of Savage*, in any case, these questions seem not to have been asked, presumably because Johnson was convinced that Savage's outrage and quest for justice were the natural responses of someone in his position. The seamlessness of Johnson's narrative therefore reflects the unquestioning behaviour of his subject; Johnson is indignant at the neglect and cruel treatment that this discovery reveals (and provokes) rather than intrigued by the psychological complexity of the discovery itself. Savage may have been better off, he suggests, as an unsuspecting apprentice at the shoemaker's awl, but this is a judgement concerning Savage's capacity for happiness, not an invitation to consider how human character is formed.

When Savage approaches his mother for the first time, he is motivated by a desire, which he now construes as his 'Right', to share in her affluence; when he is rebuffed, he attempts to awaken her tenderness. He clamours for recognition and financial restitution; when he fails, he seeks revenge against a society that has illicitly engendered and then ruthlessly discarded him. But if Savage's eventual despair and sad demise seem inevitable, it is not because Johnson has placed him in a stereotyped role or schematic structure, but rather because we have grown to understand Savage and his illusions so well. Although modern readers persist in describing Savage in categorical terms—as the magnanimous man, the imprudent man, the masochistic parasite, the distressed poet—Johnson

refuses to characterize him as any particular type.[70] Savage *is* magnanimous, imprudent, parasitic, and a beleaguered writer, but he is also more
complex than even the sum of these various parts. Johnson may not ask
the same questions we would raise about Savage, but his portrait is never
psychologically reductive. Savage's identity may remain a mystery, but we
understand his character as well as anyone's.

[70] See, respectively, Folkenflik, *Samuel Johnson, Biographer*, pp. 198–201; Brady, 'The Strategies of
Biography', pp. 254–5; Edmund Bergler, 'Samuel Johnson's "Life of the Poet Richard Savage"—a
Paradigm for a Type', *American Imago*, 4 (Dec. 1947), 42–63; and Fussell, *Samuel Johnson and the Life of
Writing*, p. 264.

8

Reynolds and 'The Genius of Life'

BOSWELL'S response to the *Life of Savage* was highly ambivalent, as we have seen. He had difficulties, on the one hand, understanding how such a consummate biographer could be taken in by such a roguish subject; on the other hand, he dutifully laboured to extract the 'useful lesson' to be learned from Johnson's text, which was that the book would 'guard men of warm passions from a too free indulgence of them' (a dictum Boswell had often applied to himself in his journals). But beyond this rather dry, didactic response, Boswell was also able to sense the fascinating hold the text had on its readers: 'the various incidents are related in so clear and animated a manner, and illuminated throughout with so much philosophy, that it is one of the most interesting narratives in the English language.' To support this claim, Boswell inserted an anecdote that has long been cherished as one of the most vivid examples of a contemporary reader's response to an eighteenth-century text:

Sir Joshua Reynolds told me, that upon his return from Italy he met with it in Devonshire, knowing nothing of its authour, and began to read it while he was standing with his arm leaning against a chimney-piece. It seized his attention so strongly, that, not being able to lay down the book till he had finished it, when he attempted to move, he found his arm totally benumbed. (i. 165)

Reynolds eventually met Johnson four years later, in 1756, and painted his first portrait of him soon afterwards; and although Reynolds could boast of many other close friends—Goldsmith, Boswell, and Burke in particular—the rest of his life was intertwined with Johnson's to an extraordinary degree.[1] The nature of their relationship is well known; what deserves renewed attention is the fact that the most successful portrait-painter of the century continued to be fascinated by biography throughout his lifetime, and that this enduring interest usually had Johnson and Boswell as its catalysts.

Reynolds apparently attempted his first biographical sketch in 1776.[2]

---

[1] The dating of this portrait and of Reynolds's first meeting with Johnson cannot be precisely determined; see e.g. Yung, p. 79. Boswell claimed, in 1791, that the portrait was painted in 1756 (ibid. 83).

[2] My summary of the composition of Reynolds's biographical sketches is based on Hilles's account in Reynolds, *Portraits*, pp. 29–31, 59–63, 81–5, 89–90. Further references are provided in the text.

His friend Thomas Percy had agreed to undertake the task of writing a life of Goldsmith, who had died two years before, and he turned to Reynolds, among others, for various forms of assistance. The circumstances surrounding the progress of this larger work—which was never written—are sketchy at best, but it appears that Reynolds prepared a character of Goldsmith at about the same time that Percy relinquished his task to Johnson; the project reverted to Percy upon Johnson's death, and Reynolds's manuscript eventually found its way to Boswell, who made no use of it before he died. Boswell did, however, ask Reynolds to write down his observations of Johnson's character after their friend's death in 1784, and he later drew upon them in writing his two-volume biography. Reynolds's character of Johnson is much more ambitious than Boswell's references to it indicate, though, especially when it is paired with the two dialogues in which Reynolds attempted to reveal Johnson's character in action. A fourth biographical fragment, an unfinished sketch of Garrick, cannot be confidently dated, nor do we know whether a particular event or solicitation occasioned it. It is intriguing, however, to recall Frederick W. Hilles's suggestion that the two Johnsonian dialogues may have been prompted by Reynolds listening to Boswell read the proof-sheets of the *Life of Johnson* at a time when the painter, now visually impaired, was forced to turn to verbal rather than graphic representations of his friend.[3] In the following pages I want to consider these verbal portraits—and the miscellaneous manuscripts associated with them—in some detail, for although they have been readily available for examination since Hilles published them together in 1952, Reynolds's critics have refrained from assessing their significance either as independent sketches or as indications of how Reynolds may have conceived of human character. I speculate later, in the second and third sections of this chapter, on how such a theory of character might shed fresh light on several of Reynolds's most famous images of his contemporaries.

---

[3] It is interesting to note that many of the sayings that Reynolds puts into Johnson's mouth are also recorded by Boswell in the *Life*: on Foote's limitations as an actor (ii. 154); on the public and private Goldsmith (ii. 236); on Garrick's variety as an actor (iii. 35); and on Garrick's consciousness that he was not actually Richard III when he played that role on the stage (iv. 244). Boswell also records Garrick's remarks on Johnson's contradictions (iii. 24). There would seem to be three explanations for these echoes: Boswell was reminded of them by reading Reynolds's dialogues; Reynolds read them in the *Life* while it was in proof; or both actually heard—and remembered—Johnson's pronouncements and then, with or without reinforcement from each other, introduced them into their texts. The question is not whether Reynolds was accurate (although it is reassuring to learn that he was), but whether he was original in including these sayings and in characterizing Johnson as he did. At present there does not appear to be sufficient evidence to draw a conclusion.

i. A Theory of Character

When we think of Reynolds as a theorist, we naturally think of his *Discourses on Art*, the fifteen elegant and sometimes ceremonious addresses he delivered to the Royal Academy from 1769 to 1790. The discourses, however, have often served as stumbling-blocks to those who wish to reconcile Reynolds's theory and practice as a painter. The usual charge is one of inconsistency, both within the discourses themselves and between his theoretical prescriptions and his actual career as a painter of portraits. But as Reynolds's modern editor, Robert Wark, cautions us, we must constantly keep in mind the context in which Reynolds wrote.[4] His audience included his friends and artistic colleagues, but his lectures were specifically addressed to younger artists at various stages in their training. He chose, moreover, to focus on what was still considered in the eighteenth century to be the most ambitious and prestigious genre of painting—*istoria*, in both its secular and sacred forms—and his discourses naturally turn again and again to the questions of imitation, ideal beauty, and what Reynolds called the 'great style' in painting. The discourses, in other words, were written to encourage another generation of painters to excel in a different (and nobler) artistic pursuit, and in the famous conclusion to the fifteenth discourse Reynolds conceded that his own career had taken a different turn: 'I have taken another course, one more suited to my abilities, and to the taste of the times in which I live.' And yet if he could 'begin the world again', he would try to imitate the divine Michelangelo: 'I would tread in the steps of that great master: to kiss the hem of his garment, to catch the slightest of his perfections, would be glory and distinction enough for an ambitious man' (p. 282).

This is not to say, however, that the *Discourses* have little relevance to our understanding of Reynolds as a painter. The essays are filled with examples drawn from portraiture, but Reynolds's interest lies in exploring formal rather than psychological problems; a conception of character is less important in the *Discourses* than the mode of characterization to be chosen by the ambitious student. And yet Reynolds considers knowledge of other men to be essential to any aspiring artist. In the seventh discourse, which is largely devoted to a discussion of taste, Reynolds argues that 'Every man whose business is description' ought to be

[4] Reynolds, *Discourses*, p. xvii. By far the most searching analysis of the inconsistencies, ideological context, and 'public' function of the *Discourses* can be found in John Barrell, *The Political Theory of Painting from Reynolds to Hazlitt: 'The Body of the Public'* (New Haven: Yale Univ. Press, 1986), ch. 1 and *passim*.

acquainted 'with that part of philosophy which gives an insight into human nature, and relates to the manners, characters, passions, and affections. He ought to know *something* concerning the mind, as well as *a great deal* concerning the body of man' (pp. 117–18), a suggestion that may remind us of Tristram Shandy's argument that 'A man's body and his mind . . . are exactly like a jerkin, and a jerkin's lining;—rumple the one— you rumple the other.'[5] Circling back to this subject later in his essay— and armed with a firm belief in the uniform nature of men—Reynolds states that 'A knowledge of the disposition and character of the human mind can be acquired only by experience: a great deal will be learned, I admit, by a habit of examining what passes in our bosoms, what are our own motives of action, and of what kind of sentiments we are conscious on any occasion.' And then, with a spirited twist to a common maxim, he concludes by claiming that, 'as he who does not know himself does not know others, so it may be said with equal truth, that he who does not know others, knows himself but very imperfectly' (p. 132).

What, then, is the nature of man? Reynolds's most direct statement on this subject occurs not in the *Discourses* but in an essay on Shakespeare that he left unfinished and unpublished during his lifetime. Much of what Reynolds says about Shakespeare is consistent with what Johnson had written in the preface to his edition as many as fifteen years earlier, but Reynolds returns to particular subjects—especially the justification of tragicomedy—as if he had to work out a specific argument to his own satisfaction. Shakespeare is warranted in mixing his serious with his comic characters because man is 'what he is,' Reynolds argues, 'an inconsistent being, a professed lover of art and nature, of order, of regularity, and of variety, and who therefore cannot long continue his attention without some recreation; hence it is that the poet relieves the mind of the reader, professedly by episodes, and in a more private manner by similes and illustrations, with which he proceeds so far that it would be open to ridicule but for this reason of variety'.[6] The desire to experience a 'pure' form of tragedy, divorced from anything that would divert us, would be attainable only if we were 'endued with perfect wisdom and taste. But that is not the case. We are governed by our passions as well as our reason.'

[5] Laurence Sterne, *The Life and Opinions of Tristram Shandy, Gentleman*, ed. Ian Campbell Ross (Oxford: Clarendon Press, 1983), 127 (III. iv). Reynolds must also have in mind the Juvenalian commonplace about a sound mind in a sound body.

[6] Reynolds, *Portraits*, p. 118. Arthur Sherbo, *The Birth of Shakespeare Studies: Commentators from Rowe (1709) to Boswell-Malone (1821)* (East Lansing, Michigan: Colleagues Press, 1986), 134–5, points out that the missing part of this essay was printed in Edmond Malone's edition of Shakespeare (1790), I. i. 143–4 n., where Reynolds argues that 'we should acknowledge this passion for variety and contrarieties [i.e. for tragicomedy] to be the vice of our nature . . .'.

Man is both a consistent and an inconsistent being, he continues: 'a lover of art when it imitates nature and of nature when it imitates art, of uniformity and of variety, a creature of habit that loves novelty'. Critics, on the other hand, depict man as 'too uniformly wise, and in their rules make no account for the playful part of the mind' (pp. 118–19).

In the following paragraph, as Reynolds proceeds to explore this 'playful part of the mind' in more detail, we begin to sense the restlessness that the painter sees in himself and, by extension, in others.

The mind appears to me of that nature and construction that it requires being employed on two things in order that it may do one thing well. Perhaps this disposition proceeds from the mind having always been accustomed to do many things at once, as in reading and writing, in which, from long habit, the operation of the mind comes to be no operation, or at least not perceptible. This double operation, what it has been so long accustomed to, begins at last to be a thing necessary, and required even, in affairs where a man would wish the whole powers of his mind to concentrate. Hence I would infer that that simplicity which is so much boasted in the ancient drama, or in whatever works of imagination, is even not natural to the mind of man. If I was to judge from my own experience, the mind always desires to double, to entertain two objects at a time. (p. 119)

Robert Moore, the only scholar to comment on this remarkable passage, sees this description of the workings of the mind as an example of the artist's mental habit of generalizing and particularizing at the same time.[7] This may be true, but it is an interpretation that leads us back once again to the question of characterization—of how subjects are to be represented—rather than towards a conception of character that would determine the appropriateness of particular forms of representation. Reynolds's argument here and in the preceding passages is actually twofold. Man is fundamentally an inconsistent being because he is torn between his reason and his passions; much as he may attempt to 'regulate' and 'guard' himself, he is always vulnerable to old habits and fresh desires. But Reynolds endows this traditional view of man with renewed force by associating it with the tensions that play upon the human mind at all times and in the most minute ways: the mind desires 'to double', to entertain two objects at once. This is a description of how the mind works, however, not an analysis of why it works in this particular way. Johnson, who investigated these problems with great care throughout the 1750s, argued that the mind ranges back in memory and forward in anticipation

---

[7] Robert E. Moore, 'Reynolds and the Art of Characterization', in *Studies in Criticism and Aesthetics, 1660–1800*, ed. Howard Anderson and John S. Shea (Minneapolis: Univ. of Minnesota Press, 1967), 340.

because it is always dissatisfied with the vacuity of life held out by the present moment. Reynolds offers a perhaps less penetrating answer, but he too realizes that man is a lover of both regularity and variety, a creature who 'cannot long continue his attention without some recreation'.

Similar statements about the nature of the human mind are dispersed throughout Reynolds's miscellaneous jottings, even if they did not find their way into the *Discourses*. In a fragment that may have been associated with the composition of the fourth discourse, for example, Reynolds writes that 'Shaftsbury says men have too [*sic*] minds—they have too minds to be pleased ... The mind has two qualities, or two different modes of receiving pleasure', one approaching the divine just as the other approaches sensuality.[8] And works of art, he adds, are always addressed to 'one or the other of those passions ...'. Another short note, this one intended to elucidate Lear's final speech in the fifth act of Shakespeare's play, illustrates Reynolds's belief that the mind can entertain two objects even in the most painful of circumstances. Lear's reference to his poor fool being hanged had been interpreted by Malone and Steevens as a reference to Cordelia, but Reynolds maintained that it was a stroke of genius 'or of nature' on Shakespeare's part to have this 'good-natured, passionate, and rather weak old man' bestow a thought on his fool at a time when he himself was in still greater distress.[9] A third fragment, entitled 'On Prejudice', reinforces Reynolds's cautionary statements about the conflict between reason and passion (or, as he will reformulate it elsewhere, between principles and habits):

> In forming the understanding and judgment to acquire the character of what is called a right-headed man, perhaps no part of our conduct is more necessary to be watched and attended than our prejudices, the difficulty lying in distinguishing between those which are to be eradicated and those which ought to be received with respect and reverence.[10]

It is precisely this power of distinguishing between salutary and vicious prejudices 'that makes what may truly be called the genius of life'. The man who lacks this ability, 'which is above all rules, is a wrong-headed man, whatever powers of argument he may possess to prove that he acts from reason and (as he is likely to say himself) is superior to vulgar prejudices'.

Scattered observations such as these do not in themselves, of course,

---

[8] *The Literary Career of Sir Joshua Reynolds*, ed. Frederick Whiley Hilles (Cambridge: Cambridge Univ. Press, 1936; rpt. [Hamden, Conn.]: Archon, 1967), 222.

[9] Ibid. 99.

[10] Reynolds, *Portraits*, pp. 157–8.

constitute a coherent and formal theory of character, but taken together they do suggest something of the seriousness and care with which Reynolds approached the question of human behaviour. Theory itself, Reynolds insisted, has its limitations. In the essay on Shakespeare he wrote that 'Theoretical systems appear to have a great propensity to separate in theory what is inseparable in nature', and the example he cites is man's inability to 'separate his intellectual from his sensual desires' (p. 118). It is therefore not surprising that Reynolds began his first verbal portrait, his character of Goldsmith, not only by commenting on the contradictions inherent in human character, but also by arguing that these very complications afford the portraitist his most promising materials:

> Those only are the favourite characters of a biographer in which are united qualities which seem incompatible with each other, which appear impossible to exist together at the same time and in the same person. The writer reigns here and revels. An opportunity is presented to him of displaying his sagacity and those nicer powers of discriminating between things which to an ordinary observer appear to have no marks of distinction, as well as of reconciling seeming contradictions. (p. 40)

Here we see what Reynolds calls 'the genius of life'—the ability to discriminate between, and thereby reconcile, one's conflicting prejudices and desires—applied to the act of biography itself, which must interpret both the subtle and the strikingly paradoxical marks of human character.

In Reynolds's character of Goldsmith, the biographer's task is of the second kind, for he must endeavour to show 'what indeed is self-apparent, that such a genius could not be a fool or such a weak man as many people thought him'. Reynolds's essay is therefore a work of sympathy and restitution; he must redeem the reputation and character that Goldsmith's booksellers and friends 'have lived upon' ever since his death. If Goldsmith was a walking contradiction to many who knew him—an inspired idiot, in Walpole's withering phrase—his folly and absurdities proceeded partly from what Reynolds calls 'principle' and partly from 'a want of early acquaintance with that life to which his reputation afterwards introduced him' (p. 42). A stout defender of his friend's intellectual powers and literary talent, Reynolds nevertheless argues that Goldsmith entertained such a strong desire to be liked, 'to have his company sought after by his friends', that he consciously 'abandoned his respectable character as a writer or a man of observation to that of a character which nobody was afraid of being humiliated in his presence'. This was 'a system' with Goldsmith; it served as 'his general principle'.

Goldsmith existed, in effect, as two distinct individuals: in his closet he was penetrating and shrewd; in conversation he was easy and complacent. But when he attempted to combine these two personalities at once—when he resolved to 'be more formal and to carry his character about with him'—the result was disastrous, for he found that 'he could not unite both' of them (p. 43).

Reynolds offers two explanations for the difficulties Goldsmith experienced when he attempted to engage in serious conversation. In the first place, Goldsmith 'came late into the great world. He had lived a great part of his life with mean people. All his old habits were against him. It was too late to learn new ones, or at least for the new to sit easy on him.' Like the young Boswell of the *London Journal*, he patterned his behaviour on the conduct of others, but his 'anxious desire and impatience to distinguish himself, brought him often into ridiculous situations' (p. 43). In a dramatic illustration of this point, Reynolds wryly depicts Goldsmith striving ' "to tell a story as well as Mr. Garrick" ', but inevitably subverting his own success: ' "There lived a cobbler—some people do laugh at this story and some do not; however, the story is this—there lived a cobbler in a stall ..." ' (p. 47). And yet, paradoxically, it was this buffoonishness and ineptitude that made his company so 'greedily sought after, for in his company the ignorant and illiterate were not only easy and free from any mortifying restraint, but even their vanity was gratified to find so admirable a writer so much upon a level, or inferior to themselves, in the arts of conversation' (p. 44).

But Goldsmith's perplexing behaviour in polite (and not so polite) society also had its origin in the very nature of his learning and intelligence. Reynolds characterizes Goldsmith's mental powers as instinctual, his manner of writing as peculiarly organic:

He felt with great exactness, far above what words can teach, the propriety in composition, how one sentiment breeds another in the mind, preferring this as naturally to grow out of the preceding and rejecting another, though more brilliant, as breaking the chain of ideas. In short, he felt by a kind of instinct or intuition all those nice discriminations which to grosser minds appear to have no difference. (p. 52)

This unusual talent, which echoes Reynolds's description of the biographer's task at the opening of this sketch, 'is real genius if anything can be so called'. But little of it, Reynolds adds, ever appeared in his conversation; 'it came when he took up the pen and quitted him when he laid it down.' His mind was 'entirely unfurnished' (p. 50). When he was engaged in a work, 'he had all his knowledge to find, which when he found, he knew how to use, but forgot it immediately after he had used it'.

Reynolds's fascination with apparent contradictions, his interest in exploring the warfare between fixed principles and inferior habits and prejudices, also characterizes his verbal portraits of Garrick and Johnson. The sketch of Garrick is extremely brief—a bare two pages—but in his few remarks Reynolds manages to strike at the heart of his friend's public success and private failings. Once again he scrutinizes a pattern of behaviour that had its roots in his subject's early development: 'Garrick from his early youth, when he used to repeat passages in plays and act whole parts in private theatres, naturally imbibed a desire for popular applause. Afterwards, when he entered the great world and had enlarged his circle, this universal passion was not likely to be much abated ...' (p. 86). But the qualities that made Garrick such a consummate artist on the stage undermined his relations with close friends, for here too he left nothing to chance, 'had too much the same habit of preparing himself, as if he was to act a principal part'. Reynolds dispassionately observes that it was difficult to woo him to one's table and just as difficult to keep him there: 'He never came into company but with a plot how to get out of it.' Unlike Goldsmith, Garrick understood his own powers only too well and consequently 'made himself a slave to his reputation'. The strict 'rules' by which he governed himself in public and his habit of seeking fame made him unfit for the cultivation of private friendship. Worse, Reynolds argues, this passion for fame, 'however proper when within due bounds as a link in the social chain, as a spur to our exertions to acquire and deserve the affections of our brethren, yet when this passion is carried to excess, like every other excess it becomes a vice, either ridiculous, or odious, or sometimes criminal' (p. 87). By degrees, he sadly comments, every principle of right or wrong, 'whatever dignifies human nature, is lost, or not attended to when in competition with the shadow of fame'. At the conclusion of this brief sketch, Garrick loses his own individuality as Reynolds points the moral to his tale: 'From having no great general principle they live in perpetual anxiety what conduct to take on every occasion to insure this petty praise' (p. 88).

Reynolds's portrait of Johnson is much more well rounded and warm hearted, but it is no more relenting in its analysis of the complexities of Johnson's character. 'It is always to be remembered that I am giving a portrait, not a panegyric, of Dr. Johnson', Reynolds writes; at another point he tells Boswell that 'You will wonder to hear a person who loved him so sincerely speak thus freely of his friend, but you must recollect I am not writing his panegyric, but as if upon oath not only to give the truth but the whole truth' (pp. 72–3). Above all else, Reynolds admires the quality of Johnson's intellect. Despite his disclaimer at the beginning of his sketch that the portrait-painter normally considers 'so much only of character as lies on the surface', his is indeed an attempt 'to go deeper and investigate the peculiar colouring of his mind, as distinguished from all other minds . . .' (p. 66). The distinctive feature of Johnson's mind is that it was 'always ready for use'; he had the habit of 'applying his knowledge to the matter in hand which I believe was never exceeded by any man' (p. 67). Reynolds graciously acknowledges his own debt to Johnson, who 'may be said to have formed my mind and to have brushed off from it a deal of rubbish' (p. 66), and he reminds Boswell that any criticism they may have of Johnson is indebted to Johnson's own enabling influence in their lives.

Reynolds therefore chooses to praise Johnson as a living (and some-times overbearing) presence rather than as an author, and he naturally draws particular attention to Johnson's powers as a conversationalist: 'It has been frequently observed that he was a singular instance of a man who had so much distinguished himself by his writings that his conversation not only supported his character as an author, which is very rarely seen, but what is still rarer, in the opinion of many was superior.' Reynolds, who had previously explored the causes of Goldsmith's difficulties in holding his own in polite conversation, now examines the forces that compelled Johnson to invest his talk with so much importance. Once again his explanation takes two forms. On the one hand, he realizes that Johnson was drawn to others because of his 'horror' of solitude. Reynolds had invoked the same word earlier to describe the 'horror which [Goldsmith] entertained of being overlooked' by his friends (p. 46); here he applies it to Johnson's fear that his mind will prey upon itself, an anxiety that could only be relieved by the 'necessity' of living as much as possible in the company of others. This was one 'habit'; the other was an 'exertion' that eventually became a fixed 'rule', which was always to speak his best, even if his audience could not completely understand him.

It is but a short step, however, from speaking one's best to 'talking for victory', and Reynolds is quick to draw this troubling connection; 'The drawback to his character is entertaining prejudices on very slight foundation, giving an opinion perhaps first at random, but from its being contradicted he thinks himself obliged always stubbornly to support—or if he could not support, still not to acquiesce' (p. 71). Here is where Johnson's 'genius of life' at least partially failed him. 'From passion, from the prevalence of his disposition for the minute, he was continually acting contrary to his reason, to his own principles' (pp. 73–4). Reynolds's conclusion, which is so painfully consistent with his other remarks on the contradictory nature of man, leads to an exasperated outburst that would not be out of place in the *Life of Savage*:

> But what appears extraordinary is that a man who so well saw, himself, the folly of this ambition of shining, of speaking or acting always according to the character you imagined you possessed in the world, should produce in himself the greatest example of a contrary conduct.
>
> Were I to write the life of Dr. Johnson, I would labour this point, to separate his conduct that proceeded from his passions, and what proceeded from his reason, from his natural disposition seen in his quiet hours. (p. 74)

At the same time, Reynolds realizes that actions produced by stubbornness and pride—even when they are closely related to the deepest contradictions between passion and reason in Johnson's character—must be kept in strict proportion by the successful biographer. 'That Johnson was rude at times cannot be denied', he writes, but he also complains that 'by reading any account of him you would shrink at the idea of being in his company. Every prominent part of a man's character, every eccentric action when exerted, counts for ten, like some particular cards in games' (p. 78). A sensitive biographer must therefore 'proportion the eccentric parts of his character to the proportion of his book', advice that Reynolds himself follows by emphasizing Johnson's 'piety and virtue' as a man and as a writer (the very words that Jonathan Richardson had chosen to characterize Milton's life and works), and by suggesting—as Boswell also would—that Johnson should serve as a model to be imitated by other men and women.[11]

Reynolds's insistence on biographical proportion can be seen even more clearly in the artful construction of his two Johnsonian dialogues. The format of each imaginary conversation is the same: the subject is human greatness, the example is David Garrick, and the principal—if somewhat reluctant—speaker is Johnson, who knew Garrick longer, and perhaps more thoroughly, than any of the actor's other friends. Reynolds serves as Johnson's verbal combatant in the first dialogue, Edward Gibbon in the second; in each case, however, the friend who attempts to draw Johnson out (or lead him on) receives a serious drubbing. Alluding to Reynolds's deafness, Johnson suggests that 'you may not have

---

[11] Reynolds invokes this phrase three times in extolling Johnson. For Richardson's use of it, see above, p. 142; for Boswell's, see *Boswell's Journal of a Tour to the Hebrides*, ed. Frederick A. Pottle and Charles H. Bennett (London: Heinemann; New York: McGraw-Hill, 1936), 6.

understood me; you misapprehended me; you may not have heard me'
(p. 94). Even the voluminous Gibbon is cut off in mid-sentence:

Gibbon. I don't understand—
Johnson. Sir, I can't help that.   (p. 102)

But the reasons behind these harsh replies are quite different. In the first
dialogue, Johnson is coaxed into conversation only with difficulty, for the
initial subject is predestination and free will, and the very mention of
Garrick in this solemn context elicits Johnson's chariest evaluation of his
old friend. In the following conversation, however, which is four times as
long as its counterpart, Gibbon emerges as Garrick's detractor and
Johnson as his champion. Having dismissed all common conceptions of
greatness and Garrick's tenuous claims to them in the first dialogue,
Johnson must now both redefine the various meanings of that word and
then show how well Garrick—let alone other men—could measure up to
them. Johnson emerges in both dialogues as a formidable and stubborn
opponent, but by proportioning the conversations as he does, Reynolds
reveals the warmth and generosity of his friend without concealing his
peculiarities.

We should not be surprised, moreover, to discover that the consistency
between Reynolds's character-sketches and the imaginary dialogues
extends not only to his portrayal of Johnson but to Johnson's assessment
of Garrick as well. Both conversations are filled with echoes of phrases
and entire judgements that Reynolds had used elsewhere, but it is to his
credit as a writer that these opinions emerge only as the result of a skilful
dialectic. When Johnson distinguishes between Garrick's habits and
principles, when he examines the causes that produced both his virtues
and his failings, when he states that 'Garrick left nothing to chance' or
that 'Garrick, no more than another man, could unite what, in their
natures, are incompatible', we feel that Reynolds has earned his conclusions even though he has placed them in his protagonist's mouth.[12] Even
after his death Garrick provoked strong reactions among those who
understood what a complicated man he had been. The very format of
Reynolds's dialogues reinforces the contradictions in Garrick's character,
while also revealing the equally complex nature of those who attempted to
sort these contradictions out.

The humour and intelligence of these conversations demonstrate how
keen an observer Reynolds was even when he forsook his studio for the

---

[12] See Reynolds, *Portraits*, pp. 96, 104, 105, 103.

company of his friends. Despite his notorious deafness, these sketches show him to have been a good listener, especially in the surroundings he found most congenial. He once wrote to Boswell that 'Everybody has their taste. I love the correspondence of *viva voce* over a bottle with a great deal of noise and a great deal of nonsense', and he punctuated his defence of tragicomedy in the essay on Shakespeare by referring to 'our habits, to what we are used to at a table'.[13] This was the dramatic scene he relished most, when men and women who respected each other's abilities spoke their own minds freely. According to Hannah More, these dialogues were uncannily accurate:

Dear Sir Joshua, even with his inimitable pencil, never drew more interesting, more resembling portraits. I hear them all speak, I see every action, every gesture which accompanied every word. I hear the deep-toned and indignant accents of our friend Johnson; I hear the affected periods of Gibbon; the natural, the easy, the friendly, the elegant language, the polished sarcasm, softened with the sweet temper, of Sir Joshua.[14]

But these imaginary conversations are not important merely because they provide an accurate imitation of how this extraordinary group of men sounded to each other; Reynolds is more ambitious than this. In a revealing passage in the second dialogue, Johnson extols Garrick's abilities as an actor by comparing him with the mimic Samuel Foote. Foote went out of himself, Johnson argues, 'but without going into another man'. Garrick, on the other hand, could not only produce an exact imitation of the voice and gestures of his original, but could also exhibit 'the mind and mode of thinking of the person imitated' (pp. 98–9). This is Johnson's greatest praise of the actor's art, delivered within a sketch that demonstrates just how well Reynolds understood the complexities of verbal as well as visual portraiture.

ii. Divided Selves

When Reynolds wrote that 'The habits of my profession unluckily extend to the consideration of so much only of character as lies on the surface, as is expressed in the lineaments of the countenance', he was expressing an opinion that we must consider rather carefully, even if we make allowances for its modesty and politeness. Similarly, when Johnson argues in Reynolds's tendentious first dialogue that 'I have often lamented how

---

[13] Ibid. 16, 121; see also *The Literary Career of Sir Joshua Reynolds*, pp. 91–2.
[14] Charles Robert Leslie and Tom Taylor, *Life and Times of Sir Joshua Reynolds* (1865), ii. 260.

dangerous it is to investigate and to discriminate character, to men who
have no discriminative powers' (p. 94), he encapsulated a view that might
be applied to much of the portrait-painting of the age in which he lived.
Of the many hundreds of canvases that Reynolds painted, the vast
majority are portraits in which likeness and appropriateness of representation are necessarily more important than the careful discrimination of
character. A significant part of Reynolds's reputation will always rest on
the suppleness and dexterity with which he, like Van Dyck, captured and
inevitably moulded the appearance of the influential men and women of
his generation. Any serious attempt to delineate character, to disclose its
complexities and explore 'the genius of life', would necessarily be at odds
with the primary function of public and commemorative portraiture. And
we should not forget that Reynolds's speculations on human character
appear in essentially private sources—unpublished, often unfinished,
usually focused on his own character or on those men whose characters he
knew best. It is only by turning to more intimate or fanciful portraits that
we shall be able to begin to gauge the extent to which Reynolds's theory
of character can be reconciled with his practice as an artist. In the
following sections I therefore want to consider (and in some cases return
to) a number of images in which the pose, the subject's profession, the
sitting itself, the notorious 'borrowed attitudes', or the interplay among
several portraits of the same person will enable us to judge the relevance
of Reynolds's theoretical writings.

  One of Reynolds's most famous paintings, the portrait of *Garrick
between Tragedy and Comedy* (Plate 61), provides perhaps the most vivid
reminder of the artist's fascination with the divided self.[15] Commentators
from Walpole to Panofsky have recognized the painting's affinity with the
visual and verbal motif of 'The Choice of Hercules', in which the central
figure must decide between the stern figure of Virtue or the seductive path
of Vice.[16] As Walpole noted, Tragedy 'exhorts him to follow her exalted
vocation, but Comedy drags him away, and he seems to yield willingly,
though endeavouring to excuse himself, and pleading that he is forced.
Tragedy is a good antique figure, but wants more dignity in the
expression of her face. Comedy is a beautiful and winning girl . . .'[17]. More
recent criticism, however, has focused on the implied rather than the
explicit subject of the portrait. Waterhouse was the first to notice that the

---

[15] Penny, no. 42; Ellis Waterhouse, *Reynolds* (London: Phaidon Press, 1973), pl. 31.

[16] Erwin Panofsky, *Hercules am Scheidewege und andere antike Bildstoffe in der neueren Kunst* (Leipzig and
Berlin: Teubner, 1930), 133.

[17] Walpole, *Anecdotes of Painting in England*, vol. v, ed. Frederick W. Hilles and Philip B. Daghlian
(New Haven: Yale Univ. Press; London: Oxford Univ. Press, 1937), 61.

figure of Comedy is painted in the manner of Correggio and Tragedy in the style of Guido Reni, an opposition that not only accentuates the directions in which Garrick is torn but also suggests the choice Reynolds himself was forced to make between intimate and heroic portraiture.[18] Garrick's dilemma (which must also be read as a triumph) is thus Reynolds's as well, for both artists were successful in each of the genres at which they tried their hand. The brilliance of Reynolds's portrait therefore lies not merely in the playful tension betwen the pose of these three figures and the classical motif they evoke—in which Garrick's Herculean elevation is also a witty comment on modern heroism—but also in Reynolds's ability to introduce the opposing figures of Comedy and Tragedy within the same frame and paint them in pictorial styles that are both different and yet complementary. Reynolds's portrait of Garrick is no less complex than the character he chooses to paint; it serves as a fitting tribute to Garrick because it is serious and comical at the same time, a pictorial approximation of the dramatic tragicomedy that Reynolds attempted to justify in his own writings.

David Mannings, who has written the most extensive analysis of this painting, summarizes the relation between Garrick and Reynolds quite eloquently when he argues that 'this picture is about conflicts that take place and decisions that must be taken at the deepest and most secret levels of creativity'.[19] This is surely true, but Reynolds's concise character-sketch of Garrick suggests that many of the misgivings Reynolds harboured about Garrick as a private character—as the man behind the dramatic mask—can also be sensed in this compelling portrait. Like other commentators, Mannings is uncomfortable with the traditional association of *Garrick between Tragedy and Comedy* with 'The Choice of Hercules', and he therefore introduces other visual analogues (Reni's *Lot and his Daughters* and Rubens's *Triumph of Silenus*) to explain the precise configuration in Reynolds's painting. Garrick is indeed pictured 'between' Tragedy and Comedy, but there is no choice to be made: his body is already turned in the direction of Walpole's 'beautiful and winning girl', and his facial expression and outstretched hands communicate an apologetic but inevitable denial to the regally painted figure of Tragedy on the right of the canvas. But this is not a bacchanalian procession in the manner of Rubens, nor is Garrick (like Lot) manipulated in one direction by the other figure in the painting. Garrick is genuinely torn between these two women, but

---

[18] Waterhouse, p. 225.
[19] David Mannings, 'Reynolds, Garrick, and the Choice of Hercules', *Eighteenth-Century Studies*, 17 (1983–4), 283.

the scene is essentially one of seduction and imminent departure. The actor is about to be carried away by the force of Comedy, an uncannily prophetic hypothesis that Garrick would eventually verify by choosing, after prolonged indecision, to play a comic role in his last performance on the London stage.[20]

Reynolds handles this indecisiveness with great dexterity. Robert Moore has argued, for instance, that Garrick is 'the master of both ladies', and Paulson, as we saw earlier, acutely noted that the actor's pre-eminence in both tragedy and comedy made no choice possible or even necessary.[21] These observations are consistent with Garrick's status as an actor, but they are actually at odds with the dilemma Reynolds depicts in this portrait. In the painting itself Garrick is—for the moment—master of neither lady; lacking the very control of which he was thought to be the master, he attempts to make the most graceful exit he can manage under the circumstances. We may wish to read the expression on Garrick's face as one of genuine regret, but we must also remember that Garrick 'left nothing to chance. Every attitude, however it might have the appearance of immediate impulse, was the result of various trials in his closet' (p. 86). The situation in which Reynolds places him is therefore entirely consonant with the painter's depiction of his private character:

Amongst the variety of arts observed by his friends to preserve [his] reputation, one of them was to make himself rare. It was difficult to get him and when you had him, as difficult to keep him. He never came into company but with a plot how to get out of it. He was for ever receiving messages of his being wanted in another place. It was a rule with him never to leave any company saturated. (pp. 86–7)

This in itself might be excusable—the stuff of comedy—but Reynolds also knew that 'An inordinate desire after fame produces an entire neglect of their old friends, or we may rather say they never have any friends; their whole desire and ambition is centred in extending their reputation by showing their tricks before fresh new men' (p. 87). And what Reynolds accused Garrick of in his private life, others would attack in his professional career. A caricature appearing in 1772 and modelled on the structure of *Garrick between Tragedy and Comedy* (Plate 65) reveals the actor torn between traditional dramatic values on the left—represented by both Comedy *and* Tragedy—and stage mechanics on the right, who will enable Garrick to present the newest farces, spectacles, and pantomimes. Manu-

---

[20] Burke, p. 208, whose source is Joseph Knight, *David Garrick* (1894), 276–80.
[21] Moore, 'Reynolds and the Art of Characterization', p. 334; for Paulson, see above, p. 188.

scripts labelled 'Shakespeare', 'Jonson', and 'Rowe', meanwhile, are trampled beneath the wavering Garrick's feet.[22]

In painting *Garrick between Tragedy and Comedy*, Reynolds is unlikely to have worried that Garrick 'seems to yield willingly' to Comedy, as Walpole put it, nor can it be argued that the painter had Garrick's private failings uppermost in his mind. But what I find most intriguing about this rich portrait is the extent to which the very terms in which Garrick is praised for his professional talents are consistent with a much darker reading of his private character. As the caricature will later make clear in a rather crude way, the central tableau of the painting can also be read against itself and ultimately subverted: the painting confirms what Reynolds maintained about Garrick on several occasions, that the characteristics that made him a great actor undercut his value as a friend. His studied appearance and unquenchable thirst for fame made him forfeit 'what is truly praiseworthy, steadiness of conduct' (p. 88). Even the beautiful and touching portrait of *Garrick Reading to His Wife* (Plate 62) depicts a husband eagerly awaiting the judgement of his spouse as she concentrates on the lines he has just read. There can be little doubt that Reynolds admired Garrick and that he understood the extent to which both he and his friend were forced to make difficult artistic choices. But his ambitious portrait takes as its subject not only the self-consciousness and divided loyalties that Reynolds sensed in most men's characters, but the more specific situation in which a man in pursuit of fame lives 'in perpetual anxiety what condut to take on every occasion to insure this petty praise' (p. 88).

Reynolds painted at least two other portraits of Garrick—one in the character of Kiteley in *Every Man in His Humour* and later an intimate portrait for the Thrales' library at Streatham—and in 1772 he was said to be contemplating a multiple portrait of the actor that would 'show him as himself, in the centre, surrounded by fifteen other Garricks in the costume of some of the most remarkable characters he has played'.[23] If it was natural that Reynolds should paint several portraits of someone whose countenance was so much in demand, it is just as appropriate that a painter interested in character should turn to the stage or the greenroom as frequently as Reynolds did, for the affinities between acting and portraiture, though rarely mentioned, are remarkably strong. Painting a portrait

---

[22] Penny, pl. 195.

[23] Derek Hudson, *Sir Joshua Reynolds: A Personal Study* (London: Bles, 1958), 122 (Hudson provides no source). For portraits by Reynolds's contemporaries, see *Thirty Different Likenesses: David Garrick in portrait and in performance* (exhib. cat.; Buxton Museum and Art Gallery, 1981).

of *Garrick in the Character of Kiteley*, for instance, produces an inherent visual drama that is similar to the tension we experience when we attend the theatre. When we watch a dramatic performance, we are naturally interested in how actors will interpret characters with which we are already familiar (such as Kiteley), or how actors whose work we know quite well will handle a part that is new to them—or to us. In each case we begin with a known quantity and then gauge the differences that interpretation or method produce; it is precisely this emphasis on difference and even variety that would make a portrait of fifteen characters surrounding Garrick 'himself' of such dramatic interest. This is part of the intrinsic drama we sense in portraits of someone 'as' or 'in the guise of' someone else, and it is a form of drama that occurs much more naturally in portraits of actors than in the 'composite' portraiture of Reynolds's more ambitious paintings.

It is also natural for us to consider the relation between the dramatic character portrayed and the character of the actor, for portraiture can, like drama itself, reveal the figure behind the mask. This is literally and figuratively the case in Reynolds's portrait of Harry Woodward (Plate 66), an actor in Garrick's company best known for his comic roles in Shakespeare (hence his 'Van Dyck' dress).[24] Portraits such as this—and Reynolds painted many of them—perform a double role by commemorating a specific performance for the sitter's immediate audience and by introducing a particular actor to posthumous viewers in an activity associated with his or her profession. But the essential interest of this kind of portrait lies in the act of unveiling, a gesture that asks us to study the man or woman who is normally hidden behind the mask or within the theatrical costume. Reynolds's portrait of Woodward forces us to think once again of the difference between public and private roles and of the personal qualities that make these successful impersonations possible. It is clear from the second of Reynolds's Johnsonian dialogues, moreover, that he considered both acting and painting to be creative activities in which the artist did not relinquish control of his or her own emotions. As we have seen, Reynolds's Johnson distinguishes between Garrick and Foote by arguing that his friend could go 'into another man', but he later clarifies this assertion by refuting Gibbon's statement that Garrick's sensibility, his fine feelings, made him the great actor he was:

Johnson. This is all cant, fit only for kitchen-wenches and chambermaids.

[24] Penny, pl. 47.

Garrick's trade was to represent passion, not to feel it. Ask Reynolds whether he felt the distress of Count Ugolino when he drew it.

Gibbon. But surely he feels the passion at the moment he is representing it.

Johnson. About as much as Punch feels. (pp. 104–5)

Johnson's view of acting here should remind us of Reynolds's exploration of how the mind 'desires to double', to entertain two objects at the same time. But Johnson's argument, with its disarming glance at Reynolds himself, also reaffirms a traditional view of art as representation rather than expression in a way that draws attention once again to the discrepancy between private lives and public roles, even if in Garrick's case the two were tragically confused.

It might therefore be argued that every successful theatrical portrait encapsulates the portrait-painter's central dilemma, which is to preserve likeness—to keep up appearances—while simultaneously penetrating beneath the surface to reveal the essential character that lies within.[25] This analogy between portraiture and theatre provides another twist, however, when we think about the relationship between painter and sitter or about the dramatic nature of the sitting itself. These issues can be illustrated most clearly in Reynolds's splendid portrait of *Mrs Siddons as the Tragic Muse* (Plate 3), a portrait in which, as I have argued earlier, both spatial and temporal form are blurred in order to produce an impression of transcendence. Although Mrs Siddons appears to us as a fully recognizable figure, she is also portrayed 'out of herself' as she takes on the more ambitious role of the tragic muse. According to the actor, this was a pose that she and Reynolds carefully worked out in concert with each other:

In tribute to his triumphant Genius I cannot but remark his instantaneus decission on the attitude and expression. In short, it was in the twinkling of an eye.

When I attended him for the first sitting, after many more gratifying encomiums than I dare repeat, he took me by the hand, saying, 'Ascend your undisputed throne, and graciously bestow upon me some grand Idea of the Tragick Muse'. I walkd up the steps & seated myself instantly in the attitude in which She now appears. This idea satisfyd him so well that he, without one moments hesitation, determined not to alter it.[26]

It is highly doubtful, of course, that Reynolds made an 'instantaneus'

[25] Edgar Wind, 'Hume and the Heroic Portrait', in *Hume and the Heroic Portrait: Studies in Eighteenth-Century Imagery*, ed. Jaynie Anderson (Oxford: Clarendon Press, 1986), 34, has argued that portraits of actors provide the 'acid test' for his comparison of Reynolds and Gainsborough; he shrewdly observes that 'the actor is, so to speak, a living metaphor . . .'.

[26] Quoted by Roger Manvell, *Sarah Siddons: Portrait of an Actress* (New York: Putnam, 1971), 98.

decision to depict Sarah Siddons in this particular role; Romney had painted Mrs Yates as the tragic muse ten years earlier, and Mrs Siddons had already been praised in a poem bearing this exact title.[27] Mrs Siddons's insistence throughout this passage on the unhesitating and even effortless manner in which both painter and sitter determined and then realized this pose, however, reinforces the impression she wishes to produce here, which is that it was both appropriate and natural for her to be cast as the tragic muse. Her version of the sitting, in other words, provides further substantiation for the claims this painting makes on her behalf, and it simultaneously compliments Reynolds as well. The painter, generous with his 'gratifying encomiums', takes the actor by the hand and seats her on her throne, elevating her in the studio just as he will symbolically elevate her in the painting by crowning her as the 'undisputed' queen of the English stage. And by elevating Sarah Siddons, he is in effect elevating his own art of impersonation and representation as well. His famous remark about the placement of his signature on this canvas—'I have resolved to go down to posterity upon the hem of *your* Garment'—is both a compliment to Mrs Siddons and an implicit affirmation of the importance of his own work.

If we had only Mrs Siddons's account of its genesis, we would be forced to view Reynolds's painting as the record of a remarkably close collaboration of kindred spirits. We have already discovered such a relationship between painter and patron in Van Dyck's portrait of Venetia Stanley, the wife of Sir Kenelm Digby, and it is possible that Sarah Siddons did indeed seat herself 'instantly' in the attitude of the tragic muse. But on another occasion Mrs Siddons told the painter Thomas Phillips that the unusual pose 'was the production of pure accident':

Sir Joshua had begun the head and figure in a different view; but while he was occupied in the preparation of some colour she changed her position to look at a picture hanging on the wall of the room. When he looked at her, and saw the action she had assumed, he requested her not to move; and thus arose the beautiful and expressive figure we now see in the picture.[28]

A third version of this sitting, related by Samuel Rogers, affirms the accidental nature of Mrs Siddon's pose, but provides a different explanation for it:

[27] See Leslie and Taylor, *Life and Times of Sir Joshua Reynolds*, ii. 420–1. Edgar Wind, 'Hume and the Heroic Portrait', pp. 44–5, adds valuable information about Mrs Yates's performance as the Tragic Muse at the Shakespeare Jubilee and subsequently on the London stage; Mrs Siddons had apparently not yet performed this role herself, and Reynolds's portrait of her may therefore have helped to promote her career.

[28] Leslie and Taylor, *Life and Times of Sir Joshua Reynolds*, ii. 422.

I was at Sir Joshua's studio when Mrs. Siddons came in, having walked rapidly to be in time for her appointment. She threw herself, out of breath, into an armchair; having taken off her bonnet and dropped her head upon her left hand—the other hand drooping over the arm of the chair. Suddenly lifting her head she said, 'How shall I sit?' 'Just as you are,' said Sir Joshua, and so she is painted.[29]

These conflicting accounts of the composition of *Mrs Siddons as the Tragic Muse*—which range from the mundane and the adventitious to the self-aggrandizing and the inevitable—nicely mirror the tension Reynolds depicted in the painting itself between the actual historical figure and the more idealized character under which she is subsumed. Samuel Rogers's insistence on the accidental determination of the pose may undercut some of Mrs Siddons's rather extravagant claims in her first version of the sitting, but it nevertheless pays tribute to Reynolds's ability to discern the ideal in the actual, to take advantage of the accidents that nature produces. Reynolds drew attention to this very situation later in the same year when he delivered his twelfth discourse: 'It is better to possess the model with the attitude you require, than to place him with your own hands: by this means it happens often that the model puts himself in an action superior to your own imagination. It is a great matter to be in the way of accident, and to be watchful and ready to take advantage of it ...' (pp. 222–3). A painting may serve as the record of artistic collaboration, but it may also serve as the record of a sitting in which the drama is of a very different kind: not collaboration, but experimentation and even confrontation; not the effortless realization of a predetermined idea, but the imaginative transformation of the accidental into an unexpectedly more appropriate image.

Of the three explanations that have survived, Mrs Siddons's second version of her sitting to Sir Joshua is finally the most intriguing, for it suggests that the pose she accidentally assumed was superior to the position in which the artist had initially placed her. Reynolds immediately sensed the appropriateness of the altered pose because his sitter was *naturally* absorbed in the activity of viewing a painting on the wall of his studio, and this is precisely the impression he wished to convey of the tragic muse herself in his finished portrait. In this version of the story, the drama enacted within Reynolds's studio is identical to that pictured in the painting that serves as the idealized record of it, and it is therefore fitting that the object of the actor's absorption should itself be a painting. The power of the image on the wall produces an effect that no amount of

[29] William T. Whitley, *Artists and Their Friends in England 1700–1799* (London and Boston: Medici Society, 1928), ii. 5.

rehearsing within the studio could achieve. In this account, at least, the power of painting is commensurate with the dramatic power to which Reynolds's portrait of Mrs Siddons pays tribute.

The relation between image and beholder represents Reynolds's most ambitious and sophisticated attempt to embody in his painting the conflicts and discrepancies that he found rooted in human character. In the portraits we have considered so far, we have confined ourselves to the conflicts or tensions inherent in the image itself: Garrick's pose, or the play between an actor's face and his discarded mask, or the canvas as a record of the process that produces it. The implicit relationship between Garrick and Hercules, however, turns the table on us as viewers. The tensions and conflicts that we previously detected in the visual text have now been extended to the process of interpretation; as viewers, we are necessarily implicated in the complexities of representation.[30] In Reynolds's hands, composite portraiture demands that we 'entertain two objects at the same time', that we produce a literate response to the image we contemplate by comparing it to a prototype with which it is visually or verbally associated. For the portrait of *Garrick between Tragedy and Comedy* we must construct an equation that will enable us to measure the relation between Garrick and Hercules, Tragedy and Virtue, Comedy and Vice. In viewing borrowed attitudes, we must perform that 'double operation' which Reynolds described in his essay on Shakespeare. This phenomenon of 'seeing double' can be illustrated most clearly in Reynolds's humorous portrait of *Cupid as Link Boy* (Plate 67), which is a composite portrait in a literal sense because it actually merges the figure of Cupid with that of a contemporary child.[31] The urchin's wings allow us to see both Cupid as a link boy and the link boy as a modern-day cupid, carrying his phallic torch to light the way for lovers through the darkened streets of London.

Reynolds's extensive use of visual allusion eventually earned him a reputation as a plagiarist, but Walpole argued that these borrowed attitudes were a witty form of quotation. 'A quotation from a great author,' he wrote, 'with a novel application of the sense, has always been allowed to be an instance of parts and taste; and may have more merit than the original', an opinion that Reynolds affirmed in the *Discourses* when he stated that 'What is taken from a model, though the first idea may have been suggested by another, you have a just right to consider as your own

---

[30] I am building here, at least in part, on Wind's classic studies of composite portraiture and its inherent tensions, now collected in *Hume and the Heroic Portrait*, ed. Anderson.

[31] Penny, pl. 92; Waterhouse, *Reynolds*, pl. 79.

property'.[32] In his portrait of *Master Crewe as Henry VIII* (Plate 68), for example, Reynolds has 'appropriated' Holbein's—and Eworth's—portrayal of the king to suit his own purposes.[33] 'Is not there humour and satire,' Walpole remarked, 'in Sir Joshua's reducing Holbein's swaggering and colossal haughtiness of Henry VIII. to the boyish jollity of Master Crewe?'[34] There is diminishment here, to be sure; even the boy's denomination as 'Master' Crewe reminds us of how much his title, like the iconic image of the king, has deteriorated with the passage of time. But the painting does not exert its comical sway over us merely by building upon discrepancy; there is a certain appropriateness here as well. Reynolds's allusion suggests that, if there is a measure of the tyrant in the boy, so there is also an element of boyishness in the tyrant. The child's costume and pose enable us to see his character in a new light, or at least to sense more vividly the self-satisfaction and budding imperiousness that he shares with other boys of similar age and social standing. As the dog in the lower left-hand corner of the painting suggests, this portrait works by a process of de-familiarization: just as the dog must sniff the boy's leg to make sure that this is indeed his master, so we too must sort out the congruence or discrepancy implicit in this double image. The delighted boy, moreover, is himself unconscious of the dilemma he has provoked. Here, as in all of Reynolds's composite portraits, the suggestion of tension or conflict has been transferred from the subject of the painting to its beholder. To signify this reversal, the dog on the right turns his head in our direction as if to ask what all the fuss is about. Any sense of incongruity or witty analogy remains ours alone.

iii. Images of a Life

The tensions and discrepancies that we sense within Reynolds's composite portraits function much as the argumentative dialectic does within (and between) his imaginary dialogues. Both the portraits and the verbal texts serve as dramatic forms in which the complexity of the subject's character is introduced indirectly, as an interpretative challenge to the reader or beholder. But even the relative sophistication of composite portraiture cannot fully suggest the development of a man or woman whom the

[32] Walpole, *Anecdotes of Painting in England*, ed. Ralph N. Wornum (1849), i. xvii n.; Reynolds, *Discourses*, p. 222.

[33] Penny, pl. 97; Waterhouse, *Reynolds*, pl. 60. For an interesting discussion of this portrait in the context of composite portraiture, see Paulson, *Emblem*, p. 88.

[34] Walpole, *Anecdotes of Painting in England*, ed. Wornum, i. xvii n.

painter has known for many years. If he or she is to chart the growth of an individual, the artist must produce a series of portraits that will reveal the sitter engaged in several roles, captured in different poses and formats, or experiencing those signs of advancing age that Hogarth noted with such incisive objectivity in *The Analysis of Beauty*.[35] Reynolds's four portraits of Garrick, for instance, depict his friend in a variety of ways: as a husband, awaiting his wife's response; as a celebrated friend (in the Streatham portrait); as an actor submerging himself in another character's personality (in the portrait of the jealous Kiteley); and as *the* actor of his generation, torn between his tragic and comic roles. These multiple images—taken as a whole or played off against each other—create a far more complex representation of Garrick than any single portrait can itself sustain, and yet even in these four portraits there is very little sense of personal or professional growth. The painting of *Garrick between Tragedy and Comedy*, which presumably celebrates the actor at the height of his powers, was actually painted seven years before the portrait of Garrick as Kiteley. Perhaps only the double portrait of Garrick and his wife Eva, which places him in a tranquil, domestic scene, is capable of suggesting a more contemplative and less volatile artist during the latter part of his career. If we are to explore Reynolds's changing conception of a friend's character, however, we must turn to his portrayal of the figure who also holds centre stage in his attempts at verbal portraiture in the character-sketches and Johnsonian dialogues.[36] Here, in the portraits of one of his closest friends, we shall continue to sense Reynolds's exploration of the contradictions and warring impulses that are inherent in Johnson's character as well as in his own.

Reynolds painted at least five portraits of Johnson over a period of twenty-five years, and the first of these portraits was almost certainly revised by Reynolds himself at the very end of his career as a painter. Reynolds had known Johnson for only a year or two when he painted his first portrait of him in 1756 or 1757, soon after the publication of the great *Dictionary* (Plate 2).[37] It was therefore appropriate that Reynolds chose to represent Johnson in the traditional pose of the man of letters, seated at a small writing-desk, with his left hand resting upon a sheaf of papers and his right hand holding a quill pen. Like Eworth's Lady Dacre, Johnson is captured in a moment of meditation or reverie, his head cocked slightly to

[35] See above, p. 175.

[36] Reynolds also painted his original patron, Viscount Keppel, at four different times in his life; for a shrewd analysis of three of these portraits, see Lawrence Lipking, *The Ordering of the Arts in Eighteenth-Century England* (Princeton: Princeton Univ. Press, 1970), 174–5.

[37] Boswell, *Life*, iv. 448; Yung, no. 39.

his right and the mechanical activity of writing suspended: yet another example of how Reynolds could suggest psychological complexity through the development of a 'suspended' pose. The portrait is of a man in his mid-forties, and yet the features of Johnson's face—without being idealized—are relatively youthful. The composition itself is essentially monochromatic, with the checkered pattern on the back of the chair reinforcing the play between the few light areas in the painting—Johnson's head, hands, and the sheaf of paper—and the dark greys and blacks of the figure and its background. And yet in spite of the conventional format of the painting, there are elements of interest and even surprise to be found here, especially in the contrast between Johnson's active right eye and his unfocused left eye, in which he was blind, and between Johnson's forceful left hand, with its clenched knuckles bearing down upon the papers beneath them, and the comparatively relaxed attitude of the right hand, in which he loosely holds his pen.[38]

This is the only portrait in which Reynolds depicted Johnson in a seated position, which suggests that the painter may have found this to be an awkward and difficult way in which to pose his friend.[39] Johnson's sprawling figure is placed somewhat obliquely on the chair, and it is possible that Reynolds added the checkered shawl or fabric to ensure that the massiveness of Johnson's body would not appear to dwarf the chair itself. Similarly, the small writing-desk, with the folds of its green tablecloth pulled sharply back to the right of the canvas, lacks any clear spatial definition, and this may have been one of the reasons why Boswell noted, in the manuscript of the *Life of Johnson*, that the picture 'has never been finished ...'.[40] When Reynolds next painted Johnson's portrait (twelve or thirteen years later, in 1769), he chose to paint him standing upright, with his hands striking a dramatic attitude directly in front of his chest (Plate 69).[41] This is the most complicated of Reynolds's images of Johnson, for it combines a classical pose and costumes with other features that are far more intimate. David Piper has suggested that the statuesque pose may derive from one of the disputing figures in Raphael's *School of*

[38] The first scholar to draw attention to these aspects of the painting was Herman W. Liebert in 'Portraits of the Author: Lifetime Likenesses of Samuel Johnson', in *English Portraits of the Seventeenth and Eighteenth Centuries* (Los Angeles: William Andrews Clark Memorial Library, 1974), 52–3. Liebert discusses each of Reynolds's portraits of Johnson, but his scholarship does not supersede the standard commentary, which is still Birkbeck Hill's appendix to Boswell, *Life*, iv. 448–53.

[39] It might be argued that the third portrait—of Johnson reading—or the fourth—the Streatham portrait—could conceivably depict a sitting figure; but no chair is included in either of these paintings, where the focus is squarely on Johnson's head and torso.

[40] Quoted by Yung, p. 80.

[41] Boswell, *Life*, iv. 448–9; Penny, no. 73. I reproduce the studio copy.

Athens (which Reynolds had caricatured early in his career), and yet the focus in this portrait is on one solitary, isolated figure, struggling with himself, 'wrenching, half physically, thought into words'.[42] Johnson wears his own hair, which is both consistent with his toga and pose and suitable to a privileged glimpse of a writer pictured in the seclusion of his study. The choice of the toga was apparently prompted by Reynolds's desire to ennoble his subject—to endow him with the timeless simplicity of the busts of Roman poets and orators—and to draw attention to his recent appointment as Professor of Ancient History at the Royal Academy. At the same time, Johnson also wears a simple linen shirt, open at the collar. The few iconographical objects associated with the life of writing in the first portrait of Johnson have been augmented in this second image; to the right of his head we find a pen, an inkwell, several books, and a scroll—the traditional emblem of the *logos* that had long since found its way into secular portraiture[43]—and yet these objects have been placed in the background, where they function both as a reminder of what Johnson has already written and as an intimation of what this intense activity will eventually produce. Like the draped character in Raphael's *St Paul Preaching at Athens*, which Reynolds extols in the *Discourses*, the figure of Johnson in this portrait 'appears to think from head to foot' (p. 221).

Reynolds exhibited this painting at the Royal Academy in 1770, where it was paired with a portrait in which Reynolds depicted Goldsmith in an extremely similar pose. Both portraits were purchased by the Duke of Dorset, who collected them as images—presumably as *classical* images—of illustrious contemporary writers.[44] A studio copy of the portrait of Johnson was then sent to his stepdaughter, Lucy Porter, in Lichfield, where it was a great success, as Johnson happily confided in a letter to Reynolds: 'When I came to Lichfield I found that my portrait had been much visited and much admired. Every man has a lurking wish to appear considerable in his native place, and I was pleased with the dignity

---

[42] Piper, *Image of the Poet*, p. 94; the quotation is from Piper, *English Face*, p. 204. Yung (p. 103) quotes Reynolds and his sister Frances on Johnson's famous gesticulations, which he suggests the painter may have had in mind when he painted this portrait. Liebert, however, asks whether we can believe 'that the painter posed his subject in a classic robe, idealized his face and hair, surrounded him with attributes of learning, and then drew his hands in some convulsive paroxysm?' (p. 55). Penny (p. 240) believes that 'The gestures here are surely intended as a dignified version of these "gesticulations".'

[43] For the symbolic function of the scroll, see Sixten Ringbom, *Icon to Narrative: The Rise of the Dramatic Close-Up in Fifteenth-Century Devotional Painting* (Acta Academiae Aboensis, ser. *a*, xxxi. 2; Åbo: Åbo Akademi, 1965), 60.

[44] Yung, p. 103.

conferred by such a testimony of your regard.'[45] We have every reason to believe, moreover, that Reynolds's portrait was also a testimony of friendship: the two men had spent much of the preceding twelve years in each other's company, and when James Watson produced a mezzotint of the painting in 1770, it was accompanied by a similar engraving, of identical size, of a self-portrait of Reynolds.[46] And yet one cannot escape the 'dignity' and 'considerable' appearance that Johnson noted in his letter, and it is intriguing to think of how this classicizing portrait—so unusual in its pose and in the action it depicts—functioned as an icon in Johnson's native town. At the very least it reminds us, as it did those old friends who chose to live their lives in Lichfield, of the writer and moralist Johnson had become and of the intellectual activity that had prompted Reynolds to paint him as a modern worthy.

But for all of its dignity and gravity—and even the relative youthfulness of the face—this is not a flattering portrait of Johnson. The heavy features and the squint of the right eye are prominently displayed, and there is little of the soft moulding that led Frances Reynolds to remark of the companion portrait of Goldsmith that 'it was a very great likeness of the Doctor; but the most flattered picture she ever knew her brother to have painted.'[47] It is therefore interesting that Johnson was pleased with this 'official' but essentially faithful portrait—exhibited both in a nobleman's collection and in the much more modest surroundings of Lichfield—whereas he objected strongly to Reynolds's subsequent likeness of him, which was painted for his friend Edmond Malone (Plate 70).[48] In this third portrait of Johnson, painted in 1775, Reynolds moves Johnson's body much closer to the picture surface and fills virtually the entire canvas with the image of his friend absorbed in the act of reading. In her *Anecdotes*, Mrs Piozzi attempted to explain Johnson's antipathy towards this painting:

When Sir Joshua Reynolds had painted his portrait looking into the slit of his pen [*sic*], and holding it almost close to his eye, as was his general custom, he felt displeased, and told me 'he would not be known by posterity for his *defects* only, let Sir Joshua do his worst.' I said in reply, that Reynolds had no such difficulties

[45] *The Letters of Samuel Johnson*, ed. R. W. Chapman (Oxford: Clarendon Press, 1952), i. 260–1. Surely Nadia Tscherny is wrong here in arguing that 'It is precisely this view of himself, self-absorbed, with "mind ... preying on itself," that Johnson could not have had, nor would have wished to be perpetuated for posterity.' See 'Likeness in Early Romantic Portraiture', *Art Journal*, 46 (1987), 194.

[46] Penny, p. 240.

[47] James Northcote, *The Life of Sir Joshua Reynolds*, 2nd edn. (1819), i. 326.

[48] Boswell, *Life*, iv. 449–50; Yung, no. 78.

about himself, and that he might observe the picture which hung up in the room where we were talking, represented Sir Joshua holding his ear in his hand to catch the sound. 'He may paint himself as deaf if he chuses (replied Johnson); but I will not be *blinking Sam*.' (p. 142)

Mrs Piozzi might have added that Reynolds painted Baretti in a similar pose, and that the acknowledgement of a physical impairment or disability was both an act of artistic integrity, an attempt to capture a sitter in a characteristic attitude, and an index of the intimacy that existed between the painter and his subject.

In this third portrait, almost all of the earlier props associated with authorship have disappeared; only the book remains, with an oblivious Johnson holding it tightly—even roughly—in his hands as he studies its contents. The intensity of this encounter between the critic and the material on which he feeds should remind us of the many passages in the *Life of Johnson* in which Boswell comments on Johnson's unusual reading habits, especially his ability to grasp 'at once what was valuable in any book, without submitting to the labour of perusing it from beginning to end' (i. 71). Later Boswell recalls a dinner at Dilly's in April 1778—only three years after this portrait was painted—in which this voracious appetite for literature (or for distraction) overshadowed the feast itself:

Before dinner Dr. Johnson seized upon Mr. Charles Sheridan's 'Account of the late Revolution in Sweden,' and seemed to read it ravenously, as if he devoured it, which was to all appearance his method of studying. 'He knows how to read better than any one (said Mrs. Knowles;) he gets at the substance of a book directly; he tears out the heart of it.' He kept it wrapt up in the tablecloth in his lap during the time of dinner, from an avidity to have one entertainment in readiness when he should have finished another; resembling (if I may use so coarse a simile) a dog who holds a bone in his paws in reserve, while he eats something else which has been thrown to him. (iii. 284–5)

Reynolds's fourth image of Johnson bears a close resemblance in many ways to the portrait of '*blinking Sam*', especially in its focus on the massive torso and the intense activity of the countenance (Plate 71).[49] The precise dating of this famous portrait remains uncertain: the version painted for Johnson's friend Topham Beauclerk was paid for in 1779; the version for the Thrales' library at Streatham has traditionally been dated 1778, although Mrs Piozzi remarked in her annotations to Johnson's letters that it had been painted in 1772; all of the Streatham portraits, moreover, were apparently in Reynolds's studio in 1780, when he was said to be 'touching

⁴⁹ Boswell, *Life*, iv. 450–2; Yung, no. 83; Penny, no. 80.

up' the series and ordering frames.[50] Johnson wrote to Mrs Thrale twice in October 1778 to tell her that Reynolds was pleased with his own performance and that the painting 'seems to please every body, but I shall wait to see how it pleases You'.[51] This is the first portrait in which the paraphernalia of authorship has been completely abandoned, and yet the rendering of Johnson's face, which is now caught in an almost full frontal pose, continues to suggest the solemnity and power of his intelligence. As Sir John Hawkins remarked in his biography of Johnson, 'there is in it that appearance of a labouring working mind, of an indolent reposing body, which he had to a very great degree.'[52] Although only one hand is shown, the full bend of the arm at the elbow and the play of the thumb above the clenched fingers reinforce the intensity of Johnson's face. In William Doughty's popular engraving (to which Hawkins himself refers), Johnson appears to stare off into space, his eyes not quite focused upon his audience. In the original painting, however, Johnson's right eye engages us directly and holds us within its powerful gaze, and it is surely this evocation of Johnson's powerful intellectual presence that led one of the original owners of this image to speculate on the discrepancy between the inner and the outer man. Here is Boswell's account:

> On the frame of his portrait, Mr. Beauclerk had inscribed,
>
>> '——*Ingenium ingens*
>> *Inculto latet hoc sub corpore.*'
>> ['–Underneath this rude, uncouth disguise,
>> A genius of extensive knowledge lies.']

After Mr. Beauclerk's death, when it became Mr. Langton's property, he made the inscription be defaced. Johnson said complacently, 'It was kind in you to take it off;' and then after a short pause, added, 'and not unkind in him to put it on.' (iv. 180–1)

Reynolds painted his last and most moving portrait of Johnson a year or two before Johnson died (Plate 73).[53] Johnson continues to fill the canvas, but his torso is virtually unaccented here, for Reynolds has chosen to paint neither his hands nor the buttons on his coat, which almost disappears against the dark colours of the drapery in the background. It is possible, in fact, to examine the face alone without sacrificing the dramatic

[50] The fullest accounts are in Yung, pp. 117–18, and Penny, pp. 249–50.

[51] *The Letters of Samuel Johnson*, ed. Chapman, ii. 257, 263.

[52] *Johnsonian Miscellanies*, ed. George Birkbeck Hill (1897), ii. 10.

[53] Boswell, *Life*, iv. 452; Yung, no. 103, where the attribution to Reynolds is challenged on stylistic grounds.

intensity of the composition, which focuses so poignantly and yet unflinchingly on the elongated features of a dying man (Plate 74). It is a face filled with suffering and experience, the face of a writer who, in the month preceding his own death, would turn to a translation of Horace's *Odes*:

> The changing year's successive plan
> Proclaims mortality to Man.
> Rough Winter's blasts to Spring give way,
> Spring yield[s] to Summer['s] sovereign ray,
> Then Summer sinks in Autumn's reign,
> And Winter chils the World again.
> Her losses soon the Moon supplies,
> But wretched Man, when once he lies
> Where Priam and his sons are laid,
> Is naught but Ashes and a Shade.[54]

This final portrait was painted for Dr John Taylor of Ashbourne, one of Johnson's oldest and dearest friends, the person, he told Mrs Piozzi, who 'is better acquainted with my *heart* than any man or woman now alive . . .'.[55]

But the history of Reynolds's Johnsonian iconography does not end with this extraordinary portrait of his dying friend. Reynolds's first portrait of Johnson had remained in his own possession for many years; he had neither exhibited nor sold it, and it had never been engraved. After Johnson's death, Reynolds made a present of it to Boswell, who was then busily engaged in the task of completing his great biography. Perhaps because the painting had never been reproduced—perhaps because it was a recent gift from Reynolds, an image that he could now claim as his own—Boswell chose this portrait as the appropriate frontispiece to the *Life* when it appeared in 1791 and referred to it at that crucial moment in his narrative when he described his first encounter with Johnson in Tom Davies's bookshop. Boswell's dramatic introduction of this portrait in the *Life* constitutes a rather complicated gesture (and I shall therefore return to this scene in the following chapter), but it is no more problematical than the actual history of the image itself during its transformation from the painted portrait to the engraved frontispiece by James Heath (Plate 72).[56] Until quite recently the changes we see in Heath's engraving were

---

[54] *The Poems of Samuel Johnson*, ed. David Nichol Smith and Edward L. McAdam, 2nd edn. (Oxford: Clarendon Press, 1974), 265.

[55] Piozzi, *Anecdotes*, p. 70.

[56] For a further discussion, see pp. 285–90, below.

also present in the portrait itself; it was not until the painting was cleaned by Bettina Jessell in 1977 that it was discovered that the larger table, the inkstand, and second quill pen, the volumes in the background (including the great *Dictionary*), and the arm on the chair were all added to the original portrait (Plate 2), which, after its cleaning and restoration, also reveals a much more youthful, even dreamier look on Johnson's face. Jessell has argued that Boswell employed a painter to make most of these alterations, and that the wooden table was probably a nineteenth-century addition.[57] More recent scholarship by Irma Lustig and Kai Kin Yung, however, which draws upon Boswell's manuscripts and the successive states of Heath's engraving (there are four in all), has confirmed my own conjecture that Reynolds was responsible for these changes, even if he supervised some of these revisions when he was no longer able to execute them himself.[58]

But why would Reynolds wish to tamper with his original composition, and why would Boswell serve as his accomplice? We know, in the first place, that Reynolds was not only notorious for his technical experiments but that he often revised his work as well. His portrait of *Mrs Abington as the Comic Muse*—another figure of an actor with a mask in her hand—was painted in 1769 and significantly revised in 1772 and 1773; his portrait of his niece, Offy, originally painted in 1776, was retouched following her marriage in 1781 to reflect the changing hairstyles of the times.[59] It is therefore clear that Reynolds was not afraid to alter his work, and he was in fact infamous not only for the strenuously reworked passages in his own compositions (perhaps a result of his relatively weak skills as a draughtsman), but also for the alacrity with which he revised paintings by other artists in his own collection.[60] Yung has suggested that the inkwell, second quill pen, and set of books were such common accessories in Reynolds's portraits of literary men at mid-century that they may have been painted in long before 1789,[61] and I would argue that the introduction of a larger writing-desk, which lacks the green tablecloth of the

[57] 'A Study of the Paint Layers of a Portrait of Dr. Johnson by Sir Joshua Reynolds P.R.A.', *The Conservator*, 5 (1981), 36–40.

[58] See Lustig, 'Facts and Deductions: The Curious History of Reynolds's First Portrait of Johnson, 1756', in *The Age of Johnson*, i (1987), 161–80, and Yung, pp. 79–81. I posed my own doubts in '*Ut Pictura Biographia*: Biography and Portrait Painting as Sister Arts', in *Articulate Images: The Sister Arts from Hogarth to Tennyson*, ed. Wendorf (Minneapolis: Univ. of Minnesota Press, 1983), 123 n. 65.

[59] Penny, p. 247; Hudson, *Sir Joshua Reynolds*, p. 152.

[60] See M. Kirby Talley, jun., ' "All good pictures crack": Sir Joshua Reynolds's practice and studio', in Penny, pp. 55–70.

[61] Yung, p. 81.

original painting, provides much sharper definition to the space immediately in front of Johnson's sprawling figure.

For the change of expression on Johnson's face we must turn to Boswell's commentary on the successive impressions of Heath's engraving. Below the plate of the second impression—which Boswell thought was the first—he wrote that

This is the first impression of the Plate after M.ʳ Heath the Engraver thought it was finished. He went with me to Sir Joshua Reynolds who suggested that the countenance was too young and not thoughtful enough. M.ʳ Heath therefore altered it so much to its advantage that Sir Joshua was quite satisfied, and Heath then saw such a difference that he said he would not for a hundred pounds have had it remained as it was.[62]

In his first two states, in other words, Heath dutifully reproduced the head of Johnson as it appeared in Reynolds's original painting; in his third and fourth states, however, he altered Johnson's face by introducing a frown and gradually ageing his features. Reynolds, for his part, must then have revised his own painting so that it would correspond to the published image of it; these, in turn, are presumably the alterations that prompted Boswell to suppress his original statements that the picture 'has never been finished' and 'has never been produced' and to insert, instead, a passage informing his readers that this was the painting 'which Sir Joshua very kindly presented to me, and from which an engraving has been made for this work' (i. 392).[63]

The facts concerning the revision of Boswell's manuscript, Reynolds's painting, and Heath's engraved print are worth rehearsing in some detail because they reveal how closely Johnson's biographer and portrait-painter collaborated on a common image of their celebrated friend. We have already seen how seriously Reynolds approached the task of sketching a verbal portrait of Johnson, one that Boswell would make use of in his biography; later he was not only willing to present his younger friend with his own image of Johnson, but was willing to have it reproduced and even changed. The alterations to the original portrait are strictly in keeping, moreover, with the decorum of Boswell's *Life*: the revised image associates the seated figure of the writer with his most famous publication—the work with which his own name had proved to be synonymous—and the altered countenance is consistent with a more conventional conception of the moralist, especially in the final three

---

[62] Quoted by Yung, 82.

[63] The quotations from Boswell's manuscript are provided by Yung, p. 80.

portraits that Reynolds himself painted. This retrospective image of Johnson reveals an attempt by both artists to recapture their friend as they most vividly remembered him. The original image had been painted at least six years before Boswell first met Johnson, and for Reynolds it may, at best, have served as a distant image of the past, not as a reminder of the man he later knew so well. For both men, moreover, this conscious act of revision was closely tied to the common impulse of visual and verbal portraiture to fix an individual in time, to reconstruct—and even re-envision—the past, to bring renewed life to 'Ashes and a Shade'.

Considered as a succession of images, these six representations of Johnson suggest not only the different ways in which Reynolds conceived of his friend's character, but also the changing nature of the relationship between the painter and his subject. Taken together, these portraits also bear tribute to the inventiveness with which Reynolds approached fairly conventional poses, a severely restricted number of accessories, and even rather intractable material—'this rude, uncouth disguise'. Ultimately these three issues are closely bound together. Reynolds's decision to forego the use of any traditional literary props in the fourth portrait, for example, marks the growing extent of Johnson's own fame: because he was now universally known as a scholar and moralist, there was no longer any convincing reason in the late 1770s to provide the normal iconographical attributes, replete with their conventional identifications. Johnson was, after all, much more than a mere writer; he was, in Mrs Piozzi's phrase, a 'living book', and it was therefore appropriate for Reynolds to attempt to create this impression of his physical and intellectual presence by limiting himself to the figure alone. In this portrait no less than in the earlier images of Johnson as a writer or reader, Reynolds was able to depict what Johnson had himself praised in his imaginary tribute to Garrick: 'the mind and mode of thinking of the person imitated'. We continue to sense Johnson's struggles in this central portrait, but by freeing Johnson of any authorial properties Reynolds has been able to portray a man whose hand now reflects either meditation or emphatic discourse. This fourth portrait therefore represents both a continuation and a refinement of the images that preceded it; if it reveals growth, it also—like the verbal portraits of Garrick and Goldsmith, and the tribute to Gainsborough in the four-teenth discourse—reminds us that character is an evolving entity, that the behaviour of mature men often has its origins in patterns and deficiencies that were imposed long ago. As Johnson says of himself in a fascinating passage in the second of Reynolds's dialogues,

I looked on David [Garrick] with some degree of envy, not so much for the respect he received, as for the manner of its being acquired. What fell into his lap unsought, I have been forced to claim. I began the world by fighting my way. There was something about me that invited insult, or at least a disposition to neglect; and I was equally disposed to repel insult and to claim attention, and, I fear, continue too much in this disposition now it is no longer necessary. (p. 101)

This portrait, moreover, was intended to hang in a specific setting at Streatham; it was commissioned as an act of friendship and admiration by the Thrales, and later reproduced for Topham Beauclerk, whose widow then presented it to another close friend, Bennet Langton. One can in fact trace a consistent pattern in the collection of these portraits, for with the exception of the Duke of Dorset's purchase of the second painting, each of these images was closely tied to Johnson's friends. The studio version of the second portrait was given to Lucy Porter; the depiction of '*blinking Sam*' was appropriately commissioned by Malone, one of the most prominent bookmen of the century; the fourth image was shared by Beauclerk and the Thrales; the fifth was owned by Taylor; and the revised first, which had been held so long by Reynolds himself, was given to Boswell, as we have seen. These associations should not be overlooked, for they remind us of how conscious Reynolds must have been that he was creating images for patrons who cared about Johnson as much as he did. Reynolds, moreover, shared with these friends an increasing intimacy with the man they all wished to commemorate. When we consider the disappearance of authorial attributes in the final two portraits, the straightforward gaze in Johnson's eyes, and the close proximity of the figure to the surface of the painting, we can begin to account for these pictorial developments by referring (as I have) to the changes in Johnson's reputation and character, the artistic compulsion to invent fresh poses, or the patronage that would determine where these images would be hung and who would view them. But we must also recognize that this increasing simplicity, directness, and spatial proximity also reflect Reynolds's growing familiarity with his subject and his willingness to confront the Johnson he knew as directly as he could.

9

Boswell's Flemish Picture

AMONG the maxims that James Northcote collected in his two-volume biography of Reynolds is one that raises important questions about the role of distinctiveness and particularly in verbal or visual portraiture: 'Portraits, as well as written characters of men, should be decidedly marked, otherwise they will be insipid.'[1] Reynolds's statement should remind us of Jonathan Richardson's justification for heightening the characters of his subjects nearly fifty years earlier. 'Life would be an Insipid thing indeed,' he wrote in *An Essay on the Theory of Painting*, 'if we never saw, or had Ideas of any thing but what we commonly see.'[2] Reynolds, who championed the role of ideal form in painting by arguing that 'the whole beauty and grandeur of the art consists, in my opinion, in being able to get above all singular forms, local customs, particularities, and details of every kind',[3] nevertheless recognized that the task of successfully 'marking' the characters of men and women was extremely complex. If Reynolds shunned excessive particularity, he also realized that an attempt to distinguish characters through extensive exaggeration could be equally hazardous. Boswell, for example, often praised Johnson for his 'strong, yet nice portraits' (iii. 20), for his ability to depict characters 'as they appeared to him, both in light and shade' (ii. 306). In 1775, Reynolds joined Boswell by remarking that their friend ' "was fond of discrimination, which he could not show without pointing out the bad as well as the good in every character; and as his friends were those whose characters he knew best, they afforded him the best opportunity for showing the acuteness of his judgement" ' (ii. 306). In a later conversation, however, he tempered his opinion:

BOSWELL. 'His power of reasoning is very strong, and he has a peculiar art of drawing characters, which is as rare as good portrait painting.' SIR JOSHUA REYNOLDS. 'He is undoubtedly admirable in this; but, in order to mark the characters which he draws, he overcharges them, and gives people more than they really have, whether of good or bad.' (iii. 332)[4]

---

[1] *The Life of Sir Joshua Reynolds*, 2nd edn. (1819), ii. 55.
[2] Richardson, *Essay*, p. 183; see pp. 138, 150, above.
[3] Reynolds, *Discourses*, p. 44.
[4] Cf. Northcote's conversation with Boswell on this same topic in *The Life of Sir Joshua Reynolds*, ii. 76–7.

Contending (and even contradictory) remarks such as these constitute a running debate in the pages of *The Life of Johnson*—and in Mrs Piozzi's *Anecdotes* as well—for they reflect the concerted effort of Johnson's friends to characterize his temperament and social deportment as well as his powers of mind. Boswell clearly shared Reynolds's concern with marking, discriminating, even over-charging individual characters; but while he systematically drew his analogies from his friend's practice as a painter, his own biographical enterprise led him in a different direction.

i. The General and the Particular

By insisting on accuracy, fullness, and vividness in his biographical writings, Boswell became the supreme proponent of the particular—of 'the fact imagined', in Wimsatt's shrewd phrase—and in relying so extensively on detail, on the minutiae of everyday life, he therefore broke decisively with what both Reynolds and Johnson had taught him.[5] Reynolds's preoccupation with the general and the particular surfaces again and again in the *Discourses*, where he worries about the tendency of minute representation (what Northrop Frye would call low mimetic style) to subvert the artist's quest for beauty and grandeur. In the fourth discourse, for example, he argues that 'minute peculiarities' of dress, furniture, or location should not draw our attention from the 'ideal picture' that a story or painting presents. Some 'circumstances of minuteness and particularity frequently tend to give an air of truth to a piece,' he concedes, but 'the usual and most dangerous error is on the side of minuteness,' even in portraits, where 'the grace, and, we may add, the likeness, consists more in taking the general air, than in observing the exact similitude of every feature' (pp. 58–9). Reynolds returns to this point in the eleventh discourse, where he observes that there are 'great characteristick distinctions, which press strongly on the senses, and therefore fix the imagination. These are by no means, as some persons think, an aggregate of all the small discriminating particulars; nor will such an accumulation of particulars ever express them' (p. 192). Only the general effect of the whole, rather than its parts, 'can give to objects their true and touching character' (p. 193), a conclusion that Reynolds then dramatically reaffirms for his audience by drawing upon memories of his own early days as a student of painting:

[5] William K. Wimsatt, jun., 'James Boswell: The Fact Imagined', in *Hateful Contraries: Studies in Literature and Criticism* (Lexington: Univ. of Kentucky Press, 1965), 165–83.

I REMEMBER a Landscape-Painter in Rome, who was known by the name of STUDIO, from his patience in high finishing, in which he thought the whole excellence of art consisted; so that he once endeavoured, as he said, to represent every individual leaf on a tree. This picture I never saw; but I am very sure that an artist, who looked only at the general character of the species, the order of the branches, and the masses of the foliage, would in a few minutes produce a more true resemblance of trees, than this Painter in as many months. (p. 199)

Reynolds then extends these observations to his own practice as a painter by declaring that 'The excellence of Portrait-Painting, and we may add even the likeness, the character, and the countenance, as I have observed in another place, depend more upon the general effect produced by the painter, than on the exact expression of the peculiarities, or minute discrimination of the parts' (p. 200).

It is not accidental, of course, that Reynolds's pronouncements on the general and the particular resonate with echoes of Johnson's own remarks, in *Rasselas*, on the streaks of the tulip, or his belief that 'Shakespeare always makes nature predominate over accident; and if he preserves the essential character, is not very careful of distinctions superinduced, and adventitious.' A poet, Johnson reminded Shakespeare's eighteenth-century readers, 'overlooks the casual distinction of country and condition, as a painter, satisfied with the figure, neglects the drapery'.[6] But there is another side to Reynolds's concern with the particular, for if he was critical of paintings that were too finely 'finished', he was also wary of images that left too much to the viewer's imagination. This concern emerges for the first time in his discussion, in the eighth discourse, of sketches and preliminary drawings, which he introduces by drawing a literary analogy: 'A great part of the beauty of the celebrated description of EVE in Milton's Paradise Lost, consists in using only general indistinct expressions, every reader making out the detail according to his own particular imagination,—his own idea of beauty, grace, expression, dignity, or loveliness: but a painter, when he represents EVE on a canvas, is obliged to give a determined form, and his own ideal of beauty distinctly expressed.' When we look at a drawing, he argues, our imagination may supply more 'than the painter himself, probably, could produce', but Reynolds cannot recommend 'an undeterminate manner, or vague ideas of any kind, in a completed and finished picture'. The notion

---

[6] 'Preface to Shakespeare' (1765), in *Johnson on Shakespeare*, ed. Arthur Sherbo (New Haven: Yale Univ. Press, 1968), i. 66 (vol. vii of *The Yale Edition of the Works of Samuel Johnson*). For a different perspective on Johnson's neoclassical aesthetic, see C. R. Tracy, 'Johnson and the Art of Anecdote', *University of Toronto Quarterly*, 15 (1945), 86–93.

of leaving anything to the imagination 'opposes a very fixed and indispensable rule in our art,—that every thing shall be carefully and distinctly expressed . . .' (p. 164).

Reynolds raises this issue again exactly ten years later when, in his penultimate discourse, he attempts to evaluate Gainsborough's success as a painter. Although Gainsborough's portraits were filled with indeterminate forms, they were nevertheless attentive to 'the general effect', the 'whole together', and they therefore served as faithful likenesses of the subjects they portrayed. And paradoxically, Reynolds continues, it may be precisely Gainsborough's unfinished manner that makes his resemblances so striking: 'It is presupposed that in this undetermined manner there is the general effect; enough to remind the spectator of the original; the imagination supplies the rest, and perhaps more satisfactorily to himself, if not more exactly, than the artist, with all his care, could possibly have done.' This is a generous tribute to Gainsborough—and an even greater concession to the power of indeterminate form—and yet Reynolds remains keenly aware of its limitations. What would happen, for example, if the portrait were to be viewed by those who had no knowledge of the 'original'? Different people would form different ideas, he argues, 'and all would be disappointed at not finding the original correspond with their own conceptions; under the great latitude which indistinctness gives to the imagination, to assume almost what character or form it pleases' (p. 259).

Like Reynolds, Johnson feared excessive 'finishing' and adventitious details no less than he worried about indeterminate form and an unleashed imagination. In the most extended passage on the nature of visual and verbal art in the *Life*, Boswell mentions Johnson's high regard for Reynolds's discourses (although Johnson himself 'had no taste for painting'), and then poses a dilemma that is very close to Reynolds's response to Gainsborough's work:

> When I observed to him that Painting was so far inferiour to Poetry, that the story or even emblem which it communicates must be previously known, and mentioned as a natural and laughable instance of this, that a little Miss on seeing a picture of Justice with the scales, had exclaimed to me, 'See, there's a woman selling sweetmeats;' he said, 'Painting, Sir, can illustrate, but cannot inform.' (iv. 321)

According to this view—which Reynolds implicitly seems to share with Boswell and Johnson—painting may be, in the semiotic sense, a more directly iconic language than writing, but it nevertheless functions as a

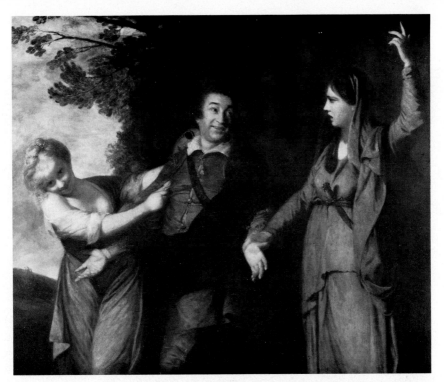

61. Sir Joshua Reynolds, *Garrick between Tragedy and Comedy*, 1761, private collection

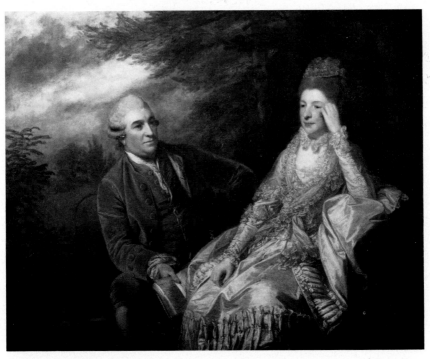

62. Sir Joshua Reynolds, *Garrick Reading to His Wife*, 1773, National Portrait Gallery, London

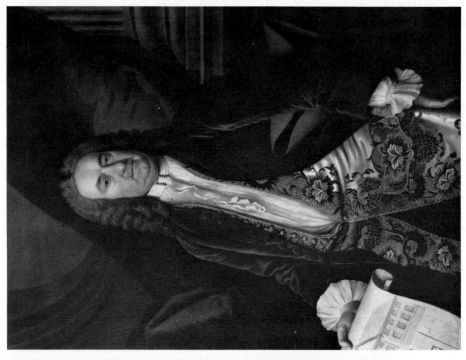

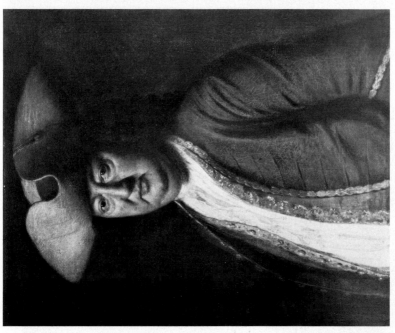

63. (*above*) William Hoare, *Richard Nash, c.*1761, Victoria Art Gallery, Bath

64. (*right*) Unknown artist, *Richard Nash*, Town Hall, Tunbridge Wells

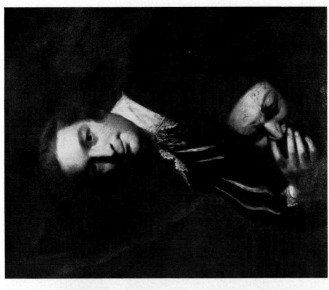

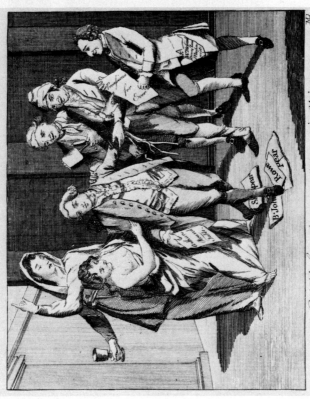

Suppose JOB living 'midst the Critic train,
Our Theatres would ope his angry vein.

Behold the Mimic ROSCIUS sue in Vain,
Taylors & Carpenters usurp their Reign.

LONDON:

PRINTED FOR JOHN BELL, IN THE STRAND, AND C. ETHERINGTON, AT YORK.

M.DCC.LXXII.

66. (*above*) Sir Joshua Reynolds, *Harry Woodward,* 1759–62, Lord Egremont, Petworth House

65. (*left*) Matthew Darly, caricature of Reynolds, *Garrick between Tragedy and Comedy,* title-page of *The Theatres. A Poetical Dissection. By Sir Nicholas Nipclose,* 1772

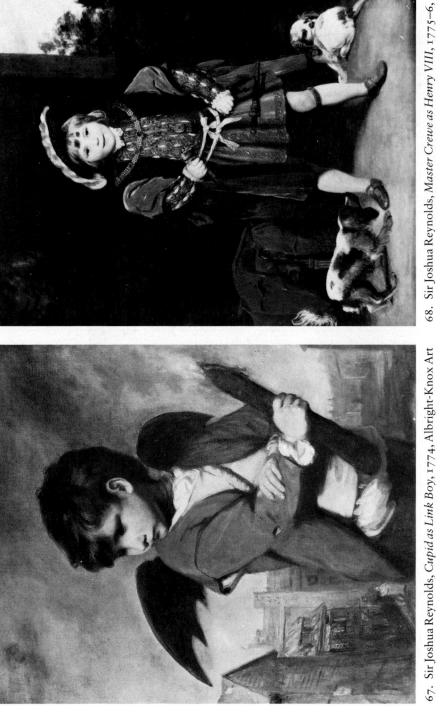

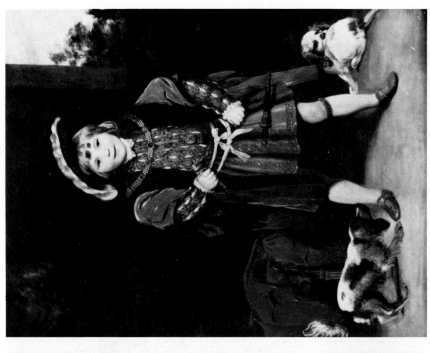

68. Sir Joshua Reynolds, *Master Crewe as Henry VIII*, 1775–6, private collection

67. Sir Joshua Reynolds, *Cupid as Link Boy*, 1774, Albright-Knox Art Gallery, Buffalo, New York

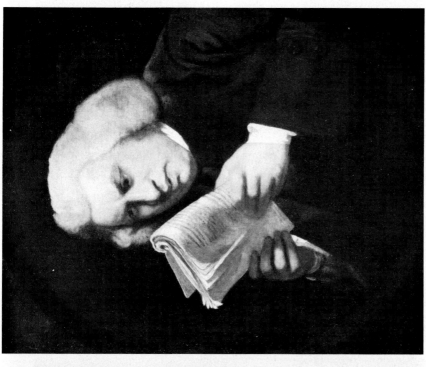

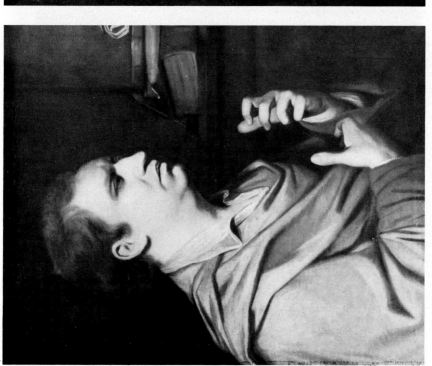

70. Sir Joshua Reynolds, *Samuel Johnson*, 1775, Loren R. Rothschild

69. Sir Joshua Reynolds, *Samuel Johnson*, 1769, Houghton
Library, Harvard University

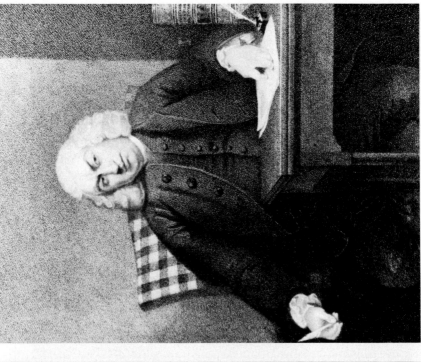

72. Sir Joshua Reynolds, *Samuel Johnson*, 1756–7, engraved by
James Heath, frontispiece to Boswell's *Life of Samuel Johnson*,
1791

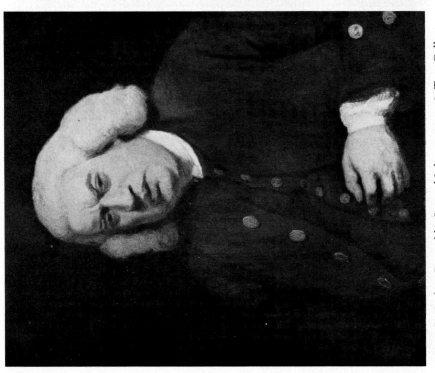

71. Sir Joshua Reynolds, *Samuel Johnson*, c.1778, Tate Gallery

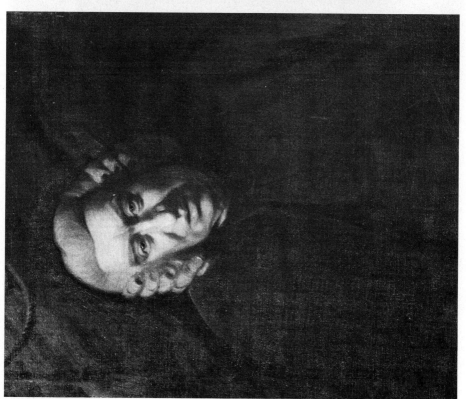

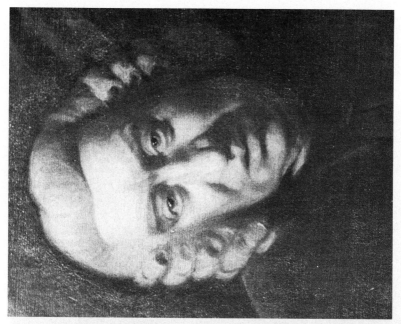

74. (*above*) Detail, Reynolds, *Samuel Johnson, c.1782*

73. (*left*) Sir Joshua Reynolds, *Samuel Johnson, c.1782*, Magill Library, Haverford College

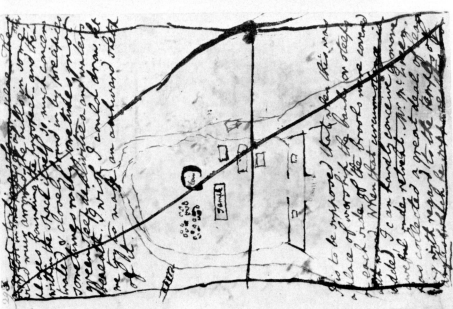

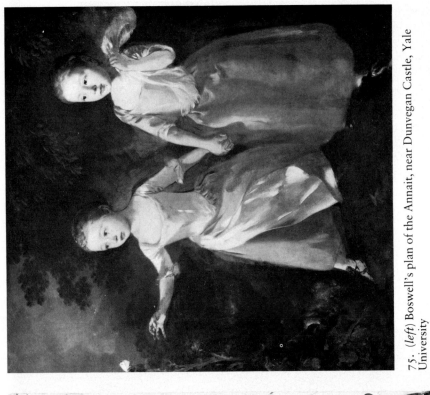

75. (*left*) Boswell's plan of the Annait, near Dunvegan Castle, Yale University

76. (*above*) Thomas Gainsborough, *The Painter's Daughters Chasing a Butterfly*, *c.*1756, National Gallery, London

form of secondary discourse, dependent upon previously articulated ideas, images, 'originals', or stories. When Boswell asks Johnson during their travels in Scotland whether he would rather have 'fine portraits or faithful ones,' Johnson argues that ' "their chief excellence is in being like."—*Boswell.* "Are you of that opinion as to the portraits of ancestors, whom one has never seen?"—*Johnson.* "It then becomes of more consequence that they should be like; and I would have them in the dress of the times, which makes a piece of history" ' (v. 219). Even here, as Johnson attempts to align portrait-painting with truthfulness and historical accuracy, he reveals his anxiety about the instability of visual images. As Robert Folkenflik has suggested, 'his strongest reservations arise because he is aware that paintings cannot do what he believes language can do, fix meanings.'[7]

If we return to the crucial passage that Boswell entered in his journal in 1775, we shall see that the nascent biographer harboured reservations of a very different kind:

The great lines of characters may be put down. But I doubt much if it be possible to preserve in words the peculiar features of mind which distinguish individuals as certainly as the features of different countenances. The art of portrait painting fixes the last, and musical sounds with all their nice gradations can also be fixed. Perhaps language may be improved to such a degree as to picture the varieties of mind as minutely.[8]

This is both a tribute to the power of painted images and an acknowledgement that biography nourishes even greater aspirations, for it strives to depict the peculiar features of mind that distinguish one person from another. The great lines of character may be 'put down'; they may, in Reynolds's phrase, be 'decidedly marked'. But how does one 'picture the varieties of mind as minutely'? The answer, of course, already existed in the very journal in which Boswell raised these questions. By relying upon the extraordinarily rich record of his life with Johnson—and by shaping

---

[7] 'Samuel Johnson and Art', in *Samuel Johnson: Pictures and Words* (Los Angeles: William Andrews Clark Memorial Library, 1984), 109.

[8] *Boswell: The Ominous Years, 1774–1776*, ed. Charles Ryskamp and Frederick A. Pottle (London: Heinemann; New York: McGraw-Hill, 1963), 168; see pp. 2–3, above. Cf. a journal passage for 16 Sept. 1769, published in *Boswell in Search of a Wife: 1766–1769*, ed. Frank Brady and Frederick A. Pottle (London: Heinemann; New York: McGraw-Hill, 1957), 311:

I observe continually how imperfectly, upon most occasions, words preserve our ideas. . . . all I have said of the Stratford Jubilee is very dim in comparison with the scene itself. In description we omit insensibly many little touches which give life to objects. With how small a speck does a painter give life to an eye! The vivid glances of Garrick's features, which cannot be copied in words, will illuminate an extent of sensation, if that term may be used, as a spark from a flint will throw a lustre in a dark night for a considerable space around it.

this material to meet the formal requirements of biography—Boswell would be able to complete a full-dress portrait that combined the broad outlines of character with its peculiar features. And it is for this reason that Boswell turned to portrait-painting when he wanted to suggest the unusual qualities of his own work. Recalling his efforts to help Johnson remove a dead cat from an obstructed waterfall, he notes that this 'may be laughed at as too trifling to record; but it is a small characteristick trait in the Flemish picture which I give of my friend, and in which, therefore, I mark the most minute particulars' (iii. 191). Or, in another journal entry for 1775, he reports that 'I am so nice in recording him that every trifle must be authentic. I draw him in the style of a Flemish painter. I am not satisfied with hitting the large features. I must be exact as to every hair, or even every spot on his countenance.'[9]

By invoking the Flemish style of painting, Boswell did not intend to denigrate the seriousness of his own work.[10] Reynolds praised Gainsborough, we should remember, for gleaning the best features from his Flemish models: 'the harmony of colouring, the management and disposition of light and shadow, and every means which the masters of it practised, to ornament and give splendour to their works' (p. 253). Each of these characteristics could be applied to Boswell's *Life*—and Boswell himself was assiduous in drawing precisely these intricate parallels—but it was clearly the minute and highly finished qualities of Flemish painting that he found most congenial, even to the point of cherishing those quotidian details that Reynolds, elsewhere in the *Discourses*, would deprecatingly associate with the low mimetic style of Flemish landscape, still-life, and genre painting. Boswell was not content with merely relating the most important events of Johnson's life; as he argued in his opening pages, only by interweaving 'what he privately wrote, and said, and thought' could Boswell force his reader 'to see him live, and to "live o'er each scene" with him'; only by gathering together an unprecedented amount of diverse material—some of which would certainly appear to be trivial in *other* biographical texts—could Boswell ensure that 'he will be seen in this work more completely than any man who has ever yet lived' (i. 30).

---

[9] *Boswell: The Ominous Years*, p. 103.

[10] Richard B. Schwartz, *Boswell's Johnson: A Preface to the 'Life'* (Madison: Univ. of Wisconsin Press, 1978), 17 and *passim*, attempts to turn the metaphor of the Flemish portrait against Boswell by arguing that 'minute detail may involve the portraitist with the trivial and cause him to lose sight of the important.' This is possible, of course, but Schwartz does not convince me that it is true of the *Life of Johnson*. For a more approving association of the Flemish picture with 'minuteness of graphic depiction', see Pottle, 'James Boswell, Journalist', in *The Age of Johnson: Essays Presented to Chauncey Brewster Tinker*, ed. Frederick W. Hilles (New Haven: Yale Univ. Press, 1949), 23.

But for all of Boswell's obsession with particulars, he himself believed (at least early in his career as a writer) that he could not render them accurately or vividly. One of the revelations of the manuscript version of the *Journal of a Tour to the Hebrides* is the frequency and urgency with which Boswell lamented his inability to describe the physical world. After struggling with his verbal portrait of the cave at Raasay, for instance, he writes that 'I find a wretched deficiency in expressing visible objects',[11] a complaint that he renews several days later when he attempts to survey the temple and its surroundings at Dunvegan:

Whatever this place has been it has been a most striking solemn scene. The sight lost in some places on a wild moor around; the hills in some other places bounding the prospect; and then, within, the space itself, so much concentrated and closely bound in by precipices, sometimes rocky, sometimes just green steep declivities—and water beneath. I wish I could draw. Let me try to make an awkward sketch of it. . . . My sketch of it may convey some idea. But there is no exactness in it. I may truly be said to

Write about it, Goddess, and about it. (p. 180)[12]

This is a fascinating passage, and no less so given the opinion of Boswell's editors that his sketches 'are of little value from any point of view' (p. xiii). The sketch they reproduce (Plate 75) is crude enough, but it is eloquent testimony to Boswell's desire to fix his subject, even at the expense of surrounding his drawing with dark phalanxes of prose and belittling his own plight by quoting from the *Dunciad*: 'For thee [we] explain a thing till all men doubt it, / And write about it, Goddess, and about it' (iv. 251–2). A few days later he will continue his awkward sketching and repeat his earlier lament: 'I can do nothing in the way of description of any visible object whatever. Whether it is owing to my not seeing with accuracy, or to my not having the use of words fitted to such sort of description, I cannot say' (p. 220).[13]

Complaints such as these reveal the seriousness of Boswell's dilemma. On the one hand—as the sketches themselves attest—Boswell lacked the graphic skills of Aubrey and North; he could not rely on actual visual images to supplement or replace his verbal descriptions. And thus, on the other hand, he worried all the more about his ability to find a language

[11] *Boswell's Journal of A Tour of the Hebrides with Samuel Johnson, LL.D.*, ed. Frederick A. Pottle and Charles H. Bennett (London: Heinemann, 1936), 148; further references are provided in the text. Cf. *Tour* (vol. v of Boswell, *Life*), 173, where the passage remains unchanged. Wimsatt mentions Boswell's difficulty in describing objects in 'James Boswell: The Fact Imagined', p. 168.
[12] Cf. *Tour* (Boswell, *Life*, v), 219, where all mention of Boswell's sketches disappears.
[13] Omitted in the *Tour*.

suited to the objects he wished to fix. Observing an 'old woman grinding
with the quern', he says that 'I cannot draw it. ... I must try if Mr.
Johnson can describe it' (p. 219), and in the *Life* itself he expands upon
this surprising comparison of their abilities by praising Johnson's descriptive powers:

> Johnson described it [a 'romantick scene'] distinctly and vividly, at which I could
> not but express to him my wonder; because, though my eyes, as he observed,
> were better than his, I could not by any means equal him in representing visible
> objects. I said, the difference between us in this respect was as that between a man
> who has a bad instrument, but plays well on it, and a man who has a good
> instrument, on which he can play very imperfectly. (iii. 187)

Boswell was much more successful when he turned to descriptions of the
men and women he met, although even here he noted that 'I find it in vain
to try to draw a portrait of a young lady. I cannot discriminate' (*Tour*, p.
153). During his Highland journey he wished to have a picture, presumably an engraved portrait, of Malcom MacLeod 'just as he was', a desire
that he had essentially already satisfied by jotting down a verbal sketch
that is remarkably detailed and crisp (pp. 126–7). But even when he
contemplated those innumerable conversations that he boasted would
constitute the 'peculiar value' of the *Life* (i. 31), he inherently worried
about his ability to capture them in their entirety.[14]

Boswell touches on this issue most vividly when he tells us that he was
successful in transcribing Johnson's speech only after he had been
'*impregnated with the Johnsonian æther*' (i. 421), but there are lively reminders
of this struggle throughout his earlier biographical work. In the *Tour*, for
instance, he faced the difficulty of recording two speeches at once when
Johnson and Hector, neither of whom 'heard very quickly', debated
Leibnitz's confutation of Bayle:

> During the time that Mr. Johnson was thus going on, old Mr. Hector was
> standing with his back to the fire, cresting up erect, pulling down the front of his
> periwig, and talking what a great man Leibnitz was. To give an idea of the scene
> would require a page with two columns; but it could not be quite well
> represented but by two players. (p. 256)

But capturing Johnson's speech alone posed difficulties enough for

[14] William C. Dowling, *Language and Logos in Boswell's 'Life of Johnson'* (Princeton: Princeton Univ.
Press, 1981), ch. 4, is the only recent critic to re-examine the role of speech in the *Life*. Although his
discussion is filled with acute perceptions of the power of verbal utterance to create a 'real and present
Johnson' (pp. 28–9), he appears to forget that Boswell himself records and refashions Johnson's
conversations: 'Yet speech, precisely because it is unmediated, may always expose the illusion,
threaten or subvert or deny the unreality one constructs' (p. 88).

Boswell, who characterized it as 'the business of this work' (*Life*, ii. 242). Drawing upon organic metaphors, Boswell described these conversations as crops to be harvested (iii. 376, 400); to record them 'after some distance of time, was like preserving or pickling long-kept and faded fruits, or other vegetables, which, when in that state, have little or nothing of their taste when fresh' (iii. 183).

In attempting to describe the particular quality of Johnson's conversation, however, Boswell drew most heavily upon an analogy with music, for 'musical sounds with all their nice gradations can also be fixed'. Boswell initiates this parallel in his character-sketch of Johnson in the opening pages of the *Tour*: 'The *Messiah* played upon the Canterbury organ is more sublime than when played upon an inferior instrument, but very slight music will seem grand when conveyed to the ear through that majestic medium. *While therefore Doctor Johnson's sayings are read, let his manner be taken along with them.*' And then perhaps wondering if his analogy would be misconstrued, he adds that 'the sayings themselves are generally great; that, though he might be an ordinary composer at times, he was for the most part a Handel' (p. 8). Later, during their stay in Aberdeen, he writes that he 'was sensible today, to a very striking degree, of Mr. Johnson's excellent English conversation. I cannot account for it, how it struck me more now than any other day. But it was as if new to me; and I listened to every sentence which he spoke as to a musical composition' (pp. 59–60). This mode of thinking about Johnson's conversation, his 'deliberate and strong utterance', leads eventually to a remarkable proposition. 'His mode of speaking was indeed very impressive,' Boswell notes, 'and I wish it could be preserved as musick is written, according to the very ingenious method of Mr. Steele, who has shown how the recitation of Mr. Garrick, and other eminent speakers, might be transmitted to posterity *in score*' (ii. 326–7). Here we sense, perhaps even more dramatically than in Boswell's worries about his visual powers, his interest in preservation, in full and accurate transcription, in committing the evanescence of spoken speech to the permanent record of written systems: either his own form of stenography, or the 'peculiar Symbols' that Steele advertised in the subtitle of his treatise.[15]

---

[15] Boswell tells us that Steele's treatise was entitled '*Prosodia Rationalis*: or, an Essay towards establishing the Melody and Measure of Speech, to be expressed and perpetuated by peculiar Symbols'. Cf. the following remark in *Boswell's Column*, ed. Margery Bailey (London: Kimber, 1951), 332: 'Sometimes it has occurred to me that a man should not live more than he can record, as a farmer should not have a larger crop than he can gather in. And I have regretted that there is no invention for getting an immediate and exact transcript of the mind, like that instrument by which a copy of a letter is at once taken off.'

There are times, moreover, when this insistence on recording and reliving takes precedence over life itself. In the *Tour*, for instance, Johnson asks Boswell why they 'were so little together. I told him my Journal took up so much time. But at the same time, it is curious that although I will run from one end of London to another to have an hour with him, I should omit to seize any spare time to be in his company when I am in the house with him. But my Journal is really a task of much time and labour, and Mr. Johnson forbids me to contract it' (p. 188). Occasionally, of course, sheer intertia carries the day: 'I felt a kind of lethargy of indolence. I did not exert myself to get Mr. Johnson to talk, that I might not have the labour of writing down his conversation' (p. 122). But Boswell's normal practice here, and in the *Life*, is to treasure whatever 'gold dust' or 'diamonds' come his way or—as is so often the case—he can prompt his friend to produce. And when Boswell pauses to characterize these gleanings or to defend his predilection for the particular, more often than not he draws a parallel with the art of portrait-painting. In the *Tour* he notes that 'I am most scrupulously exact in this Journal. Mr. Johnson said it was a very exact picture of his life' (p. 245), and in the biography he concedes that he is 'fully aware how very obvious an occasion I here give for the sneering jocularity of such as have no relish of an exact likeness; which, to render complete, he who draws it must not disdain the slightest strokes' (i. 486).

Often these finer strokes of the brush will not be flattering, as Boswell admits in the introductory pages of the *Life*: 'in every picture there should be shade as well as light, and when I delineate him without reserve, I do what he himself recommended, both by his precept and his example' (i. 30). But Boswell has the authority of Reynolds to appeal to as well. In the dedication he immediately attempts to establish the fairness and scope of his work by declaring that 'luminous as he was upon the whole, you perceived all the shades which mingled in the grand composition; all the little peculiarities and slight blemishes which marked the literary Colossus' (i. 2). This biographical principle will be tested throughout the quotidian texture of the *Life*, but nowhere more dramatically than in the pages near the conclusion of the book in which Boswell faces 'the most difficult and dangerous part of my biographical work', the decision to investigate the 'propensities which were ever "warring against the law of his mind" ', and which sometimes overcame his pious resolutions (iv. 398, 396). Boswell's 'sacred love of truth' will force him to approach these criminal 'indulgences' as 'a shade in so great a character . . .' (iv. 397).

When Boswell delineated Johnson without reserve, he was indeed following his friend's precepts in *Rambler* no. 60 and his examples in *The Lives of the English Poets*. But much as Johnson sought to distinguish the lights and shades in the characters of the men he portrayed, it was customary for him to do so by formulating moral judgements rather than by lingering on the minute episodes in anyone's life. Although Boswell referred to Johnson's interest in the significant detail in his very first attempt at biographical portraiture—in the sketch of Paoli—his pursuit of the particular in his later work is manifestly at odds with the texture of even the most extended of Johnson's narratives.[16] We might say, in fact, that his relation to Johnsonian biography is similar to his adaptation of the models he found in Mrs Piozzi and William Mason: Boswell's accumulation of telling particulars, or of table talk, or of Johnson's letters is vastly more ambitious; and the very weight of these materials requires, in turn, a dexterity in shaping them into a coherent design that was simply not called for in Boswell's models. Sometimes, of course, these particulars will defy even the most sympathetic biographer's attempt to interpret them. Thus in the *Tour* Boswell confesses that 'It is in vain to try to find a meaning in every one of Mr Johnson's particularities, which I suppose are mere habits contracted by chance; of which every man has some which are more or less remarkable' (p. 297). But throughout his career Boswell was buoyed up by Johnson's affirmation that ' "There is nothing, Sir, too little for so little a creature as man. It is by studying little things that we attain the great art of having as little misery and as much happiness as possible" ' (i. 433).

It is not surprising, then, that when Boswell speculates about what distinguishes one person from another he characteristically turns to these 'little things' in order to make his point. Consider, for example, one short passage from his description of their journey through the Midlands in the autumn of 1777, when Boswell experiences an 'immediate sensation of novelty' in walking about Derby, a city he has never visited before:

. . . one speculates on the way in which life is passed in it, which, although there is a sameness every where upon the whole, is yet minutely diversified. The minute diversities in every thing are wonderful. Talking of shaving the other night at Dr. Taylor's, Dr. Johnson said, 'Sir, of a thousand shavers, two do not shave so much alike as not to be distinguished.' I thought this not possible, till he specified so many of the varieties in shaving;—holding the razor more or less perpendicu-lar;—drawing long or short strokes;—beginning at the upper part of the face, or

---

[16] For the early citation of Johnson, see *Boswell on the Grand Tour: Italy, Corsica, and France 1765–1766*, ed. Frank Brady and Frederick A. Pottle (London: Heinemann; New York: McGraw-Hill, 1955), 190.

the under;—at the right side or the left side. Indeed, when one considers what variety of sounds can be uttered by the wind-pipe, in the compass of a very small aperture, we may be convinced how many degrees of difference there may be in the application of a razor. (iii. 163)

Or of a pen or brush, we might add, for the significance of a passage such as this lies not only in Boswell's fascination with the 'minute diversities' that make life 'wonderful' for him, but also in his characteristic examination of the 'degrees of difference' that distinguish one shaver (or one town, or one person) from another. What begins as Boswell's exploration of the 'new' immediately takes the form of a meditation both on the uniform nature of contemporary life and on the ways in which it is 'minutely diversified'. Although the controlling metaphor is drawn from Johnson's conversation, the incident itself would arguably be out of place in Johnson's own work. In Boswell's hands, however, this tale 'of a thousand shavers' serves as an appropriate emblem of the biographical scrutiny and dexterity that are needed to make the characters of men and women 'decidedly marked'.

ii. Biographical Legitimacy

For Boswell, to be particular was to be authentic.[17] 'And sure I am,' he wrote at the close of his narrative for 1769, 'that, however inconsiderable many of the particulars recorded at this time may appear to some, they will be esteemed by the best part of my readers as genuine traits of his character, contributing together to give a full, fair, and distinct view of it' (ii. 111). Full, fair, distinct—these are precisely the ways in which he believed that his text would supersede the biographies his predecessors had already published. But these rivals were always on Boswell's mind: even the tribute to Johnson's biographical skills with which his narrative opens acknowledges that, had Johnson written his own life, 'the world would probably have had the most perfect example of biography that was ever exhibited' (i. 25). An absent text—Johnson's own text—stands as the ideal to which Boswell's own work must aspire. Other texts, those written by John Hawkins and Mrs Piozzi, could be supplanted more easily, although the persistence with which Boswell refutes their portraits of Johnson betrays the anxiety he feels as a relative latecomer to Johnsonian

---

[17] Schwartz, *Boswell's Johnson: A Preface to the 'Life'*, pp. 14–15, questions Boswell's use of words such as 'certainty', 'completeness', 'authenticity', and 'perfection', but fails to notice Boswell's careful insertion of modifiers whenever he makes a claim for the thoroughness and accuracy of his own research, which, by contemporary biographical or historical standards, were indeed quite remarkable.

biography. As we have seen, Mrs Piozzi knew Johnson intimately, and in a domestic environment that was often closed to Boswell's prying eye. But Boswell strenuously objects to her almost constitutional inaccuracy, and to the 'unfavourable and unjust impression' she gives of Johnson's long residence under Henry Thrale's roof (iv. 347). Hawkins, moreover, knew Johnson as a young man; he was both Johnson's contemporary and one of his executors, and thus into his hands passed 'such fragments of a diary and other papers as were left; of which, before delivering them up to the residuary legatee, whose property they were, he endeavoured to extract the substance'. But Hawkins did not know what to do with this precious trust. His memoir contains 'a dark uncharitable cast, by which the most unfavourable construction is put upon almost every circumstance in the character and conduct of my illustrious friend; who,' Boswell trusts, 'will, by a true and fair delineation [i.e. Boswell's own narrative], be vindicated' (i. 27–8). And thus Johnson's papers were eventually transferred to Boswell, who portrays himself—with considerable justice—as Johnson's spiritual heir, his biographical successor, his figurative 'residuary legatee'.

Part of the drama of the *Life of Johnson* therefore lies in Boswell's attempt to legitimize his own claims as a biographer. These claims may appear to be self-evident to us today, but we must keep in mind both the number of close friends who intended to write biographies of Johnson, and the important role that predetermined succession played in the careers of biographers as well as in the more firmly established profession of portrait-painting. This sense of legitimate succession was especially strong among English painters in the eighteenth century: Hogarth was Sir John Thornhill's son-in-law as well as his former student; another tradition of English painters and apprentices extended in an unbroken line from Riley to Richardson, Richardson to Hudson, Hudson to Reynolds, and Reynolds to Northcote, who wrote Reynolds's biography. Boswell would also have known that Roper was Sir Thomas More's son-in-law, that Edward Phillips was Milton's nephew, that Sprat was Cowley's executor, that Roger North was both Lely's executor and his brothers' keeper. Walton inherited his biographical duties upon the death of Sir Henry Wotton; Lucy Hutchinson wrote a biography of her husband, Evelyn a memoir of the unworldly woman with whom he had pledged vows of divine friendship. Throughout the eighteenth and nineteenth centuries, moreover, the executors of literary estates often believed that their duties included publishing a formal tribute to their relatives or friends, and it is in this context that Hawkins wrote his memoir of Johnson and John

Gibson Lockhart his much more ambitious life of his father-in-law, Sir Walter Scott.[18]

It should therefore not surprise us that issues of succession and legitimacy pervade the *Life of Johnson*.[19] Boswell was, in the first place, an ardent believer in primogeniture and the lawful succession of males, and it was thus with great distress that he finally acquiesced in his father's decision to entail his estate to 'heirs general, that is, males and females indiscriminately' (ii. 414). Boswell held a 'zealous partiality for heirs male', and although he necessarily agreed to be the first member of his family to be restrained by his father's will, his heated opposition—in a lengthy footnote—to the 'indiscriminate' succession of males or females literally undermines the tone of resignation in his text. Throughout this stormy episode, Johnson provides soothing counsel and frees his friend from 'scruples of conscientious obligation' (ii. 421 n.). Earlier Johnson had congratulated him on the birth of his second child: ' "Of your second daughter you certainly gave the account yourself, though you have forgotten it. While Mrs. Boswell is well, never doubt of a boy. Mrs. Thrale brought, I think, five girls running, but while I was with you she had a boy" ' (ii. 280). A year later he can write that ' "I am glad that the young Laird is born, and an end, as I hope, put to the only difference that you can ever have with Mrs. Boswell" ' (ii. 387). But the birth of Boswell's son is partially eclipsed by the death of Thrale's:

He said, 'This is a total extinction to their family, as much as if they were sold into captivity.' Upon my mentioning that Mr. Thrale had daughters, who might inherit his wealth;—'Daughters, (said Johnson, warmly,) he'll no more value his daughters than—' I was going to speak.—'Sir, (said he,) don't you know how you yourself think? Sir, he wishes to propagate his name.' In short, I saw male succession strong in his mind, even where there was no name, no family of any long standing. (ii. 468–9)

Boswell's belief in the importance of rightful inheritance leads to his radical scepticism about the claims of Richard Savage and—by extension—the credibility of Johnson's biography of his friend; but this same belief also compels him to devote a great deal of energy to the disputes

[18] Lockhart was already an accomplished biographer and novelist by the time he turned to his father-in-law's life; see Joseph W. Reed, jun., *English Biography in the Early Nineteenth Century: 1801–1838* (New Haven: Yale Univ. Press, 1966), ch. 7. An interesting survey of writers who chose biography as a profession, particularly during the 19th cent., is provided by Ira B. Nadel, *Biography: Fiction, Fact and Form* (New York: St. Martin's, 1984), ch. 2.

[19] For a similar focus on legitimacy and primogeniture in the quite different context of labour and credit in the *Life*, see William H. Epstein, *Recognizing Biography* (Philadelphia: Univ. of Pennsylvania Press, 1987), ch. 6.

surrounding the Douglas case, even to the point of fictionalizing this famous Scottish controversy in *Dorando, A Tale*. The question in each case was whether a 'supposititious' child, a young pretender, had been fraudulently presented as the rightful heir. But both cases also raised questions about female chastity, about which both Johnson and Boswell held strong views. When Boswell asked Johnson about his opinion of legitimation by a subsequent marriage, which was sanctioned by Roman and Scottish law, Johnson argued against it by contending that female chastity was ' " of the utmost importance, as all property depends upon it ..." ' (ii. 457), an economic argument that resonates throughout the *Life* and in much contemporary writing. In addition, Boswell was even more adamant than Johnson in his belief that one's *literary* offspring should also be attributed to their rightful author. Just as it was clearly understood that adopted children 'were not of the blood of their nominal parents,'

So in literary children, an authour may give the profits and fame of his composition to another man, but cannot make that other the real authour. A Highland gentleman, a younger branch of a family, once consulted me if he could not validly purchase the Chieftainship of his family, from the Chief who was willing to sell it. I told him it was impossible for him to acquire, by purchase, a right to be a different person from what he really was; for that the right of Chieftainship attached to the blood of primogeniture, and, therefore, was incapable of being transferred. (i. 254–5)

Boswell argues much the same brief when he discusses the fraudulent publication of Mackenzie's *Man of Feeling*: 'The *Filiation* of a literary performance is difficult of proof; seldom is there any witness present at its birth.' The true author, he argues, 'may not be able to make his title clear', unless, like Johnson, the 'peculiar features of his literary offspring' will 'bid defiance to any attempt to appropriate them to others: "But Shakespeare's magick could not copied be, / Within that circle none durst walk but he!" ' (i. 360–1).

Boswell's concern with forgery therefore compels him to examine with great care the most famous contemporary cases of imposture—the Cock-lane ghost, the unfortunate Dr Dodd, the publications of Ossian and Chatterton—and to become a zealous defender of Johnson's own literary reputation. In a beautifully self-contained scene in which Boswell and Johnson cross the Thames to Blackfriars, Boswell asks his friend whether any action should be taken against those who have recently published a little volume entitled *Johnsoniana*, filled with 'dull stupid nonsense' and profane speech.

BOSWELL. 'I think, Sir, you should at least disavow such a publication, because the world and posterity might with much plausible foundation say, "Here is a volume which was publickly advertised and came out in Dr. Johnson's own time, and, by his silence, was admitted by him to be genuine."'
JOHNSON. 'I shall give myself no trouble about the matter.' (ii. 433)

Johnson will eventually turn, in this conversation, to a discussion of the 'importance of strict and scrupulous veracity', but it remains Boswell's task to preserve the sanctity of the Johnsonian canon. His biography opens, we should remember, not with a chronology of Johnson's life but with 'A Chronological Catalogue of the Prose works of Samuel Johnson, LL.D.', which Boswell annotates as either acknowledged publications or 'those which may be fully believed to be his from internal evidence' (i. 16); later in the *Life* he will mark the 'avowed' works 'with an *asterisk* accordingly' (i. 309). In a similar manner Boswell preserves the addresses of each of Johnson's residences, and even attempts to 'recollect all the [literary] passages that I heard Johnson repeat: it stamps a value on them' (iii. 29). Here—and throughout the *Life*—Boswell strives to emulate his friend's 'principle and habit' of truthfulness by ensuring the absolute authenticity of his own narrative. After its publication he would write that his book was 'a *real history*, and not a *novel*', and that he was therefore forced to 'suppress all erroneous particulars, however entertaining' (ii 467 n.), but in the text itself he continually emphasizes his own biographical practice and castigates the laxity of others:

one of the gentlemen said, he had seen three folio volumes of Dr. Johnson's sayings collected by me. 'I must put you right, Sir, (said I;) for I am very exact in authenticity. You could not see folio volumes, for I have none: you might have seen some in quarto and octavo. This is inattention which one should guard against.' JOHNSON. 'Sir, it is a want of concern about veracity. He does not know that he saw *any* volumes. If he had seen them he could have remembered their size.' (iv. 83–4)

When Boswell turns to the most important (or controversial) events in Johnson's life—the creation of *Rasselas*, the letter to Chesterfield, or the receipt of the king's pension—he takes great pains to demonstrate the thoroughness of his own research and the comparative negligence of his rivals. Hawkins, for instance, 'guesses vaguely and idly' about the origins of *Rasselas* (i. 341); various 'stories, all equally erroneous, have been propagated' about the king's pension, but Boswell has taken care 'to have it in my power to refute them from the most authentick information' (i. 372–3). Similarly, both Hawkins and Mrs Piozzi 'have strangely misstated the history' of the publication of Goldsmith's *Vicar of Wakefield*: 'I shall give it authentically from Johnson's own exact narration ...' (i. 415–16). Boswell clearly thought that he was neither as uncharitable as Hawkins nor as intellectually unchaste as Mrs Piozzi, who was, in Johnson's words, ' " "contented to hear every day said to you, what the highest of mankind have died for, rather than bear.'—You know, Sir, the highest of mankind have died rather than bear to be told they had uttered a falsehood. Do talk to her of it: I am weary." ' (iii. 243).[20] There is good reason to believe that authentic biography was indelibly associated in Boswell's mind with his own patriarchal view of the family and of family history. By the same token, however, his own claim to biographical legitimacy clearly rested upon the precision and comprehensiveness with which he enabled his readers to see Johnson live, and to 'live o'er each scene' with him.

iii. The Life of an Image

In his quest for fullness and authenticity, Boswell was especially interested in discovering those 'marks' or 'traces' by which Johnson's career could be substantiated, particularly during the early years of his life. When he turns to Johnson's translation of Father Lobo, for instance, he finds it 'a curious object of inquiry how much may be traced in it of that style which marks his subsequent writings with such peculiar excellence' (i. 87), and later he rejoices that a 'very diligent observer may trace him where we should not easily suppose him to be found', in a short historical essay in the *Gentleman's Magazine* (i. 154). Boswell takes pleasure, moreover, 'in tracing so great a man through all his different habitations' (i. 111), an activity that not only fixes Johnson in the various stages of his career but also enables his biographer to heighten the illusion of presence in his text.

Absence and presence always play a double role in the *Life*, for Boswell's struggle to embody Johnson in the pages of his narrative also reflects the dynamics of their personal relationship.[21] A fit of the spleen during their journey through the Highlands, for example, forces Boswell to confront the nature of his dependency: 'had it not been that I had Mr. Johnson to contemplate, I should have been very sickly in mind. His

---

[20] Cf. my discussion of Mrs Piozzi's *Anecdotes* above, p. 201.

[21] The issue of absence and presence permeated Boswellian scholarship long before the emergence of a deconstructive poetics. For the more recent examinations, see Dowling, *Language and Logos*, ch. 3; Elizabeth W. Bruss, *Autobiographical Acts: The Changing Situation of a Literary Genre* (Baltimore: The Johns Hopkins Univ. Press, 1976), esp. 71; and Fredric V. Bogel, *Literature and Insubstantiality in Later Eighteenth-Century England* (Princeton: Princeton Univ. Press, 1984), 186 ff.

firmness kept me steady. I looked at him as a man whose head is turning at sea looks at a rock or any fixed object' (*Tour*, p. 118). Later, in the *Life*, he confesses that Johnson's 'steady vigorous mind held firm before me those objects which my own feeble and tremulous imagination frequently presented, in such a wavering state, that my reason could not judge well of them' (iii. 193). By creating his own representation of Johnson's character, Boswell was thus also paying tribute to the decisive influence Johnson had on those who continually looked to him for emotional support and moral guidance.

It may surprise us that, despite Boswell's relish for the particular, the minute, and the vivid—for the sense of *enargeia* we so often find in his narrative—the text of the *Life of Johnson* is not actually built upon visual detail. We might expect this to be the case in the early sections of the life, in which the biographer must retail his materials at second hand; but even in Johnson's later years (in what is now the fourth volume of the text) Boswell rarely relies upon a pictorial method in shaping his most successful scenes. Consider, for example, a dinner at Sir Joshua's on 30 March 1781: 'a most agreeable day, of which I regret that every circumstance is not preserved; but it is unreasonable to require such a multiplication of felicity' (iv. 78). For Boswell, of course, writing is the ultimate multiplier of felicity; his career as a writer is predicated on the belief that life must be recorded in its entirety if its significance is to be sifted and its moments of happiness to be lived over again. But the scenes that he delineates—even one as agreeable as this—normally owe their afterlife to the give and take of conversation and to the comforting superiority of Johnson's own voice; and these, presumably, are the circumstances that even Boswell could not entirely preserve. Less than a month later he was to record yet another memorable day, 'one of the happiest days that I remember to have enjoyed in the whole course of my life'. The company included, in addition to Reynolds and Burney, a number of their blue-stocking friends—Hannah More, Elizabeth Carter, and Mrs Boscowan—and was hosted by David Garrick's widow. Like Reynolds's drawing-room, Mrs Garrick's flat in the Adelphi is never described; for Boswell, it is enough to mention his fond associations with a place 'where I have passed many a pleasing hour with him "who gladdened life" '. The spirit of Garrick permeates this entire scene: his widow 'looked very well, talked of her husband with complacency, and while she cast her eyes on his portrait, which hung over the chimney-piece, said, that "death was now the most agreeable object to her." The very semblance of David Garrick was cheering.'

Memorable as this day is for Boswell, it is nevertheless composed of a disquieting series of substitutions. The 'semblance' of Garrick must stand in place of their departed friend; his widow provides her guests with a 'splendid entertainment' and regales them with Lichfield ale, but she wistfully looks beyond their merriment to a reunion with her departed husband. Even Boswell, who whispers to Mrs Boscowan that ' "this is as much as can be made of life" ' and remarks that 'The general effect of this day dwells upon my mind in fond remembrance', must also confess that 'I do not find much conversation recorded. What I have preserved shall be faithfully given' (iv. 96–7). The portrait of Garrick thus emerges as the ruling image in this bitter-sweet passage: both because we are able to gauge the responses of various characters to it (including Beauclerk's inscribed quotation from Shakespeare), and because of the transitory note it introduces into even the liveliest and most ludicrous of scenes. Boswell will eventually record his companions' hilarious response to Johnson's pronouncement that someone's wife 'had a bottom of good sense', but as this passage draws to a close, Boswell quietly notes that

He and I walked away together; we stopped a little while by the rails of the Adelphi, looking on the Thames, and I said to him with some emotion that I was now thinking of two friends we had lost, who once lived in the buildings behind us, Beauclerk and Garrick. 'Ay, Sir, (said he, tenderly) and two such friends as cannot be supplied.' (iv. 99)

Our own response to this episode, like Boswell's, is necessarily tempered by our increasing awareness of Johnson's own mortality; *his* death, as William Hamilton put it, ' "has made a chasm, which not only nothing can fill up, but which nothing has a tendency to fill up" ' (iv. 420). Paul Fussell pointed out years ago that much of Boswell's narrative is necessarily infused with this elegiac tone;[22] and the very format of the book—with the date and Johnson's age supplied at the top of each opening—reminds us that it is always, among other things, an irrevocable march towards the grave. And yet given the emotional timbre of Boswell's text, it is remarkable how careful he is not to sentimentalize his hero. The few pictorial details we are given in this particular scene—the portrait of Garrick and the parting near the railing of the Adelphi—may be emotionally charged, but they are also carefully balanced against the vitality and good humour of the intervening conversations. To adapt Boswell's own terms, he aspires to animate character while avoiding the

[22] Fussell, *The Rhetorical World of Augustan Humanism: Ethics and Imagery from Swift to Burke* (Oxford: Clarendon Press, 1965), 284.

pitfalls of a florid or manipulative style that does not rely upon empirical observation:

BOSWELL. 'Will you not admit the superiority of Robertson, in whose History we find such penetration—such painting?' JOHNSON. 'Sir, you must consider how that penetration and that painting are employed. It is not history, it is imagination. He who describes what he never saw, draws from fancy. Robertson paints minds as Sir Joshua paints faces in a history-piece: he imagines an heroick countenance. You must look upon Robertson's work as romance, and try it by that standard.' (ii. 237)

Johnson will repeat this distinction years later, this time disparaging Lord Hailes's *Annals of Scotland* for its 'dry particulars' while simultaneously taking both Robertson and Mrs Piozzi to task for their carelessness: ' "Robertson paints; but the misfortune is, you are sure he does not know the people whom he paints; so you cannot suppose a likeness" ' (iii. 404).

Boswell clearly understood the dangers of painting in prose, but penetration—the ability to discover the wellsprings of character— remained the ambitious goal of his biographical enterprise. Much as he relied upon particulars, he nevertheless attempted to shape them into episodes and scenes that revealed more than the mere surface texture of an individual life. His text is filled with passages that emphasize the disparity between external behaviour and inner conflict: 'What philosophick hero- ism was it in him to appear with such manly fortitude to the world, while he was inwardly so distressed!' (ii. 190). And thus the most dramatic moments in the *Life* occur not simply when Boswell is carefully stage- managing important encounters that will display Johnson in a new light—the famous dinner at Dilly's or the accidental reunion with his old friend Edwards—but also when Boswell can pierce into the heart of an event that has been shrouded in mystery or surrounded by controversy. He introduces his account of the well-known letter to Chesterfield, for example, by commenting that 'There is, perhaps, in every thing of any consequence, a secret history which it would be amusing to know, could we have it authentically communicated' (i. 183). In this case—and in many others—Johnson's own co-operation ensures that this 'secret history' will be divulged, and Boswell therefore rightfully treasures those infrequent moments when he is afforded a privileged glimpse into Johnson's private world. Consider, for instance, Boswell's barely suppressed excitement when Levet shows him the two garrets that constitute Johnson's library:

I found a number of good books, but very dusty and in great confusion. The floor was strewed with manuscript leaves, in Johnson's own hand-writing, which

I beheld with a degree of veneration, supposing they perhaps might contain portions of the Rambler, or of Rasselas. I observed an apparatus for chymical experiments, of which Johnson was all his life very fond. The place seemed to be very favourable for retirement and meditation. (i. 435–6)

Like so many other passages, this one will end with a moral observation (about Johnson's refusal to allow his servants to announce that he is out when he is actually at home), but of at least equal importance here is Boswell's sense of having penetrated to those private recesses—the study, the heap of books, the scattered manuscripts, the natural experiments—in which Johnson's mind was most vigorously engaged.

As Boswell's co-conspirators, we treasure similar moments of penetration and disclosure: Boswell analysing Johnson's 'Comprehension of mind' as 'the mould of his language' (i. 222), receiving an unprecedented invitation to join Johnson and his domestic companions for an Easter dinner (ii. 215), puzzling over the significance of the notorious orange-peels that Johnson stores in his pockets (ii. 330), or accompanying him to Wirgman's toyshop in search of a new set of silver buckles for his shoes (iii. 324–5). This last episode is particularly interesting, for it follows upon Boswell's description of how Johnson loved to keep his affairs 'floating in conjecture: *Omne ignotum pro magnifico est*. I believe I ventured to dissipate the cloud, to unveil the mystery, more freely and frequently than any of his friends.' This emphasis on secret history and the penetration of character should remind us, moreover, of the famous distinction Johnson drew between Richardson and Fielding—and of Boswell's thoughtful rejoinder to it. Fielding's characters of manners, Johnson argued, ' " are very entertaining; but they are to be understood, by a more superficial observer, than characters of nature, where a man must dive into the recesses of the human heart" ' (ii. 49). There was as much difference between Richardson and Fielding, he continued, ' "as between a man who knew how a watch was made, and a man who could tell the hour by looking on the dial-plate" '. Boswell, however, believed that the terms of this comparison short-changed Fielding's broader but equally successful technique. The 'neat' watches of Fielding, he maintained, 'are as well constructed as the large clocks of Richardson, and . . . his dial-plates are brighter. Fielding's characters, though they do not expand themselves so widely in dissertation, are just pictures of human nature, and I will venture to say, have more striking features, and nicer touches of the pencil . . .' (ii. 49).

The great threat of Johnsonian mythography, even in Boswell's time, was that his friend would emerge only as a character of manners. If Boswell were to reveal Johnson as the great character of nature whom his friends knew so well, then he would have to adopt the intricate Richardsonian model in which characters were allowed to 'expand themselves' in dissertation and readers were allowed to 'dive into the recesses of the human heart'. But psychological complexity in Boswell's work is not necessarily at odds with the 'striking features' and vivid strokes of the brush that he associates with Fielding. Like the portrait of Garrick, the extended metaphor of the watch functions as a distinctive controlling image that allows precisely these subtle discriminations to be made. If Boswell constructed a much larger and more complicated biographical 'clock' than his rivals, his dial-plate was brighter as well.

The construction of a ruling image was particularly important to Boswell when he attempted to 'go deeper', in Reynolds's words, 'and investigate the peculiar colouring of his mind, as distinguished from all other minds . . .'. But none of the figures he chose to elaborate—the watch (appropriated from Johnson),[23] a mill, a set of scales—is *visually* minute, not even Boswell's most memorable image, which is embedded in a moving discussion of Johnson's fear of death:

His mind resembled the vast amphitheatre, the Colisæum at Rome. In the centre stood his judgement, which, like a mighty gladiator, combated those apprehensions [of death] that, like the wild beasts of the *Arena* were all around in cells, ready to be let out upon him. After a conflict, he drove them back into their dens; but not killing them, they were still assailing him. (ii. 106)

Surely this episode, in which Boswell maintains (against Johnson himself) that the fear of death filled his friend with 'dismal apprehensions', is one of the most successful in Boswell's entire narrative. But Boswell's metaphor is detailed only in the sense that it invokes a specific image—the Roman Coliseum—that is subsequently broken down into its smaller (but more frightening) components: those compartmentalized cells that house the wild beasts of Johnson's imagination. The primary emphasis in this passage falls on more general notions of danger, combat, and heroism that the mere mention of the Coliseum evokes ('We who are about to die salute you'). Boswell explicitly chooses a 'vast' image to convey his own sense of Johnson's grandeur; to borrow Carlyle's phrase, he depicts Johnson as

---

[23] Allan Ingram has analysed Boswell's comparison of Johnson's mind with a watch (and with several other images) in *Boswell's Creative Gloom: A Study of Imagery and Melancholy in the Writings of James Boswell* (Totowa, New Jersey: Barnes and Noble; London: Macmillan, 1981), 33, 48, and *passim*. See also David L. Passler, *Time, Form, and Style in Boswell's 'Life of Johnson'* (New Haven: Yale Univ. Press, 1971), who also examines the notion of spatial form in Boswell's narrative.

'Brave old Samuel: *ultimus Romanorum!*'[24] We have already seen that Boswell intended to raise a biographical 'Monument' in Johnson's honour; here we view him portraying Johnson himself as a monument of equal stature.

Even a specific and complex spatial image, in other words, can be counted upon to raise traditional, abstract associations in the reader's mind; and the tension Boswell suggests in his visual metaphor—between the judgement and its apprehensions—is also the product of a temporal scheme in which this scene of psychological combat is one of perpetual strife. Boswell's careful choice of tenses emphasizes his conviction that Johnson, successful as he may be in any single encounter with these fears, must content himself with victories that are temporary at best: Johnson 'ever looked upon' this subject with horror; his judgement 'combated' those apprehensions that 'were all around' in cells; he 'drove' them back, 'but not killing them, they were still assailing him'. Boswell's metaphor thus insists that Johnson's fears are constantly present, in spite of the finality of Johnson's pronouncements in his writings (written when he was 'in a celestial frame') and in conversation with his intimate friends: ' "The act of dying is not of importance, it lasts so short a time." He added, (with an earnest look,) "A man knows it must be so, and submits. It will do him no good to whine" ' (ii. 107). Even the conclusion of this passage bears out Boswell's characterization of his friend. When Boswell attempts to continue their conversation, Johnson, knowing that further talk will only revitalize his own fears, abruptly terminates their meeting: ' "Give us no more of this; . . . Don't let us meet to-morrow." '

Boswell's strategy in this powerful passage corroborates what Paul Alkon and others have skilfully drawn attention to in the *Life of Johnson* as a whole: Boswell manipulates both spatial and temporal design to produce a portrait of Johnson that is both static and complex.[25] If Boswell views his subject with a painter's eye, he nevertheless suppresses any exact description that might distract the reader–viewer from the importance of his central image. Just as Reynolds's most pronounced effects in his portraits of Johnson are produced by spatial design—the construction of strong masses and lines, the play of light and shadow, the implied tension between a relaxed and an exercised hand or a focused and a vacant eye—so Boswell's most distinctive experiments lie in his handling of time,

[24] *On Heroes, Hero-Worship and the Heroic in History*, ed. Carl Niemeyer (Lincoln: Univ. of Nebraska Press, 1966), 184.
[25] Alkon, 'Boswellian Time', *Studies in Burke and His Time*, 14 (1973), 239–56; see also Passler, *Time, Form, and Style in Boswell's 'Life of Johnson'*, 14–15, 32–3, and *passim*.

especially in his attempt to re-create the experience of accompanying
Johnson throughout his life. Biography is iconic here—in the semiotic
sense—not so much in the visual metaphors it creates as in its emphasis on
conversation, in its dramatization of action, and in its ability to provide a
sense either of the passing of time or of an emotion fearfully and
perpetually present. It is largely through these devices that Boswell
approaches what Hagstrum has described as rhetorical *enargeia*: 'the ability
of the writer to achieve palpability, to make readers believe that objects,
persons, and scenes actually appeared before their eyes'.[26]

Thus in this famous scene Boswell makes Johnson come alive for us by
letting us know how greatly Johnson's abrupt behaviour has upset him.
He tells us that Johnson 'was thrown into such a state of agitation, that he
expressed himself in a way that alarmed and distressed me . . .'. Johnson's
apprehensions of death are thus balanced by Boswell's own fears that he
has offended his friend—that he might even lose his intimate footing with
him—and his description of his own predicament extends the metaphor
with which he has already portrayed Johnson's: 'I seemed to myself,' he
writes, 'like the man who had put his head into the lion's mouth a great
many times with perfect safety, but at last had it bit off.' In this new
scenario, Johnson becomes the lion and Boswell—the perpetual
lionizer—becomes the gladiator. And it is precisely this quality of
dramatic re-enactment and even emotional transference that charges
Boswell's narrative with the immediacy and palpability that he considered
to be the pre-eminent qualities of biography's sister art.

The figure of the Coliseum is all the more compelling, moreover,
because it reflects so many other suggestive images in the *Life* and in
Boswell's earlier writings. Much later in his narrative he will describe his
attempt to harvest Bennet Langton's 'rich fruits of *Johnsonian* wit and
wisdom' in terms that suggest an archaeological excavation: 'a good store
of *Johnsoniana* was treasured in his mind; and I compared it to Hercula-
neum, or some old Roman field, which, when dug, fully rewards the
labour employed. The authenticity of every article is unquestionable'
(iv. 1–2). It is not surprising that, having sifted through the various layers
of biographical sedimentation, Boswell should describe what he has
unearthed in appropriately classical terms. Having already described both
his father and Johnson as 'intellectual gladiators' in the *Tour* (p. 375), it
was natural for him to expand that image in the *Life* by focusing on the
arena itself, which Gibbon had extolled as both a symbol of enduring

---

[26] Review of Hugh Witemeyer, *George Eliot and the Visual Arts*, in *Nineteenth-Century Fiction*, 34
(1979), 218; see also Hagstrum, pp. 11–12.

monumentality and as a scene of perpetual conflict and internal dissolu-
tion.[27] Even Boswell's emphasis on the isolated cells of the Coliseum
echoes those intriguing entries in his journals in which he compares the
mind of man to a series of rooms, or to a central room containing a
number of different—and ever changing—pictures.[28] And in the *Life* itself
he confessed that he was bewildered by the disparity between Milton's
power and sensibility as a poet and his religious, political, and domestic
severity: 'It is proof that in the human mind the departments of judgement
and imagination, perception and temper, may sometimes be divided by
strong partitions; and that the light and shade in the same character may
be kept so distinct as never to be blended' (iv. 42).

Boswell's invocation of the Coliseum must be interpreted, in short, as
his own way of making sense not just of Johnson's inner struggles—the
recesses of one human heart—but of the human mind itself. As an image
embedded in one scene within an extraordinarily long narrative, it can
make no claim to be the only, or perhaps even the most important
unifying image in the *Life*. Ralph Rader regards it, in fact, as a potentially
dangerous metaphor whose pretensions must be justified in the ensuing
exchange between Johnson and his tormentor.[29] But the episode as a
whole not only validates the grandeur of Boswell's image, I would argue,
but also reinforces one of the most fervently argued conclusions of the
entire biography: 'This little incidental quarrel and reconciliation, which,
perhaps, I may be thought to have detailed too minutely, must be
esteemed as one of the many proofs which his friends had, that though he
might be charged with *bad humour* at times, he was always a *good-natured*
man ...' (ii. 109). Like the figure of the Flemish picture, moreover, the
image of the Coliseum serves as a metaphor for the shape Boswell's
biographical text would itself take: a static structure that strives to restrain
its own contending forces, a symbol of the fragility of human achievement
and a reminder of our own mortality.

iv. First Encounters and Last Farewells

Boswell arranged for the *Life* to be published on the anniversary of his

[27] *The History of the Decline and Fall of the Roman Empire*, ed. J. B. Bury (London: Methuen, 1914;
rpt. New York: AMS, 1974), vii. 329–33.

[28] *Boswell's London Journal: 1762–1763*, ed. Frederick A. Pottle (London: Heinemann; New York:
McGraw-Hill, 1950), 203; *Boswell in Search of a Wife*, pp. 137–8.

[29] Ralph W. Rader, 'Literary Form in Factual Narrative: The Example of Boswell's *Johnson*', in
Essays in Eighteenth-Century Biography, ed. Philip B. Daghlian (Bloomington: Indiana Univ. Press,
1968), 3–42, rpt. in *Boswell's 'Life of Johnson': New Questions, New Answers*, ed. John A. Vance (Athens:
Univ. of Georgia Press, 1985), 25–52 (see 43–4).

first meeting with Johnson in the back-parlour of Tom Davies's book-shop on 16 May 1763. Boswell's depiction of this famous scene has been admired by generations of readers; even those who chafe at the chronological disproportions of the book must sense the dramatic transformation of the narrative once Boswell steps into Johnson's life and hence into the pages of his own text. The discovery of the London journal, moreover, has enabled us to appreciate the conscious artistry with which Boswell revised the relatively short and non-committal entry in his original account of this fateful encounter. Both the original entry and the episode in the *Life* recount Boswell's surprise at suddenly confronting the man he had so often attempted to meet, but the task of re-creating this scene almost thirty years later enabled Boswell to compensate for his initial helplessness by exerting control over the manner in which his narrative would unfold. As many of Boswell's commentators have pointed out, this crucial scene—like the dinner at Dilly's—relies for its success upon the artful management of adumbration, suspense, dramatic complication, and eventual revelation and closure. In his second telling of the tale, Boswell places us, his readers, in the role he originally played himself; no longer the *ingénu*, he can now poke fun at his earlier behaviour and manipulate our own responses at the same time.

What I find particularly intriguing in this scene is not simply the artful strategy by which Boswell nurtures our interest and thwarts our curiosity, but the unusual nature of these succeeding stages in his text. Each step towards the eventual disclosure of Johnson contains a representation of this still distant figure, and the measure of our distance can be gauged by the comparative deficiencies in each of these representational forms. Boswell opens this episode in the *Life* by noting how his initial understanding of Johnson was entirely based on Johnson's work as a writer:

Though then but two-and-twenty, I had for several years read his works with delight and instruction, and had the highest reverence for their authour, which had grown up in my fancy into a kind of mysterious veneration, by figuring to myself a state of solemn elevated abstraction, in which I supposed him to live in the immense metropolis of London. (i. 383–4)

Boswell's task in the *Life* is therefore one of demystification; he must replace his own notion of an elevated abstraction with a concrete figure—a character of nature—and he must therefore learn to know Johnson as intimately as the 'immense metropolis' with which he so closely associates him.

But how will he accomplish this initial act of penetration? The Irish actor Francis Gentleman is the first to raise Boswell's hopes, for Gentleman had provided Boswell with 'a representation of the figure and manner of DICTIONARY JOHNSON! as he was then generally called; and during my first visit to London, which was for three months in 1760, Mr. Derrick the poet, who was Gentleman's friend and countryman, flattered me with hopes that he would introduce me to Johnson, an honour of which I was very ambitious' (i. 385). But this dramatic imitation of Johnson is all that Gentleman can produce, and Boswell therefore turned to another actor, Thomas Sheridan, who taught 'the English Language and Publick Speaking' to audiences in Edinburgh in the summer of 1761. Sheridan was an even more promising intermediary, for he knew Johnson quite well and was teaching the young Boswell how to speak like an Englishman. Boswell heard Sheridan 'frequently expatiate upon Johnson's extraordinary knowledge, talents, and virtues, repeat his pointed sayings, describe his particularities, and boast of his being his guest sometimes till two or three in the morning' (i. 385). A year later, however, the friendship between Johnson and Sheridan had completely ruptured; Sheridan's admiration had turned to vicious resentment, and in his biography of Swift he later characterized his former friend as ' "A writer of gigantick fame in these days of little men" ' (i. 388–9).

Boswell was therefore forced to rely on a third actor, Tom Davies, for his introduction to Johnson, who often came to take tea with Davies in the back of his bookshop. Like Gentleman and Sheridan, Davies also regaled Boswell with his dramatic representations of Johnson: he 'recollected several of Johnson's remarkable sayings, and was one of the best of the many imitators of his voice and manner, while relating them. He increased my impatience more and more to see the extraordinary man whose works I highly valued, and whose conversation was reported to be so peculiarly excellent' (i. 391). And thus into Tom Davies's back-parlour Johnson finally, but unexpectedly, walked, his 'aweful approach' announced by Davies 'somewhat in the manner of an actor in the part of Horatio, when he addresses Hamlet on the appearance of his father's ghost, "Look, my Lord, it comes." ' But this is no apparition, no theatrical illusion; the figure of Johnson finally steps into Boswell's life, and into ours. The frustration of knowing Johnson only at second-hand ends as soon as Davies symbolically glimpses his figure through the glass doors of his back-parlour; the series of representational substitutions, of mediations through luckless intermediaries, is now superseded by the entrance of a living and breathing character who can be described at first-hand and speak in his own voice, his presence fully felt for the first time.

   Such, at least, is the compelling illusion of Boswell's own representational artistry. The carefully contrived sequence of deficient representations—literary texts, anecdotes, reported conversation, dramatic gestures—marks the boundary between an account that has relied upon research and good faith and the voluminous, authentic narrative that now lies before us. But why, at such an important turning-point in his text, would Boswell decide to introduce yet another mediating representation—Reynolds's portrait of 'Dictionary Johnson'—rather than control the narrative through his own words, as he originally did in his journal? There, we should remember, Boswell described Johnson as 'a man of a most dreadful appearance':

He is a very big man, is troubled with sore eyes, the palsy, and the king's evil. He is very slovenly in his dress and speaks with a most uncouth voice. Yet his great knowledge and strength of expression command vast respect and render him very excellent company. He has great humour and is a worthy man. But his dogmatical roughness of manners is disagreeable.[30]

In the *Life*, as we have seen, Boswell says only that he 'had a very perfect idea of Johnson's figure, from the portrait of him painted by Sir Joshua Reynolds soon after he had published his Dictionary, in the attitude of sitting in his easy chair in deep meditation, which was the first picture his friend did for him, which Sir Joshua very kindly presented to me, and from which an engraving has been made for this work' (i. 392).

   There are several plausible explanations for this curious substitution. It has been argued, for instance, that the engraved portrait is a much more flattering likeness of Johnson, that the omission of the prose sketch ensures that Boswell's readers will not harbour any initial prejudices against him, and that by suppressing his own reaction to Johnson's appearance, Boswell was simultaneously able to control our own response. It has also been pointed out that the omission of the short physical description of Johnson is not really an act of suppression, for each of Boswell's descriptive details in the journal finds its way into the pages of the *Life*.[31] But where, precisely, do these particular comments emerge in

   [30] *Boswell's London Journal*, p. 260.

   [31] See Irma S. Lustig, 'Fact into Art: James Boswell's Notes, Journals, and the *Life of Johnson*', in *Biography in the 18th Century*, ed. J. D. Browning (New York: Garland, 1980), 128–46 (esp. 145–6), and William R. Siebenschuh, *Fictional Techniques and Factual Works* (Athens: Univ. of Georgia Press, 1983), 70–1. Also of interest are Frank Brady, 'Fictional Techniques in Factual Works', *The Eighteenth Century: Theory and Interpretation*, 26 (1985), 158–70 (a review of Siebenschuh's book), and Felicity A. Nussbaum, 'Boswell's Treatment of Johnson's Temper: "A Warm West-Indian Climate"', *Studies in English Literature*, 14 (1974), 421–33.

the text? We should not be surprised, I think, to find that Boswell introduces the kernel of his original description of Johnson earlier in the narrative, and that he presents it in the context of someone else's response to Johnson—as yet another mediating representation. Like Boswell, Bennet Langton had read the *Rambler* with great admiration, and as a young man 'he came to London chiefly with the view of endeavouring to be introduced to its authour' (i. 247). Levet served as his intermediary, but failed to prepare him for his first encounter with Johnson:

Mr. Langton was exceedingly surprized when the sage first appeared. He had not received the smallest intimation of his figure, dress, or manner. From perusing his writings, he fancied he should see a decent, well-drest, in short, a remarkably decorous philosopher. Instead of which, down from his bed-chamber, about noon, came, as newly risen, a huge uncouth figure, with a little dark wig which scarcely covered his head, and his clothes hanging loose about him. But his conversation was so rich, so animated, and so forcible, and his religious and political notions so congenial with those in which Mr. Langton had been educated, that he conceived for him that veneration and attachment which he ever preserved. (i. 247–8)

In the *Life*, in other words, Boswell has not only substituted Reynolds's portrait for his original verbal depiction, but has also forced the young Bennet Langton to bear his own initial responses to Johnson's terrifying—but ultimately edifying—appearance.[32] Having introduced this physical description earlier in his narrative (and, characteristically, through an intermediary), he can turn to the painted portrait as a mode of representational shorthand. Because Reynolds's painting is more direct, more efficient, more immediate than a full-length portrait in prose, it works to keep the drama alive at this crucial point in the text. As a ruling image, moreover, it encapsulates the many particulars we have already encountered, thereby reinforcing what Boswell had called the 'great art of biography, which is to keep the person whose life we are giving always in the reader's view'.[33]

I have already argued that Boswell chose to introduce Reynolds's portrait at this point in his narrative because the painting had served as

[32] Boswell's own description of Johnson's appearance—which is very much like Langton's—appears a few pages later in the *Life*, when he first pays a visit to Johnson's house (i. 396). Dowling, *Language and Logos*, pp. 27–8, cites Langton's meeting with Johnson as a further corroboration of Boswell's own view of Johnson, in which an abstract and idealized earlier conception is supplanted by Johnson's actual physical presence, which in turn is superseded by Johnson's powerful conversation; for Dowling, Johnson's uncouth physical appearance represents an illusion that is shattered by the intellectual power of his speech and thought.

[33] Quoted by Lustig, 'Fact into Art', p. 141, from *The Private Papers of James Boswell*, ed. Geoffrey Scott and Frederick A. Pottle (Mt Vernon, New York: privately printed, 1928–34), xv. 268.

Boswell's own introduction to Johnson's appearance. This, at least, is what Boswell claims. What he does not tell us is that he did not meet Reynolds until after he had met Johnson, and that if he had seen this particular portrait, which Reynolds never exhibited, it would have been during a public visit to the painter's gallery in Leicester-Fields.[34] Although the exact chronology of these events may well remain a mystery, it is clear that Boswell regarded his possession and manipulation of this image as a personal and biographical coup. As we have seen in the previous chapter, it is quite likely that Boswell was influential in suggesting or at least supervising the revisions to both the painting and the engraved frontispiece; his collaboration with Reynolds produced an image of a mature writer—his lexicographical tasks now literally behind him—that perfectly suited both Boswell's own conception of Johnson and the demands of his biographical narrative. The painting served, moreover, as yet another authentic image in his text. Reynolds, who would not part with the portrait during Johnson's lifetime, 'very kindly presented' it to his own (and to Johnson's) successor as a portraitist, thereby reinforcing, in Boswell's eyes at least, his own claims to biographical legitimacy.

We should ask one final question, however, of this famous portrait and of Boswell's use of it. To what extent does this particular image—or any of the central images we have examined—differ from the engraved portraits or carved monuments that Walton introduced into his text more than a century and a half earlier? We should remember that at different times both Johnson and Boswell intended to edit Walton's *Lives*, Johnson arguing that the *Life of Donne* 'was the most perfect of them', and concluding that Walton ' "was a great panegyrist" ' (ii. 363–4). Boswell praised Walton's 'sincere admiration' for his subjects, and in conversation with Johnson two days earlier maintained that admiration was 'one of the most agreeable of all our feelings', a conclusion that Johnson dismissed by stating that ' "as a man advances in life, he gets what is better than admiration—judgment, to estimate things at their true value" ' (ii. 360). But Boswell resolutely believed that admiration was more 'pleasing' than judgement, just as love is more pleasing than friendship, and in one of the most notorious passages in the *Life* he confessed that he worshipped Johnson: 'ROBERTSON. "But some of you spoil him; you should not worship him; you should worship no man." BOSWELL. "I cannot help worshipping him, he is so much superiour to other men" ' (iii. 331). In spite of his careful research and reliance upon particulars, is Boswell

---

[34] See the discussion of these issues in the previous chapter and footnotes, pp. 256–8.

therefore essentially a latter-day Walton, relying upon iconic images to convince his audience that the more they consider Johnson's character (as he put it in the final sentence of his book), 'the more he will be regarded by the present age, and by posterity, with admiration and reverence'?

Boswell clearly did not think so. Like Reynolds, he promised that he would portray Johnson 'as he really was', for 'To be as he was, is indeed subject of panegyrick enough to any man in this state of being . . .' (i. 30). By March of 1778, moreover, we find him confiding to his journal that he was now quite 'easy' with Johnson, quite his companion. He now misses 'that aweful reverence with which I used to contemplate Mr. SAMUEL JOHNSON, in the complex magnitude of his literary, moral, and religious character' (iii. 225). But this easiness—with its accompanying banishment of '*mystery*'—produces just that sense of judgement which Johnson would extol: 'I should be glad that I am more advanced in my progress of being, so that I can view Dr. Johnson with a steadier and clearer eye.' To glimpse Johnson through the haze of reverence, Boswell continues, is to see through a glass darkly; now, as in a future state, he can observe him face to face. Even the typography in this interesting passage underscores the distinction that Boswell wishes to draw: a Johnson contemplated through the 'cloudy darkness' of the young Boswell's mind will be elevated—and thus set apart—in small capitals, whereas the Johnson he has grown to know will remain immersed in the lower-case characters of Boswell's text.[35]

At the same time, it is clear that Boswell, like any successful writer, marshalled his images and scenes to convince his readers of the essential accuracy and validity of his own conclusions. But unlike most of his seventeenth-century predecessors (and many of his contemporaries) he refused to excite his readers' sense of admiration and reverence at the expense of his own complicated conception of Johnson's character. Walton, we should remember, attempted to collapse the text of the *Life of Donne* into two symbolic images, and in doing so he managed to evade many of the inherent conflicts in his own portrait of Donne, especially the process by which a secular poet became the learned divine who would wrap himself in his own funereal shroud. In the *Life of Johnson*, Boswell does not invoke images in order to collapse his verbal argument; ruling images may serve to sharpen the focus in a particular scene, but they never overrule the words themselves, nor stall the progress of the narrative. Unlike iconic images, therefore, Boswell's figures tend to expand rather

[35] The typographical setting of Johnson's name is inconsistent throughout the *Life*, but the contrast of styles appears to be quite clear in this particular passage.

than limit his verbal structures, and they do so throughout the entire text, not only at important turning-points, as in Walton's biography (or even Goldsmith's). Thus no one individual image can finally fix Johnson's character and thereby encapsulate the entire text, and this is why the analogy Boswell draws with the Flemish portrait works so well. Like the image of the Roman Coliseum, it figures a static external structure that contains within it a number of dynamic and often contending forces. We read Johnson through the innumerable particulars of the text, but not at the expense of intervening metaphors or of the overall coherence of the narrative itself.

The ambitious scope and local texture of the *Life of Johnson* necessarily thwart the reductiveness that we associate with iconicism; if anything, Boswell's readers have wished for greater structural coherence as well as for an even more sophisticated conception of how Johnson became the man whom Boswell met in 1763.[36] And it is difficult to fault Boswell's critics. Faced with the prospect of reading through yet another legal controversy, we may wish to respond much as Johnson did: ' "Why, Sir, (said he,) I do not take much delight in it; but I'll go through it" ' (ii. 157). The issue at stake here has already been articulated by Reynolds, who argued in the eleventh discourse that there are 'great characteristick distinctions, which press strongly on the senses, and therefore fix the imagination. These are by no means, as some persons think, an aggregate of all the small discriminating particulars; nor will such an accumulation of particulars ever express them' (p. 192). We might argue that for Johnson—and even more so for Evelyn and Walton—these 'great characteristick distinctions' represent the controlling structure of the biographical text; when particulars are introduced, they are almost always subsumed under these general heads. Perhaps only of Aubrey can it be said that his lives constitute an 'aggregate of all the small discriminating particulars'; but Aubrey, as we have seen, was able to pursue this method only because he intended to present his own 'accumulations' to others— and they had designs of their own.

Judged by Reynolds's criteria—and against the examples of his predecessors—Boswell's solution will inevitably be seen as a compromise, but one that has had an immense influence on his successors. Never simply an aggregate or mere accumulation of particulars, his text none the less comprises an unusual diversity of material, some of which is not fully integrated into the narrative itself. A more complete integration of the

---

[36] See e.g. Leopold Damrosch, jun., '*The Life of Johnson*: An Anti-Theory', *Eighteenth-Century Studies*, 6 (1972–3), 486–505.

general and the particular, on the other hand, might well have jeopardized his endeavour to represent life as it is actually experienced: sometimes with a clear sense of its patterns, but often with a healthy tolerance for our own curtailed vision. Boswell was clearly aware of the dilemma his own ambitions had created. During the winter of 1791 he asked Malone how he should conclude his narrative: 'Pray how shall I wind up. Shall I give the Character in my *Tour*, somewhat enlarged?'[37] Boswell's decision to close with an expanded version of his earlier sketch should not be interpreted, however, as a gesture in the direction of Waltonian biography, in which an iconic text yields so easily to an encapsulating conclusion. Deliberately placed at the opening of the *Tour*, the original character-sketch of Johnson did, in fact, function in an iconic manner, determining much of our conception of a static Johnson even before the narrative proper had begun.[38] By placing his 'character' at the end of the *Life*, on the other hand, Boswell was able to present his findings as hard-fought conclusions rather than as predetermining propositions.

The nature of this 'somewhat enlarged' sketch is also telling, for Boswell's additions reflect a much more mature conception of Johnson's character. Entirely consistent with the accumulating scenes in the narrative, for instance, is Boswell's conviction that Johnson's 'superiority over other learned men consisted chiefly in what may be called the art of thinking, the art of using his mind; a certain continual power of seizing the useful substance of all that he knew, and exhibiting it in a clear and forcible manner; so that knowledge, which we often see to be no better than lumber in men of dull understanding, was, in him, true, evident, and actual wisdom' (iv. 427–8). Like Reynolds, he also observed that 'Man is, in general, made up of contradictory qualities' that will show themselves in 'strange succession'; at different times, he continues, 'he seemed a different man, in some respects; not, however, in any great or essential article, upon which he had fully employed his mind, and settled certain principles of duty, but only in his manners, and in the display of argument and fancy in his talk' (iv. 426).

But for all of Boswell's increased suppleness of characterization in these pages, the sketch itself will continue to evoke ambivalent responses. We can argue, on the one hand, that the breadth and particularity of the text throw the comparative compression and generalization of the concluding

---

[37] *The Correspondence and Other Papers of James Boswell Relating to the Making of the 'Life of Johnson'*, ed. Marshall Waingrow (New York: McGraw-Hill, n.d. [1969]), 384.

[38] See William Siebenschuh, *Form and Purpose in Boswell's Biographical Works* (Berkeley and Los Angeles: Univ. of California Press, 1972), 31–3.

sketch into high relief. After working our way for so long through such varied scenes, we may well sense that the character-sketch of Johnson is outdated and ultimately unnecessary. But we might also argue that the very existence of this eloquent conclusion—outmoded as it may be— forces us to acknowledge the consistency of Boswell's characterization of Johnson throughout the preceding pages. Because Boswell's generalizations emerge so smoothly from the many accumulated particulars that precede them, we are forcibly reminded of the essential coherence of Boswell's narrative. But not even this response is likely to convince us that Boswell's conclusion to the *Life* is entirely successful. What Boswell's own difficulty in deciding how to close his narrative does suggest, however, is how complex biographical form and the representation of character had become in his hands.

Epilogue
Gainsborough's Butterfly

IN 1834, just three years after Croker published his inflated 'edition' of the *Life of Johnson*, Allan Cunningham offered the following comparison of Johnson's and Boswell's divergent biographical methods:

The chief fault of [Boswell's] performance is, that it wants the splendid summary, and final judgment of character, which forms the crowning glory to the 'Lives of the Poets.' We are left to draw our own conclusions from the anecdotes and indications of Boswell, and the consequence is, that every one forms a mental character according to his abilities or prejudices, and nothing is fixed or defined.[1]

Nothing fixed or defined: Cunningham's verdict is manifestly at odds with Boswell's own belief that he was presenting 'A full, fair, and distinct view' of Johnson's character. Even Boswell's final deference to the dead hand of biographical tradition—his decision to resuscitate the venerable character-sketch his audience expected—was surely based, as we have seen, on his conviction that the anecdotal accumulations of his narrative could be reconciled with 'the splendid summary, and final judgment of character' that Cunningham associated with Johnson.

But a later generation thought otherwise. Preferring, instead, the grand Johnsonian synthesis, Cunningham posed his reservations about the *Life* in terms that are remarkably similar to Reynolds's pronouncements on indeterminate form in the *Discourses*, where Gainsborough's 'indistinctness' enables the imagination 'to assume almost what character or form it pleases'.[2] But the irony of Reynolds's remarks—and of Cunningham's as well—is that even the most innovative and naturalistic portraitists of the late eighteenth century could not entirely resist the influence of biographical or pictorial convention. In the seventeenth century, we should remember, a 'character' normally typified a group, whereas a biography or portrait painting served to separate a man or woman *from* the group; and

---

[1] *Biographical and Critical History of the British Literature of the Last Fifty Years* (1834), 244–5, quoted by Joseph W. Reed, jun., *English Biography in the Early Nineteenth Century: 1801–1838* (New Haven: Yale Univ. Press, 1966), 27. The Boswellian aftermath has also been carefully traced by Francis R. Hart, 'Boswell and the Romantics: A Chapter in the History of Biographical Theory', *ELH* 27 (1960), 44–65, and by A. O. J. Cockshut, *Truth to Life: The Art of Biography in the Nineteenth Century* (New York and London: Harcourt, 1974).

[2] Reynolds, *Discourses*, p. 259; see my discussion above, p. 264.

the character sketch, as it worked its way into biographical narratives, retained its original tendency to generalize and encapsulate at the same time, even within the confines of Boswell's lengthy text.[3] Even William Mason, who had carefully edited Gray's letters so that the poet could speak for himself, found himself locked in the same dilemma. Near the end of his memoir he could quite correctly claim that 'The method in which I have arranged the foregoing pages, has, I trust, one degree of merit, that it makes the reader so well acquainted with the man himself, as to render it totally unnecessary to conclude the whole with his character.' One page later, however, he would add that, although he could now 'lay down my pen, yet if any reader should still want his character, I will give him one', and the epitome he inserts is not even his own, but an anonymous piece culled from one of the monthly magazines.[4]

This accommodation of convention can also be seen in Gainsborough, the painter whose work has most persistently been placed in opposition to the iconic canvases of Van Dyck, Hogarth and Reynolds. Let me introduce, as an extreme but telling example, the picture entitled *The Painter's Daughters Chasing a Butterfly* (Plate 76), which Gainsborough completed early in his career, before moving from Ipswich to Bath.[5] Rarely has any painting received such uniformity of description and praise. Waterhouse singles it out as 'one of the most enchanting, most original, most native, and most natural things in English painting'; John Hayes extols it as an 'entrancing little canvas' in which Gainsborough excels Ramsay and Hogarth 'not only in vividness of detail but in inspired informality'.[6] And Edgar Wind, who more than any other modern critic has attempted to oppose the learned Reynolds to the simple and unfettered Gainsborough, argues that 'For all their elegant manner, Gainsborough's portraits of children always leave the child undisturbed in its natural surroundings.' Citing this painting in particular (and comparing it with Reynolds's *Master Crewe as Henry VIII*), Wind notes that the girls 'are wearing their everyday dress and the general impression is lyrical. Any attempts to heighten the effect, if made at all, tend towards emphasizing the natural, easy, occasionally even gypsy-like appearance of

[3] In posing this dichotomy, I am adapting the model suggested by Benjamin Boyce, *The Polemic Character 1640–1661: A Chapter in English Literary History* (Lincoln: Univ. of Nebraska Press, 1955; rpt. New York: Octagon, 1969), 46.

[4] *The Poems of Mr. Gray. To Which Are Prefixed Memoirs of His Life and Writings by W. Mason, M.A.*, 2nd edn. (1755), 400–1.

[5] Ellis Waterhouse, *Gainsborough* (London: Hulton, 1958), no. 285 (pl. 52); John Hayes, *Gainsborough: Paintings and drawings* (London: Phaidon Press, 1975), fig. 12; Martin Davies, *National Gallery Catalogues: The British School*, 2nd edn. (London: National Gallery, 1959), no. 1811 (pp. 38–9).

[6] Waterhouse, p. 252; John Hayes, *Gainsborough: Paintings and drawings*, p. 37 (see also n. 31).

the figures. Gainsborough never imposes theatrical action or a rigid statuesque pose on these subjects.'[7]

This is surely true—to a point; but anyone who has worked through the history of pictorial representation that I have presented in this book should immediately recognize the affinities between this picture and Van Dyck's *Self-portrait with a Sunflower* (Plate 32) or Hogarth's *The Mackinnon Children* (Plate 57).[8] Gainsborough's portrait might in fact be considered a *terminus a quem* in the history of iconic form, for while it is true that his Margaret and Mary are depicted with unprecedented informality and warmth, it is also true that their delicacy and the transitory nature of their youth are consistent not only with the naturalistic image of the butterfly but with its emblematic significance as well. Michael Levey, the only critic to notice that 'The instinctive attempt to grasp the butterfly is perhaps consciously weighted to possess some symbolic value', points out that the 'sky over the dark woodland might presage a storm or the approach of night. . . . Childhood may be an enchanted state, but it does not last. Beyond the wood lies the world.'[9] Those who praise the naturalness of this painting are therefore entirely justified so long as their focus falls on the positioning of Gainsborough's daughters, their simple clothing and unguarded expressions, or the free handling of paint on what is thought to be an unfinished canvas. But even the syntax of the girls' rhythmic pose— in which the clasped hands on the right are juxtaposed to the grasping hand and the insect resting on the thistle to the left—suggests that the action which will complete this sequence will also reinforce the iconic undercurrent of change and mortality.

If, as I have argued, the iconographical features of the *Self-portrait with a Sunflower* appear to have blinded Van Dyck's critics to the actual objects depicted on that canvas, then, by the same token, the apparent naturalism of Gainsborough's picture has prevented his admirers from noticing the intriguing ways in which his painting continues to represent children in a familiar pose and in pursuit of an emblematic creature. The similarities between this painting and *The Mackinnon Children* are particularly telling, for the pictorial emphasis of each artist on the transience of his youthful subjects re-enacts the representational drama in which the painter

[7] 'Hume and the Heroic Portrait', in *Hume and the Heroic Portrait: Studies in Eighteenth-Century Imagery*, ed. Jaynie Anderson (Oxford: Clarendon Press, 1986), 22.

[8] See the discussions above, pp. 95–8 (Van Dyck) and pp. 182–3 (Hogarth).

[9] *Gainsborough: The Painter's Daughters chasing a butterfly* (Painting in Focus, no. 4; London: National Gallery, 1975), no pag. [1]. Levey introduces *The Mackinnon Children* as the first English painting to make use of the butterfly motif, 'perhaps with allegorical significance'. In spite of the tentative phrasing in this pamphlet, it is clear that Levey wants to combat the traditional conception of 'an entirely natural Gainsborough' (p. [7]).

attempts to capture these fleeting moments on canvas.[10] And like
Hogarth's spirited conversation piece, Gainsborough's charming portrait
of his daughters also introduces its symbolic material in a problematical
way: not because two iconographical objects compete with one another
(as in Hogarth's depiction of the butterfly atop the sunflower in the centre
of his picture), but because Gainsborough has literally pushed his
butterfly as far to one side of the canvas as he can. He may, like Boswell,
strive as much as possible to marginalize the convention he has inherited.
But isolated as it is, Gainsborough's butterfly continues to provide the
conceptual structure for his painting, while also serving as the catalyst for
a much simpler drama.

[10] See my discussion above, pp. 182–3.

Index

All figures, authors, and editors cited in the text and notes are included in the index with the exception of frequently cited reference works listed among the 'Abbreviations' (e.g. Millar, *Tudor, Stuart*) and passing references to historical figures (e.g. the Earl of Somerset, St Paul).

Percy, Thomas 228
Perrault, Charles 12
Perry, Ruth 191 n. 6
Petersson, R. T. 93 nn. 97–8, 94 nn. 99, 103
Pevsner, Nikolaus 72
Phillips, Edward 22–3, 140, 273
Phillips, John 24 n. 8
Phillips, Thomas 246
Pieresc, Nicolas Claude Fabri de 22 n. 3
Pinto, Vivian De Sola 10 n. 29
Piozzi, Gabriel 197
Piozzi, Hester Thrale: *Anecdotes of Johnson* 191–206; mentioned 10, 253–4, 255, 259, 262, 271, 272–4, 276–7, 280
Piper, David 12 n. 38, 16 n. 54, 68 n. 14, 75 n. 35, 78 n. 40, 89 n. 80, 100, 123–5, 136, 251; *see also* 'Abbreviations'
Plutarch 8, 22 n. 3, 23, 24, 25, 29, 206, 214
Pond, Arthur 138 n. 8
Ponsonby, Arthur 53 n. 58, 64 n. 80
Pope, Alexander 5, 13, 57, 71 n. 22, 99, 103, 146–9, 224
Popham, Sir John 113
Portrait-painting: historical and theoretical interrelations with biography 1–21, 134–5, and *passim*; portraits as documents 9; temporal design in 15–17; formulaic poses 65–70; grammar of poses 80–1; allegorical 89–98; and acting 185–8; general v. particular in 261–72 *passim*; *see also* Iconicism, Miniatures
Porter, Lucy 252, 260
Pottle, Frederick A. 2 n. 8, 201 n. 24, 202 n. 28, 237 n. 11, 265 n. 8, 266 n. 10, 267 n. 11, 271 n. 16, 285 n. 28, 289 n. 33
Powell, Anthony 1 n. 1, 108 n. 1, 109 nn. 3–4, 110–11, 115 n. 15, 118
Powell, L. F. 11 n. 32
Price, Martin 18 n. 60, 222 n. 62

Rader, Ralph W. 8 n. 24, 285
Raines, Robert 73 n. 28
Rand, Benjamin 21 n. 69
Raphael 251–2
Ray, John 1, 108
Redford, Bruce 29 n. 19
Redgrave, Richard and Samuel 179, 183
Reed, Joseph W., jun. 274 n. 18, 295 n. 1

Reni, Guido 241
Reynolds, Edward 35
Reynolds, Frances 252 n. 42, 253
Reynolds, Graham 123 n. 30, 125 n. 37
Reynolds, Sir Joshua: and Boswell 2–3, 256–9; theory of character 227–39; char.-sketches of Johnson, Garrick, and Goldsmith 233–9; as a port.-painter 239–60; *Mrs Siddons as the Tragic Muse (Plate 3)* 16–17, 245–8, *Samuel Johnson, 1756–7 (Plate 2)* 16, 250–1, 256–9, *Master Crewe as Henry VIII (Plate 68)* 90, 248–9, *Garrick between Tragedy and Comedy (Plate 61)* 188, 240–3, 248, *Garrick Reading to His Wife (Plate 62)* 188, 243, *Harry Woodward (Plate 66)* 244, *Cupid as Link Boy (Plate 67)* 248, *Samuel Johnson, 1769 (Plate 69)* 251–3, *Samuel Johnson, 1775 (Plate 70)* 253–4, *Samuel Johnson, c.1778 (Plate 71)* 254–5, *Samuel Johnson, c.1782 (Plates 73–4)* 255–6; mentioned 11, 13, 14, 15, 69, 136, 137, 150 n. 35, 176, 203, 261–96 *passim*
Ribeiro, Alvaro 12 n. 38, 47 n. 46
Richardson, Jonathan: *Life of Milton* and work as a port.-painter 135–50; *John Milton (Plate 44)* 145–6, *A. Pope, as Milton (Plate 45)* 147, composite port. of Milton and Pope *(Plate 46)* 147–8, *Self-portrait (Plate 47)* 148, *The Richardsons with Milton (Plate 48)* 149, *Martin Folkes (Plate 53)* 180; mentioned 5, 7, 11, 14, 15, 18–19, 71 n. 22, 106, 176, 178, 202 n. 29, 237, 261, 273
Richardson, Samuel 281–2
Ricks, Christopher 28 n. 18
Riely, John C. 191 n. 6
Riley, John 106, 136, 273
Ringbom, Sixten 21 n. 70, 252 n. 43
Rivers, the Earl 189, 220
Roberts, Sydney Castle 4 n. 10
Robertson, Dr William 280
Rochester, Henrietta Boyle, Countess of 67–8
Rochester, John Wilmot, 2nd Earl of 23, 25
Rogers, Malcolm 95 n. 105
Rogers, Samuel 246–7
Romney, George 246